The Combined Problems Of
ALCOHOLISM,
DRUG ADDICTION AND AGING

The Combined Problems of
ALCOHOLISM,
DRUG ADDICTION
AND AGING

Edited by

EDWARD GOTTHEIL, M.D., Ph.D.

Professor of Psychiatry and Human Behavior
Director of Jefferson Center for Studies of Alcohol and Addictions
Thomas Jefferson University, Philadelphia, Pennsylvania
Consultant, VA Medical Center, Coatesville, Pennsylvania

KEITH A. DRULEY, Ph.D.

Chief, Substance Abuse Treatment Unit
VA Medical Center, Coatesville, Pennsylvania

Associate Professor of Psychiatry and Human Behavior
Thomas Jefferson University, Philadelphia, Pennsylvania

THOMAS E. SKOLODA, Ph.D.

Coordinator, Drug and Alcohol Admission Ward
Substance Abuse Treatment Unit
VA Medical Center, Coatesville, Pennsylvania

Research Assistant Professor (Psychology)
Thomas Jefferson University, Philadelphia, Pennsylvania

HOWARD M. WAXMAN, Ph.D.

Assistant Professor of Psychiatry and Human Behavior
Thomas Jefferson University, Philadelphia, Pennsylvania

CHARLES C THOMAS • PUBLISHER
Springfield • Illinois • U.S.A.

Published and Distributed Throughout the World by

CHARLES C THOMAS • PUBLISHER
2600 South First Street
Springfield, Illinois 62717

© *1985 by* CHARLES C THOMAS • PUBLISHER

ISBN 0-398-05046-5

Library of Congress Catalog Card Number: 84-8627

With THOMAS BOOKS *careful attention is given to all details of manufacturing and design. It is the Publisher's desire to present books that are satisfactory as to their physical qualities and artistic possibilities and appropriate for their particular use.* THOMAS BOOKS *will be true to those laws of quality that assure a good name and good will.*

Printed in the United States of America
SC-R-3

Library of Congress Cataloging in Publication Data
Main entry under title:

The Combined problems of alcoholism, drug addiction, and aging.

Papers presented at the 6th annual Coatesville-Jefferson conference, held Nov. 1983 at the Coatesville VA Medical Center and sponsored by the Center's Substance Abuse Treatment Unit and the Jefferson Center for the Study of Alcoholism and Addiction.
Includes bibliographies and index.
1. Aged—United States—Alcohol use—Congresses.
2. Aged—United States—Drug use—Congresses.
3. Alcoholism—Treatment—United States—Congresses.
4. Drug abuse—Treatment—United States—Congresses.
5. Aged—United States—Psychology—Congresses.
I. Gottheil, Edward L.   II. Coatesville VA Medical Center. Substance Abuse Treatment Unit.   III. Jefferson Center for the Study of Alcoholism and Addiction.   IV. Title: Alcoholism, drug addiction, and aging. [DNLM: 1. Aged—psychology—congresses. 2. Alcoholism—in old age—congresses. 3. Substance Abuse—in old age—congresses. WM 270 C731 1983]
HV5138.C65   1984   362.2'92'0880565   84-8672
ISBN 0-398-05046-5

CONTRIBUTORS

STEWART L. BAKER, M.D.
Associate Director, Mental Health and Behavioral Sciences Services
Veterans Administration Central Office
Washington, D.C.
Clinical Professor of Psychiatry, Uniformed Services
University of Health Sciences
Bethesda, Maryland

WALTER W. BAKER, Ph.D.
Professor, Department of Psychiatry and Human Behavior
Thomas Jefferson University
Philadelphia, Pennsylvania
Professor, Physiology/Pharmacology,
Philadelphia College of Osteopathic Medicine
Philadelphia, Pennsylvania

HARRIETT BARR, PH.D.
Director of Research and Evaluation
Eagleville Hospital
Eagleville, Pennsylvania

LISA F. BERKMAN, Ph.D.
Associate Professor, Department of Epidemiology
    and Public Health
Yale University, School of Medicine
New Haven, Connecticut

JOHN BLAND, ACSW, LCSW
Director of the Alcoholism Control Administration
Maryland Department of Health and Mental Hygiene
Baltimore, Maryland
Faculty Member/Teacher

Rutger's Summer School of Alcohol Studies
New Brunswick, New Jersey

JACOB A. BRODY, M.D.
Associate Director for Epidemiology, Demography, and
    Biometry Program
National Institute on Aging
National Institutes of Health
Bethesda, Maryland
Senior Associate, Department of Epidemiology
Johns Hopkins University, School of Hygiene and Public Health
Baltimore, Maryland

ERWIN A. CARNER, Ed.D.
Director of the Division of Geropsychiatry
Clinical Assistant Professor, Department of Psychiatry and Human
    Behavior
Thomas Jefferson University
Philadelphia, Pennsylvania

LAIRD S. CERMAK, Ph.D.
Research Career Scientist
VA Medical Center
Boston, Massachusetts
Professor of Neurology
Boston University, School of Medicine
Adjunct Professor
Sargent College
Boston, Massachusetts

DONNA COHEN, M.D.
Associate Professor of Psychiatry and Neuroscience
Director, Division of Aging and Geriatric Psychiatry
Montefiore Medical Center and
Albert Einstein College of Medicine
Director of Research and Evaluation
Beth Abraham Hospital of the Montefiore Medical Center
New York, New York

DAVID T. COURTWRIGHT
Chairman, History Department

University of Hartford
West Hartford, Connecticut

DON C. DES JARLAIS, Ph.D.
Assistant Deputy Director for Substance Abuse Research
    and Evaluation
Division of Substance Abuse Services
Office of Alcoholism and Substance Abuse
New York, New York

KEITH A. DRULEY, Ph.D.
Chief, Substance Abuse Treatment Unit
Coatesville VA Medical Center
Coatesville, Pennsylvania
Associate Professor of Psychiatry and Human Behavior
Thomas Jefferson University
Philadelphia, Pennsylvania

NANCY ELLIOTT, R.N.
Head Nurse and Coordinator of Supportive Alcohol
    Rehabilitation Program
Substance Abuse Treatment Unit
VA Medical Center
Coatesville, Pennsylvania

ROBERT H. FORTIER, Ph.D.
Associate Professor, Department of Psychology
Purdue School of Science
Indiana University-Purdue University
Indianapolis, Indiana

FREDRICA MANN FRIEDMAN, Ph.D.
Family Therapist
Program Director, Creative Human Services for the Aging
Ardmore, Pennsylvania

C. JACK FRIEDMAN, Ph.D.
President, Creative Human Services for the Aging
Ardmore, Pennsylvania
Associate Professor, Department of Psychiatry and
    Human Behavior
Thomas Jefferson University
Philadelphia, Pennsylvania

MEYER D. GLANTZ, Ph.D.
Clinical Research Psychologist,
Division of Research, Psychological Sciences Branch
National Institute on Drug Abuse
Rockville, Maryland
Lecturer
George Mason University
Fairfax, Virginia
Clinical Practice
Bethesda, Maryland

EDITH LISANSKY GOMBERG, Ph.D.
Professor, School of Social Work
Research Scientist
Institute of Gerontology
Faculty Associate
Institute for Social Research
University of Michigan
Ann Arbor, Michigan

EDWARD GOTTHEIL, M.D., Ph.D.
Professor of Psychiatry and Human Behavior
Director of Jefferson Center for Studies of Alcohol and Addictions
Thomas Jefferson University
Philadelphia, Pennsylvania
Consultant, Coatesville VA Medical Center
Coatesville, Pennsylvania

MERTON M. HYMAN, MA
Assistant Research Specialist (Sociologist-Statistician)
Researcher, Editorial Referee
Rutger's University
New Brunswick, New Jersey

HERMAN JOSEPH
Research Scientist for the Bureau of Cost Effectiveness
    and Research
New York State Division of Substance Abuse Services
New York, New York

ROBERT W. KENNEDY, Ph.D.
Psychologist, Psychology Service

VA Medical Center
Coatesville, Pennsylvania
Instructor, Department of Psychiatry and Human Behavior
Thomas Jefferson University
Philadelphia, Pennsylvania

MELISSA KLEIN, M.A., M.C.P.
Research Associate, Center for the Study of Geropsychiatry
Thomas Jefferson University
Philadelphia, Pennsylvania

GARY D. KUNZ, Ph.D.
Coordinator, Alcohol Rehabilitation Program
Substance Abuse Treatment Unit
VA Medical Center
Coatesville, Pennsylvania

PETER P. LAMY, PH.D., F.A.G.S.
Professor and Director, Institutional Pharmacy Programs
Chairman, Department and Administrative Science
University of Maryland School of Pharmacy
Baltimore, Maryland

LUIS A. MARCO, M.D.
Associate Chief of Staff for Research and Development
VA Medical Center
Coatesville, Pennsylvania
Professor, Department of Psychiatry and Human Behavior
Professor, Pharmacology
Thomas Jefferson University
Philadelphia, Pennsylvania

ALLAN MEYERS, Ph.D.
Associate Director of the School of Public Health
Boston University School of Medicine
Boston, Massachusetts

BRIAN L. MISHARA, Ph.D.
Professor, Department of Psychology
University of Quebec
Montreal, Quebec, Canada

ALAN P. MITTELMAN, MSW
Coordinator, Re-Entry House

VA Medical Center
Coatesville, Pennsylvania

CAROL A. NOWAK, Ph.D.
Director, Social Science Research Center for the Study of Aging
Research Assistant Professor, Department of Psychology
State University of New York
Buffalo, New York

EMIL F. PASCARELLI, M.D.
Medical Director of Affiliated Physicians of St. Vincent
Adjunct Associate Professor of Clinical Public Health
New York Hospital
Cornell Medical Center
New York, New York

STEVEN PASHKO, Ph.D.
Coordinator and Social Science Analyst
Substance Abuse Treatment Unit
VA Medical Center
Coatesville, Pennsylvania

HENRY PINSKER, M.D.
Associate Director, Department of Psychiatry
Beth Israel Medical Center
Professor, Department of Psychiatry
Mount Sinai School of Medicine
New York, New York

PATRICIA M. RANDELS, M.D.
Chief, Psychogeriatric Unit
VA Medical Center
Coatesville, Pennsylvania
Clinical Professor, Department of Psychiatry and Human Behavior
Thomas Jefferson University
Philadelphia, Pennsylvania

THOMAS E. SKOLODA, Ph.D.
Coordinator, Drug and Alcohol Admission Ward
Substance Abuse Treatment Unit
VA Medical Center
Coatesville, Pennsylvania

Research Assistant Professor
Thomas Jefferson University
Philadelphia, Pennsylvania

DONNA G. SMITH, R.N.
Head Nurse, Admission/Evaluation Program
Substance Abuse Treatment Unit
VA Medical Center
Coatesville, Pennsylvania

THOMAS STAMMERS, M.D.
Physician Fellow, Substance Abuse Treatment Unit
VA Medical Center
Coatesville, Pennsylvania
Department of Psychiatry and Human Behavior
Thomas Jefferson University
Philadelphia, Pennsylvania

HOWARD M. WAXMAN, Ph.D.
Assistant Professor, Department of Psychiatry and Human
    Behavior
Thomas Jefferson University
Philadelphia, Pennsylvania

W. GIBSON WOOD, Ph.D.
Evaluation Coordinator, Geriatric Research, Education, and Clini-
    cal Center (GRECC)
VA Medical Center
St. Louis, Missouri
Assistant Research Professor, Department of Internal Medicine
St. Louis University School of Medicine
St. Louis, Missouri

SHELDON ZIMBERG, M.D.
Director, Department of Psychiatry, Joint Diseases
North General Hospital
Associate Professor, Department of Psychiatry
Mount Sinai School of Medicine
New York, New York

PREFACE

Some alcohol and drug abusers "mature out" as they grow older, but many maintain their addiction and become elderly addicts. In addition, a number of previously non-addicted individuals turn to alcohol and/or drugs as they grow older and some of them become elderly addicts. In recent years there has been a growing awareness of the existence of this increasing population of elderly alcohol and drug dependent individuals and of the difficult research and treatment problems presented. Since the fields of addiction and aging are still very young, however, it is perhaps not surprising that there have been so few reported studies of the complex interacting problems of patients who are both aged and addicted.

A main and continuing purpose of our Coatesville-Jefferson series of conferences has been to provide a forum for researchers to communicate their findings to clinicians and for clinicians to present their observations and questions to researchers about new or developing areas. Elderly alcohol and other substance abuse seemed to us to represent such an area. For our Sixth Annual Conference, then, we brought together an outstanding group of clinicians and researchers from the fields of alcoholism, drug addiction, geriatrics, and general psychiatry to share their findings and ideas regarding the combined problems of aging and addiction.

We asked our invited experts to consider issues such as the following: incidence and prevalence estimates of substance abuse among the elderly; patterns of alcohol and drug use and abuse in the elderly; incidence, prevalence, and causes of abuse and misuse of OTC and prescribed medications; implications of early as compared to late-onset alcoholism; factors in the aging process which prompt or support substance abuse; problems in the recognition of abuse in the elderly; specific problems in the treatment of older substance abusers; coping methods of the elderly; expected course and outcome of aged substance abuse; special considerations regarding nursing home patients, recent retirees, VA medical center patients; the role of AA, church, and self-help communities; preventive approaches; and relationships of stress and social supports to substance abuse in the elderly. The contributions, coming from psychology, psychiatry, neuropharmacology, epidemiology, geriatrics (geropsychiatry, psychogeriatrics), public health, neuropsychology, alcoholism, drug addiction, substance abuse, social work, family therapy, nursing and pharmacy, strongly suggest that there is a growing body of literature on elderly addiction, that much is known even though the information tends to be scattered across many disciplines, and that important issues and questions are being recognized and clarified.

Presentation of the conference was made possible through the cooperative efforts of the Substance Abuse Treatment Unit of the Coatesville VA Medical Center and the Jefferson Center for the Study of Alcoholism and Addiction of Thomas Jefferson University. We are indebted to Mr. James Parsons, Director of the Coatesville VA Medical Center, and Dr. Paul J. Fink, Professor and Chairman of the Department of Psychiatry of Thomas Jefferson University, for their support and guidance. The conference coordinators gratefully acknowledge the financial assistance provided to the conference by Mead Johnson Pharmaceuticals, Merrell Dow Pharmaceuticals, Inc., McNeil Pharmaceutical, and The Upjohn Company. We wish to thank the individual contributors for their cooperation in completing their manuscripts and especially Kathy Migrala and Karen Mullen for their dedicated assistance.

E.G.

K.A.D.

T.E.S.

H.W.M.

INTRODUCTION

For many years, the aged, the alcoholic, and the drug addict have not been included among the favorite subjects of most clinicians or researchers. Little was known about these conditions, little was done for them other than to provide symptomatic care, and, indeed, it was felt that little could be done for them. This has changed somewhat in recent decades.

Alcoholism was the first of these areas to gain a measure of recognition and respectability. It did not come easily, however, and did not occur until after alcoholic individuals themselves had demonstrated that alcoholics could be helped. The formation and growth of Alcoholics Anonymous and the National Council of Alcoholism provided a constituency and the continuing accumulation of evidence regarding the treatability of alcoholic individuals provided a rationale, which together generated the pressure necessary to stimulate the development of organized services for alcoholic patients. As the treatment network expanded, professional clinicians and researchers became interested in the field which gained further recognition and status with the establishment of a National Institute on Alcoholism and Alcohol Abuse.

Public and professional awareness of, and interest in, drug addiction came about quite differently. The sudden epidemic of drug use and abuse in the 1960s created immediate and widespread alarm. The need for knowledge and services was apparent and a field of drug abuse developed almost instantaneously. In the case of geriatrics, progress has been slow but seems to be gaining some momentum at the present time. There is an increasing realization of the steadily growing proportion of aged individuals in the population. New knowledge is accumulating regarding the treatment responsiveness of symptoms and conditions previously thought to be progressive and irreversible. In addition, elderly citizens with the help of groups such as the Gray Panthers and the Association of Retired Persons have become much more politically aware and active.

The fields of alcoholism, drug addiction, and geriatrics each now have a national institute, organized networks of treatment services, research centers, and respected professional journals. Nevertheless, they are historically very young and remain beset with funding, administrative, conceptual, and methodological problems. Although some progress has been made, the fields of aging and addiction are still relatively unattractive to new professional clinicians and researchers.

The major issues of concern in these fields still revolve, for the most part, around basic definitions and field boundaries. Thus, the complex overlapping problems of the elderly addict tend to receive less immediate priority. Moreover, only a small proportion of the elderly are found to be addicted, and only a small proportion of addicts are elderly. As a consequence, most program administrators have not established specialized units for elderly addicts but, instead, assign such patients to their standard geriatric or addiction treatment programs. Similarly, most researchers have avoided the combined problems of the elderly addict by excluding individuals with addiction from studies of the aged, and by excluding the aged from studies of addiction. Clinicians, however, do not have the option of avoiding the substance abuse problems of their geriatric patients or the geriatric problems of their addict patients. Whether the administrators or researchers are ready or not, the clinician must attempt to manage these patients with the best resources and techniques available. From these attempts come the observations, the questions, and the impetus for the development of research projects and treatment programs.

A search of the literature revealed that there actually were considerable numbers of clinical, theoretical, and research papers dealing with the problems of the elderly addict. Much useful information was available but it was found to be scattered across the journals of many different disciplines. The purpose of our conference, and of this volume, then, was to bring together the leading experts from the various disciplines, obtain updates on research and theory in their respective fields, initiate dialogue among them, and provide a compilation of currently available information on the combined problems of aging and addiction.

Four chapters on the "Psychosocial Aspects of Aging and Substance Abuse" make up the first section of this book. Brody sets the stage by describing the changing numbers, demographics, living patterns, and characteristics of our elderly population. He then reviews studies of the prevalence of older alcoholics and notes the difference in estimates provided by epidemiological as compared to clinical investigations. He concludes by discussing prevention, case finding, and treatment strategies which are most likely to be cost efficient.

The effects of social and community ties, stress, and life events on substance-abusing behavior are considered in the next two chapters by Berkman and Nowak. In the final chapter of this section, Gomberg discusses the vagueness and lack of specificity of a number of our concepts. Late-onset drinking, for example, could include individuals who began having problems with drinking in their forties and who at age 65 would have been alcoholics for over 20 years. Since we usually think of late-onset drinking as reactive or situational, she suggests that it might be useful to differentiate out a recent-onset group of elderly alcoholics whose difficulties do not begin until they are about 60 years of age. Gomberg also suggests that we need to know much more about gerontology than we do at the present time and indicates a number of areas requiring further study.

Section II, entitled "Differential Drug Effects in the Aged" includes chapters by Cermak, Cohen, and Wood. Using a variety of memory tasks, Cermak found different patterns of memory deficits in younger and older alcoholic subjects which were not found in controls and which he interpreted as supporting a premature aging hypothesis. In Cohen's chapter, a series of studies are described in which serum immunoglobulin levels were found to be related to cognitive performances in healthy older persons, individuals with nonreversible dementias of later life, and patients with chronic alcoholism.

Laboratory data, reviewed by Wood, indicate that at the same blood level, alcohol has a greater effect on certain responses (e.g., righting behavior) of older than younger animals. Such findings cannot be explained by differences in metabolism, elimination, or water distribution but suggest, instead, that the sensitivity of the brain to alcohol is somehow altered with aging. Supporting this hypothesis are experiments demonstrating that biological membranes from aged animals differ in their response to ethanol from those of younger animals. Clearly, this is an exciting and developing area. Having shown that the effects of acute and chronic alcohol administration are greater in older than in younger organisms, we are now beginning to learn more about the types and patterns of deficits that occur and the underlying mechanisms responsible for these age differences.

Five chapters on "Drug Use and Misuse by the Elderly" constitute the third section of the book. While the extent of illicit drug abuse by the elderly is increasing, it still constitutes but a small percentage of the total amount of inappropriate use in the geriatric population. Misuse is much more frequent and may involve underuse, overuse, or taking the wrong drugs. The drugs may be illicit, prescribed, or over-the-counter remedies and the inappropriate use may be either active or passive. Thus, Glantz points out, although researchers have developed considerable expertise in assessing levels and types of drug abuse among young populations, these techniques may not be as effective or reliable in assessing inappropriate use in older populations. He then reviews the various types of assessment problems encountered in conducting such studies and closes with recommendations for managing them.

Misuse in the elderly usually occurs against a background of chronic diseases and the drugs taken for them, changes in metabolism, slower elimination, and poor circulation. Each additional drug compounds the problem of possible interactions which may not always be well known or even considered. Side effects may be misinterpreted as psychiatric symptoms or as representing organic changes due to age while underlying drug toxicities may be overlooked. These problems are discussed by Lamy for drugs in general and by Baker for psychoactive drugs.

Frequency of use of over-the-counter and prescription drugs, possession of CNS drugs, drug misuse, and non-compliance with prescriptions were compared with socio-psychological data collected from a normal group of elderly men and women by Fortier and Maultsby. Using cluster analytic techniques, they were able to demonstrate the influence of personality, health, and social factors on drug use patterns of the elderly.

Waxman et al. examined the problem of psychoactive drug misuse in nursing homes. While this is usually discussed as an example of passive misuse by the elderly, the authors take the view that it may represent active misuse by the institution. They offer the interesting thesis that medication misuse by a long-term facility is similar to substance abuse by an individual. It is suggested that an understanding of the factors promoting psychotropic medication misuse in institutions is necessary if we hope to help them withdraw from their "addiction."

Section IV is concerned with "Coping Tactics of Elderly Substance Abusers." Two of the chapters involve follow-up studies. Barr reports that mortality rates of alcohol and other drug addicts at two and eight years following treatment were significantly increased relative to the general population. Older patients who responded favorably to treatment did not evidence this increased mortality despite long histories of abuse, whereas the outcomes for those who persisted in their abuse were generally progressive deterioration or premature death. Hyman describes what happened to a group of alcoholics 15 years following treatment in a public outpatient clinic and compares the resources and intervening treatment involvement of those who were abstaining, drinking moderately, still abusing, mentally deteriorated, or dead. A major implication of the study was that while neither legal pressure, psychiatric hospitalization, or other form of treatment was alone adequate to insure a favorable outcome, each little bit appeared to help and to add to the likelihood of a favorable outcome.

Some addicts who do not mature out, recover, or die enter methadone programs as their contacts and sources of supply dwindle and they become too old to continue hustling drugs. Desjarlais and his coworkers and Pasacarelli turned to this group of elderly methadone patients in order to learn what coping tactics they had used to achieve their longevity. Seven factors emerged which appeared to contribute to their ability to outlive most of their peers. Another finding was that the methadone programs had become a major source of social interactions and support for these patients and an integral part of their lives.

In contrast to investigations of patients in treatment or at various lengths of time following treatment, Meyers's approach to the study of elderly addicts was by means of a probability sampling of the population of Metropolitan Boston in which 1 percent of the respondents over 60 years of age indicated that they had a drinking problem. The findings of this community survey differed from those reported in previous clinical studies with respect to issues such as late-onset drinking, the importance of stresses due to aging, and the influence of social supports. Although all of the subjects reported a current drinking problem, only one was in treatment at the time of the survey. Whether this speaks to the need for special programs or better access to existing ones is not clear. Moreover, Meyers suggests that the treatment problems of this group may have as much to do with the long-term duration of their drinking problems which had not responded to previous treatment efforts as with their age.

"Treatment Strategies" are discussed in Section V. Mishara emphasizes the importance, in treatment planning, of recognizing that each cohort of elderly alcoholics represents a different cultural and historical era in terms of education, sex roles, attitudes toward drinking, and other values typical of that specific period of time. He describes a developmental model of alcoholism from which treatment implications are derived and then reviews some of the techniques and difficulties involved in primary, secondary, and tertiary prevention approaches for elderly alcoholics.

The next three chapters are concerned with particular attempts to develop appropriate treatment services for the elderly. Bland, for example, describes a successful effort to increase treatment availability for older alcoholics in the state of Maryland by bringing together representatives from alcoholism and geriatric treatment facilities for meetings, information exchange, and cross training over a two-year period. Friedman et al., concerned with the limited range of treatment options exercised in most nursing homes, explored the utility of a short-term family oriented therapeutic approach. A combination of evaluation and management techniques were developed which were applicable to elderly nursing home residents and decreased the need for psychotropic drugs. Pinsker attempted to establish a special socialization and activity group for patients over the age of 55 who were attending an alcoholism outpatient clinic. Possible reasons for the somewhat disappointing results are discussed which pertain to the types of services that are needed and appropriate for older addicts.

In the last chapter of this section on treatment strategies, Zimberg discusses classification systems in relation to treatment planning, the contribution of psychosocial stresses to geriatric alcoholism, and the importance and efficacy of psychosocial interventions in the treatment of elderly alcoholics. He then provides a comprehensive description and discussion of principles, staff utilization, treatment location, and therapeutic techniques that are useful in treating alcoholism in aged patients.

The sixth and final section of the volume is titled "Issues in Dealing with Substance Abuses Among Older Veterans." Baker reviews the problems of substance use, misuse, and abuse as they relate to the increasing population of older veterans in our country. Projections regarding the increased demand for services are staggering and will require changes in the VA health care delivery system. Awareness of the problems and projections has resulted in the establishment of geriatric and substance abuse treatment, education, and research centers that should help in the planning and development of an appropriate system response.

An overview of the diagnosis and treatment of elderly alcoholics is provided by Marco and Randels who also describe the characteristics of a sample of such patients on the combined geriatric and extended service at the Coatesville Veterans Administration Medical Center. Elliott and Smith discuss practical nursing considerations, and Mittelman outlines the dispositional alternatives available to aging alcoholic veterans at the Coatesville facility and the process whereby patients are helped to select from among these options.

Druley and Pashko describe the development of a nurse-coordinated therapeutic community program for older veterans with combined psychiatric and addictive problems. In-treatment and post-treatment assessments indicated that the program was cost effective as well as cost efficient. In the last chapter of the section, Kunz et al. address the issue of assigning older patients to addiction rehabilitation programs on the basis of their particular psychological characteristics rather than merely by age.

It is evident that there is increasing interest in and research on the combined problems of aging and addiction as well as a growing body of literature. This is fortunate from a number of points of view. Many of the most controversial issues in the field of addiction have been related to the course of the disease. We are now beginning to obtain more reliable information about those who follow a progressively downhill and deteriorating course, who end up on skid row or in institutions, who die in a variety of accidents or commit suicide, who succumb to physical disease, or who mature out. Data are being gathered with respect to the characteristics, social factors, and life events that contribute to persistent abuse, moderated use, or abstinence. We are learning more about underlying biological processes and about which treatments have been helpful for which patients. These accumulating data, emerging from the studies of aged addicts reported in this volume, are related to basic issues regarding the etiology, description, diagnosis, treatment, course, prognosis, and prevention of addiction. They are also important to a better understanding of aging, the role of stress factors in the aging process, and the coping mechanisms employed by aged individuals. Finally, they should help improve our ability to reach and treat elderly addicts.

E.G.
K.A.D.
T.E.S.
H.M.W.

CONTENTS

The Combined Problems Of
ALCOHOLISM,
DRUG ADDICTION AND AGING

SECTION I
PSYCHOSOCIAL ASPECTS OF
AGING AND SUBSTANCE ABUSE

Chapter 1

ALCOHOL AND AGING—
THE EXTENT OF THE PROBLEM
FROM LIMITED DATA

Jacob A. Brody

C areful studies of the degree and extent of the problems of aging and alcohol abuse do not exist (1). Common sense and common experiences do suggest however that the elderly are a highly susceptible group for having alcohol problems. Retirement comes with the potential for failure of an individual to deal with the sudden increase in leisure time, a lowering of demands and role status, and loss of income. Deaths occuring among relatives and friends may lead to morbid gloom and depression augmented by the awareness that more deaths are coming. Poor health and physical discomfort increase with age. Finally, loneliness and isolation tend to grow, particularly among elderly women.

Thrown into this background is the imponderable effect created by the fact that all those who are more than 65 years old in 1982 were born no later than 1917. Thus, the entire population lived through the period of Prohibition, experiencing not only the moral outrage that produced this social experiment but the problems engendered by its failure. We lack knowledge of the impact of Prohibition on these people over 65, an obstacle in trying to understand and deal with the target population.

The above a priori scenario is, perhaps, the most negative view of potential alcohol related problems. We tend to stereotype and presume the bulk of the elderly population are abandoned in decaying nursing homes throughout the land.

This allows us to muster up a full measure of guilt about the sad and forsaken older sector of the country. In fact, however, only 5 percent of the people over age 65 are in nursing homes. The rest are out there, and, for the most part, doing rather well. Riley and Foner (2) noted, "The typical older person seems to have a strong sense of his own worth, to minimize his self-doubts, and not even to regard himself as old. The older person seems at least as likely as the younger person to feel adequate and to have a sense of satisfaction in playing his various marital, parental, occupational, or housekeeping roles. To be sure, he does not perceive old age as the happiest period of his life. Nevertheless, he does not worry any more than the young person about his health, his finances, or any of the other difficulties to which he is subject."

In 1978 (3), one in nine, or approximately 24.1 million, Americans were 65 years old or older. Among whites, 11 percent of the population was over 65, while among blacks 8 percent were in this age group and among Spanish-surname populations the figure was approximately 4 percent. The net increase per day of the population 65 years old or older is approximately 1,500 people. This takes into account the number of people becoming 65 and subtracts the deaths in the age group 65 and over. Modestly projecting to the year 2000, there will be 32 million people over the age of 65 in the United States. Between 3.5 and 6.7 million individuals will be 85 years of age or older. Currently, 45 percent of those 65 or older live in seven states. There are more than 2 million in this age group in California and New York. More than 1 million people over age 65 live in Florida, Illinois, Ohio, Pennsylvania, and Texas. There is a slight tendency for more elderly to live in rural areas and in the central cores of large cities.

In 1977, about 14 percent of the elderly population lived below poverty level. Massachusetts had the lowest rate, with approximately 6 percent below the poverty line, while Mississippi and Georgia had the highest percentages, 37 and 32 percent, respectively.

Life expectancy in the United States in 1978 was 73 years, or approximately 69 years for males and 77 for females. An infant girl born today has a 50–50 chance of surviving until age 80. Of those 65 and over, almost 40 percent are over 75 years of age. At age 65 the subgroup with the most favorable life expectancy is the black female. Approximately 82 percent of females and only 65 percent of males survive to age 65. At age 65, the average male can expect to live another 14 years, while females can expect to live another 18 years. The differential survivorship between males and females causes a potentially devastating imbalance over age 65. For every 100 males there are approximately 150 females.

In terms of living arrangements, somewhere between 4 and 5 percent over age 65 are in institutions, the great majority, of course, being in nursing homes. The average age in nursing homes is approximately 82 years, with two thirds of the population being female. Almost 50 percent of people in nursing homes have no living relatives. Among those residing in the community, 1.6 million males, or 17 percent of the total male population over age 65, live alone or with non-relatives. An almost staggering 6.0 million females in this age group, 42 percent of the total female population over 65, live alone or with non-relatives. Because women live longer but tend to marry older men, and older men who are widowed find it easier to remarry, at present, of those over the age of 65, 77 percent of men, and only 48 percent of women are married.

The present cohort aged 65 or more has an average of 9.5 years of education. About a third have finished high school, and 8 percent have finished college. Along with the increase in the absolute number of people aged 65 or older, the median level of education is rising, so that within the next few decades there will be little difference in educational levels at any adult age. This has considerable significance in terms of planning, since the people who will be joining the ranks of the elderly will be better educated and hence more vocal and demanding than the present constituency.

At present 8 percent of women over age 65 are working. This is not a great departure from the past. Among men, however, only 20 percent of the population are working. In 1900, 67 percent of the male population over age 65 were employed. Leisure time, however, may be diminishing in recent years as financial needs cause more elderly people to remain employed.

A total of 40 percent of people 65 or older have a serious health problem that causes some limitation in conducting normal daily activities. This compares with approximately 7 percent of the population under age 65. Each year 17 percent of those over 65 are hospitalized at least once, and each hospitalization lasts for an average of 12 days. For those under 65, 10 percent are hospitalized annually and stay approximately 7 days. The average annual cost for health, per capita, per year, for those over age 65 is estimated to be approximately $1,500, while for those under age 65 it is $550.

ISSUES

Major clinical observations by Zinberg (4) and by Rosin and Glatt (5) were made in the early 1970's or before. None of their work has been expanded or repeated. Their initial reports described fewer than 200 patients, and their populations tended to be atypical, in that they contained an excess of females, from urban and impoverished areas such as Harlem or parts of London.

Key points have emerged from their studies. These authors tend to agree that there are two broad types of elderly alcohol abusers. One is the long-term abuser or survivor, who has the constitutional stamina to reach old age. Estimates suggest that two thirds of the elderly alcoholics are in this group. The second group includes those in whom the onset of alcoholism occurs late in life. In contradistinction to the former, these are referred to alcohol specialists through geriatric practice rather than psychiatric practice. Their drinking is generally situational, exacerbated by failing physical and mental health and by emotional and environmental stresses.

A notable claim is that elderly alcoholics, with either early or late onset, are easier to treat than younger alcoholics. It is further suggested that their treatment need not be through classic mechanisms used for younger alcoholics such as intensive inpatient therapy, Alcoholics Anonymous (AA) and routine alcohol counseling, but that their alcoholism is amendable to simple socialization. When in treatment programs, the elderly tend to be more responsive and more faithful in attendance.

The claim that therapeutic methods, which are of little use in earlier years, are successful for both early-onset and late-onset elderly alcohol abusers, — arouses both skepticism and optimism in researchers and therapists. It is of critical importance to confirm or refute these data.

There are few hard data about drinking patterns in the elderly population. Reviews are available (6, 7), and I shall attempt only to cull out data and concepts that relate to areas of potential development and progress. Various surveys of the general population suggest that the absolute number of abstainers increases, and the total amount of alcohol consumed decreases, with age. Estimates of alcoholism range from about 1 to 5 percent of the population over age 65. Thus, in a survey to detect about 25 patients we would have to interview 1,000 people, assuming total cooperation and candor in responses. Not knowing the effects of Prohibition, the female preponderance, etc., on this age group, and giving some credence to the belief that this population and their families are inclined to deny alcohol problems, this estimate of sample size may be too low. It would appear that surveys are a costly and potentially unreliable measure of alcoholism in the elderly.

A pragmatic approach which may give insight into a large portion of the problems of alcohol abuse in the elderly involves individuals being hospitalized or being seen by physician or other health providers for any and all reasons. Within this population it is estimated that 10 to 15 percent have a drinking problem that is in some way related to the presenting illness. Both Zimberg (4) and Schuckit (8) discuss this issue and the attendant difficulty in establishing the diagnosis of an alcohol-related problem in this population. There is some evidence that alcohol has unusual effects on elderly people. They appear to be less tolerant at lower doses of alcohol, and since many have heart conditions and alcohol is a cardiac muscle irritant, the role of alcohol on the patients' cardiovascular condition is difficult to evaluate. Approximately 25 percent of the population 65 and over is on some form of medication. Knowledge of drug and alcohol interactions is limited, and the possibility that reaction may be idiosyncratic and dangerous, even in small doses, is extremely disquieting. Finally, alcohol seems to produce transient syndromes in the elderly which are indistinguishable from senile dementia. This is potentially tragic, because a person could easily be labeled as having senile dementia when he has only a mild alcohol problem. Once the diagnosis of dementia is made, a person's chances of spending the rest of his life in an institution increase considerably.

DISCUSSION

We presented evidence, suggesting that there are many elderly alcoholics of both the early-onset and late-onset categories who would be easy to cure. While the rates of alcohol abuse and drinking are low, and decline with advancing age, it is reported that 10 to 15 percent of all those seeking medical help have an alcohol-related problem.

If these studies can be confirmed, they will offer a rational modus operandi to find and treat large numbers of elderly alcoholics. This should certainly be investigated immediately since the rate of 10 to 15 percent is sufficiently high that a fairly intensive effort would yield a large number of suffering individuals. If we find that the yield is high, we must develop methods to make care-givers more sophisticated so that they can diagnose the alcohol problems in the patients they see. If the treatment is as simple and successful as is suggested by the classic writers, then we have a relatively efficacious and available mechanism to deliver a great deal of medical and social help to a large group of people. Please note that I am emphasizing that the early studies and assumptions must be confirmed before massive programs can be embarked upon with optimism.

A persistent source of anecdotes that do not appear in the literature comes from people who run housing authorities or large housing projects, or manage retirement communities. Since urban housing and retirement communities are becoming more numerous, these observations demand attention and evaluation. Informants tell me that one of their most distressing and persistent problems is alcoholism and alcohol abuse, which causes an inordinately high proportion of serious and nagging difficulties. The rates of alcohol-associated fires, falls, starvation and neglect, and violence are simply unknown, but increasingly whispered about in communities for the elderly.

Confounding the establishment of the veracity of these anecdotes is the barrier to collecting accurate data. There is no research in this age group concerning how to question about alcohol and to get reliable answers. The nuances in working include the fact that there are more women, that their attitudes were formed and influenced before and during Prohibition, that surveys themselves are very expensive, and if the anecdotes are only partially true, it would take about a hundred interviews to find one patient given a predictably high denial rate. Some survey research should be done but my opinion is that firm data will not emanate from the age group currently under investigation. It is likely that studies of the natural history and factors related to the decline in alcohol consumption with age would be rewarding, possibly in ways not immediately apparent. Another promising route of investigation is to learn more about late-onset problem drinkers. Case-control studies might identify the people at high risk as well as the precipitating circumstances. This should be accompanied by intense research to determine whether and why alcohol has an exceptionally deleterious effect on aging individuals and whether addiction is easily cured. Finally, I would give highest priority to straightforward case-finding studies in hospitalized series and to carefully documented treatment trials.

CONCLUSIONS

Concomitantly with survey research and clinical treatment research we should contemplate prevention efforts of the type that have done relatively poorly in the adolescent and young ages. As I have previously argued (1), it is likely that preventive efforts would find a much more responsive audience in the population that is now 55–64 years of age. A major prevention and education program would be of great interest to unions, management, the government, and anyone paying pensions or involved in health insurance. The staging would be to instruct this population that they are growing older and with age comes those risks that we know are associated with a greater likelihood for developing and perpetuating problems with alcohol. To repeat them once again, we would educate the target population that with retirement will come less money, a change in status and role, and free time to which they are unaccustomed. We must openly discuss the fact that death will be increasingly visible as they enter into the period when relatives and friends are passing away.

We must present forcibly the information that health declines with age and that major and minor illnesses are an inevitable risk to the individual and to his loved ones. Finally, we must emphasize the problem of loneliness and physically living alone, particularly for women but really for all elderly people. Throughout this, the message to be maintained is that alcohol, while tempting and abundant, is very likely to make things worse.

Encompassed in these suggestions are two goals. The first is to prevent alcohol problems from arising after age 65 by targeting the population aged 55 to 64. Secondly, it is likely that this is a fairly effective way to reach people already older than 65. This population is know to be sophisticated to the extent that they read newspapers and watch television more than most of their younger counterparts. Many of those who do have alcohol-related problems will identify with the messages being presented for the younger cohort and will seek help through medical sources, Alcoholics Anonymous, and other community resources. Thus, through practicing good prevention in one cohort we may be practicing good case detection in another. This is a time for research and a time for action. Our problems will be growing worse until our commitment becomes greater. In 18 years there will be no fewer than 32 million people over age 65 in the United States.

SUMMARY

Demographic information suggests that the problems of alcohol abuse among the elderly will increase at least in proportion to the population growth of that sector. While fewer older people drink and average consumption declines, four factors that promote alcohol abuse are noted. These are: 1) retirement, with its attendant boredom, change of role status, and loss of income; 2) deaths occurring among relatives and friends and the awareness that more deaths are coming; 3) poor health and discomfort; and 4) loneliness, a particular problem among elderly women. Surveys in older age groups, in addition to being costly, are of questionable value. Anecdotal evidence and several early studies, however, suggest that a high proportion of elderly (10 to 15 percent) who seek medical attention for any reason have an alcohol-related problem, and that elderly alcoholics, whether alcoholism is of early or recent onset, are relatively easy to treat. If these findings can be confirmed, then detection during health-seeking encounters could have great potential value. Research in detection and treatment is critical. A prevention strategy involving the cohort 55 to 64 years of age could have the dual effect of preventing subsequent alcohol problems among these people and offering a message that would be heard by those at older and less accessible ages.

REFERENCES

1. Brody, J. A. Aging and alcohol abuse. *J Am Geriatrics Society,* 1982, 123–126.
2. Riley, M. W., and Foner, A. *Aging and Society,* (Vol. I), 1. New York: Russell Sage Foundation, 1968.
3. Brock, D. B., and Brody, J. A. Statistical and epidemiologic characteristics of the United States elderly population. In R. Andres, E. L. Bierman, and W. R. Hazzard (Eds.), *Principles of Geriatric Medicine.* New York: McGraw-Hill. In press.
4. Zimberg, S. The elderly alcoholic. *Gerontologist,* June 1974, 221.
5. Rosin, A. J., and Glatt, M. M. Alcohol excess in the elderly, *Q. J. Stud. Alcohol,* 1971, 32, 53.
6. Keller, M., Promisel, D. M., and Spiegler, D. et al. (Eds.), *Second Special Report to the U.S. Congress on Alcohol and Health June 1974 Chapter II. Alcohol and Older Persons.* USDHEW, PHS, M E Chafetz, Chairman of the Task Force, p. 27.
7. Cahalan, D., and Room, R. Problem Drinking Among American Men. Monograph No. 7. New Brunswick, NJ: Rutgers Center of Alcohol Studies, 1974.
8. Schuckit, M. A., and Pastor, P. A., Jr. The elderly as a unique population: Alcoholism. *Alcoholism Clin Exp Res,* 1978, 2, 31.

Chapter 2

STRESS, SOCIAL NETWORKS AND AGING

Lisa F. Berkman

S tereotypes of older people as frail and vulnerable abound in our society. We frequently think of chronic debilitating disease as an inevitable part of the aging process. We think of older people as fragile and vulnerable to even minor social stresses. We think of them as isolated, lonely, and "disengaged." In the medical community, these images have come about largely because our contacts with older people occur when in fact they are hospitalized, ill, recently bereaved or otherwise not feeling well. Furthermore much of the research on older people is conducted among highly selected groups, frequently institutionalized, who are comprised of very elderly people with severe physical and mental disabilities, many of whom have completely severed social contacts. Rarely do we get to see healthy, socially active older people because they have no reason to come to our attention. Thus it is not surprising that based on clinic populations or those in nursing homes we have developed the stereotypes we have.

As understandable as this situation is, it is not helpful to have so little information on the vast majority of men and women over 65 who are living in communities independently. I say this for two reasons. The first is that based on whom we observe and the research we read, we develop certain expectations about what is normal for people of a certain age. We then plan interventions or treatment regimens based on our expectations for what is "normally" attainable. For instance if most people we see exhibit some degree of cognitive impairment, we may come to think of this impairment

Parts of this chapter have been reproduced from Kasl, S., Berkman, L. F.: Some psychosocial influences on the health status of the elderly: the perspective of social epidemiology. In *Aging: Biology and Behavior.* Ed. by J. McGaugh and S. Kiesler, Academic Press, 1981.

as a normal part of the aging process and not consider its causes or potential treatment. On the other hand, if we knew that only 5 percent of the population over 65 manifested that degree of cognitive impairment we might consider it in a rather different light. The second reason is that unless we have data on healthy individuals, it is impossible to develop estimates of risk or to understand the etiology of diseases. This is especially important because there is some evidence that risk factors change in their predictability with age. For instance, some data show that the risk ratio for incidence of coronary events in men goes up with age for blood pressure but down with age for serum cholesterol, cigarettes and relative weight (1). Thus we may not be able to extrapolate from well-known findings of middle-aged samples to older groups. For these reasons we are in critical need of studies of general populations representative of the entire population of men and women 65 and over.

If we focus attention on studies which include representative samples of the elderly population, do the data conform to our stereotyped images of the elderly? Let us take the social issues raised at the beginning of this paper and examine them in this regard.

ARE THE ELDERLY A LONELY AND ISOLATED GROUP?

It is frequently assumed that increasing social isolation comes with old age. Widowhood, retirement, and grown children leaving home are thought to bring about an irreversible loss of social attachments and community ties. Physical disabilities and functional limitations make it more difficult to maintain active social relations with others. While social losses are certainly common in old age, what is the evidence that increasing social isolation is an age-linked phenomenon or may even be a part of the normal aging process?

In terms of the most obvious of social contacts, those which result from living arrangements, it is interesting to note that the majority of men and women older than 65 (79 percent of men and 59 percent of women) live with other family members, including spouses (2). Among the widowed, this situation is different and appears to have changed substantially over the last 30 years. Chevan and Korson (3) in an analysis of United States census data, report that 50.4 percent of widows and 47.0 percent of widowers in 1970 reported living alone. These percentages are double what they were in 1940. In this analysis, black widows and widowers were less likely to live alone than white widows and widowers; and those with more children and less income and education lived alone more than people with fewer children and in higher status groups. Among blacks but not whites, women were less likely to live alone than men.

While living with others protects one from the most severe forms of social isolation, living alone should not be automatically equated with social isolation. Much research indicates that older single people prefer to live alone but close to their children (4, 5). Shanas (6) has presented international data suggesting that among older people with living children, for more than three-fourths, the nearest child was either in the household or within an hour or less distance from him or her. The growing literature on parents and grown children (7–10) also indicates an effective, modified extended family structure in the United States and other modern European countries.

Data from the Human Population Laboratory (HPL) Survey of almost 7000 adults in Alameda County, California, in 1965 reveal few decreases in social contacts with age, with a few important exceptions. Table 2-I reveals that only group membership shows a consistent inverse relationship with age. Other investigators have reported somewhat weaker inverse relationships for men but no association with age for women (11) or a weak relationship without controlling for sex (12). Among women, church membership increases with age. Contacts with friends and relatives do not vary greatly by age except among non-married men aged 60 to 69 who show a sharp decrease in contacts. The finding that single men in this age group are more than twice as likely as their married counterparts to report few contacts agrees with earlier findings (13). The older single man is likely to be in a particularly deviant position since few men aged 60 to 69 are single. Having possibly lost old sources of friendship, originally established through work contacts, marriage, and other social affairs, he is now likely to be an odd person at social gatherings with friends and family. The older woman, in contrast, is likely to know more people in her similar situation (since there are more) and is likely to have an easier time making social contacts. Blau (13) also notes that, incidentally, this situation disappears for people over 70 when the incidence of widowhood increases dramatically. This diminished difference is also evident in the HPL data. The greater ability of women, compared with men, to maintain intimate friendships with both family and friends has been reported at several other life stages besides the elderly (11, 14–16).

The elderly, particularly elderly women, are increasingly likely to lose a spouse with advancing years, Jacobs and Ostfeld (17), in a comprehensive review on the mortality of bereavement, estimate that 2–3 percent of married Americans over the age of 50 will become widowed each year. Between the ages of 65 and 74, 10 percent of men and 43 percent of women are widowed. For those 75 years and older the respective percentages are 29.5 and 70.2 (18). Clearly, this is an extremely frequent event among the elderly. However, there is also some evidence to suggest that the nature of bereavement is in some ways modified for the elderly. Several investigators (19–22) indicate that grief among the elderly is not the same as grief at younger ages. Jacobs and Douglas (23) have summarized this work, reporting that among the elderly, a loss is faced with more cognitive acceptance and is associated with less numbness, denial, and guilt. However, hallucinations and illusions and psychosomatic symptoms may occur with greater frequency. Jacobs and Douglas (23) suggest that these differential characteristics of grief among the elderly may be the result of the process of anticipation of death, which is probably associated with older age. This ability to anticipate and accept widowhood may also play some role in the decreased relative risks associated with bereavement at older ages reported by researchers (24, 25). This finding also supports Neugarten's (26) viewpoint that what makes events traumatic is their being "off time" and unanticipated. "Major stresses," she emphasizes, "are caused by events that upset the sequence and rhythm of the life cycle ... when the empty nest, grandparenthood, widowhood, or retirement occur *off time* [pp. 86–87]." It may also be that the experience of becoming a widow or

TABLE 2-I

PERCENTAGE OF MEN AND WOMEN WITHOUT SOCIAL CONTACT
BY MARITAL STATUS AND AGE AND SOURCE OF CONTACT,
ALAMEDA COUNTY, CALIFORNIA, 1965[a,b]

	30-49		50-59		60-69		70+	
	Percentage	Number	Percentage	Number	Percentage	Number	Percentage	Number
MEN								
None or few contacts with friends and relatives								
Married	16.4	(1209)	12.0	(446)	15.3	(268)	18.2	(143)
Nonmarried	21.8	(175)	16.4	(55)	34.5	(58)	23.9	(71)
No group membership								
Married	22.4	(1227)	19.7	(446)	28.7	(268)	42.7	(143)
Nonmarried	34.9	(175)	34.5	(55)	44.8	(58)	52.3	(76)
No church membership								
Married	71.1	(1227)	65.9	(446)	70.5	(268)	68.5	(143)
Nonmarried	78.9	(175)	70.9	(55)	80.7	(58)	75.0	(76)
WOMEN								
None or few contacts with friends and relatives								
Married	15.4	(1249)	10.0	(401)	9.4	(202)	12.8	(86)
Nonmarried	16.1	(286)	10.2	(167)	12.9	(179)	13.3	(241)
No group membership								
Married	32.7	(1249)	37.3	(407)	55.8	(208)	56.2	(89)
Nonmarried	42.3	(286)	44.9	(167)	54.7	(179)	62.1	(256)
No church membership								
Married	66.7	(1249)	60.9	(407)	58.7	(208)	57.3	(89)
Nonmarried	76.9	(286)	65.2	(167)	63.1	(179)	54.3	(256)

[a]From Human Population Laboratory.
[b]Lower totals in age cells are due to missing data.

widower at a time when one's peers are also becoming single provides a structural support that buffers against some of the stressful circumstances encountered by younger widows and widowers. This topic is discussed in greater detail in the next section.

To summarize the association of social and community ties with age, we might say that the elderly are less likely than younger men and women to maintain extensive contacts from many sources; however, in most cases these differences are not large. There are important exceptions to this pattern. People who are in structurally deviant positions appear to have a more difficult time maintaining contacts, that is, widowers aged 60 to 69. Clearly, older people are more likely to become widowed than younger and middle-aged people. Furthermore, although space does not permit a review of this evidence, both socioeconomic status and health status exert a powerful influence on the elderly person's ability to see other people.

ARE THE ELDERLY MORE VULNERABLE
THAN OTHERS TO SOCIAL STRESSES?

Much of the research on the biology and physiology of aging indicates that with time men and women are less physiologically adaptable and resilient to stresses, that is they take longer to "bounce back" from environmental or bodily insults. Older people are less immunologically competent, have slowed homeostatic and regulatory functions, and show significant declines in kidney function, insulin uptake, muscle function (27, 28). All of these physiologic changes should indicate that when exposed to a similar stressor, social or physical, the older person will respond more severely, that is be more vulnerable to physical illnesses, than younger or middle-aged individuals. In terms of physical stressors such as exposure to colder temperatures, surgery, and ingestion of toxic substances, their impact does seem to be greater among older people. But, can we say the same about social stressors? Let us take the case of social isolation or loss of social networks.

Perhaps the most profound tie maintained by individuals is between husband and wife. It has been repeatedly observed that those who are married have lower mortality rates than those who are single, widowed, or divorced (29–31). Contrary to our intuitions, this mortality risk does not appear to be as great for women as for men and actually seems to decline with age. Some evidence also suggests that the relationship between marital status and health is independent of many "traditional" physiological risk factors. In a random sample of 6672 men and women between the ages of 18 and 79, Weiss (32) examined the relationship between marital status, coronary heart disease (CHD) and serum cholesterol, systolic and diastolic blood pressure, and a ponderal index. Although Weiss found increased CHD mortality rates present among the non-married to some extent at all ages above 25, his results revealed that no differences in any risk factor explained the married/non-married CHD mortality differential. In fact, there were no consistent differences in any of the risk factor levels between married and nonmarried men and women at any age levels.

Recent evidence also indicates that mortality from ischemic heart disease (IHD) is higher among divorced and widowed people even when controlling for social class. In a study of death certificates in Finland, Koskenvuo et al. (33) found that differences in IHD rates by marital status were greatest for men between the ages of 25 and 54, evident for women in that same age group, and weaker though still observable for older men and women.

The association between widowhood and increased morbidity and mortality is particularly striking. Maddison and Viola (34), Marris (10), and early studies by Parkes (35) indicate that widows, especially in the first year following bereavement, report many more complaints about their health, both mental and physical, and believe they have sustained a lasting deterioration to their health. The relationship between widowhood and increased mortality risk from a wide variety of diseases has been reported both in studies using vital statistics (24, 25, 36, 37) and in cohort studies (21, 38–40).

In one of the more conclusive studies, Parkes, Benjamin, and Fitzgerald (41) report that of 4486 widowers 55 and older, 213 died during the first six months following bereavement. This is 40 percent above the expected rate for married men the same age. After 6 months, the rates gradually fell back to those of married men and remained at that level. Through an analysis of husbands' and wives' concordance rates for cause of death, the authors concluded that neither the sharing of a similar pathogenic environment nor the tendency toward the selection of the unfit to marry the unfit (homogamy) was likely to explain more than a part of the increased 6-month mortality rate.

In a more recent study, Helsing and colleagues (42, 43) identified from a non-official census conducted in 1963, in Washington County, Maryland all men and women who lost a spouse between 1963 and 1975. These 1204 men and 2828 women were each matched to a married person of the same race, sex, year of birth and geography of residence. Mortality rates based on person—years at risk, were virtually no different for female widowed than married but significantly higher for male widowed than married, even after adjustment for a number of demographic, socioeconomic and behavioral variables. The male widowed in all age groups experienced higher mortality than male married, the relative risk attaining statistical significance only in age groups 55–64 and 65–74, although the indicated relative risk was even higher in the younger age groups. This finding is shown clearly in Table 2-II where the relative risk of dying for widowed versus married men decreases steadily with age though the confidence intervals are much wider in lower ages based as they are on smaller numbers of deaths. For women, the relative risks in any age group are never higher than 1.34 and generally remain close to one.

Two other observations are of interest here. The first is that the investigators observed no significantly higher mortality immediately following bereavement, rather than later, for either the male or female widowed. The excess deaths found by Parkes et al. in the first six months were not found in these data; rather the risks were maintained over the twelve year follow-up period. If replicated in further work, these findings would suggest that being widowed is a chronically stressful situation rather than an acute event whose effects pass quickly.

The second area of interest is in the causes of death which are responsible for the increased mortality rates. In a paper on this topic (43) the authors note that deaths from infectious diseases, accidents, and suicides were significantly higher than expected

TABLE 2-II

RELATIVE RISK OF MORTALITY AMONG WIDOWED/MARRIED MEN AND WOMEN
BASED ON PERSON YEARS AT RISK, WASHINGTON COUNTY, MARYLAND, 1963–1975

Age	Relative Risk	95% Confidence Limits
MEN		
18–44	2.61	0.5–13.4
45–54	1.61	0.9– 2.9
55–64	1.61	1.1– 2.3
65–74	1.28	1.0– 1.6
75+	1.16	0.9– 1.4
WOMEN		
18–44	1.02	0.4– 2.9
45–54	1.34	0.7– 2.5
55–64	1.09	0.8– 1.5
65–74	1.14	0.9– 1.4
75+	1.03	0.8– 1.3

SOURCE: Adapted from Helsing, K., Szklo, M.: Mortality after bereavement. *Amer J. Epidemiol*, 114:41–52, 1981

among widowed males, and death from cirrhosis of the liver were significantly higher than expected among women. However, while individually statistically significant findings were found for these causes of death, they were but a very small portion of the overall excess in mortality. For almost every cause of death, the widowed men and women had substantially higher rates than the married. In fact, the authors conclude that this study adds to the weight of evidence that the greater mortality of the widowed is remarkably non-specific as to its causes.

The existence of a supportive marriage has been shown to mediate between stressful life events and poor health outcomes. In one study of the mental and physical health consequences of job loss due to a factory shutdown, Gore (44) reports that those men who had "the emotional support of their wives while unemployed for several weeks had few illness symptoms, low cholesterol levels, and did not blame themselves for loss of job." In general, men who were both unemployed for a longer time and unsupported tended to have the worst health outcomes (45). In another study of psychiatric disturbance among women, Brown et al. (46) found that having a husband or boy friend who was a confidant served as a powerful mediator between a severe event or major difficulty and onset of psychiatric disorder. In this sample of women aged 18 to 65, 38 percent of those who had a stressful event and no husband or boy friend as confidant experienced the onset of a disturbance. (For those without such a confidant and without a severe event, the percentage of psychiatric disturbance was under 4 percent.) When the confidant named was a sister, mother, or friend seen weekly, the relationship was not observed to mediate between live events and psychiatric disturbance.

These data suggest that there is something protective about a supportive spouse or partner that is capable of shielding an individual against the otherwise deleterious effects of some objective life circumstances. The morbidity and mortality findings also indicate that the loss of a spouse, a major enduring tie to another person, may be at least a precipitating factor in the increased death rates found among widowers.

However, they also indicate that widowhood does not have a greater impact on older people in terms of mortality risk. In fact, it appears that widowhood may actually have a less severe effect on older people or that in some way the older are more adaptable to this severe social stress.

OTHER SOCIAL TIES

Apart from spouses, other social ties are relied on by most people to fulfill a variety of emotional and pragmatic needs. Some of these ties are characterized by enduring and emotionally important relationships, while other contacts are characterized primarily by their task orientation. Some people in these links may fulfill a variety of needs; others may have one specific need for which they are relied on. Taken as a whole, these relationships and informal associations form a web or a social network in which most people spend a significant part of their lives. Although network configurations have been described in detail by many social scientists, relatively little is known about the impact that various network configurations have on health status.

Additionally, networks have been hypothesized to have direct effects on health status by effecting physiologic processes as well as having more indirect effects as buffers against the consequences of other serious life events or changes; such as widowhood. According to the buffer hypotheses, the extent to which an individual is able to maintain social support in certain situations may have a profound effect on: 1) the way the situation is ultimately resolved and 2) the emotional impact the situation has on the individual. These factors, in turn, may influence the degree to which the event itself is stressful and has serious disease consequences. For example, McKinley (47) suggests that social networks, more than any other variable, "may determine how the crisis of death is responded to or coped with." Other investigators (48) note that different kinds of network ties are important at different times in the bereavement process. Early in the process, soon after the death of a spouse, individuals need emotional support which is best supplied by other close, intimate relations and friends. However, there soon may be a discrepancy, especially in Westernized cultures, between the needs of the bereaved individual to complete "grief work" and to make a transition, and the ability of those most intimate with the individual to supply the necessary resources and support. During these later phases, less intimate or weaker ties may aid in the adjustment of the bereaved by supplying new information and sources of contact.

While most researchers interested in the health effects of social networks have proceeded along the lines just described, that is by investigating the ability of an individual's network to buffer the impact of various life events, I became intrigued with the possibility that social networks, which include both intimate and extended or weaker ties, have more direct disease consequences.

Since, 1975, I have had the opportunity to examine the impact of different social relationships on mortality and morbidity risk in a cohort of a random sample of adults in a community. In 1965, the Human Population Laboratory (HPL) part of the California State Department of Health conducted a survey of an area probability sample of non-institutionalized adult residents of Alameda County, California. Questionnaires were returned for 86 percent of the enumerated population yielding, 6,928 respondents. Mortality data were collected for the 9-year period between 1965 and 1974 when respondents were resurveyed. Death certificates from both in and out-of-state were located for 682 respondents. The collection of mortality data between 1965 and 1974 seems to be reasonably complete since only 4 percent of the total sample could not be located at the end of the 9-year follow-up period, and those lost to follow-up did not differ markedly on health measures in the 1965 survey.

In the survey, basic information on many essential aspects of an individual's personal network, was collected. A Social Network Index was developed based on four types of social connections: (1) marriage, (2) contacts with extended family and close friends, (3) church membership, and (4) other group affiliations. Contacts with friends and relatives were measured by the number of close friends and relatives a respondent reported and the frequency with which he/she saw them.

Analysis of the relationship between the Social Network Index and nine year mortality risk shows that people who lack social and community ties are at a substantially increased risk of dying (49). Table 2-III shows that relative risk for different age and sex groups reveal only a slightly lower relative risk in older age groups, and that the dimunition in relative risk by age was not very regular. Calculations done on the 70 and older group, in which a little more than 50 percent died during the follow-up period, still reveal the predictive power of the Social Network Index. It thus appears that social isolation does not particularly diminish or increase in its potency as a risk factor for mortality in higher age groups. Since the mortality data by marital status discussed earlier reveal a dimunition of risk with age, this difference in results may suggest that other items in the Social Network Index are particularly notable predictors of mortality in the older population.

In Tecumseh, Michigan, House et al. have extended and partially reproduced the findings observed in Alameda County (50). In their study of men and women aged 35–69 they found that men reporting a higher level of social relationships and activities were significantly less likely to die during the follow-up period of 9–12 years. Trends for women were similar, but generally non-significant once age and other risk factors were controlled. These latter findings stand in contrast to those reported for Alameda County where womens' risks were generally equal to mens'. The investigators comment that this may reflect differing processes of social integra-

TABLE 2-III

MORTALITY RATES FROM ALL CAUSES (PER 100) BY SOCIAL NETWORK INDEX. AGE,
SEX-SPECIFIC RATES, ALAMEDA COUNTY, CALIFORNIA, 1965–1974

Social Network Index	30-49 Percentage	Number	50-59 Percentage	Number	60-69 Percentage	Number	70+ Percentage	Number
MEN								
I (Most connections)	2.4	(457)	9.6	(197)	21.8	(110)	50.0	(54)
II	3.1	(450)	12.1	(157)	26.3	(95)	59.5	(42)
III	5.3	(396)	18.2	(121)	33.0	(88)	65.2	(89)
IV (Least connections)	6.1	(99)	30.8	(26)	39.4	(33)	88.2	(34)
WOMEN								
I (Most connections)	1.5	(460)	7.3	(205)	9.7	(93)	30.4	(56)
II	2.0	(402)	4.9	(122)	16.7	(78)	46.3	(41)
III	4.3	(514)	8.0	(188)	17.7	(158)	44.2	(156)
IV (Lease connections)	6.9	(159)	15.3	(59)	29.4	(58)	55.4	(92)

tion in a small city in a rural area such as Tecumseh versus a more metropolitan area such as Alameda County. Thus social relationships and activities are more likely to occur casually as part of the normal fabric of daily life, especially among women in Tecumseh. Women may not report or think of these relationships as "visits" or formal interactions in Tecumseh as they might in Alameda County.

The Tecumseh findings indicate that less active solitary activities such as watching television, listening to the radio, and reading are actually associated with some *increase* rather than decrease in mortality risk. While this may be due to the physical impairments of people, it is clear that such factors are not effective in reducing a person's risk of dying. To have such beneficial effects, these data suggest that an activity must involve greater active effort by the individual and some contact with other people. These findings have important implications for some of the elderly whose major activities involve only watching or listening to the radio and TV.

House et al. (50) also had the opportunity to assess the importance of self-reported satisfaction with social relationships in conjunction with the intensity and frequency of such relationships. They found no association between satisfaction and mortality risk. They hypothesize that the satisfaction measures used may be too unreliable to produce significant effects on mortality or that satisfaction may not be the critical aspect of a relationship which affects mortality. For instance it may be that some minimal level of relationship is more important than the subjective perception of the quality of that relationship.

While the Tecumseh study did not include people 70 and over in their analyses, a recent study in which many of these same issues were explored has just been reported on 331 men and women 65 and over and living in Durham County, North Carolina (51). In this study with a 30 month follow-up period, three measures of social support were found to predict mortality. The measures were: (1) impaired roles and available attachments — measured by marital status and number of living children and siblings; (2) impaired frequency of social interaction measured by telephone calls and visits with friends or relatives made during the past week, and; (3) impaired perception of social support — measured by feeling lonely, like no one understands you, and not having someone to help you if you were ill or disabled, or who cares what happens to you. After controlling for ten potentially confounding factors such as age, race, economic status, physical and mental health status, capacity for self-care, stressful life events and cigarette smoking, all three variables remained significant predictors of mortality. In contrast to the Tecumseh findings, the strongest predictor of mortality was the perceived support variable. Whether this variable is actually more important to older people or reflects differences in measurement between the studies is unclear. Nevertheless after controlling for confounding variables, the relative risk for this factor was 3.40, compared to 2.04 and 1.88 for the other support factors.

What can we conclude from these findings? The findings reviewed strongly suggest that people, young or old, who are isolated, disconnected, or who have recently lost an intimate relationship, are subject to increasing mortality risk. They do not however indicate that the elderly are more vulnerable to those losses and isolation than others. If anything, it appears that the impact of social disconnections are weaker in the elderly than others—that is, they survive these conditions better than younger and middle-aged people. This is especially surprising since, as stated earlier, the elderly are less resilient to physical stresses and are less adaptable physiologically. However, there may be some perspective which makes this finding more logical and comprehensible. First, it may be that elderly cohorts represent, in a sense, the survival of the "fittest" so that there has been prior attrition of the more vulnerable. Any such process could explain why risk factors predictive of disease in middle-age could "wash out" in older cohorts. In order to understand this process better, cohorts would have to be identified in young or middle-age and followed longitudinally for decades.

It is also possible that past learning facilitates adaptation to the next experience—that in fact, we do get wiser as we age. Older people may also have reduced adaptive demands if societal role expectations become more openended. Or it is likely as Neugarten has hypothesized that there is a diminishing psychosocial significance of events because of life-cycle changes in aspirations, expectations, and perceptions.

While the evidence seems to favor the perspective of a diminishing impact of events and experiences on the health of the elderly, it would also seem that many of us are not comfortable with such a perspective. After all, the elderly seem to live in a state in which mounting social losses, physical debilitation, economic deprivation, and loss of (conventionally defined) useful work activities are taking place with great inevitability, but we do not seem to be able to detect the intuitively expected corresponding impact, such as in clinical depression or physical illness (52). It is possible, then, that we have an incomplete grasp of the various positive factors in the lives of the elderly—the resources in their social environment, the adaptive strategies available to them—that serve to diminish the impact of the presumptively stressful experiences. Furthermore, we may not have a good understanding of what is specifically stressful to the elderly. That is, if we accept the approximate definition of stress as "demands that tax the adaptive resources," we may well ask if particular events and experiences represent social and personal demands equally for the elderly as for the younger person.

DO OLDER PEOPLE UNDER STRESS
HAVE HIGH RISK HEALTH PRACTICES?

I would like to review briefly some of the findings from Alameda County regarding the relationship between social networks and such health practices as smoking, physical activity, obesity, and particularly alcohol consumption. As stated earlier both social networks and health practices have an independent impact on mortality risk in the Alameda County data. However, they are also associated with each other, cross-sectionally in the 1965 baseline survey. The question of interest here is whether people who are isolated or lacking in social and community ties are more likely than others to maintain certain practices which may be detrimental to their health, particularly whether they are more likely to drink heavily. We are also interested in knowing whether this relationship is different for older men and women than younger people.

Table 2-IV shows the percentage of men and women who maintain 3 or more high risk health practices (of a possible 5) by varying level of social network. The table is age and sex specific. The table reveals that with the exception of men 70 years and over, people who are lacking social and community ties are much more likely, about 3 times as likely, to maintain high risk practices than their counterparts with the most social contacts. Specifically, the more isolated one becomes, the more likely he or she is to smoke, drink heavily, be physically inactive, obese or severely underweight, and sleep either more or less than 7 or 8 hours per night.

TABLE 2-IV
PERCENTAGE OF MEN AND WOMEN
WITH THREE OR MORE (OF 5) HIGH-RISK HEALTH PRACTICES
BY SOCIAL NETWORK INDEX (AGE AND SPECIFIC RATES),
ALAMEDA COUNTY, 1965

Social Network Group	30–49	50–59	60–69	70+
MEN				
I least connections	30.3	42.3	45.5	29.4
II	23.7	25.6	20.5	24.7
III	15.8	21.0	10.5	14.3
IV most connections	11.4	10.7	16.4	27.8
WOMEN				
I least connections	25.2	37.3	27.6	32.6
II	19.8	24.5	20.9	14.7
III	12.7	22.1	21.8	12.2
IV most connections	9.6	9.3	9.7	8.9

If one examines the relationship between alcohol consumption alone, and social networks, similar associations are revealed (see Table 2-V). Again people who are lacking social and community ties are more likely to drink heavily than those with more extended and varied contacts. This pattern is most clear in men and is weaker in women. Only women with the most connections, group IV, have a consistently lower percentage of heavy drinkers than the other three network groups. It is important to note that this measure of alcohol consumption is measured by quantity per sitting and frequency of consuming wine, beer, and liquor. It is not a measure of extremely heavy consumption or, in any way, of alcoholism or substance abuse. However, the measure as it has been devised, is predictive of mortality risk over the nine year period. Thus, people who consume 46 or more drinks per month are found to have an elevated mortality risk in the Alameda County data.

TABLE 2-V

PERCENTAGE OF MEN AND WOMEN DRINKING 46+ ALCOHOLIC BEVERAGES PER MONTH
BY SOCIAL NETWORK INDEX (AGE AND SEX-SPECIFIC RATES), ALAMEDA COUNTY, 1965

Social Network Index		30–49	50–59	60–69	70+
		MEN			
I	least connections	23.2	34.6	24.2	23.5
II		26.8	21.5	15.9	11.2
III		24.4	25.5	14.7	9.5
IV	most connections	19.9	13.7	11.8	7.4
		WOMEN			
I	least connections	13.2	13.6	3.4	1.1
II		9.7	9.0	3.2	3.2
III		13.9	6.6	3.8	2.4
IV	most connections	8.3	4.4	2.2	0

Considering the question of whether the association between networks and health practices changes with age, again the data show a fairly consistent relationship across all age ranges. Thus, while health practices and social networks are associated with one another, this is no more true for the elderly than for other age groups.

In a review of the effects of bereavement, a severe social loss, Klerman and Izen (53) report marked increases in the consumption of drugs, alcohol and tobacco among recently bereaved men and women. Parkes (35) reports that sedative drugs were prescribed seven times more frequently for widows under the age of 65 years during the first six months of bereavement than in the period preceding bereavement. No differences were observed for those over 65. In two later studies, Parkes and Brown (54) and Maddison and Viola (34) showed significant increases in smoking, alcohol consumption and use of sedatives among widows during the first 13 months after bereavement when compared to non-bereaved controls.

Although these studies are far from conclusive and are limited in number, they do illustrate the possibility that health practices are responses to stressful circumstances and may, in fact, be used as coping mechanisms to mitigate the negative emotional impact such situations have. However, the evidence also indicates that older people are no more likely than others to employ such high-risk practices.

SUMMARY

Professional stereotypes of older people are based primarly on exposure to the institutionalized elderly. This results in a highly biased image as the vast majority of older people live independently in the community. This bias has serious consequences as we attempt to develop public policy, plan treatment interventions, attempt to develop estimates of risk and to understand the etiology of diseases of the elderly. This paper examines three popular stereotypes. First that the elderly are a lonely and isolated group. Second, that the elderly are more vulnerable to social stress. Finally that the lack of social network configurations causes older people to be more likely to maintain health risk practices and to be more vulnerable to health risks. A review of numerous research studies based on non-institutionalized older people indicates that these stereotypes are for the most part in error or in need of drastic modification. Social networks do change with age and some segments of our older population may be at greater risk. In addition, there is considerable evidence to suggest that they may, in fact, handle psychological stressors, such as social disconnections, with less negative consequence than younger and middle-aged people. The paper urges further exploration of the resources available in the social environment of the elderly and of the adaptive strategies that serve to diminish the impact of the presumptively stressful experiences associated with growing older.

REFERENCES

1. Pooling Project Research Group. Relationship of blood pressure, serum cholesterol, smoking habit, relative weight and ECG abnormalities to incidence of major coronary events: Final report of the pooling project. *Journal of Chronic Diseases*, 1978, 31, 201–306.
2. Sussman, M. B. The family life of old people. In R. H. Binstock and E. Shanas (Eds.), *Handbook of Aging and the Social Sciences*. New York: Van Nostrand Reinhold Co., 1976.
3. Chevan, A., and Korson, J. H. The widowed who live alone: An examination of social and demographic factors. *Social Forces*, 1972, 51, 45–53.
4. Troll, L. The family of later life: A decade review. *Journal of Marriage and Family*, 1971, 33, 263–290.
5. Rosenmayr, L., and Kockeis, E. Housing conditions and family relations of the elderly. In F. M. Carp and N. M. Burnett (Eds.), *Patterns of Living and Housing of Middle-Aged and Older People. Public Health Service Publication No. 1496*, 29–46. Washington, D.C.: U.S. Department of Health, Education and Welfare, 1966.
6. Shanas, E. Family help patterns and social class in three countries. *Journal of Marriage and Family*, 1967, 29(2), 257–266.
7. Adams, B. N. The middle-class adult and his widowed or still married mother. *Social Problems*, 1968, 16(1), 50–59.
8. Sussman, M. B. The help pattern in the middle-class family. *American Sociological Review*, 1953, 18, 22–28.
9. Townsend, P. *The Family Life of Old People*. London: Routledge and Kegan Paul, 1957.
10. Marris, R. *Widows and Their Families*. London: Routledge and Kegan Paul, 1958.
11. Booth, A. Sex and social participation. *American Sociological Review*, 1972, 27, 183–193.
12. Harvey, C., and Bahr, H. Widowhood, morale, and affiliation. *Journal of Marriage and the Family*, 1974, 36(1), 97–106.
13. Blau, Z. *Old Age in a Changing Society*. New York: Franklin Watts, 1973.
14. Arth, M. American culture and the phenomenon of friendship in the aged. In C. Tibbits and W. Donahue (Eds.), *Social and Psychological Aspects of Aging*, 529–534. New York: Columbia University Press, 1962.
15. Lowenthal, M. F., Thurnher, M., Chiriboga, D., and Associates. *Four Stages of Life*. San Francisco, Calif.,: Jossey-Bass, 1975.
16. Powers, E. A., and Bultena, G. L. Sex differences in intimate friendships of old age. *Journal of Marriage and Family*, 1976, 38(4), 739–747.
17. Jacobs, S., and Ostfeld, A. An epidemiological review of the mortality of bereavement. *Psychosomatic Medicine*, 1977, 39(5), 344–357.
18. Siegel, J. S. Some demographic aspects of aging in the United States. In A. M. Ostfeld and D. C. Gibson (Eds.), *Epidemiology of Aging*. Publication No.

77–711. National Institute of Health, Washington, D.C.: U.S. Department of Health, Education and Welfare, 1975.

19. Stern, K., and Williams, G. M. Grief reactions in later life. *American Journal of Psychiatry*, 1951, 108, 289–294.

20. Gramlich, E. P. Recognition and management of grief in elderly patients. *Geriatrics*, 1968, 23, 87–92.

21. Gerber, I., Rusualem, R., Hannon, N., Battin, D., and Arkin, A. Anticipatory grief and widowhood. *British Journal of Psychiatry*, 1975, 122, 47–51.

22. Heyman, D. K., and Gianturco, D. T. Long term adaptation by the elderly to bereavement. *Journal of Gerontology*, 1973, 28, 259–262.

23. Jacobs, S., and Douglas, L. Grief: A mediating process between loss and illness. *Comprehensive Psychiatry*, 1979, 20(2), 165–174.

24. Kraus, A. S., and Lilienfeld, A. M. Some epidemiologic aspects of the high mortality rate in the young widowed group. *Journal of Chronic Diseases*, 1959, 10, 207–217.

25. McNeil, D. N. Mortality among the widowed in Connecticut. M.P.H. essay. New Haven, Conn.: Yale University, 1973.

26. Neugarten, B. Adaptation and the life cycle. *Journal of Geriatric Psychiatry*, 1970, 4, 71–100.

27. Timiras, P. *Developmental Physiology and Aging.* New York: Macmillan, 1972.

28. Finch, C. E., and Hayflick, L., (Eds.), *Handbook of the Biology of Aging.* New York: Van Nostrand Reinhold, 1977.

29. Ortmeyer, C. Variations in mortality, morbidity, and health care by marital status. In C. F. Erhardt and J. E. Berlin, (eds.), *Mortality and Morbidity in the United States*, 159–188. Cambridge, Mass: Harvard University Press, 1974.

30. Durkheim, E. *Suicide.* Glencoe, Ill.: The Free Press, 1951.

31. Price, J. S., Slater, E., and Hare, E. H. Marital status of first admissions to psychiatric beds in England and Wales in 1965 and 1966. *Social Biology*, 1971, 18, 574–594.

32. Weiss, N. S. Marital status and risk factors for coronary heart disease. *British Journal of Preventive and Social Medicine*, 1973, 27, 41–43.

33. Koskenvuo, M., Kaprio, J., Kesaniemi, A., and Sarna, S. Differences in mortality form ischemic heart disease by marital status and social class. *Journal of Chronic Disease*, 1980, 33, 95–106.

34. Maddision, D., and Viola, A. The health of widows in the year following bereavement. *Journal of Psychosomatic Resources*, 1968, 12, 297–306.

35. Parkes, C. M. The effects of bereavement on physical and mental health: A study of the medical records of widows. *British Medical Journal*, 1964, 2, 274–279.

36. Young, M., Benjamin, B., and Wallis, C. The mortality of widows. *Lancet*, 1963, 2, 454–457.

37. Co, P. R., and Ford, J. R. The mortality of widows shortly after widowhood. *Lancet*, 1964, 1, 163.

38. Rees, W. P., and Lutkins, S. G. Mortality of bereavement. *British Medical Journal*, 1967, 4, 13–16.

39. Clayton, P. J. Mortality and morbidity in the first year of widowhood. *Archives of General Psychiatry*, 1974, 30, 747–750.
40. Ward, A. W. Mortality of bereavement. *British Medical Journal*, 1976, 1, 700–702.
41. Parkes, C. M., Benjamin, B., and Fitzgerald, R. G. Broken heart: A statistical study of increased mortality among widowers. *British Medical Journal*, 1969, 1, 740–743.
42. Helsing, K., and Szklo, M. Mortality after bereavement. *American Journal of Epidemiology*, 1981, 114 (1), 41–52.
43. Helsing, K., Comstock, G., and Szklo, M. Causes of death in a widowed population. *American Journal of Epidemiology*, 1982, 116(3), 524–532.
44. Gore, S. The effect of social support in moderating the health consequences of unemployment. *Journal of Health and Social Behavior*, 1978, 19; 157–165.
45. Cobb, S., and Kasl, S. V. *Termination: The Consequences of Job Loss.* (NIOSH) Publication No. 77–224. Cincinnati, Ohio: U.S. Department of Health, Education, and Welfare, 1977.
46. Brown, G. W., Bhrolchain, M. N., and Harris, T. Social class and psychiatric disturbance among women in an urban population. *Sociology*, 1975, 9, 225–254.
47. McKinlay, J. B. Social networks, lay consultation, and help-seeking behavior. *Social Forces*, 1973, 51, 275–292.
48. Walker, N. K., MacBride, A., and Vachon, M. L. Social support networks and the crisis of bereavement. *Social Science and Medicine*, 1977, 11, 35–41.
49. Berkman, L. F., and Syme, S. L. Social networks, host resistance, and mortality: A nine-year follow-up study of Alameda County residents. *American Journal of Epidemiology*, 1979, 109, 186–204.
50. House, J. S., Robbins, L., and Metzner, H. The association of social relationships and activities with mortality: Prospective evidence from the Tecumseh Community Health Study. *American Journal of Epidemiology*, 1982, 116(1), 123–140.
51. Blazer, D. G. Social support and mortality in an elderly community population. *American Journal of Epidemiology*, 1982, 115(5), 684–694.
52. Jarvik, L. F. Aging and depression: Some unanswered questions. *Journal of Gerontology*, 1976, 31(3), 324–326.
53. Klerman, G. L., and Izen, J. The effects of bereavement and grief on physical health and general well-being. *Advances in Psychomatic Medicine*, 1977, 9, 63–101.
54. Parkes, C. M., and Brown, R. Health after bereavement. A controlled study of young Boston widows and widowers. *Psychosomatic Medicine*, 1972, 34, 449–461.

Chapter 3

LIFE EVENTS AND DRINKING BEHAVIOR IN LATER YEARS[1]

Carol A. Nowak

S imon (1) defines an alcoholic as a person whose dependence upon alcohol has reached such a degree as to interfere with his health, interpersonal relationships, social adjustment, and economic functioning. Most of the literature on these nonadaptive correlates of alcohol abuse has addressed their relevance to individual functioning in the first half of life. Relatively few investigations of their dynamics in mid-and later life have been explored despite research findings to suggest that both alcoholism and death due to alcohol abuse peak in the late-middle and early-old ages (19, 20). Similarly, etiological investigations have reported distinct differences between young and old onset problem drinkers, the latter reliably possessing characteristics which suggest "drinking-to-cope" adaptive styles in reaction to stressful life events (24). Despite this classification of late onset drinkers as stress-reactive rather than process alcoholics, and despite several intriguing findings about the nature of events which precipitate such problems (23, 21), no systematic effort has yet been made to explore the etiology of late life drinking behavior within a stressful life events framework. This is particularly surprising in the light of findings which suggest that the most stressful periods of adult life are those nearly identical to the most problematic years for alcohol abuse and illness.

---

[1]Nowak, C. A reconceptualization of life events. Manuscript in progress, 1982.

ALCOHOL USE IN MID- AND LATER LIFE

While there has been extensive theoretical and empirical work reported in the area of mid- and late-life stress and coping, there have been very few investigations of alcohol use among the elderly in general, and among aged who drink in reaction to stressful episodes in particular (1). There is practically nothing known of those individuals whose drinking can be predicted from stress and coping histories as opposed to personality type and psychiatric pathology throughout the latter half of life. Most empirical knowledge of the aged drinker is, in fact, of the aged *alcoholic*, derived from hospitalized or institutionalized samples of elderly who are differentiated either on the basis of presence or absence of organic brain syndrome (OBS) (see, for example, 2, 3, 4, 5), or, in the latter case, on MMPI or comparable personality measure subtest scores (6, 7, 8). (Recent works by Meyers and by Hingson are notable exceptions (43, 44).) The apparent preoccupation of researchers with facility-admitted aged alcoholics may be attributed to several predisposing factors. First, their pathology is generally obvious once an examination beyond their presenting complaint is made (9, 1), while community-bound alcoholics may be less visible for a variety of well-documented reasons (1). Secondly, the incidence of alcoholism has been shown to decline in later life (10, 11, 12), and may thus represent a lower research priority among gerontological investigators than do those variables more closely linked to later life pathology, except where the problem is so blatant as to require hospitalization. Thirdly, the suggestion that alcoholism may, in fact, be a self-limiting disease that reverses itself in the latter half of life (13) may be interpreted by some investigators to suggest that alcoholism is an affliction suffered by the less physiologically hearty elderly, and is thus an issue of clinical rather than community significance. Lastly, considerable naivete among medical and mental health investigators about the developmentally normal vs. sterotypically expected changes which accompany the aging process has still been shown to exist (14). Thus, signs of alcohol-related pathology in community-dwelling elderly may go unnoticed as their symptoms are mistaken for the effects of age, chronic illness, or "senility" (1).

Despite the somewhat encouraging, (although potentially mis-
leading), picture painted by these data which suggest the non-
prevalence and/or reversibility of alcoholism in the latter half of
life, there is also substantial evidence to suggest that non-adaptive
drinking is a matter of considerable concern during this period.
Epidemiological studies indicate that well over 10 percent of individuals 60 and over are heavy drinkers, most of them with serious
or severe diagnoses (2). Mortality rates are higher for mid- and for
late life alcoholics than for any other age groups, with greatest
incidence of death in the age ranges between 50–59 and 60–69
respectively (15, 16). While it isn't clear if most late-life alcoholism
is processual from youthful onset to full-blown symptomatology
in old age, or characterized instead by actual mid- or later
life onset, it has been established, that among the latter type,
heavy drinking is more often associated with illness or age—
related environmental stresses such as the empty nest (17), bereavement, retirement, loneliness leading to depression (18), or
other interpersonal circumstances regardless of specific event
occurrences (43).

These latter findings are especially interesting when examined
in the light of research relevant to stressful life events in mid-and
later life. There is considerable empirical evidence, for example,
to suggest that the peak years for stressful life change (whether
positive or negative), and the reorganization of coping strategies
are between 45–55, and 65–75—years which overlap with those
that peak for alcohol abuse, and follow closely those believed to be
the typical onset age for late life drinking (19, 20). Furthermore,
where investigations have even tangentially explored the characteristics of late-life onset alcoholics, they have found them to be
more inundated with stress; more depressed; more likely to have
developed inappropriate or unchallenged reserves of strength to
cope with stress in their adult years; more involved in situationally
anchored rather than psychologically elusive incidents of stress;
more likely to have better prognoses for recovery; and more
responsive to and active in their plans for treatment and rehabilitation (21, 22, 20, 23, 1). While strongly suggestive of the linkage
between mid- and late-life drinking behavior and the ability to
cope with the stresses of adult life events, however, several recent

investigators have indicated that research has not only *not* established any causal or empirically correlative relationship between the two (43, for example), but is sorely needed to do so (1, 18). This paper proposes to explore the linkage between adult life events and drinking behaviors in middle and old age within the innovative conceptual and methodological life events framework described below. It seems important to do so for several reasons: (1.) It is well-documented in the developmental-social psychological literature on later life that type, nature and circumstances surrounding accumulated and compounded life experiences over time are better indicators of coping and adaptation than are physiological, social or psychological criteria by themselves and at *given* points in time (see 42, for example). (2.) Increasingly serious attention is being paid to the late—life community mental health literature, which suggests several issues pertinent to late—onset maladaptive reactions to stressful life events. These issues include the relative merits of primary and secondary crisis intervention for the amelioration of mental distress (including alcohol abuse), over long-term psychotherapy; the need to develop innovative epidemiological strategies for assessing the prevalence and etiology of maladaptive behavior in later life, because of low community visibility of the elderly, and their reluctance to present themselves for psychological assistance; and the need for better techniques to differentially diagnose such things as alcohol and drug misuse from chronic organicity in later life.

A LIFE EVENTS APPROACH TO THE
STUDY OF ADULT STRESS AND COPING

The study of life events is currently a theoretically and empirically "hot" approach to the understanding of human development in the middle and late adult years. Of particular interest to researchers in the arena of community mental health is the relationship of these events to socially and psychologically adaptive coping behaviors. Classic life event investigators envision certain events as catalysts for excessive stress and the breakdown of previously adaptive coping behaviors (25, 26). They have developed weighted checklists of relatively expectable adult life "crises," and assume an additive, compounding relationship between the number and intensity of events experienced by an individual, and the development of psychosomatic illness or other maladaptive responses to life stress. Contemporary life event investigators, however, view this classic approach as both limiting and simplistic.[2] Espousing what might best be called a "structural" approach to life events (27), lifespan developmental psychologists believes that individual development occurs in the more complex, interrelated context of biocultural change (28), and this "change" results from dynamic competition and resolution among individual, ecological, and societal event components and contexts (28, 29). As a result, life cycle investigators have come to favor models of development that characterize human growth as continuous, interrelated segments of several different, thematic life trajectories (for example, career, interpersonal, family, social, and so forth). Each profoundly influences the other; each varies within and between individuals, and each is amenable to prediction, optimization, and enhancement of adaptive behavior over the course of time (27, 28, 29). The central feature of this more contemporary view of life events is their delineation of antecedent event classes which are processed by the individual, and eventuate in behavioral or psychological outcomes that are either facilitative of, or inocuous or disruptive to, individual coping at given points in time. It is this structural view of life events that guides the present discussion of the relationship between life events, stress, and drinking behavior in the latter half of life. In order to maximally understand the methodology and implications of this linkage, however, some definitions and interpretations should first be operationalized.

CATEGORIES OF LIFE EVENTS

Contemporary life event theorists conceptualize life events categorically as either individual, societal, or non-normative. Each of these event classes is presumed to profoundly influence an individual's developmental growth and adaptation.

---

[2]Ibid.

Individual-life events

Individual influences upon human development refer to those events that correlate chronologically to a person's life cycle (28). They are in part determined by biological readiness or capability, and in part by socialization, representing what are more commonly referred to as "normative life crises" (30, 31, 32).

They are predictable, pivotal landmarks which demarcate an individual's specific developmental domains across the life cycle. Thus, marriage, birth of a first child, emptying of the nest, and widowhood all represent events presumed to anchor the *family* life cycle. Choosing a career, landing a promotion, and retirement similarly demarcate the life course of *work,* and so on. Their primary impact coincides with the time of event onset, since such occurrences typically function as "turning points" which require new adjustments, decisions, behaviors, or growth (30, 27). Nowak,[3] however, suggests that it is not the occurrence of the life event itself which exerts its impact upon the person experiencing it, but the competing demands of the context within which it occurs. She suggests that pivotal life events actually occur in three competing contexts, the interactions among which mediate the meaning and significance of the event for the experiencing individual. The first, and simplest, context is that of the actual domain within which the event is located (31). For example, launching one's last child occurs in the context of the *family* life cycle. *Secondly,* there is the context of multiple, concurrent life-course domains, or as Elder (34) suggests, "multiple, interlocking career lines, (with their) resulting problems of synchronization and resource management" (p. 15). Launching one's last child for example, might occur simultaneously with one's retirement from the work life cycle, adding, among other things, an economic dimension to the empty nest. *Thirdly,* there exists the context of the multiple career lines of significant others at the point during which an individual is experiencing a so-called "critical life event" (33). For example, one's last child may be launched just as a previously launched child is about to give birth to a first grandchild. It is the

---

[3]Ibid.

ebb and flow of events that are simultaneously embedded within these three contexts—that is, their timing and sequencing—that are crucial determinants in the assessment of just how "critical" a "critical event" is.

Elder (34), however, notes that the stressfulness of a life change is *not* only dependent upon "the temporal context of the change, its position within the life cycle, and its relation to other (life course) events" (p. 25). Other event and person characteristics are also important. "The nature of the change, whether drastic—or not, incremental or decremental, anticipated or unexpected, (as well as) the life history of experience, expectations, and adaptive skills that one brings to the new situation . . . " (34), (p. 25) are also determinants. The individual's perceptions of, and attitudes toward, the event can likewise be added to these. All of them help determine the stress levels and coping styles of the individual who experiences the event. Individual events as discussed above generate some implicit assumptions about the nature of normative life changes. The complex interplay of life course contexts, event, and person characteristics render naive, at best, the view that "life events" are discrete occurrences with discernible onset, definable parameters, and measurable impact. A more accurate representation might be to envision them as "event processes," with interconnecting anticipatory cues, event competition, interwoven affect, and gradual resolution along multiple life-career lines. Unique interindividual configurations of multiple life influences also make it difficult to accept, as given, "a priori" notions of just what events are, in fact, normatively critical. Although it is true that societal requirements for appropriate timing and sequencing of various life events exist, the clarity and rigor of enforcement of these social criteria are not as firmly established as has been believed (31). Thus, conceptually reasonable representations of individual life events should probably look toward predictors of individual impact that consider event *structure* and patterning, rather than just their societally meaningful content. Unfortunately, life event research to date has shied away from such considerations. Instead, its focus has been basically unidimensional, non-dyadic, and post event oriented.

Societal Life Events

Societal life events are a second antecedent influence system upon life change and adaptation. Unlike individual events, whose impact is primarily personal and immediate, societal events unfold in the slow-moving context of biosocial change within which individual development proceeds (28, 29). They represent what is more commonly referred to in the literature as "historical" or "cultural" change. The impetus for such change might be some major historical event such as the Great Depression (35), some less discernible but nevertheless impactful secular trend, such as floods, tornados and earthquakes,[4] or matters of local, state, or national politics. The "bumping and grinding" of these societal events against various demographic, career, and community contexts at any given time provide the impetus which then give rise, Ryder (36) tells us, to "a set of conventions for moving individuals in and out of social patterns" (p. 8). Thus, changes in societal priorities, community resources, and job availability, in concert with changes in cohort size and composition which affect family structure and friendship networks, collectively contribute to the allocation of role assignments and expectations and the process which socializes individuals into them (34). Modell and his collaborators (37) thus point out that "the timing (and sequencing) of any (given) transition in our complex society is rarely a simple reflection of an age norm. (It) is rather the cumulative outcome of the allocational needs of the society, the time required for adequate socialization for the performance of these roles, and individual volition" (p. 9). They suggest that cohort level analysis considerations of on or off timing, in or out of sequencing, and impact of life events in

---

[4]See the following:

Hartshough, D. Meddling with "Acts of God," A disaster recovery intervention. Paper presented at the American Psychological Association Convention, Chicago, 1975.

Hartshough, D. Lafayette crisis center volunteer training program. Paper presented at the Southern Psychological Convention, New Orleans, 1976.

Hartshough, D. Monticello in retrospect: Confessions of a mental health disaster recovery worker. Paper presented at the American Psychological Association Convention, San Francisco, 1977.

proper perspective. Thus, the popular notion of societal, or social, clocking of normative life events is useful for targeting potential adaptation difficulties in an individual context, but oversimplified when examined outside of that context. Thus simple judgements about the timing and the sequencing of individual life events independent of cohort referents are less rich, less meaningful, and less predictive than are those mindful of the historical milieu within which they are embedded. Unfortunately, most empirical work in life events is of the former variety.

Non-Normative, Low-Probability, Life Events

Non-normative life events represent what most theorists consider a third major antecedent life change system. Baltes and others (28, 29) define these events as significant influences upon development, but not for everyone, and not in easily predictable or detectable ways. Danish, Smyer and Nowak (27) prefer to think of these events as low-probability occurrences in either the individual or societal domain. The latter might include such things as floods, health epidemics, or "Acts of God," while the former might be illness, divorce, job loss, or other such low-probability life changes. Very little research has been done on societally low-probability events (27); considerably more has addressed individual such events.

Those individual events most studied have been related to illness. Holmes and Rahe (25), and the Dohrenwends (26), have pioneered the investigations in this realm. Interestingly enough, their studies have actually centered about illness *in response to* other major life changes. Although their work virtually spearheaded the life-events approach *qua* approach as it has come to be developed, their work, too, suffers from some of the operational limitations noted earlier in this discussion.

Antecedent Event Classes, Summarized

Three classes of events antecedent to life change — individual, societal, and non-normative — have so far been operationally reviewed. It has been suggested that empirical inquiries utilizing a so-called life events framework have actually lagged behind more sophisticated *theoretical* conceptualizations of event research. Elder (34) and others have variable attributed this to lack of appropriate and innovative research designs and data collection techniques, inadequate methodologies, lack of sufficient seed funds to investigate new strategies, and insufficient time for researchers to employ complicated life history interview and charting procedures. Whatever the reasons, it is clear that life events research has basically impassed at the point of studying life changes with respect to their content rather than structure, their post-event impact rather than processual unfolding, and their proximal, to the exclusion of distal, implications for adjustment. Thus, the richness of a life-events approach to the study and prediction of adult psychological development can only be realized if operational innovations in methodology keep apace of the conceptually more complex and exciting thought behind the framework.

AN OPERATIONAL ALTERNATIVE: THE STUDY OF THE STRUCTURAL CHARACTERISTICS OF LIFE EVENTS

Danish, Smyer, and Nowak (27) suggest that the prominent view of life events which has just been discussed is one which designates them "markers," or milestones, that give shape and direction to the various aspects of individual lives. They also suggest, however, that life events can more meaningfully be viewed as processes, with their own developmental histories from time of anticipation, through onset, until their immediate and future aftermaths have been resolved and experienced. In this view, actual life event occurences are but a point in time, and not necessarily the critical point of impact. It is important to remember that "events do not occur in a vacuum, (but in) the rich life space of the individual, including competing demands from a variety of areas (e.g., work, family life, physical development) and people significant to the individual" (27) (p. 342). Simply to choose "an event" and examine its impact for psychological adjustment and growth thus becomes simplistic. A way to determine when, where, why and how events operate, through their process of unfolding in multiple life contexts, seems a richer, more predictive direction to take than the latter "content-oriented" approach. As an alternative, the study of the so-called structural characteristics of life events — those properties common to all events regardless of their history or content — is now proposed.

Structural Characteristics of Life Events.

Nowak and others (27, 38) propose several structural life event characteristics presumed important to an understanding of psychological adjustment to life change. Significant among them are the following: event timing, duration, sequencing, cohort specificity, contextual purity, and probability of occurence. *Event timing* refers to its congruence with either personal or societal expectations of when it *should* occur; *event duration* refers to the length of time it is experienced, including its anticipation, its actual occurrence, and its aftermath and resolution; *event sequencing* refers to whether or not life events appear in personally or societally expected order; *cohort specificity* of life events refers to the notion that given occurences have different meanings and effects for different cohorts or generations; *contextual purity* pertains to the extent to which events interfere with the resolution of other, concurrent life events, either one's own or those of one's significant others; and lastly, *probability of occurrence* refers to the likelihood that certain events will be experienced by large proportions of the population over time. Each of these structural life event properties has implications in and of themselves for the way in which an individual perceives transition and ultimately adjusts to it. Taken together, their impact becomes complex and multi-determined. When event characteristics such as these are considered, it becomes clear that any one event can have multiple sources of impact, and indicators of adjustment may be a subtle combination of seemingly low-relevance, but actually quite powerful, individual circumstances. If it is, in fact, true that a life events perspective does have considerable potential for mental health intervention in adulthood, then assessment techniques for personalizing effective therapeutic interventions must be sensitive to the unique predictive capabilities of interacting life event properties, and *less* influenced by the affective, singular, and immediate post-impact indices so characteristic of life event research to date.

THE RELATIONSHIP OF LIFE EVENTS
TO THE DRINKING BEHAVIORS OF LATER LIFE:
SUMMARY AND INTENT

Several things have been established: There is a striking similarity between the previously unlinked alcohol use and life events literatures in the established peaks for alcoholism and for life stresses in mid—and older age; there is a small but sound literature suggesting the relationship of life events to the onset of alcohol abuse in later life; and there is a rich and innovative life—events framework within which to explore the relationships among these variables. The structural approach to studying the relationship between life event properties and later life drinking behaviors proposed here would allow the exploration of the patterning, timing, accumulation, and significance of life events over time and their differential relationships to styles of and resources for coping among alcohol users and non-users in middle and old age. It will further allow more traditional event content analyses of life stress impacts upon drinking behavior, and thus "event occurrence" versus structural methodologies can be compared for their contributions to an etiological understanding of the correlates of alcohol use and abuse in later life. Finally the structural relationship of life transitions to drinking behavior will have significant implications for differential diagnosis and treatment of late life mental disorder.

SUMMARY

While extensive theoretical and empirical work has been reported in the area of later life stress and coping, very few investigations have addressed alcohol use among the elderly in general, and among older persons who drink in reaction to stressful episodes in particular. There is practically nothing known of those individuals whose drinking can be predicted from stress and coping histories as opposed to personality type and psychiatric pathology throughout the latter half of life. Evidence is suggestive, however, that the peak years for alcohol abuse and mortality due to alcoholism are in mid– and later life respectively, almost identically paralleling what life event researchers consider peak years for life stress (45–55 and 65–75 respectively). The present paper urges the exploration of the relationship between drinking behavior and stressful life events, using a conceptually and methodologically innovative framework for examining life crises over time.

REFERENCES

1. Simon, A. The neuroses, epersonality disorders, alcoholism, drug use and misuse, and crime in teh aged. In J. Birren and R. B. Sloane (Eds.), *Handbook of Mental Health and Aging,* 653–670. Englewood Cliffs: Prentice-Hall, 1980.
2. Gaitz, C. and Baer, P. Characteristics of elderly patients with alcoholism. *Arch. Gen. Psychiatry,* 1971, 24, 372–378.
3. Overall, J., Hoffman, N. and Levin, H. Effects of aging, organicity, alcoholism, and functional psychopathology on WAIS subtest profiles. *J. Consulting and Clinical Psychology,* 46(6), 1315–1322.
4. Harrington, L. G. and Price, C. Alcoholism in a geriatric setting v. incidence of mental disorders. *J. American Geriatrics Soc.,* 1962, 10, 209–211.
5. Mack, J. and Carlson, N. J. Conceptual deficits and aging: the category test. *Perceptual and Motor Skills,* 1978, 46, 123–128.
6. Libb, J. W. and Taulbee, E. S. Psychotic-appearing MMPI profiles among alcoholics. *J. Clinical Psychology,* 1971, 27, 101–02.
7. Lorberg, T. MMPI-based personality subtypes of alcoholics. *J. of Studies on Alcoholism,* 1981, 42(9), 766–782.
8. Hoffman H. Personality characteristics of alcoholics in relation to age. *Psych Reports,* 1970, 27, 167–171.
9. Brody, J. A. Epidemiological characteristics of alcohol in the elderly. *Advances in Alcoholism,* 1981, 2, 7.
10. Cahalan, D. *Problem drinkers.* San Francisco: Jassey-Bass, 1970.
11. Cahalan, D., Cisin, I., and Crossley, H. *American drinking practices.* New Brunswick, NJ: Rutgers University Press, 1969.
12. Knupfer, G. and Room, R. Age, sex, and social class as factors in amount of drinking in a metropolitan community. *Social Problems,* 1964, 12, 224–240.
13. Drew, L. R. Alcoholism as a self-limiting disease. *Q. J. Stud. Alc.,* 1968, 29, 906–907.
14. Troll, L., and Nowak, C. How old are you? The question of age-bias among counselors. *J. Counseling Psychology,* 1976, 6(1), 41–44.

15. Lipscomb, W. Mortality among treated alcoholics: A three year follow-up study. *Q. J. Stud Alc.,* 1959, 20, 596–603.
16. Metropolitan Life Insurance Company. Mortality from alcoholism. *Statistical Bulletin,* 1977, 58, 3–7.
17. Curlee, J. Alcoholism and the empty nest. *Bull. Menn. Clinic,* 1969, 33, 165–171.
18. Schuckit, M. Geriatric alcoholism and drug abuse. *Gerontologist,* 1977, 17, 168–174.
19. Bailey, M., Haberman, P., and Alksne, H. The epidemiology of alcoholism in an urban residential area. *Q. J. Stud Alc.,* 1965, 26, 19–40.
20. Schuckit, M., Morrissey, E., and O'Leary, M. Alcohol problems in the elderly men and women. *Addictive Diseases,* 3(3), 405–406.
21. Rosin, A., and Glatt, M. Alcohol excess in the elderly. *Q. J. Stud Alc.,* 1971, 32, 53–59.
22. Droller, H. Some aspects of alcoholism in the elderly. *Lancet,* 1964, 2, 137–139.
23. Fiske, M. Tasks and crises of the second half of life: The interrelationship of committment, coping, and adaptation. In J. Birren and R. B. Sloane (Eds.), *The handbook of mental health and aging,* 337–373. Englewood Cliffs: Prentice-Hall, 1980.
24. Zimberg, S. The elderly alcoholic. *Gerontologist,* 1974, 14, 221–224.
25. Holmes, T., and Rahe, R. The social readjustment rating scale. *J. of Psychosomatic Research,* 1976, 11, 213–218.
26. Dohrenwend, B., and Dohrenwend, B. (Eds.), *Stressful life events: Their nature and effects.* New York: Wiley, 1974.
27. Danish, S., Smyer, M., and Nowak, C. Development intervention: Enhancing life-event processes. In P. Baltes and O. H. Brim, Jr., (Eds.), *Life-span development and behavior,* (Vol. 3). New York: Academic Press, 1980.
28. Baltes, P., and Willis, S. Lifespan developmental psychology, cognitive functioning, and social policy. In M. Riley (Ed.), *Aging from birth to death.* Boulder: Westview Press, 1979.
29. Baltes, P., Cornelius, S., and Nesselroade, J. Cohort effects in developmental psychology. In J. Nesselroade and P. Baltes (Eds.), *Longitudinal research in human development: Design and analysis.* New York: Academic Press, 1979.
30. Neugarten, B. Adaptation and the life cycle. *The Counseling Psychologist,* 1976, 6, 16–20,
31. Neugarten, B., and Hagestad, G. Age and the life course. In R. Binstock and E. Shanas (Eds.), *Handbook of aging and the social sciences,* 35–37. New York: Van Nostrand Reinhold, 1976.
32. Datan, N., and H. Ginsberg (Eds.), *Life-span developmental psychology: Normative life crisis.* New York: Academic Press, 1975.
33. Hultsch, D., and Plemons, J. Life-events and lifespan development. In P. Baltes and O. H. Brim (Eds.), *Life-span development and behavior* (Vo. 2), 1–36. New York: Academic Press, 1979.
34. Elder, G. Family history and life course. *Journal of Family History,* 1977, 2, 279–304.

35. Elder, G. *Children of the great depression.* Chicago: University of Chicago, 1974.
36. Ryder, N. The demography of youth. In J. Coleman (Ed.), *Youth: Transition to adulthood.* Chicago: University of Chicago Press, 1974.
37. Modell, J., Furstenberg, F., and Hershberg, T. Social change and transitions to adulthood in historical perspective. *Journal of Family History,* 1976, 1, 7–33.
38. Brim, O., and Ryff, C. On the properties of life events. In P. Baltes and O. H. Brim (Eds.), *Life-span development and behavior* (Vol. 3), 367–388. New York: Academic Press, 1980.
39. Cahalan, D. *Problem drinkers: A national survey.* San Francisco: Jossey Bass, 1970.
40. Wanberg, K., Horn, J., and Foster, F. A differential assessment model for alcoholism: The scales of the alcohol use inventory. *J. Stud. Alc.,* 1977, 38, 512–543.
41. Balan, J., Browing, H., Jelin, E., and Litxler, R. A computerized approach to the processing an analysis of life histories obtained in sample surveys. *Behavioral Science,* 1969, 14, 105–120.
42. Neugarten, B. Personality and aging. In J. Birren and K. W. Schaie (Eds.), *Handbook of the psychology of aging,* 626–646. New York: Van Nostrand, 1977.
43. Meyers, A., Hingston, R. Mucatel, M., and Golden, E. Social and psychological correlates of problem drinking in old age. *Journal of the American Geriatrics Society,* 1982, 30(7), 452–456.
44. Hingson, R. Life satisfaction and drinking practices in the Boston Metropolitan area. *Journal of Studies in Alcoholism,* 1981, 42, 24–37.

Chapter 4

GERONTOLOGY AND ALCOHOL STUDIES

Edith Lisansky Gomberg

Although there are many issues relating to the problems of alcohol and aging, the fact is that, unfortunately, we have only limited bits of information. One datum is that older people, in general, drink less than younger people. Another datum: the population of persons 60 and older does include people who have alcohol problems.

The conference organizers have circulated a list of questions and two of these questions are quite fundamental and raise issues which need discussion. I would like to talk about these two questions.

FIRST QUESTION. Is there such an issue as early versus late onset alcoholism? What indeed do we mean by "late onset"? Can an alcohol problem *begin* late in life? If persons 60 and older who behave alcoholically have long histories of problems with alcohol or histories of intermittent alcohol episodes throughout their lives, the related question of elderly stress becomes irrelevant. But if there are elderly people whose alcohol problems are of *recent* origin, might these problems be linked to "stresses of aging," and in that case, which stresses of aging?

SECOND QUESTION. What in the aging process supports or causes substance abuse? That may be "the stresses of aging" question all over again but we propose to ask a more basic question here: What in the aging process is related to the decision to drink, not drink, quit drinking, start drinking, change the amount? In addition to concerns and research questions about heavy or alcoholic drinking, we need some basic research about the customs, choices, behaviors of older persons in relation to alcohol and to medications.

INTRODUCTION

First let's look at some percentages. In an urban alcoholism education and referral service, records were kept about people who telephoned the service, looking for information and referral about drinking problems (1). The help sought might be for the person calling or it might be for a relative or friend. There was no special interest in older persons; these are simply the percentages of people in different age groups who called about themselves or about someone they cared about (See Table 4-I).

TABLE 4-I
PERCENTAGES OF PEOPLE IN DIFFERENT AGE GROUPS
CALLING FOR INFORMATION AND REFERRAL ABOUT DRINKING PROBLEMS

Age	Self-Callers	Called About
20–29	15%	8%
30–39	25%	31%
40–49	35%	28%
50–59	19%	19%
60 and over	6%	14%

SOURCE: From Corrigan, E. M. *Problem Drinkers Seeking Treatment*, Monographs of the Rutgers Center of Alcohol Studies, No. 8, 1974, page 14.

In this report, Corrigan states: "... among those aged 60 and over, more than twice as many problem drinkers were *called about.* In this way, we may be seeing the concern expressed by family and friends either about alcoholism among the retired and aging, or about a problem of long duration ... " (p. 15).

Problem drinking is not a major problem among older people. The available data show that older problem drinkers represent a *small* percentage of the elderly population and a *small* percentage of the alcoholic population. But the problem *does* exist and it obviously troubles the people who comprise the social network of the older person and the drinker himself or herself. It seems to me a particularly poignant problem. Older people, as a rule, must adapt to a diminishing work and parental role. Losses are heavier. It is an area of controversy whether they adapt better or worse than younger people to the life events which are part of the human condition, but it does seem tragic when the response to loss is a resort to alcohol.

Parenthetically, it might be well to state here that there is no apparent reason why older persons cannot drink moderately unless there are illnesses or medications which contraindicate any drinking. It needs to be stated because we are, in this business, so often carried away by the problems which alcohol generates that we overlook the pleasures and benefits of social drinking.

QUESTION 1: IS THERE SUCH AN ISSUE AS EARLY VS. LATE-ONSET ALCOHOLISM?

This question has been raised because there are contradictory lines of evidence. Clinical observations report a phenomenon: recent-onset older persons with alcohol problems. Survey researchers, studying the general population, report some difficulty in finding these persons. (Interestingly enough, the conflict is usually the reverse, i.e., epidemiologists report phenomenally high proportions of alcohol-related problems in segments of the population who are minimally represented in treatment facilities.) People working in housing projects and social services for older persons, emergency room personnel, law enforcement personnel, and relatives (see Table 4-I) say that such people exist.

No worker in facilities for alcohol and drug abusers will argue that older persons make up a large percentage of the problem drinkers. In alcoholism agencies — unless they are designed specifically to reach older people — the elderly will make up less than 10% of the intake. But they are there.

Nor is the existence of elderly problem drinkers, even if they constitute a small percentage of those coming to a treatment facility, a trivial matter. A triage principle argues that limited rehabilitation resources should go to young and middle aged adults but here we get into moral and ethical issues best set aside for now.

To carry this a step further: if all older alcoholic persons who show up at a treatment facility of any sort are long-term alcoholics who have survived into their sixties and seventies, just how much is there to say about prevention and treatment? For this aging chronic alcoholic, it is too late to talk about primary or secondary prevention, and, for the most part, our treatments consist of minimizing the sequelae and making the last years of his/her life more comfortable. But if late-onset or, preferably *recent*-onset older alcoholic persons exist, several new lines of inquiry open. How does one treat an older person who has recently begun drinking heavily and consequently has alcohol-related problems? What is such behavior related to, what are the antecedents, what are the vulnerabilities, what are the precipitants of heavy drinking, and how may knowledge of these help us to develop programs of early intervention and programs of primary prevention for older individuals?

The question of "early versus late alcoholism" should be separated into two hypotheses:

> *Hypothesis I.* Recent onset problem drinkers exist in the 60+ population.
> *Hypothesis II.* Recent onset problem drinking originates in loss and other stresses which accompany the process of aging.

HYPOTHESIS I

One of the first suggestions that late onset alcohol problems might exist in an elderly group came as a serendipitous findings in an epidemiological study of health issues in a New York City sample (2). Questions about drinking problems manifested by a family member were included in the interview schedule and those identified by the study criteria as "probable alcoholics" showed some unexpected age and marital status patterning (see Table 4-II).

The expectation was that rates would begin dropping off in the 55 to 64 year old age group and continue dropping; this was anticipated because of "the high mortality associated with alcoholism." However, an increase appeared in the 65 to 74 year old group, apparently due to the number of elderly widowers who acknowledged drinking problems. The upward rate turn in this age group did not characterize the women in the sample; for women, the alcoholism rate among widows — presumably the oldest age group —

TABLE 4-II

EPIDEMIOLOGY OF ALCOHOLISM: RATES OF PROBABLY ALCOHOLICS PER 1,000 PERSONS
AGED 20 YEARS AND OVER IN TOTAL POPULATION AND IN SELECTED SUBGROUPS,
WASHINGTON HEIGHTS MASTER SAMPLE SURVEY, 1960–61[a]

	Rates		Rates
All Persons	19	**Marital Status - Men**[d]	
		Married	25
Sex and Race[b]		Widowed	105
Men	32	Divorced, separated	68
Women	9	Never married	29
Whites	16		
Negroes	28	**Marital Status - Women**	
White men	31	Married	8
White women	5	Widowed	5
Negro men	37	Divorced, separated	19
Negro women	20	Never married	9
Religion[c]		**Education**[e]	
Roman Catholic	24	None to some grade school	33
Jewish	2	Grade-school graduate	22
Baptist	40	Some high school	24
Other Protestant	20	High-school graduate	9
		Some college	17
Age, Years		College graduate and above	13
20–24	13		
25–34	22	**Race and Years of Education**[f]	
35–44	16	Negro, 9 or less	41
45–54	23	Negro, 10 or more	20
55–64	17	White, 9 or less	22
65–74	22	White, 10 or more	12
75 and over	12		

[a]Rites computed on the basis of the following observed numbers: total sample, 5,544
in the central zone and 2,538 in the north plus south zones; probably alcoholics, 90 in the
central zone and 52 in the north plus south zones. See methodology section for weights.
[b]Male rate significantly higher than female, white male rate significantly higher than
white female, and Negro female rate signficantly higher than white female (.05 level).
Puerto Ricans included with whites, since their sex ratio was similar to that of other whites.
[c]Jewish rate significantly lower and (Negro) Baptist rate significantly higher than rate
of all persons (.05 level).
[d]Rates of widowers and of divorced or separated men significantly higher than rate
of all males (.05 level).
[e]Rate of the least educated persons (none to some grade school) significantly higher
and rate of high-school graduates significantly lower than rate of all persons (.05 level).
[f]Puerto Ricans excluded from this section of table.

* From Bailey, M.P., Haberman, P.W. and Alksne, H. Table 2. The epidemiology of alcoholism in an urban residential area. Quarterly Journal of Studies on Alcohol, 1965, 26,
19–40.

was lowest; it was highest for divorced or separated marital status
women.

About the same time, Bogue (3) and Bahr (4), working in the
Skid Rows of Chicago and New York City, asked homeless men
with alcohol problems about onset after the age of 45. They
reported 4 percent and 7 percent, respectively and Bahr, asking
the same question of residents in a custodial rehabilitative institution, reported 20 percent.

The existence of late onset older problem drinkers was reported by many clinicians and researchers (5–11). Wilkinson in Australia (5) and Zimberg in New York City (9) both estimated late onset people to comprise about *one-third* of older alcoholic persons.

One problem, of course, is what "late onset" means. The studies on Skid Row noted above specified onset after the age of 45. Schuckit and Miller (12) comment that one-third to one-half of older alcoholics surveyed in a general medical ward had no alcohol problems before the age of 40. Schuckit, Morrissey and O'Leary (10), comparing 186 alcoholic patients under age 55, and 55 and over in a veterans' hospital note: "One of the more striking findings is that the older alcoholic does not experience alcohol-related problems for many more years than does his younger counterpart . . . it appeared that alcohol problems began in mid to late-life and were not just a progression of early alcoholics living into old age."

The term "late onset" is used by some to differentiate between those problem drinkers who manifest problems in their twenties and thirties and those who manifest them "late" (i.e., in their forties or later). This is *not* the same as talking about an elderly group of alcoholics, 60 or over, whose problems with alcohol are of *recent origin*, presumably linked in many cases to stressful experience like loss of a spouse or termination of unemployment. There are real and important differences between alcoholics for whom onset occurs early in adult life (or in late adolescence) and those where onset occurs later, and this appears to be true both of men (13) and women.[1]

A distinction needs to be made. In speaking of adults who have developed drinking problems, can we agree to speak of the age span from 20 to 60? And when "elderly alcoholics" or "elderly problem drinkers" are the subject for discussion, can we agree that these will refer to people 60 years of age and older? The term "reactive problem drinker" makes sense only if we are talking about older persons who are responding to events and stresses at that particular stage of life and we need to define whether "late

---

[1]Gomberg, E. S. L. Alcoholism in women: psychosocial aspects. Grant # 5 R01 AA 04143, from the National Institute on Alcohol Abuse and Alcoholism. Survey Research Center Project 462245, Institute for Social Research, University of Michigan.

onset" means no-alcohol-problems-before-age-40 or whether it means that problems have begun within the last five or ten years. A 65 year old man who began having problems with alcohol in his forties has a twenty year history and he is not a problem drinker responding to the pressures and frustrations of the aging process per se.

A recent research report by Hubbard, Santos and Santos (11) is relevant. These investigators analyzed 250 case reports and interviews obtained in a mental health outreach program for the elderly. Fifty clients, mean age 68.7 years, were judged to have alcohol-related problems. Twenty of these were described as, "chronic long-term alcoholics." Twelve persons were judged to be in a recent-onset group, some with a lifetime history of social drinking and some with a history of "sporadic episodes of heavy drinking." Another eleven persons had medical difficulties associated with interaction of moderate amounts of alcohol and medications; these synergistic effects produced injuries from falls, poor nutrition, diagnosis of dementia, etc. The investigators, then, found 20 "survivors" or long-term alcoholics, and 23 people for whom problems with alcohol had developed quite recently.

The report by Hubbard, Santos and Santos, which includes description of some elderly persons with alcohol problems as having a history of "sporadic episodes of heavy drinking" brings up another problem of definition when we speak of late-onset or recent-onset problem drinkers. The image which is evoked by the phrase, "reactive problem drinker" (14) is too limiting. *Recent-onset* is a descriptive phrase which should cover those who have *no* previous episodes of problematic drinking and those who have had *occasional,* sporadic episodes. We have reason to believe that some individuals will have alcoholic episodes or periods in their lives when they are drinking heavily and problematically and that these individuals will stop heavy drinking, with or without intervention. We have an important, unanswered research question here: if we accept the fact that there is a small but real group of older persons who will manifest drinking *problems* late in their lives, is an episodic heavy drinking history a predictor for late life trouble with alcohol?

Furthermore, including those elderly persons who are in trouble with alcohol plus medication interaction in the definition of "elderly persons with alcohol problems of recent origin" makes sense.

It is patently obvious that not all alcoholic persons will present themselves in later life at treatment facilities with long alcoholic histories going back to young adulthood. It is also logical to assume that the family, friends, and significant others will have different responses to an older person with a long history of alcoholism and to an older person who has only recently begun to present an alcohol problem (a good research question).

One of the problems in discussing these questions is the confusion which exists when terms like "early onset" and "late onset" are used. In our study of alcoholic women in treatment facilities, we find that the 40 to 50 year old group reports longer duration than do the 20 to 30 year olds, i.e., the older alcoholic women report a mean duration of 8.6 years and the younger group reports a mean of 5.4 years. Nonetheless, when age-at-onset is examined, the younger group is much more readily described as "early onset," 93 percent of them developing serious alcohol problems before the age of 24. At the same time, the older women may be described as "recent onset": only 2 percent of them developed alcohol problems before the age of 24, and almost 60 percent of them developed such problems when they were 36 or older. In the studies of the chronic drunkenness offender and Veterans Administration Medical Center patients described above (3,4,10,12), "late onset" means the beginning of alcohol-related problems in the subjects forties.

What I Propose Is The Following

Let us agree that we will call elderly-persons-with-alcohol-problems those people in treatment or in the untreated population, individuals who are 60 years of age and over. Let us further agree that we will call it *recent onset* if there is a history of 10 years or less of heavy, problematic drinking. And, finally, let us agree to include in this category of *recent-onset problem drinker 60 years of age or older* several different subgroups:

    a. Those individuals who have no previous history of heavy drinking, no history of problems related to alcohol in adult years but who now—with a history of 10 years or less—are engaged in heavy drinking creating family, medical, social and legal problems for themselves and those around them. These people have either been moderate drinkers or abstainers throughout their lifetimes.

b. Those individuals who have histories of sporadic episodes of heavy drinking during the years before 60 (*sporadic* needs more precise definition). Such persons may have manifested spontaneous recovery from these episodes or they may have received help from some intervention.

c. Those individuals who have drunk moderately most of their adult lives and who continue to drink moderately but who manifest problems, usually medical, because of the synergistic effects of alcohol combined with prescription drugs or over-the-counter medications.

That *recent-onset problem drinkers* exist in an older population is often a by-product or serendipitous finding in research investigating other phenomena. A longitudinal study,[2] for example, begun in 1935 when respondents were in their twenties, has collected data from the same subjects when they were in their forties in 1955, and more recently from the same subjects when their median age was 68. This longitudinal research is a study of marriage and includes questions about alcohol-related problems of the respondent and of the spouse. In 1955, 47 of the 600 respondents were reported by their spouses to have alcohol problems. The current interview data have turned up 20 persons who were *not* reported to be abusing alcohol in 1955 but who are reported, by spouse, to be abusing alcohol at the present time. It is more than likely that this group includes a high proportion of *recent-onset problem drinkers.*

HYPOTHESIS 2

If we agree that recent-onset problem drinkers exist in the population of older people, the hypothesis that *recent-onset problem*

[2]Conley, J. J. The Kelley Longitudinal Study: The Antecedents of Psychological Health Status in the Aged. National Institute of Health Grant R23AG 02837-01. Personal communication.

drinking is likely to originate in loss and stressful experiences of recent origin merits consideration.[3]

First, note that there is a lively debate over the stresses and satisfactions of aging. Rather than talking about *stresses,* some investigators prefer to talk about life events, positive and negative. The distressing effects of negative life events may be modified, according to current research and theory, by mediators. One such buffering mediator is social support, i.e., the availability and active support of other people—kin, friends, etc.—who make up one's social network. In a recent study done in California, it was demonstrated through a nine year follow-up investigation that there was a strong relationship between social networks and mortality (15), those with many social and community ties were less likely to die and those with few social and community ties were more likely to die. In fact, the California Department of Mental Health has recently sponsored a campaign that, "Friends can be good medicine" On the other side of the debate, questions have been raised about the significant role of socioeconomic status in determining social relationships (16). It should be noted that economic status appears to play an important role in suicide rates of older white males (17). (The debate is really an old question: which is more important, money or friendship?)

There has been an interesting recent shift, and literature which emphasizes the strengths and advantages of the older population has begun to appear. Thus, a discussion of "psychosocial risk factors" (18) suggests that the impact of such factors may be *weaker* rather than more intense among older persons, and researchers examining older peoples' self-report of feelings of well being, describe "special satisfactions" as well as adaptive problems posed by aging (19). Perhaps older people, in the eyes of social scientists, are moving from a disadvantaged population to a population much like other age groups, i.e., there are both negative and positive aspects of their particular stage in the life cycle.

No assumption is made that the elderly lead an existence which

---

3. After presentation of this paper, a review of literature on life stressors and problem drinking among older adults, came to my attention. This review will appear in M. Galanter (Ed.) *Recent Developments in Alcoholism,* Volume 11, New York: Plenum. The authors, J. W. Finney and R. H. Moos conclude that there is a need to identify risk factors which make older persons under stress vulnerable to problems relating to drinking.

is primarily stressful. But there are a number of problems which are likely to appear or to intensify among older people. To name a few:

- Problems of declining economic resources
- Problems of health
- Problems of loss of friends and family members
- Problems of role ambiguity (vaguely defined social roles for older persons)

Most aging persons make satisfactory adaptations to retirement, to declining income, to health limitations and to loss of others. But some do not and it is from this subgroup that recent-onset problem drinkers are probably drawn. There is no inference that all older people, who must adapt to loss or change, are vulnerable to alcohol problems, but there are reports from those who work in housing for the elderly and in agencies which deal with the needs of older persons, that alcohol-related problems appear in this age group, often among persons who were not reported to have had alcohol problems earlier in life.

Bailey and her colleagues (2) suggested a linkage between the experience of widowhood and alcoholism among the 65-and-over males in the sample. The role of retirement is not clear although the epidemiological information suggests that a sizable percentage of heavy drinking men drink *less* after retirement (14).

Conclusions from two surveys which do not find a relationship between "stresses of aging" and alcoholism are, as follows:

a. "widowhood and retirement as associated with increased problem drinking . . . not confirmed" (20).
b. "no evidence of late-adult-onset alcoholism, and no evidence to suggest that widowhood, retirement or social isolation is associated with higher risks of problem drinking" (21).

The conclusions of the surveys are justified by their data, but the question remains whether these surveys have indeed investigated the relationship between negative life events and heavy drinking by older people. For example, the first survey cited above (20) is a household survey of 1041 adults in western New York state. Respondents were asked about the quantity and frequency of drinking and about several alcohol-related problems. But what is not known is whether the 13 percent of older retired men who are heavy drinkers and the 14 percent of widowed older men who are heavy drinkers, have been heavy drinkers all their lives or for many years or for a short time. Since there is some question about the definition of "heavy drinking" in this survey, enough said.

The second survey (21) also has several problems. Refusal rate is high and when refusers were urged to cooperate, less than half do so, and they are a more educated subsample than the others in the study group (22). One may raise the question whether older persons who are drinking problematically might not be among those potential respondents who refused more than one attempt by the research team. Furthermore, the interview was structured so that large numbers of these older respondents were not asked about life satisfaction with reference to critical life areas, e.g., those who were living without a spouse (widowed or divorced) were not asked about marital satisfaction, or their response to loss of the spouse. Persons without immediate families, living alone, were not questioned about their families. The investigators report a relationship between widowhood, retirement and social isolation on the one hand and the more likelihood of abstinence on the other. Is it possible that living alone and in social isolation can be linked to abstinence for some and to heavy/problematic drinking for others, and is it possible that the survey has not reached the latter group?

The results of the second survey indicate that older people who are divorced or separated "are more than twice as likely as others to have two or more drinks a day" (22), suggesting the linkage between marital disruption and relatively heavy drinking which seems to appear in *all* stages of adult life.

Results from both surveys suggest that the hypothesis: retirement produces *less* heavy drinking among men (14) has some validity. In the first study (20), among older men, 22 percent of those who are employed and 13 percent of those who are not employed report heavy drinking (this is a reversal of percentages for age groups below 60). In the second study (22), those older men who report more control over their employment situation (presumably those still working or those who chose to retire) are more likely to drink than those with less control over employment.

The question of male retirement from paid employment needs much more thought and investigation. Retirement is probably viewed by many men as stressful, a negative life event, but it is probably also viewed by many others with equanimity if not enthusiasm. It is interesting to note that the original comments made by the epidemiological team of Bailey, Haberman and Alksne (2) contained nothing about retirement; there were no data about employment status and the "probable alcoholics" are described as "elderly widowers."

On the basis of these two surveys, I would agree that a relationship between negative events in older peoples' lives and consequent heavy drinking has not been demonstrated. But it has not been ruled out either. The question is open and still to be explored.

A strong argument *against* linking negative life events and heavy drinking among older people is the simplistic assumption of a single factor causal relationship. We know how complex the etiology of alcoholism really is, and it does not make sense to put the entire burden of cause on events like widowhood or retirement, no matter how painful or traumatic they may be. Older people, like everyone else, may be depressed or not depressed, may have more adaptive or less adaptive ways of coping with loss, may participate or may not participate in heavier drinking groups, and so on. I am suggesting that there may be vulnerable individuals who have coped reasonable well until they become elderly and then they do not cope well at all. I would further suggest that this group, in the present elderly cohort, is much more likely to be composed of males than of females.

The strongest argument *for* the linkage of negative life events and heavy drinking among older men is in the evidence of relatively high rates of depression and suicide in this group. The figures for prescription of anti-depressant drugs are suggestive; although women are prescribed more psychoactive drugs in all age groups, there is a curious turnaround in the age group 60 to 74, where 4 percent of men and 2 percent of women report use of prescribed anti-depressants (23). If suicide rates are compared, women's suicide rates decline from a peak in the forties while men's suicide rates climb, level off between 55 and 70 and then climb again (24). There are some in gerontology who believe that women are better psychological and emotional survivors in old age than are men, and a good case can be made among older men for a linkage between loss and depression, suicide, and problem drinking.

It is not epidemiology, but a great psychologist, Lois Barclay Murphy, has written in a book review (25) about loss and depression and alcohol:

> I approached this book from my own recent loss of my dearly beloved husband and I had many thoughts and questions . . . about the resources of the bereaved for dealing with loss. Fourteen widows . . . dropped by to share their own losses, often of years before . . . I had also been close to ten losses by widowers, six of whom were more shaken, depressed, and more lost than the women. . . . One was chronically angry, one was deeply depressed, two drank too much alcohol. Only one widow had turned to alcohol.

QUESTION 2: WHAT IN THE AGING PROCESS SUPPORTS OR CAUSES SUBSTANCE ABUSE?

(Broadly put, what in the aging process is related to drug use and to drinking behaviors?)

During the aging process, a number of decisions must be made. Such decisions are usually not made overnight and they are often made with a minimum of awareness. The older person makes changes in diet, in sleep and rest patterns, in exercise, in work schedule, in travel, and so on. The older person also makes decisions about drinking; he/she may continue existing drinking patterns or abstain or increase the amount drunk or decrease the amount drunk. When the linkages between this choice and the physiology, attitudes, beliefs, and economics of the older person are discovered, the basis for answering a question about the relationship between factors in the aging process and substance abuse has been established. We hypothesize that *a decision about drinking is made by older persons*, and the determinants of that decision will give the clues supplying the answer to the question above.

To understand *what in the aging process supports or causes substance abuse or substance use or substance abstinence,* alcohol and drug researchers will need to know gerontology. Just as the researcher who studies alcohol and drug use by adolescents must know a great deal about adolescence as a life stage, so must the researcher who studies alcohol and drug use by older persons know a great deal about the elderly.

A mini-course in gerontology might start with three theoretical constructs much discussed in all life span literature:

1. Stress and life events
2. Coping mechanisms
3. Social supports and social networks

1. STRESS AND LIFE EVENTS. This is an area of general interest in explaining behavior and adaptation in all age groups. Sometimes stresses are classified as those relating to loss, to rejection, to powerlessness. But there is a school of thought which argues that *any* life event, negative or positive, that involves change or adaptation, is, in that sense, a stressor. Some stresses occur with more frequency at one stage of life than another, e.g., loss of friends and peers through death, occurs more frequently for elderly people than for young adults. The same or similar event may have different impacts in different stages of life. And, of course, the same event and the response to it will vary across an enormous range of individual differences within each separate age group.

It may be most useful to deal with stressors as any life event which involves change: good, bad, or neutral. Perhaps a focus on critical life events will permit us to integrate individual differences and age/cohort differences in assessing positive or negative life events.

Perhaps there has been too much talk about "stress." I do believe that Lewis Thomas speaks for many of us in these remarks (26):

> The only question I am inclined to turn aside as being impossible to respond to happens to be the one most often raised these days, not just by my biologist friends but by everyone: the question about stress, how to avoid stress, prevent stress, allay stress. I refuse to have anything to do with this matter, having made up my mind, from everything I have read or heard about it in recent years, that what people mean by stress is simply the condition of being human. . . .

2. COPING MECHANISMS. These are clearly the habitual ways with which one deals with "the condition of being human." Psychoanalysis and ego psychology has offered one way of looking at the tasks and solutions of each life stage. Thus, Erikson's (27) "eight stages of man" begins with babyhood and, after the resolution of ego identity, the adolescent person emerges into young adulthood. The last three stages of life described by Erikson involve the development of intimacy in young adulthood, then the development of parental responsibility for the next generation, and, finally, in the last of life stage, the crises and resolution of ego integrity whose themes are self-acceptance and awareness of one's own autonomy.

An old trait psychology model has been revived recently, based on the assumption of personality variables (traits) as stable. Using a variety of test measures, projective techniques, and factor analysis, Costa and McCrae (28) have devised a formal trait model including neuroticism, extroversion, and openness-to-experience. This would appear to be a useful starting point in defining coping mechanisms. In fact, the varieties of coping styles and the adequacy of coping efforts comprise the basis of individual difference models of personality. It would be most interesting to study age differences in such coping styles.

3. SOCIAL SUPPORTS AND SOCIAL NETWORKS. The importance of these phenomena in current age span and mental health research can hardly be exaggerated. The relationship of social networks to life expectancy has been described (15). Social networks play a significant role in the quality of life of older persons (29) and social network participation discriminates among older persons who are non-drinkers, social drinkers and heavy drinkers (30, 31, 32).

The relationship between social networks and drinking for older persons, as reported to date, seems to be like this: people with more social contacts (30) and people living with spouse and family (31) are more likely to be social drinkers. Those living alone are more likely to be abstainers. At the same time, it is reported that: "Aged persons with a limited or nonexistent network of social relationships drank significantly more heavily than the elderly who were socially engaged" (32).

These different results suggest a very interesting hypothesis, worthy of research investigation. It appears that those older people who live alone are more likely to be abstainers, and at the same time, older people who live alone are more likely to be heavy drinkers. There is no contradiction involved: moderate drinking is more than likely to be *social* drinking and when there is no one else, some older people do not drink at all because there is no one to drink with, and some older people apparently use alcohol to assuage feelings of aloneness and loneliness.

What *else* in the aging process supports or causes substance abuse, what factors are related to decisions about drinking? What does the alcohol studies person who approaches an older population need to know about this population to understand their behavior in relation to alcohol and other substances?

The person who will study alcohol/drugs/gerontology should know something about *THE BIOLOGY OF AGING*. Aging is a process occurring at a multiplicity of levels of biological organization, from the total person to the individual molecule (see, for example, 33). Why is the 67 year old patient with a brief history of heavy alcohol intake developing medical complications so rapidly? What is happening with the elderly widow who drinks a moderate amount on top of a number of medications and who presents a clinical picture of confusion and disorientation? It is true that we do not yet have "a substantial body of research specific to the physiological effects of alcoholic beverages on aging and the aged" (34), but study is in progress. The gerontology—alcohol expert should certainly know the available information about the metabolism of alcohol and changes with age and the differences among Alzheimer's disease, Korsakoff psychosis and Wernicke syndrome.

Related to issues about the biology of aging, one needs to be aware, working in gerontology, of the importance of *THE FUNCTIONAL HEALTH STATUS* of older persons. This includes not only the presence or absence of acute and chronic illnesses but the limitations illness may set for the aging person. What is the energy/activity level of the older person, capacity to do chores and get around alone, shop, keep house, socialize, maintain oneself? Generally, it is considered good gerontological practice to encourage older persons to maintain themselves in their own residences as long as they are able to cope.

The gerontology and alcohol studies person should know as much as possible about *THE ECONOMICS OF AGING*. There are several realities to begin with: older women contribute disproportionately to the poverty population. Inflation is threatening to everyone but particularly to those living on limited fixed incomes. Worry about money is a major source of anxiety among older people.

The most recent Gallup Survey (35) shows a decline in the percentage of Americans who drink alcoholic beverages. The decline is largest among persons whose formal education is 8th grade or less (down 23%), those with family income below $15,000 (down 11%), and those who are 50 years of age and older (down 11%). The question is: are these the same people?

The student of gerontology should know something about *HOUSING ISSUES FOR OLDER PEOPLE.* What sorts of modifications in ordinary living quarters are advisable for elderly people? About 5 percent of older people are in nursing homes and hospitals; the other 95 percent live in a variety of arrangements: with families, by themselves, with non-related persons, in housing developments of all sorts ranging from very posh housing to Single Room Occupancy (SRO) arrangements which may be far from adequate. Some older persons prefer living in a community of age peers and others would rather live in a mixed-age community. Some older persons do well living with their adult children, some do not, and some—being chronically ill and in need of care—have no choice.

To do clinical work or research in gerontology and alcohol studies, one needs to know a great deal about *THE ISSUE OF RETIREMENT AND THE WORK ROLE.* Is retirement a trauma, a blessing, a neutral event? Are we justified in calling retirement a "stress" because it is certainly a life event, a change which necessitates adaptation?

What should the work role be for older persons? A scientific donnybrook was set off some years ago when gerontologists wrote about "disengagement" of older persons. Should older people be "put out to pasture," should they continue working, should they be given a choice? What are the entitlements? Older persons are not a homogeneous group: some want full time leisure ("we've paid our dues"), some would like to continue working.

There seems to be an ambivalence in attitudes toward older people in the United States. We are supposed to love our parents and respect our elders and observe these homilies in daily life but there is often a quite destructive perception and description of older persons as "senile," dependent and demanding, "in his/her second childhood." The fact is that we have never had so many survivors before and problems of middle aged adults with elderly parents are multiplying.

The question of women's work role is an interesting one, and I do believe that one source of psychological strength and comfort for women is the continuity of homemaking roles. They are familiar roles and they continue until the elderly woman is enfeebled; at the same time the responsibility of care of a sick spouse may lay heavy burdens on the elderly woman.

What is the relationships of work and retirement to drinking? How useful it would be to have answers to these questions. What proportion of retiring men and women drink *less* heavily than they did while working? Is this because drinking companions are no longer available and the familiar contexts of drinking have vanished? Is it perhaps because working men and women (particularly white collar, managerial, professional) are no longer under heavy competitive pressures? What proportion of retired men and women drink *more* heavily because they are retired? Is post-retirement drinking linked to the aging person's choice of leisure activities? The impact of "active recreation" and "passive recreation" on the quality of life of older persons has been studied (32), and we think these recreational choices may be relating to decisions about drinking.

If you are going to do clinical work or research into questions about adolescent drinking, it is highly advisable that you know a great deal more about adolescence as a life stage other than the fact that most of us are considered adolescents from puberty through the teens. In the same way, if you wish to pose the question, *WHAT IN THE AGING PROCESS SUPPORTS OR CAUSES SUBSTANCE ABUSE OR USE*, it is essential that you know what you mean by "the aging process."

WHERE DO WE GO FROM HERE?

This is what I propose: *First,* that we alcohol and drug specialists who are interested in older people make ourselves knowledgeable about facts and issues in gerontology.

Second, that we study the drinking experiences, drinking decisions and drinking contexts, past and present, of older people who are abstainers or moderate drinkers. For what reasons does an older person shift to drinking less, more, the same amount, or nothing at all?

Third, that we treat and study older alcoholics with the question: why have they survived when many alcoholics do not?

And, *fourth,* that we treat and study older people with more recently developed alcohol problems with the question: Why? How best to treat? How best to prevent?

SUMMARY

Several questions relating to gerontology and alcohol problems are explored. Is there a group of "late onset" alcoholics and do we mean "late onset" or "recent onset"? If indeed, as clinical observations and clinic records suggest, there is such a group of alcoholics, might recent onset of alcohol problems be related to stresses of later life stages? There is some support that such a group exists and is composed of persons who experience alcohol problems for the first time in their lives, persons who have histories of heavy/problematic drinking episodes, and moderate drinkers for whom alcohol combined with medication creates problems. Studies to date have not tested the relationship between the stresses of aging and the development of new alcohol problems and there remains a need to identify risk factors which make older persons more or less vulnerable to alcohol-related problems. It is suggested that in order to be a clinician or a researcher dealing with alcohol problems among older people, the clinician or researcher needs to know about life events and stress, coping mechanisms, and social networks among older people and about the issues in gerontology in general.

REFERENCES

1. Corrigan, E. M. *Problem Drinkers Seeking Treatment.* New Brunswick, NJ: Publications Division: Rutgers Center of Alcohol Studies. Monograph No. 8, 1974.

2. Bailey, M. B., Haberman, P., and Alksne, H. The epidemiology of alcoholism in an urban residential area. *Quarterly Journal of Studies on Alcohol,* 1965, 26, 19–40.

3. Bogue, D. J. *Skid Row in American Cities.* Chicago: University of Chicago Community and Family Center, 1963.

4. Bahr, H. M. Lifetime affiliation patterns of early and late-onset heavy drinkers on Skid Row. *Quarterly Journal of Studies on Alcohol,* 1969 30, 645–656.

5. Wilkinson, P. Alcoholism in the aged. *Australian Journal of Geriatrics,* 1971, 59–64.

6. Carruth, B, Williams, E. P., Mysak, P., and Boudreaux, L. Alcoholism and problem drinking among older persons: community care providers and the older problem drinker. New Brunswick; NJ: Rutgers Center of Alcohol Studies, 1973.

7. Mayfield, D. G. Alcohol problems in the aging patient. In W. E. Fann and G. L. Maddox (Eds.), *Drug Issues in Geropsychiatry.* Baltimore: Williams and Wilkins, 1974.

8. Cohen, S. Drug abuse in the aging patient. *Lex et Sci,* 1975, 11, 217–221.

9. Zimberg, S. Diagnosis and treatment of the elderly alcoholic. *Alcoholism: Clinical and Experimental Research,* 1978, 2, 27–29.

10. Schuckit, M. A., Morrissey, E. M., and O'Leary, M. R. Alcohol problems in elderly men and women. *Addictive Diseases,* 1978, 3, 405–416.

11. Hubbard, R. W., Santos, J. F., and Santos, M. A. Alcohol and older adults: overt and covert influences. *Social Casework,* 1979, 60, 166–170.

12. Schuckit, M. A., and Miller, P. L. Alcoholism in elderly men: survey of a general medical ward. *Annals of the N.Y. Academy of Science,* 1976, 273, 558–571.

13. Gomberg, E. S. L. The young male alcoholic: a pilot study. *Journal of Studies on Alcohol,* 1982, 43, 683–701.

14. Gomberg, E. S. L. *Drinking and Problem Drinking Among the Elderly.* Ann Arbor, MI: Institute of Gerontology, University of Michigan, 1980.

15. Berkman, L. F., and Syme, S. L. Social networks, host resistance and mortality: a 9 year follow-up study of Alameda County residents. *American Journal of Epidemiology,* 1979, 109, 186–204.

16. Fischer, C. S. *To Dwell Among Friends: Personal Networks in Town and City.* Chicago: University of Chicago Press, 1982.

17. Marshall, J. R. Changes in aged white male suicide: 1948–1972. *Journal of Gerontology,* 1978, 33, 763–768.

18. Kasl, S. V., and Berkman, L. F. Some psychosocial influences on the health status of the elderly: the perspective of social epidemiology. In *Aging: Biology and Behavior.* New York: Academic Press, 1981.

19. Herzog, A. R., Rodgers, W. L., and Woodworth, J. *Subjective Well-Being Among Different Age Groups.* Ann Arbor, MI: Institute for Social Research Reports, University of Michigan, 1982.
20. Barnes, G. M. Alcohol use among older persons: findings from a western New York State general population survey. *Journal of the American Geriatrics Society,* 1979, 24, 244–250.
21. Meyers, A. R., Hingson, R., Mucatel, M., and Goldman, E. Social and psychological correlates of problem drinking in old age. *Journal of the American Geriatrics Society,* 1982, 30, 452–457.
22. Meyers, A. R., Hingson, R., Mucatel, M., Heeren, T., and Goldman, E. The social epidemiology of alcohol use by urban older adults. *International Journal of Aging and Human Development* (in press).
23. Mellinger, G. D., Balter, M. B., Parry, H. F., Manheimer, D. I., and Cisin, I. H. An overview of psychotherapeutic drug use in the United States. In E. Josephson and E. E. Carroll (Eds.), *Drug Use: Epidemiological and Sociological Approaches.* Hemisphere Publishing Corporation, 1974.
24. Butler, R. N., and Lewis, M. I. *Aging and Mental Health: Positive Psychosocial Approaches.* St. Louis: Mosby, 1977.
25. Murphy, L. B. Review of J. Bowlby: *Loss, Sadness and Depression, Volume III.* Attachment and Loss Series. *The New Republic,* January 17, 1981, 40–41.
26. Thomas, L. *Things Unflattened by Science.* The Nineteenth Cosmos Club Award. Washington, D.C.: Cosmos Club, May 10, 1982.
27. Erikson, E. H. *Childhood and Society.* New York: W. W. Norton and Co., 1950.
28. Costa, P. T. Jr., and McCrae, R. R. Still Stable after all these years: personality as a key to some issues in adulthood and old age. In P. B. Baltes and O. G. Brim (Eds.), *Life-Span Development and Behavior,* Volume 3. New York: Academic Press, 1980.
29. Flanagan, J. C. *New Insights to Improve the Quality of Life at Age 70.* Prepared for the National Institute on Aging. Palo Alto: American Institutes for Research in the Behavioral Sciences, 1982.
30. Johnson, L. A., and Goodrich, C. H. *Use of alcohol by persons 65 years and over, upper East Side of Manhattan.* Report to the National Institute on Alcohol Abuse and Alcoholism HSM-43-73-38NIA, N.T.I.S., 1974.
31. Branch, L. G. *Understanding the Health and Social Service Needs of People Over Age 65.* Boston: Center for Survey Research, University of Massachusetts and the Joint Center for Urban Studies, M.I.T. and Harvard University, 1977.
32. Monk, A., Cryns, A. G., and Cabral, R. Alcohol consumption and alcoholism as a function of adult age. *Gerontologist,* 1977, 17, 101 (Abstract).
33. Adelman, R. C. As the body age. *Encyclopedia Brittanica Yearbook of Science and the Future,* 1982.

34. Mishara, B. L., and Kastenbaum, R. *Alcohol and Old Age.* New York: Grune and Stratton, 1980.
35. The Gallup Poll. Drinking at 13-year Low; Recession Seen As A Key Factor. September 30, 1982.

SECTION II
DIFFERENTIAL DRUG EFFECTS
IN THE AGED

Chapter 5

THE EFFECT OF ALCOHOL
ON THE AGING BRAIN

Laird S. Cermak

R yan and Butters have provided a good deal of evidence to
support the notion that chronic alcoholics demonstrate verbal memory deficits (1–3). They have also found that alcoholics
consistently perform below their age-appropriate controls, and
usually perform on a level comparable to controls in a group with
a 10-years-older age range. Because of this outcome, Ryan and
Butters have proposed that alcohol causes premature cognitive
aging. However, they also point out that their data can be used to
support Ryback's theory (4) that a continuum of cognitive abilities
exists between normals and alcoholic Korsakoffs with chronic
alcoholics' performance falling somewhere between these two
groups. The present author, however, will argue that Ryan and
Butters' data really only supports the former theory and not the
latter. Furthermore, the present report will include two studies
designed specifically to test the continuum theory in a manner
that permits differentiation from the premature aging theory.

It is important to try to distinguish between the two theories
because of the differing implications each has on our view of the
effect of alcohol on the central nervous system. The premature
aging theory presupposes the possibility that alcohol accelerates
the *general* deterioration of the CNS while the continuum theory
suggests that alcohol affects the same *specific* midline-diencephalic
structures as seen in Korsakoff's syndrome. Behaviorally, the
premature-aging hypothesis is supported by consistent deficits in
performance on any test in which alcoholics are compared to their
contemporaries. However, for the continuum theory to be correct,
the same specific "patterns" of performance seen in Korsakoff

patients ought to be approximated in alcoholics more so than would be seen for normally aging individuals. In other words, simple overall performance deficits are sufficient to support a premature aging hypothesis, but changes in patterns of performance need to exist to support the continuum theory. If alcohol does produce a patient midway between normal and brain-damaged, then we ought to see "patterns" of performance similar to Korsakoffs' begin to emerge.

Since Ryan and Butters have supplied evidence that performance by chronic alcoholics is depressed, their data supports a premature aging hypothesis but not necessarily a continuum of deficits theory. To support the latter, specific paradigms in which differential patterns of performance have been noted for Korsakoff patients would have to be used. One such paradigm taps the encoding (i.e., analytic) impairments seen in Korsakoff patients. These patients have been shown to be capable of analyzing and retaining phonemic features of words but unable to analyze the semantic features of verbal information (5–6). As a consequence, Korsakoff patients are left with little to no access routes to retrieve that material at a later time. According to the continuum theory, a similar pattern of analytic deficit ought to emerge for chronic alcoholics.

To assess this possibility, two experiments designed to measure analytic capacity were given to two separate age groups of chronic alcoholics and normal controls. The first task required that subjects utilize the associative strength of a pair of words in order to be cued for retrieval at a later point in testing. The second asked patients to remember specific features of single words (i.e., phonemic or semantic). On both of these tasks, Korsakoff patients' performance is known to be depressed but, in addition, their "pattern" of results is known to differ from that of the normals. Consequently, if only the premature aging hypothesis is correct, then the performance of alcoholics ought to be depressed on both tasks, but their pattern of performance ought to be normal. If the continuum theory is correct, then alcoholic patients' performance ought not only to be depressed but their "pattern" of performance ought to approximate that known to exist for Korsakoff patients as well.

On the first test, four groups of adult males took part. Two of the groups consisted of chronic alcoholics: 20 ·in the older group (45–60 years old; mean age 51.8) and ten in the younger group (20–35 years old; mean age 29.3). None of these alcoholic patients reported experiences of severe head injury (i.e., unconsciousness for over an hour, or hospitalization for head trauma); a history of psychiatric or neurological disorder, or histories of poly-drug abuse, electro-convulsive shock therapy, cirrhosis, or malnutrition.

There were also two control groups in this experiment. The first control group (mean age, 52.0) included 20 non-alcoholic males matched as closely as possible to the older alcoholic group for age, verbal WAIS IQ, education, and socio-economic background. The second control group included ten non-alcoholic younger males (mean age 27.6) matched to the younger alcoholic group according to the same criteria.

The subjects were told that they would be presented with a list of 12 word pairs, consisting of a capitalized to-be-recalled (TBR) word and, above this word, an associated word printed in lower case letters. Each subject was told to pay attention to the related words, as these words could serve as possible aids to recall the capitalized words later. Subjects were further informed that a recall test would be given after all the words in a given list had been presented. Then each of 12 word pairs were presented individually on index cards at a 3 sec/card rate. At the end of the presentation, the subject was given a sheet of paper containing a typed column of 12 cue words with a space beside each for him to insert the appropriate TBR word. The subject was instructed that each word on the list was a cue to help recall one of the capitalized words he had seen. He was told to write the words he remembered in the space next to the cue that helped him. Words remembered without the help of a cue were to be written separately on the page.

In this paradigm, three input conditions were combined with three output conditions to produce nine possible experimental treatment conditions, but only five of these conditions were actually used in this experiment. The input conditions were: (a) the TBR words presented alone (Input Condition O); (b) each TBR word accompanied by a weakly related word (Input W); (c) each TBR word accompanied by a strongly related word (Input S).

Output conditions were: (a) uncued recall of TBR words (Output O); (b) recall of TBR words cued by their weak associates (Output W); (c) recall of TBR words cued by their strong associates (Output S).

The five experimental conditions will henceforth be designated by the abbreviated terms of their input and output conditions: O–O, S–S, W–W, W–S, and S–W. Condition O–O was the standard no cue free recall. Condition S–S had each word accompanied by a strong associate at input and cued by the same strong associate at output. Condition W–S had each TBR word accompanied by a weak associate at input and cued by an appropriate strongly associated word at output, etc. Conditions O–S, O–W, S–O, and W–O were not tested.

The results of this task can be seen in Table 5-I, which displays the mean number of words correctly recalled by each group on each of the cueing conditions. An analysis of variance revealed a significant Group effect, a significant Age effect, and a significant Conditions effect but no significant interaction. In other words, at each age level, the alcoholics performed below their controls across all conditions. It is true that the theory of premature cognitive aging received some minor support from this experiment since the older alcoholics' performance fell significantly below that of their contemporaries while the younger alcoholics performed at a level comparable to their controls. However, the theory did not achieve the optimum level of support it would have, had the interactions been significant. What this experiment seemed to be most sensitive to was the effect of age since, overall, older subjects performed below young subjects. It was also sensitive to the effect of diagnosis since the alcoholics as a whole performed worse than the controls. Thus, deterioration on this task is primarily related to the age of the subject with alcohol increasingly enhancing the effect as the patient ages, but not accelerating it.

The continuum theory received no support from the present results. The pattern of performance across task conditions was essentially the same for all groups. In general, all groups performed best when strong cues existed both at input and output (S–S) and their second best performance occurred when strong cues existed only at output (W–S). The W–W condition was next

TABLE 5-I

PERCENTAGE OF WORDS CORRECTLY RECALLED DURING CUED RETRIEVAL
AS A FUNCTION OF INPUT-OUTPUT CONDITION

				Condition		
Group	*Age*	*S-S*	*W-W*	*W-S*	*O-O*	*S-W*
Controls	45–60	79	58	63	49	30
Alcoholics	45–60	76	50	54	43	19
Controls	20–35	91	70	67	58	33
Alcoholics	20–35	85	59	68	56	28

in line and nearly approximated the W–S performance level. It is primarily on this latter condition that the pattern of Korsakoffs' performance (5) deviates drastically from that seen here. Not only do these brain-damaged patients not profit from the repetition of a weak associate, but their retrieval is actually impaired relative to their own free recall (O–O); such a situation was not at all duplicated here. Korsakoff patients simply cannot form and/or utilize new, creative, associative relationships within this memory task. Indeed, they can rely only on pre-experimentally strong associations if they are to be facilitated by cueing at all. Not even the older alcoholics performed in this manner. They performed in a manner not at all deviate from the norm, let alone Korsakoff-like. Consequently, the continuum model was not supported by the outcome of this experiment.

The same four groups of adult males took part in the second experiment. Each subject was required to listen to a recording of 45 lists of words varying in length from 6 to 18 words per list. For 15 of these lists, the subject was instructed to raise his hand when he heard a word that was a repetition of a previous word in the list (repetition task). For another 15 of these lists, the subject was instructed to raise his hand when he heard a word that rhymed with a previous word in the list (phonemic task). For the third block of 15 lists, the subject was instructed to raise his hand when he heard a word that was a member of the same semantic category (example: golf-hockey) as a previous word in the list (semantic task).

Each of the 45 lists presented to the subject contained two target words embedded among 4 to 16 filler words. The first target word appeared in one of three possible positions—the third, the fifth, or the seventh position in the list. The second target word then occurred in one of five positions—the first, the third, the fifth, the seventh, or the ninth position after the first target word.

The subject was informed that he would be hearing prerecorded word lists presented on a cassette tape recorder and that his task would be to detect a repetition (or rhyme or same category word). He was told that when he heard this particular item he was to raise his hand. Words were presented at a one word/sec. rate.

The results for the three tasks are depicted in Figures 5-1, 5-2, and 5-3. Figure 5-1 shows each group's performance on the Repetition Task as a function of the number of intervening words between repetitions. Figure 5-2 depicts the outcome in the same manner for the Rhyme Task, and Figure 5-3 shows the results on the Category Task. An analysis of variance was performed on the number of correctly detected words as a function of the Diagnosis and Age of the patients as well as Task Condition (Repetition, Rhymes, or Categories) and the length of the delay between critical items (0, 2, 4, 6, and 8 intervening words). The analysis revealed a significant Task Condition effect, and a significant Delay effect, but no Age or Diagnostic Group effect. In addition, there was a significant Condition X Delay interaction, but none of the interactions with Diagnostic or Age Groups were significant.

The second experiment also failed to provide evidence for a continuum theory. No evidence of a Korsakoff-like encoding deficit (6) was seen here even for the older alcoholics. In fact, precisely the same pattern of encoding abilities held for all alcoholics and non-alcoholics, young or old. Where one group showed strengths, the others followed suit. Korsakoff patients, on the other hand, perform normally on the repetition task, but are impaired on both the phonemic and semantic tasks. Since there is no evidence for the existence of such an encoding disorder in the present experiment for any group, alcoholics' performance cannot be placed on a continuum between normals and Korsakoffs for this ability. The outcome of this task does differ from that of the first experiment, however, in that the overall level of performance was almost the same for all groups. Old alcoholics performed as well as the old controls, and young alcoholics' performance was on a par with

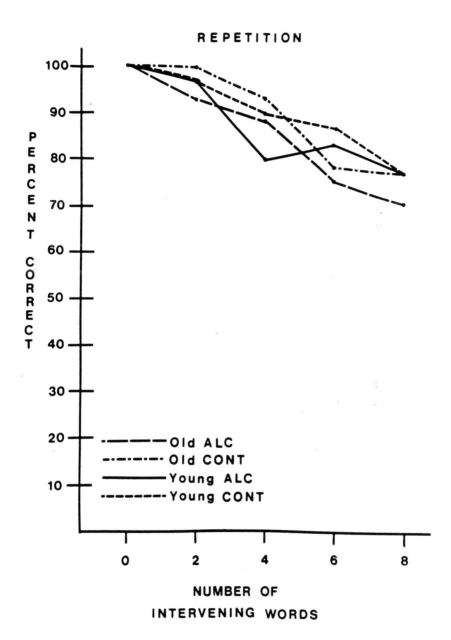

Figure 5-1. Percentage of target words correctly identified by each group on the Repetition Task as a function of the number of intervening words is shown.

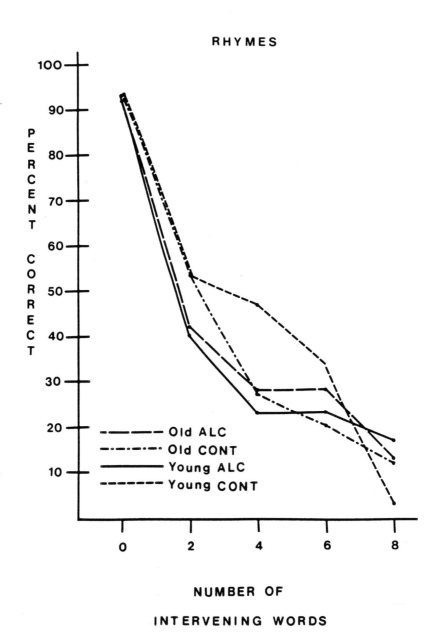

Figure 5-2. Percentage of target words correctly identified by each group on the Rhyme Task as a function of the number of intervening words is shown.

CATEGORIES

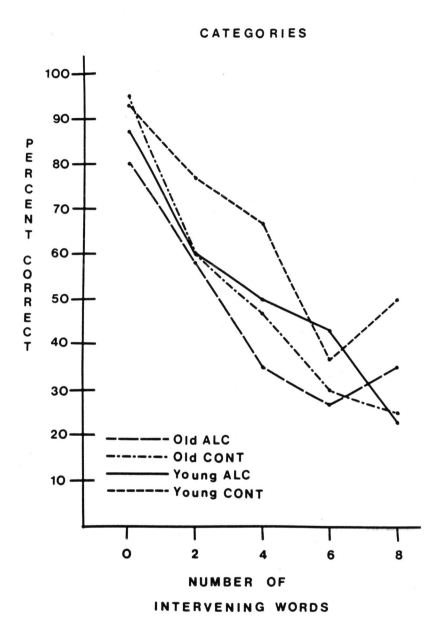

Figure 5-3. Percentage of target words correctly identified by each group on the Category Task as a function of the number of intervening words is shown.

their contemporaries. Only on the most difficult task (category detection) was there any between-group effect, and then it was one of age, not of drinking history. It would appear then, for this task at least, no difference in pattern of level of analytic ability can be seen between alcoholics and non-alcoholics. Thus neither the continuum nor the premature aging theories receives substantiation.

On both of these tasks, the older subjects' performance was below that of the young subjects; thus, each was sensitive to the effects of aging. However, only on the first task did an effect of alcohol emerge, in that older alcoholics performed significantly below their controls while younger alcoholics performed below, but not significantly below, their contemporaries. Since this effect existed for all conditions of testing rather than being sensitive to a particular type of encoding-retrieval situation, a premature-aging hypothesis received some support, but the continuum of deficits hypothesis did not receive support. In fact, the pattern of the alcoholics' performance was the same as that of the controls in both experiments. It is true that their performance was depressed in task 1, but not in a manner remotely similar to the pattern of Korsakoff patients. Thus, aging produces a retarding effect on the overall process which may be somewhat mangified by the effects of chronic alcohol consumption, but not substantially altered by it.

SUMMARY

This experiment was designed to test the continuum theory of alcoholic aging. Since the alcoholics did not show any difference in the pattern of their retrieval relative to nonalcoholics, support for a continuum of deficits between normal and Korsakoff patients has not been demonstrated. Instead, what has been shown is an accelerated depression of overall performance for some verbal memory tasks, including Experiment 1 of this report as well as experiments documented previously (1-3). Consequently, a premature aging theory can be proposed to account for those outcomes where older alcoholics' performance has been shown to be below that of their contemporaries, but the continuum model cannot be invoked. This does not mean that one or the other of these models is correct, but this report does provide parameters within which each might be tested. It might prove profitable to apply this differentiation, i.e., pattern changes versus accelerated depression, as a test for any set of experimental outcomes (even those using non-verbal materials) that seek to support the continuum model and/or the premature aging model to explain the effects of alcohol on the aging brain.

REFERENCES

1. Ryan, C., Butter, N., Montgomery, K., Adinolfi, A., and Didario, B. Memory deficits in chronic alcoholics: Continuities between the "intact" alcoholic and the alcoholic Korsakoff patient. In Begleiter, H., and Kissin B. (Eds.), *Alcohol Intoxication and Withdrawal.* New York: Plenum, 1980.
2. Ryan, C., and Butter, N. Learning and memory impairments in young and old alcoholics: evidence for the premature-aging hypothesis. *Alcoholism,* 1980, 4, 288–293.
3. Ryan, C., and Butter, N. Further evidence for a continuum-of-impairment encompassing male alcoholic Korsakoff patients and chronic alcoholic men. *Alcoholism,* 1980, 4, 190–198.
4. Ryback, R. The continuum and specificity of the effects of alcohol on memory. *Q J Stud Alcohol,* 1971, 32, 995–1016.
5. Cermak, L. S., Uhly, B., and Reale, L. Encoding specificity in the alcoholic Korsakoff patient. *Brain Lang,* 1980, 11, 119–127.
6. Cermak, L. S., and Moreines, J. Verbal retention deficits in aphasic and amnesic patients. *Brain Lang,* 1976, 3, 16–27.

Chapter 6

THE RELATIONSHIP BETWEEN SERUM IMMUNOGLOBULINS AND NEUROPSYCHOLOGICAL FUNCTIONING IN OLDER ALCOHOLICS

Donna Cohen

INTRODUCTION

The results of studies in older populations have suggested a mathematical relationship between serum immunoglobulin levels and cognitive performance in healthy older persons as well as individuals with the nonreversible dementias of later life (1–4). These observations have been interpreted within the framework of a hypothesis that immunologic factors mediate brain-behavior alterations in the aged who manifest cognitive impairment (3, 5). If serum immunoglobulins are a significant predictor of cognitive dysfunction, this relationship should also emerge in another population reported to manifest impaired cognitive performance and altered serum immunoglobulin levels, i.e., patients with chronic alcoholism.

Long-term excessive alcohol consumption is related to impaired neuropsychological functioning among alcoholics who are without overt clinical psychiatric impairment, e.g., Wernicke-Korsakoff syndrome, head trauma (6). Although there are no differences between samples of alcoholics and non-alcoholics on tests of general intelligence, the results of many investigations consistently show that more than half of alcoholics studied are significantly impaired on tests of abstraction, problem solving, decision making, visuo-motor coordination, short-term memory, and spatial-visual abilities (7–9), while verbal and long-term memory skills remain relatively intact (10). However, recovery of cognitive functioning among alcoholics has been reported with the cessation of drinking by some investigators (11) but not by all (12).

Patients with chronic alcoholism have immunologic abnormalities and are at increased risk for infections (13–16). Although *in vivo* reactivity to dinitrochlorobenzene as well as recall antigens is intact, *in vitro* defects have been observed in T-lymphocytes. Immunologic alterations in alcoholics, such as decreased lymphocyte transformation in response to mitogen stimulation and elevated serum immunoglobulin levels, have not been observed in recovered alcoholics (14). For example, serum immunoglobulin levels (IgG, IgA, and IgM) were significantly elevated in alcoholics compared to a healthy control group. However, the serum IgG levels in a population of recovered alcoholics were intermediate between those of a healthy control group and an acute alcoholic group.

The present study was designed to evaluate whether we could demonstrate a relationship between serum immunoglobulins in chronic alcoholics immediately upon cessation of drinking and three weeks after withdrawal.

A PILOT STUDY

Forty white males, aged 45–60 years, with a five to ten year history of excessive drinking, were recruited from individuals being treated in the Alcoholic Treatment Unit of a VA Medical Center. The primary diagnosis of each patient was alcohol addiction. Criteria for exclusion included known head trauma, epilepsy, history of drug abuse other than alcohol, or clinical evidence of brain damage from a source other than alcohol. No patient had any evidence of severe liver insufficiency as judged by normal prothrombin and albumin values and lack of ascites.

Subjects were first evaluated on a series of psychological and immunological parameters within a week of admission to the alcoholic detoxification inpatient unit. They were examined again approximately three weeks later. Of the 40 subjects initially accepted for the study, 34 completed the initial testing and 28 completed the predischarge evaluation.

We hypothesized that serum immunoglobulins would be directly related to psychological test performance. The cognitive test measures included selected performance subtests of the Wechsler Adult Intelligence Scale (Block Design, Digit Symbols and Picture Completion) as well as the Hooper Test of Visual Organization (17). These tests are sensitive to the neuropsychological dysfunction seen with chronic excessive alcohol intake (11).

Serum IgG, IgA, and IgM were assayed by the method of single radial immunodiffusion (using Hyland quantiplates) from 10ml blood sample drawn at each time of testing, admission and twenty one days later.

Spearman R calculations were performed separately for serum immunoglobulin levels and psychological test performance at admission and three weeks later. Furthermore, paired comparison t-tests were computed to test for significant differences in pre- and post-test measures.

No significant differences were observed in cognitive performance or serum immunoglobulin levels. At both times of testing subjects demonstrated impaired performance; the average scaled scores for each of three WAIS subtests was 14. The average serum immunoglobulin levels were within normal limits (see Table 6-I).

DISCUSSION

Although behavioral alterations due to neurotoxins have been easily related to nervous system, endocrine, and vascular parameters, immunological-behavioral relationships are a new area of research. These pilot results are consistent with the interpretation that the neuropsychological changes observed in persons with a history of long-term excessive alcohol use are evidence of a dementing psychological deterioration and change in brain function. Positive correlations between serum immunoglobulin and cognitive test performance were observed as previously reported in older persons with Alzheimer's disease and related disorders. In healthy older persons without a dementia, negative correlations between test performance and serum immunoglobulins have been reported (3, 4).

Alcohol is a powerful neurotoxin and chronic use leads to significant changes in brain function and structure (6, 18–20). Although the results reported here are only suggestive, immuno-chemical studies would improve our understanding of how the

TABLE 6-I
CORRELATION BETWEEN SERUM IMMUNOGLOBULIN LEVELS AND
PERFORMANCE IN NEUROPSYCHOLOGICAL TESTS

A.   Initial Serum Immunoglobulin Concentrations (N=34)

	IgA	IgG	IgM
Block Design	0.015	0.506** $p \leq 0.001$	0.025
Digit Symbol	0.541** $p \leq 0.00$	-0.040	0.348* $p \leq 0.02$
Picture Completion	-0.115	-0.044	0.186
Hooper Visual Organization	-0.114	-0.060	0.369* $p \leq 0.02$

B.   Final Serum Immunoglobulin Concentrations (N=28)

	IgA	IgG	IgM
Block Design	-0.109	0.519** $p \leq 0.002$	0.034
Digit Symbol	0.576** $p \leq 0.001$	0.021	0.242
Picture Completion	0.123	0.142	0.413* $p \leq 0.01$
Hooper Visual Organization	-0.095	0.045	0.516** $p \leq 0.002$

immune system responds to alcohol induced changes in the brain.

SUMMARY

Previous studies have suggested a correlation between serum immunoglobulin levels and cognitive performance in both normal and demented aged individuals. This pilot study examined chronic alcoholic patients to determine if a similar correlation existed and if changes were seen in these measures 3 weeks after admission for treatment. Results showed that, while no significant pre-treatment treatment changes in serum measures or cognitive performance were observed, some significant correlations were seen between the two types of measures. Further studies should continue to examine how the immune system responds to alcohol induced changes in the brain.

REFERENCES

1. Cohen, D., and Eisdorfer, C. Serum immunoglobulins and cognitive status in the elderly: I. A population study. *Brit J Psychiat*, 1980, 136, 33–39.
2. Eisdorfer, C., and Cohen, D. Serum immunoglobulins and cognitive status in the elderly: II. An immunologic-behavioral relationship? *Brit J Psychiat*, 1980, 136, 40–45.
3. Eisdorfer, C., Cohen, D., and Buckley, E. Serum immunoglobulins and cognition in the impaired elderly. In R. Katzman, R. D. Terry, and K. L. Bick (Eds.), *Alzheimer's Disease: Senile Dementia and Related Disorders*. New York: Raven, 1978.
4. Roseman, J. M., and Buckley, C. E. Inverse relationship between serum IgG concentration and measures of intelligence in elderly persons. *Nature (Lond)*, 1975, 254, 55–56.
5. Cohen, D., Cannarella-Nehlsen, S., Kumar, M., and Eisdorfer, C. *Alzheimer's disease: A review of the autoimmune etiology*, submitted.
6. Wells, C. Chronic brain disease: An update on alcoholism, Parkinson's disease, and dementia. *Hosp Comm Psychiaty*, 1982, 33, 111–126.
7. Parsons, O. A., and Leber, W. R. The relationship between cognitive dysfunction and brain damage in alcoholics: causal, interactive, or epiphenomenon. *Brit J Psychiat*, 1978, 133, 119–122.
8. Eckardt, J. J., Ryhack, R. S., and Paulter, C. P. Neuropsychological deficits in alcoholic men in their mid thirties. *Am J Psychiat*, 1980, 137, 932–936.
9. Grant, L., Adams, K., and Reed, R. Normal neuropsychological abilities of alcoholic men in their late thirties. *Am J Psychiaty*, 1979, 136, 1263–1269.
10. Albert, M. S., Butlers, N., and Brandt, J. Memory for remote events in alcoholics. *J Stud Alcohol*, 1980, 41, 1071–1081.
11. Schau, E. J., O'Leary, M. R., and Chaney, E. F. Reversibility of cognitive deficits in alcoholics. *J Stud Alcohol*, 1980, 41, 733–740.
12. Adams, K. M., Grant, I., and Reed, R. Neuropsychology in alcoholic men in their late thirties: A one year follow-up. *Am J Psychiat*, 1980, 137, 928–931.
13. Bjorkholm, M. Immunological and hematological abnormalities in chronic alcoholism. *Acta Med Scand*, 1980, 207, 197–200.

14. MacGregor, R. R., Gluckman, S. J., and Senior, J. R. Granulocyte function and levels of immunoglobulins and complement in patients admitted for withdrawal from alcohol. *J Infect Dis,* 1978, 138, 747–753.
15. Smith, F. E., and Palmer, D. L. Alcoholism, infection, and altered host defenses. A review of clinical and experimental observations. *J Chron Dis,* 1976, 29, 35–49.
16. Gluckman, S. J., Dvorak, V. C., and MacGregor, R. R. Host defenses during prolonged alcohol consumption in a controlled environment. *Arch Int Med,* 1977, 137, 1539–1543.
17. Hooper, E. H. *Hooper Visual Organization Test.* Los Angeles: Western Psychological Service, 1957.
18. Cala, L. A., and Mastalgia, F. L. Computerized tomography in chronic alcoholics. *Alcoholism: Clin Exp Res,* 1981, 5, 283–294.
19. Tran, V. T., Snyder, S. H., and Major, L. F. GABA receptors are decreased in brains of alcoholics. *Am Neurol,* 1981, 9, 289–292.
20. Cutting, J. The relationship between Korsakoff's syndrome and "alcoholic dementia." *Brit J Psychiat,* 1978, 132, 240–251.

Chapter 7

MECHANISMS UNDERLYING AGE-RELATED DIFFERENCES IN RESPONSE TO ETHANOL

W. Gibson Wood

Interest in the effects of alcohol on aged individuals has been increasing over the past few years. This increase is demonstrated by a wide range of endeavors including, for example, published studies (see 1–3 for reviews), books (4, 5), conferences on alcohol and aging, and the establishment of a National Alcohol Research Center to study alcohol and aging. The increased attention being given to alcohol and aging is in response to reports (6–8) that alcoholism and alcohol abuse may be problems for aged individuals. While the prevalence of alcoholism and alcohol abuse declines with increasing age (9, 10), aged individuals may be "at risk" for developing alcohol-related problems because of changes associated with aging and the pathological effects associated with chronic alcohol abuse.

Whereas more attention is being given to alcohol and the aging individual, there is still a paucity of basic data on effects of alcohol in the aged individual. For example, aged organisms are more affected generally by alcohol administered either acutely or chronically than younger organisms. It has not been determined as to the mechanism that may account for the greater effects of alcohol observed in the aged organism. The purpose of this chapter will be to examine possible mechanisms that may explain the greater sensitivity of the aged organism to effects of alcohol. The emphasis of this chapter will be on studies that have employed an

This work was supported by the Medical Research Service of the Veterans Administration and the Geriatric Research, Education and Clinical Center of the St. Louis VA Medical Center. Appreciation is extended to Cheryl Duff, Sandy Melliere, and Sharon Smith for expert secretarial assistance.

animal model as a method for studying the effects of alcohol on the aging individual.

EFFECTS OF ACUTE AND CHRONIC ETHANOL ADMINISTRATION

Acute administration (i.e., a single injection) of ethanol has a greater effect on aged animals as compared to younger animals (11–13). Aged C57BL/6NNIA male mice (24–28 mo) injected with a 3 g/kg dose of ethanol lose the righting response at lower brain and blood ethanol levels (11, 12) than younger mice (6–8 mo.). The aged mice are impaired longer and regain the righting response at lower brain and blood ethanol levels than do younger mice. Similar results have been observed in different age groups (2–3, 11–16 and 18–20 mo) of female Sprague-Dawley rats (13).

Chronic administration of ethanol has greater effects on aged animals than younger animals (14, 15). We administered ethanol in a liquid diet (Bio-Serv) for 14 days to three age groups (3, 14 and 25 mo) of C57BL/6NNIA male mice. The oldest group showed more severe signs of intoxication and withdrawal than the two younger groups. The three-month group consumed significantly more of the ethanol diet and had higher blood ethanol levels than the two older groups even though the three-month group was least affected by ethanol.

Consumption of ethanol for approximately 16 weeks affects choline acetyltransferase (Chat) activity and locomotor performance in C57BL/6J male mice tested longitudinally between 12 and 30 months of age (15). Chat activity declined with increasing age, however, ethanol consumption reduced this decline. Locomotor performance decreased with age and this decrease was augmented by ethanol consumption.

From this brief review, it is clear that aged animals differ in response to ethanol as compared to younger animals. Age differences have been reported when exposure to ethanol is either acute or chronic. The mechanism responsible for age differences in response to ethanol has not been identified. The following discussion will concentrate on the role that metabolism, body composition and brain sensitivity may have in terms of an explanation for age differences in response to ethanol.

METABOLISM

The primary system for the metabolism of ethanol is the alcohol dehydrogenase system (ADH). This system has been discussed in detail in previous reviews and the reader is referred to those reviews for a comprehensive discussion (e.g., 16–18). The ADH system includes two important enzymes, alcohol and aldehyde dehydrogenase. Alcohol dehydrogenase oxidizes ethanol to acetaldehyde. Generally, it is thought that ethanol oxidation by liver alcohol dehydrogenase is the rate-limiting step in the elimination of ethanol from the body. Acetaldehyde is catalyzed primarily by aldehyde dehydrogenase to form acetate or the activated form, acetyl coenzyme A. Data on the ADH system in relation to age is very limited. There have been no published studies that have used animals that are representative of the life span for a particular species. Most studies reporting age differences have used animals less than six months of age (e.g., 19, 20).

Wiberg, Trenholm, and Coldwell (21) studied blood and brain ethanol levels, acetaldehyde, and activity of alcohol dehydrogenase in young (3–4 mo) and adult (10–12 mo) Wistar male rats. Following a 3 g/kg ethanol injection, both brain and blood ethanol levels declined more rapidly for the younger animals. Brain and blood acetaldehyde levels did not differ clearly between the two age groups. Metabolism of ethanol was measured *in vitro* using liver slices. Liver slices from young animals metabolized ethanol at a faster rate than liver slices from older animals. The adult animals had higher levels of acetaldehyde as compared to the younger animals. It was also observed in the same study that cytoplasmic levels of alcohol dehydrogenase were significantly higher in the adult animals than the younger animals. Wiberg et al. concluded that the greater toxicity seen in adult animals could not be accounted for by changes in metabolism or enzyme activity. While this study did observe differences in both *in vivo* and *in vitro* metabolism of ethanol between young and adult rats, it did not examine aged animals. It would be well worth the effort to replicate the study using young, adult and aged animals.

Age differences have been reported for the rate of ethanol

elimination when young, adult and aged C57BL/6NNIA mice are used (11). Three age groups (6, 12, and 24 mo) of C57BL/6NNIA mice were injected with a 3 g/kg dose of ethanol. Young mice cleared ethanol at a rate of 0.53 μmol/min/gram whereas the clearance rate for the two older groups was 0.46 and 0.37 μmol/min/gram between 1 and 4 hours post-injection. The clearance rate was significantly greater for the youngest group as compared to the oldest group. In the same study, blood and brain ethanol levels were examined at 5, 15 and 30 minutes following a 3g/kg ethanol injection. Aged mice had significantly lower blood and brain ethanol levels than the other two age groups. Differences between the two older groups were small at 30 minutes, and the younger mice continued to have lower ethanol levels in brain and blood. It was concluded (11) that age differences in ethanol clearance could not account for the age differences in behavior, i.e., aged animals lost and regained the righting response at lower blood and brain ethanol levels than young animals, observed in the same study.

Ethanol elimination has also been studied using different age groups of rats (13). Three age groups (2–3, 11–12, 18–20 mo) of Sprague-Dawley female rats were injected with a 1.0 g/kg dose of ethanol. Blood ethanol levels were determined at 30, 60, 90, 120, 150 and 180 minutes post-injection. Blood ethanol levels were highest in the older animals, but with increasing time, age differences were no longer significant. The rate of ethanol elimination was reported to not be significantly different among the three age groups.

In one of the few studies that has examined aged humans, it was found that ethanol elimination does not differ with respect to age (22). Ethanol (0.57 g/kg) was administered to human subjects ranging in age from 21–81 years. Blood ethanol levels were determined at 30-minute intervals between 30 and 300 minutes following ethanol administration. Data were expressed as ethanol concentration in estimated blood water. Ethanol levels were higher in older subjects, however, the rate of ethanol elimination was not related to age.

The studies reviewed in this section demonstrate the need for additional work concerning aging and the metabolism of ethanol.

While there appears to be agreement for ethanol elimination, there are differences among the studies with respect to blood ethanol levels. These differences may be attributable to gender, species, or procedural differences. In order to understand the metabolism of ethanol in the aged organism, studies on the enzyme kinetics of alcohol dehydrogenase and aldehyde dehydrogenase will have to be performed. In addition, the role of the microsomal ethanol-oxidizing system (23) in relation to aging should be studied. Another area that has not been investigated is the relationship, if any, between acetaldehyde and the effects of ethanol in the aged organism. Based on the extant data, no definite conclusion concerning metabolism of ethanol as a mechanism for age-related differences in response to ethanol can be made.

BODY COMPOSITION

The percentage of body water to body weight and lean body mass decrease with increasing age. It has been reported that in humans the decrease in percent body water is less than 7 percent for individuals between 17–34 and 57–86 years of age (24). The decrease in body water probably results from an increase in body fat and a decline in lean body mass. Because ethanol is distributed primarily in body water, it has been hypothesized that age differences in body water may account for the greater effects of ethanol observed in aged organisms (21).

The body water hypothesis is based in a large part on a study by Wiberg, Samson, Maxwell, Coldwell, Trenholm (25), who injected two age groups (2–3 and 12–14 mo) of male Wistar rats with different doses of ethanol (1, 2, 3 g/kg). They found that pulmonary excretion of ethanol was significantly greater in the younger animals as compared to the older animals but accounted for less than 10 percent excretion of ethanol. The percentage of body water to body weight was significantly less in adult rats (52%) than in young rats (64%). Age differences in blood and brain ethanol levels were attributed to the hydrophilic properties of ethanol and the decrease in percent body water with advancing age. Wiberg et al. (25) suggested that their results may explain age difference in the acute toxicity of alcohol.

A similar conclusion has been reached using human subjects (22). Higher peak blood alcohol levels (expressed as mg/dl estimated blood water) were found for old subjects (57–81) than younger subjects (21–56). Lean body mass and total volume of distribution were observed to be correlated significantly with age: lean body mass $r = -0.533$; volume of distribution $r = 0.39$. However, when the r values are squared (yielding percent common variance shared by two variables), the contribution of lean body mass and volume of distribution was approximately 28 percent and 16 percent, respectively. Other factors, in addition to lean body mass and volume of distribution, would appear to account for age differences in response to alcohol.

Recently, a direct test of the body water hypothesis has been reported by York (26). Initially, the amount of body water was determined in two age groups (5–7 and 24–26 mo) of CD (Sprague-Dawley) female rats. Animals were then injected with different doses of ethanol based on estimated body water. The rate of ethanol elimination did not differ between the young and old animals and blood ethanol levels were similar generally. It also was observed that the distribution of ethanol in blood and brain was similar for young (7 mo) and old (28 mo) female CD strain rats. Ethanol-induced hypothermia did not differ between young and old rats when injected with ethanol based on estimated amount of body water.

Age differences in body water would appear to contribute to the greater effects of ethanol in aged animals. However, this explanation does not fully account for effects of acute and chronic ethanol administration for several reasons. Aged C57BL/6NNIA mice (24–28 mo) lose the righting response at lower brain and blood ethanol levels than younger mice (6–8 mo). In addition, the aged mice are impaired longer and regain the righting response at lower brain and blood ethanol levels than do younger mice (11, 12). Similar results have been noted for different age groups (2–3, 11–12, and 18–20 mo) of female Sprague-Dawley rats (13). When ethanol is administered chronically, aged mice (25 mo) also show a greater effect than younger animals (3, 14 mo) even though the aged mice consumed significantly less of an ethanol liquid diet and had lower blood ethanol levels as compared to the younger mice (14).

These differences suggest that ethanol is having a greater effect on brains of aged animals and not simply the result of age differences in body composition.

The body water hypothesis is interesting and should be examined further. While there are age differences in percentage of body water and lean body mass, these differences do not appear to completely explain age differences in response to ethanol. Future studies need to use different species representative of the mean life span of that species and including both male and female animals. Support for the hypothesis is based on a study (26) that used female Sprague-Dawley rats that were retired breeders. A problem with the Sprague-Dawley rat is that the aged animal becomes very obese and is not a good model of human aging.

BRAIN SENSITIVITY

Aged mice lose and regain the righting response following an injection of ethanol at lower brain and blood ethanol levels than younger mice (11, 12). We reported recently that aged mice administered ethanol in a liquid diet for 14 days showed more severe signs of intoxication and withdrawal than younger mice even though the older mice consumed less of the liquid diet (14). These results (11, 12, 14) do not support explanations for age differences in response to ethanol such as metabolism or body composition. Because responses such as loss and regaining of righting response and motor signs of intoxication and withdrawal are responses mediated primarily by brain, ethanol may be having a greater effect on brain of the aged organism as compared to the younger organism.

It has been proposed that the primary site for the pharmacological effects of ethanol is the biological membrane (27). Deterioration of biological membranes has been suggested to be a basic factor in the aging process (28). This section will discuss the role that age changes in brain membranes may have on response to ethanol.

The effects of ethanol on biological membranes has been reviewed extensively and the reader is referred to these excellent reviews (29–31). Briefly, it has been shown that when biological membranes are perturbed *in vitro* with ethanol, there is a disordering of the bulk lipids in the membrane. This disordering has been referred to as a change in the fluidity of the membrane. Fluidity refers to the viscosity of the lipid environment. The increase in fluidity (disordering) is thought to be due to the partitioning of ethanol into the hydrocarbon region of the membrane. The increase in fluidity may alter the mobility of membrane lipids which may modify the function of membrane proteins such as adenylate cyclase or Na^+K^+-ATPase (31). Ethanol also may interact directly with membrane proteins.

Changes in fluidity are dependent on whether the organism has been exposed to ethanol *in vivo*. Membranes from ethanol-tolerant animals show less change in fluidity when perturbed with ethanol *in vitro* as compared to membranes from control animals (e.g., 32, 33). The reduced response to ethanol *in vitro* has been attributed to increased cholesterol content, changes in other lipids, and reduced partitioning of ethanol into the membrane (27, 33, 34).

Biological membranes are not only affected by ethanol but also show changes with increasing age. Age-related differences in the biophysical properties of membranes have been observed for erythrocytes, lymphocytes, and liver microsomes (35–38). To our knowledge, there has not been a published study on the biophysical properties (e.g., order parameter) of brain membranes. Age differences have been reported for lipid composition of myelin (39). The ratio of cholesterol to phospholipid was greater for myelin from old C57BL/10J mice (26 mo) as compared to younger mice (3 mo). In the same study, it was observed that there was a decrease in unsaturated acyl groups of membrane phosphoglycerides with increasing age. The cholesterol/phospholipid ratio also has been found to be higher in 19-month Sprague-Dawley rats than in three-month rats (40).

Membranes from aged animals differ in fluidity and composition as compared to membranes from younger animals. Based on these differences, it is reasonable to hypothesize that membranes from aged animals would respond differently to ethanol perturbation than membranes from younger animals. We tested this hypothesis (41) using synaptic plasma membranes, brain microsomes, and erythrocytes that were prepared from C57BL/6NNIA male mice of three different age groups (3–5, 11–13, 22–24 mo). Membrane fluidity was measured using the 5-nitroxide stearic acid probe. This probe reports motion of the acyl chains of phospholipids close to the surface of the membrane. Ethanol was administered *in vitro* in two different concentrations, 250 mM and 500 mM. While these ethanol concentrations are higher than what is observed during moderate to severe intoxication, i.e. 20–40 mM, it was our intention to maximize proposed age-related differences in response to ethanol.

Fluidity of membranes at baseline (i.e., in the absence of ethanol) among the three age groups did not differ significantly for each of the membranes studied. However, age-related differences in membrane fluidity were observed when membranes were perturbed with ethanol *in vitro*. Ethanol fluidized significantly membranes from young animals in a dose-dependent manner. Ethanol had less of an effect on membranes from the two older groups. Ethanol fluidized significantly synaptic plasma membranes of the two older groups only at 500 mM and the magnitude of fluidization was not as great as membranes from young animals.

Ethanol-induced changes in fluidity of erythrocyte membranes was similar as that observed for synaptic plasma membranes. Ethanol had a greater effect on the fluidity of young erythrocyte membranes as compared to membranes from the two older groups at both ethanol concentrations.

Brain microsomes were perturbed less by ethanol than synaptic plasma membranes or erythrocytes, but the pattern of age differences was comparable to that observed for the two other membranes. Ethanol had the greatest effect on brain microsomes from young animals.

The greater resistance of membranes from aged mice to pertubation by ethanol is similar to the results of a study that measured indirectly the physical properties of liver mitochondria (42). Mitochondria from old (24 mo) male Wistar rats showed less response to increasing concentrations of KCl as compared to mitochondria from younger rats (2–4 mo).

The ability of membranes from aged animals to respond to ethanol differs as compared to the response of membranes from younger animals. These age differences in the lipid environment of the membrane may affect the activity of membrane bound enzymes, e.g., Na+K+-ATPase. Sun and Samorajski (43) examined the effects of ethanol on Na+K+-ATPase activity of synaptic plasma membranes from three different age groups of C57BL/10J male mice (3, 8, 26–29 mo). Greater ethanol-induced inhibition of ATPase activity in membranes from old animals was observed as compared to activity of membranes from younger animals. Similar results were reported in the same study using synaptic plasma membranes from human brains.

Biological membranes from aged animals differ in response to ethanol as compared to membranes from younger animals. These results occurred under conditions where metabolism and percentage of body water cannot be used as explanations for the age differences observed. Admittedly, our results are preliminary, but they do identify a possible mechanism for age differences in response to ethanol that is based on a common factor, i.e., biological membranes that are affected by ethanol and also change with increasing age.

CONCLUSIONS

Aged organisms differ in their response to both acute and chronic ethanol administration as compared to younger organisms. Generally, the effects of ethanol are greater in aged organisms. Presently, an agreed-upon explanation for age differences in response to ethanol has not been forthcoming. As discussed in this chapter, there are three different mechanisms that may account for the greater effects of ethanol in aged organisms. It is very possible that the increased effect of ethanol in aged organisms results from the interaction among the three proposed mechanisms. To date, very little data are available regarding the three mechanisms.

Data on the metabolism of ethanol is limited. Studies on the activity of enzymes such as alcohol dehydrogenase and aldehyde dehydrogenase have not been accomplished using animals representative of the life span. Related to the metabolism of ethanol is the role that acetaldehyde may play as a factor in age differences in response to ethanol. It is quite apparent that a large amount of work remains towards understanding the metabolism of ethanol in the aged organism. Moreover, the total pharmacokinetics of ethanol in the aged organism needs to be studied.

Age differences in body water as an explanation is interesting and deserves greater attention. It does appear that basing ethanol dosage on estimated body water and not body weight minimizes age differences in response to ethanol in two extreme age groups of Sprague-Dawley female rats. The body water hypothesis does not account for age differences observed both *in vivo* and *in vitro* using male C57BL mice. Much more work is needed in this area using animals representative of the life span and an animal model (e.g., Fischer 344 rat or the C57BL/6NNIA mouse) that more closely resembles the changes in body weight observed with humans.

Brain sensitivity is another possible explanation as a mechanism for age differences in response to ethanol. Age differences have been reported for enzyme activity and membrane fluidity in response to ethanol. While the exact meaning of these biochemical and biophysical changes have yet to be determined, it is very clear that ethanol affects the brain differently in aged organisms as compared to younger organisms. Future studies need to be conducted that examine membrane-bound enzymes, e.g., adenylate cyclase, and the employment of probes that report on different depths within the membrane. The composition of the membrane should also be studied for different brain membranes.

Membranes from aged animals showed less of a change in response to ethanol as compared to membranes from younger animals. The results for the aged animals are at variance with the finding that ethanol administered *in vitro* to membranes from animals not exposed previously to ethanol show increased fluidity (e.g., 32, 33). Moreover, it has been observed that long-sleep lines of mice that are more sensitive to the *in vivo* effects of ethanol than short-sleep lines of mice differ in their *in vitro* response to ethanol (44). Membranes from long-sleep mice are more disordered by ethanol as compared to membranes from short-sleep mice. The data for aged animals do not fit the positive correlation between increased *in vivo* sensitivity and increased fluidity *in vitro*. Aged animals are more sensitive to the *in vivo* effects of ethanol than younger animals, but this sensitivity is not related to increased disordering of membranes.

The inverse relationship between *in vivo* sensitivity and *in vitro* disordering observed with aged animals raises the possibility that perhaps the site of action for ethanol differs in aged animals as compared to younger animals. While this may be an explanation, there are several other explanations that need to be explored. Ethanol in the aged organism may be acting directly on membrane proteins and/or the lipids surrounding these proteins. Another explanation is that the disordering of the lipid bilayer is greater for aged organisms deeper in the membrane. We only measured the disordering at the surface of the membrane. These proposed explanations should be tested in future studies.

The age differences in membrane response to ethanol have implications for the effects of chronic ethanol abuse in younger organisms. Chronic ethanol abuse has been proposed to result in premature or accelerated aging (45). While this hypothesis is difficult to prove because an explanation for the aging process or processes has not been identified, there is a similarity in the response of membranes from aged animals and membranes from young animals who were exposed to ethanol *in vivo*. Membranes from young animals administered ethanol *in vivo* show less disordering when perturbed with ethanol *in vitro* as compared to control animals (32, 33). Whether it can be said that the young ethanol animals are aging prematurely cannot be determined presently. However, the biophysical similarity between membranes from aged animals and young animals exposed to ethanol *in vivo* is a topic that deserves closer examination. Further studies are needed in this area to determine if there is a recovery to base line of animals who have received ethanol *in vivo*. Such a recovery would suggest that the effects of ethanol and aging are not the same.

The most obvious conclusion that can be reached concerning ethanol and the aged organism is that much more work is needed. Fundamental studies on the pharmacokinetics of ethanol in aged organisms are needed. Presently, the explanation for age differences in response to ethanol is not known. The majority of studies have been studies examining effects of acute administration of ethanol. The relation between chronic ethanol consumption and aging has not been determined. To this end, the biological effects of chronic but moderate ethanol consumption across the adult life span has not been examined. This is a topic that will have increasing importance as the number of aged individuals increases.

SUMMARY

Animal studies have consistently shown that behavior is more effected by alcohol administration in older organisms than in younger ones. This chapter reviews three general physiological hypotheses for this effect. First, age-related differences in ethanol metabolism have been demonstrated in several animal studies with the result that ethanol persists longer in the bodies of older organisms. Such an age-related effect has not, however, been demonstrated with humans. Second, body composition differences also exist with age in animals and in humans with the percent of body water decreasing with age. Since ethanol is distributed primarily in body water, this may account for some of the age-related behavior effects. Finally, it is possible that age-related changes in brain sensitivity are related to alcohol sensitivity, especially the age-related deterioration of biological membranes.

REFERENCES

1. Freund, G. The interaction of chronic alcohol consumption and aging on brain structure and function. *Alcoholism: Clin Exp Res*, 1982, 56, 13–19.
2. York, J. L. The influence of age upon the physiological response to ethanol. In W. G. Wood and M. F. Elias, *Alcoholism and Aging: Advances in Research.* Boca Raton, FL: CRC Press, 1982.
3. Wood, W. G., and Armbrecht, H. J. Behavioral effects of ethanol in animals: Age differences and age changes. *Alcoholism: Clin Exp Res*, 1982, 6, 3–12.
4. Mishara, B. L., and Kastenbaum R. *Alcohol and Old Age.* New York: Grune & Stratton, 1980.
5. Wood, W. G., and Elias, M. F. *Alcoholism and Aging: Advances in Research* Boca Raton, FL: CRC Press, 1982.
6. Zimberg, S. Diagnosis and treatment of the elderly alcoholic. *Alcoholism: Clin Exp Res*, 1978, 2, 27–41.
7. Gordon, J. J., Kirchoff, K. L., and Philipps, B. K. Alcoholism and the Elderly. Iowa City: Elderly Program Development Center, 1976.
8. Carmody, A. P., and Messard, L. 1977 Supplement to Alcoholism and Problem Drinking, 1970–1975: A Statistical Analysis of VA Hospital Patients. Washington, DC, Reports and Statistics Service, Office of Controller, Veterans Administration, 1978.

9. Cahalan, D., Cisin, I. H., and Crossley, H. M. *American Drinking Practices,* (Monograph No. 6). New Brunswick, NJ: Rutgers Center of Alcohol Studies, 1969.

10. Barnes, G. M. Alcohol use among older persons: Findings from a Western New York State General Population Survey. *J Am Geriatr Soc,* 1979, 27, 244–250.

11. Ritzmann, R. F., and Springer, A. Age-differences in brain sensitivity and tolerance to ethanol in mice. *Age,* 1980, 3, 15–17.

12. Wood, W. G., and Armbrecht, H. J. Age differences in ethanol-induced hypothermia and impairment in mice. *Neurobiol Aging,* 1982, 3, 243–246.

13. Abel, E. L., and York, J. L. Age-related differences in response to ethanol in the rat. *Physiol Psychol,* 1979, 7, 391–395.

14. Wood, W. G., Armbrecht, H. J., and Wise, R. W. Ethanol intoxication and withdrawal among three age groups of C57BL/6NNIA mice. *Pharmacol Biochem Behav,* 1982, 17, 1037–1041.

15. Samorajski, T., Strong, R., and Volpendesta, D. et al. The effects of aging, ethanol, and dihydroergotoxine mesylate (Hydergine) alone and in combination on behavior, brain neurotransmitter and receptor systems. In W. G. Wood and M. F. Elias (Eds.), *Alcoholism and Aging: Advances in Research.* Boca Raton, FL: CRC Press, 1982.

16. Liber, C. S. The metabolism of alcohol. *Sci Am,* 1974, 234, 25–33.

17. von Wartburg, J. P. the metabolism of alcohol in normals and alcoholics: Enzymes. In B. Kissin and H. Begleiter (Eds.), *The Biology of Alcoholism,* (Volume 1) New York: Plenum Press, 1971.

18. Rognstad, R., and Grunnet, N. Enzymatic pathways of ethanol metabolism. In E. Majchrowiez and E. P. Noble (Eds.), *Biochemistry and Pharmacology of Ethanol* (Volume 1). New York: Plenum Press, 1979.

19. Collins, A. C., Yeager, T. N., and Lebsack, M. E. et al Variations in alcohol metabolism: Influence of sex and age. *Pharmacol Biochem Behav,* 1975, 3, 973–978.

20. Hollstedt, C., and Rydberg, U. S. Ethanol metabolism in the growing rat. *Arch Int Pharmacodyn Ther,* 1970, 188, 341–348.

21. Wiberg, G. S., Trenholm, H. L., and Coldwell, B. B. Increased ethanol toxicity in old rats: Changes in LD50, *in vivo* and *in vitro* metabolism and liver alcohol dehydrogenase activity. *Toxicol Appl Pharmacol,* 1970, 16, 718–727.

22. Vestal, R. E., McGuire, E. A., and Tobin, J. D. et al. Aging and ethanol metabolism. *Clin Pharmacol Ther,* 1977, 21, 343–354.

23. Liber, C. S., and DeCarli, L. M. The role of the hepatic microsomal ethanol oxidizing system (MEOS) for ethanol metabolism *in vivo. J Pharmacol Exp Ther,* 1972, 181, 279–287.

24. Edleman, I., Haley, H., and Schloerb, P. et al. Further observations on total body water. I. Normal values throughout the life span. *Surg Gynecol Obstet,* 1952, 94, 1–12.

25. Wiberg, G. S., Samson, J. M., and Maxwell, W. B. et al. Further studies on the

acute toxicity of ethanol in young and old rats: Relative importance of pulmonary excretion and total body water. *Toxicol Appl Pharmacol,* 1971, 20, 22–29.

26. York, J. L. Body water content, ethanol pharmacokinetics and the responsiveness to ethanol in young and old rats. *Dev Pharmacol Ther,* 1982, 4, 106–116.

27. Goldstein, D. B., and Chin, J. H. Interaction of ethanol with biological membranes. *Fed Proc,* 1981, 40, 2073–2076.

28. Sun, A. Y., and Sun, G. Y. Neurochemical aspects of the membrane hypothesis of aging. In H. P. von Hahn and S. Basel (Eds.), *Interdisciplinary Topics in Gerontology,* 1979.

29. Goldstein, D. B. Uses of electron paramagnetic resonance in alcohol research. *Alcoholism: Clin Exp Res,* 1981, 5, 137–140.

30. Rubin, E., and Rottenberg, H. Ethanol-induced injury and adaptation in biological membranes. *Fed Proc,* 1982, 41, 2465–2471.

31. Sun, A. Y. Biochemical and biophysical approaches in the study of ethanol-membrane interaction. In E. Majchrowicz and E. P. Nobel (Eds.), *Biochemistry and Pharmacology of Ethanol,* (Volume 2). New York: Plenum Press, 1979.

32. Chin, J. H., and Goldstein, D. B. Drug tolerance in biomembranes: A spin label study of the effects of ethanol. *Science,* 1977, 196, 684–685.

33. Rottenberg, H., Waring, A., and Rubin, E. Tolerance and cross-tolerance in chronic alcoholics: Reduced membrane binding of ethanol and other drugs. *Science,* 1981, 213, 583–585.

34. John, G. R., Littleton, J. M., and Jones, P. A. Membrane lipids and ethanol tolerance in the mouse. The influence of dietary fatty acid composition. *Life Sci,* 1980, 27, 545–555.

35. Butterfield, D. A., Ordaz, F. E., and Markesbery, W. R. Spin-label studies of human erythrocyte membranes in aging. *J Gerontol,* 1982, 37, 535–539.

36. Rivnay, B., Bergman, S., and Shinitzky, M. Correlations between membrane viscosity, serum cholesterol, lymphocyte activation and aging in man. *Mech Ageing Dev,* 1980, 10, 119–126.

37. Rivnay, B., Shinitzky, M., and Globerson, A. Viscosity of lymphocyte plasma membrane in aging mice and its possible relation to serum cholesterol. *Mech Ageing Dev,* 1979, 10, 71–79.

38. Armbrecht, H. J., Birnbaum, L. S., and Zenser, T. V. Changes in hepatic microsomal membrane fluidity with age. *Exp Gerontol,* 1982, 17, 41–48.

39. Sun, G. Y., and Samorajski, T. Age changes in the lipid composition of whole homogenates and isolated myelin fractions of mouse brain. *J Gerontol,* 1972, 27, 10–17.

40. Malone, M. J., and Szoke, M. C. Neurochemical studies in aging brain. I. Structural changes in myelin lipids. *J Gerontol,* 1982, 37, 262–267.

41. Wood, W. G., Armbrecht, H. J., and Wise, R. W. et al. Age-related differences in the effect of ethanol on membrane fluidity and Na^+K^+-ATPase activity *in vitro. Alcoholism: Clin Exp Res,* in press (abstract).

42. Fitzgerald, G. A., and Balcavage, W. X. Consequences of dietary ethanol on

permeability and respiration of mitochondria and liver ADH in young and aged rats. In M. Galanter (Ed.), *Currents in Alcoholism, Biomedical Issues and Clinical Effects of Alcoholism, (Volume 5).* New York: Grune & Stratton, 1979.

43. Sun, A. Y., and Samorajski, T. The effects of age and alcohol on (Na$^+$ + K$^+$)-ATPase activity of whole homogenate and synaptosomes prepared from mouse and human brain. *J Neurochem,* 1975, 24, 161–164.

44. Goldstein, D. B., Chin, J. H., and Lyon, R. C. Ethanol disordering of spin-labeled mouse brain membranes: Correlation with genetically determined ethanol sensitivity of mice. *Proc Natl Acad Sci USA,* 1982, 79, 4231–4233.

45. Courville, C. B. *Effects of Alcohol on the Nervous system of Man.* Los Angeles: San Lucas Press, 1955.

SECTION III
DRUG USE AND MISUSE
BY THE ELDERLY

Chapter 8

THE DETECTION, IDENTIFICATION
AND DIFFERENTIATION OF ELDERLY
DRUG MISUSE AND ABUSE
IN A RESEARCH SURVEY

Meyer D. Glantz

The modern study of drug abuse originally focused on opiate abusers, and, more recently, the research has kept pace with drug use and expanded its focus to include abusers of a wider range of illegal drugs. The populations involved have primarily been young adults and older adolescents, and drug abuse has come to be thought of by the general public and by the scientific community as a problem largely confined to young populations. National surveys substantiate this idea, but both surveys and anecdotal reports suggest that while the majority of abusers are in those age ranges, younger adolescents and even preadolescents and older adults are increasingly becoming involved in drug abuse.

Researchers have developed considerable expertise in assessing levels and types of drug abuse among young populations. For the most part, the techniques which are employed rely on self-reports of drug usage which the researcher then rates as to severity of abuse. As the drugs which are typically used are illegal, any use which is at more than a nominal or "experimental" level is usually considered to be drug abuse. The self-report measures are fairly simple and straightforward and have been found to be generally reliable. However, these measures rely on the subjects being willing and accurate reporters whose drug use patterns primarily involve illicit substances so that the use can be readily identified as abuse.

This chapter does not necessarily represent the views of the National Institute on Drug Abuse.

Based on the information available, it does not seem likely that this methodology can effectively be used in assessing elderly populations, both because of the characteristics of the age group as a whole and because of the patterns of drug abuse which are likely to be prevalent among the elderly. Although the available research is limited and some of the studies are methodologically flawed, some tentative statements about elderly drug abuse can be made. A very brief summary of the research will be presented. A more complete summary is available in the published reviews of the elderly drug and alcohol abuse research literature (1–4).

In terms of the abuse of illegal drugs, it does not appear that this is currently a major problem for the elderly. Only a small percentage of the elderly have ever used an illegal drug even once (5). There is a small population of elderly opiate addicts, and the small number of publicly visible elderly addicts led to the hypothesis that addicts "mature out" of their drug dependence (6). Later research indicates that only about 22 percent of an identified group of addicts mature out (7), and there is evidence that the majority of addicts adapt and conceal their drug use behaviors as they age (8, 9). Given the demographics of the current addict population, the number of elderly addicts is likely to increase over the next several decades.

A substantial number of anecdotal reports maintain that at least some elderly adults deliberately obtain multiple prescriptions for drugs, share drugs, and hoard drugs for nonprescribed usage. Unfortunately, there is no substantial research-documented information on the nature and extent of these problems. Similarly, there have been public reports of inappropriate elderly drug use which is perpetrated by individuals other than the elderly drug users themselves; these reports usually implicate nursing homes and physicians. While there has been some research to support these reports (10–13), there is no comprehensive research describing the prevalence of these types of problem.

Elderly adults account for a highly disproportionate amount of prescription drug, psychoactive drug, and over-the-counter drug use. This is assumed to be primarily related to the fact that the elderly have a disproportionate number of physical and psychological problems, but certainly the potential for inappropriate use is present. The elderly typically take a large number of different drugs and, as they metabolize many drugs more slowly and are susceptible to more side effects than younger adults, they are at much greater risk for drug interactions and other untoward use consequences.

The extent of drug misuse among the elderly is not known, although it is probable that drug misuse is more common than drug abuse. The available data indicate that underuse of drugs is the most prevalent form of elderly drug misuse (14). Studies which have attempted to determine the degree to which the elderly generally comply with prescription directions have produced highly inconsistent results (15), though it is clear that it is not a negligible problem. Potential forms of misuse other than noncompliance have also been reported. For example, Guttmann (16) found that approximately half of the subjects in his study used some type or combination of legal drugs and over-the-counter drugs in combination with alcohol.

There is no research which specifically investigated the abuse of licit drugs by the elderly. Emergency room studies imply that this is not a major problem, but, as has been suggested (17), these studies might underestimate the extent of elderly who experience drug-related emergencies, as some older people might be unwilling or unable to seek help in clinical settings. Further, it seems probable that the elderly are more likely than other populations to deny that they have an abuse problem, and, as many of the sequellae of substance abuse are similar to some of the infirmities associated with old age, abuse problems may not be readily identified by those in contact with the elderly.

Elderly alcohol abuse is integrally related to elderly drug abuse because of the very high risk for the elderly for alcohol-drug interactions. Two of the most probable forms of substance abuse among the elderly are in fact the abuse of alcohol alone and the abuse of a combination of drugs and alcohol. Estimates of elderly alcoholism range from 2–10 percent, with higher estimates for certain subgroups (18). The elderly drinker is likely to drink with the same frequency though in smaller quantities than younger drinkers (19), but there is evidence that alcohol has a greater and longer-lasting effect for the elderly. There are no available estimates of the prevalence of elderly substance abuse involving drugs in combination with alcohol.

Difficulties in research on elderly substance abuse are related to two areas of problems. The first area of problems centers around difficulties which are involved in almost any gerontological survey research. These problems have been discussed in the gerontological literature and will be mentioned only briefly here. For the most part, these general problems of gerontological research are related to sampling and to assessment issues. The sampling issues involve a variety of problems. It is often difficult to obtain a random sample of the elderly and the representativeness of any given sample is often difficult to determine. The elderly often have a lower participation rate than other age groups, and it is usually difficult to tell if the nonparticipants have self-selected themselves in such a way as to influence the representativeness of the sample in terms of the particular questions being investigated. This is likely to be especially problematic with studies of sensitive issues such as drug use. Samples may be further biased, as health and social isolation problems may make a targeted subgroup relatively unaccessible. This problem may be compounded if potential subjects with severe health problems or cognitive deficits are screened out due to the difficulties involved in assessing such individuals. The specifications of the elderly sample can also present problems. The researcher must decide whether to include both retired and currently employed elderly, healthy as well as infirm elderly, young elderly (65 to 75 years of age) and also the frail elderly (76 years and older *or* 76 to 85 years of age), elderly with various degrees of cognitive and perceptual function, elderly who reside in a variety of institutional settings and elderly living with family, or alone, etc. Each of these decisions will have a marked effect on the sample being studied and presumably on the findings. All of the issues involved in sampling the elderly become even more important when the phenomenon being investigated has a relatively low prevalence as is probably the case with at least some forms of inappropriate drug use.

The assessment technique issues revolve around the utilization of methodologies which may be valid and suitable for younger populations but which have typically not been validated for the elderly. These techniques may entail administration forms which are difficult for the elderly to handle (e.g., they may require reading small print). Of greater concern, these techniques may assess certain phenomenon in terms of research-demonstrated concomitants which might not be comparably associated for the elderly. For example, many of the symptoms assessed in several commonly used depression rating scales (e.g., sleep difficulties, changes in eating patterns) are not necessarily symptomatic of depression for an elderly individual. Similarly, substance abuse among the elderly is likely to take a different form and have different concomitants than substance abuse among younger groups.

Underlying some of the sampling and assessment difficulties and compounding the rest is the frequently made tacit assumption that the elderly are a highly homogenous population. In fact, there is tremendous variability among the elderly in terms of health, social, psychological, financial and demographic characteristics, possibly greater than with other age groups. Failure to consider the heterogeniety of the elderly may lead to the selection of an unrepresentative sample and to the selection of variables and the use of assessments that are appropriate for only an undetermined subset of the sample. Other potential problems involved in elderly research related to control groups, attributions of causality across cohort groups, follow-up obstacles in longitudinal research, etc., must be taken into account when they are relevant. All of the factors and potential problems of general gerontological research must be considered in elderly drug abuse research. The second major area of research problems which is relevant to elderly drug abuse research derives primarily from the particular nature of the most probable patterns of elderly substance abuse.

As suggested above, elderly substance abuse is more likely to involve the inappropriate use of licit rather than illicit substances; the abuse is less likely to involve use behaviors and consequences which are markedly evident and readily identified. Elderly subjects will not be aware that misuse is taking place and may be unwilling to admit to abuse. Considering the large number of prescription and over-the-counter drugs used by most elderly and the extremely large number of possibilities for misuse and abuse, in order to identify almost any inappropriate substance use, an extraordinary amount of information about drug and alcohol use and contextual factors must be collected and carefully analyzed. Many forms of inappropriate substance use will involve only subtle deviations from appropriate use, and many instances of inappropriate use will require considerable technical expertise to identify. In general, it will be necessary to first determine if inappropriate use is taking place and then to distinguish cases of misuse from abuse; there will often be insufficient information to make a positive determination. Research on elderly inappropriate substance use may well be the most difficult type of drug research to carry out.

Following is a general strategy for the collection and analysis of the information necessary to identify inappropriate substance use and to differentiate misuse from abuse. The researcher undertaking such a study will need to address the problems described above as those involved in general gerontological survey research; problems of sampling and assessment modality are not addressed here. The strategy is intended to maximize the possibility of detecting and identifying inappropriate substance use. Some of the coding recommendations, particularly those related to the distinction of misuse from abuse, are controversial and should be carefully examined.

In the data-collection stage, the elderly person should be asked in an individual interview assessment to report on all of the drugs they used in the last two weeks (including quantity/frequency use information and information about the reason the drug was prescribed, as well as the original complaint which led to the eventual prescription). Memory aids, such as pill picture cards and a prompter list of commonly used medications for common conditions, should be used as needed. Comparable information on alcohol, over-the-counter (OTC) drugs, tobacco, and caffeinated beverages should be collected. This first assessment should be supplemented with the "medicine cabinet technique" in which the interviewer (after obtaining permission from the subject) goes with the subject to the place that the subject keeps his or her medications and uses them as a memory prompt for usage information and also copies the prescription directions and any other use information (date of prescription, number of refills, number of pills used since date prescription was filled, physician's and pharmacist's name, name of person to whom prescription was given if other than subject, etc.). Information about nutrition (i.e., eating habits), health (including level of functioning and height, weight, etc.), psychological and social functioning (emphasizing ability to function normally, stress and coping factors, possible consequences of inappropriate drug use, and the assessment of any other variables which might be reasonably associated as either an antecedent or consequence of inappropriate substance use), health care sources, and a report of what drug use directions and prohibitions were given to the subject by the physician(s) and/or pharmacist(s) should also be collected. "Ever use" information and appropriate history should be collected for illegal drugs and for commonly used psychoactive drugs. Some assessment of drug and/or alcohol dependence should be made. Complete demographic information should be collected. It is recommended that when possible, variables related to general physical health, general cognitive functioning, employment status, and assignment as young or frail elderly be included.

In the second stage, it would be desirable to obtain verifying and supplementary information from the caretakers (if any), relatives, friends or roommates of the subject and from the physician(s) and pharmacist(s).

The third stage of the process would involve having a geriatric pharmacologist review the current use information. Coding of the use date would involve two major steps. The first step involves determining whether the combination of all substances taken by each individual in the context of their particular biomedical and psychosocial situations is appropriate. That is, given the physical and psychological condition of the subject, are they taking the safest (or at worst, least harmful) set of consensually accepted pharmacological substances in the recommended quantities and frequencies and following the consensually accepted directions and prohibitions related to use of the drug(s). As the elderly may metabolize and/or react to certain drugs differently than younger populations, the appropriateness of the use of and manner of use of a drug or set of drugs must be determined as it would be for an elderly population. An assessment should be made to ascertain whether it is likely that any drug interactions, duplications, illicit use, etc., have occurred. An assessment should also be made to determine if the individual violated the use directions for the drug(s). Alcoholic drinking may be said to occur if the individual drinks an average of more than 2½ or 3 (depending on their physical condition) ounces of alcohol per day or uses some combination of alcohol and drugs which has the equivalent effect of more than 2½ ounces of alcohol. It might be helpful to predetermine an elderly appropriate drug regimen standard for the most commonly prescribed drugs, a list of common psychoactive and nonpsychoactive side effects of commonly prescribed drugs at various dose levels, a list of drugs which are recommended for the most common ailments of the elderly, a list of drug-drug and drug-alcohol interactions and their consequences for commonly used substances, and a set of equivalence tables for the more commonly prescribed families of psychoactive drugs and for those drugs which may have psychoactive consequences under misuse or abuse circumstances. Some of these materials are available in the scientific literature.

The equivalence tables would facilitate the determination of the amount of a drug type that was being taken or the degree of effect which might result if a person were taking two or more drugs from a given drug family or if they were taking two or more drugs with similar effects. Two types of equivalence tables would be helpful.

The first type of table would list the equivalent doses of drugs within a particular drug family, for example, the Benzodiazepines. The most commonly prescribed drug in the drug family (for example, diazepam for the benzodiazepines) would be adopted as the standard for that category. An individual's drug regimen that included a drug in the particular drug family would, for comparison purposes, have their use of that drug also listed in terms of its dose equivalent according to the standard; a person taking 30 mg of chlordiazepoxide per day would have their drug use also listed as 10 mg per day of the benzodiazepine standard. A drug regimen which included two or more drugs from the particular family would have their use of that drug family also listed in terms of the standard. A person taking 10 mg per day of lorazepam and 30 mg per day of oxazepam would have their use also listed as 56 mg per day of the benzodiazepine drug standard.

The second type of table would list the approximate equivalent doses of drugs which have comparable psychoactive effects or consequences. The tables would be used in the same manner as those described above and should consider the side effects of non-primarily psychoactive drugs and should include OTC drugs, caffeinated beverages, alcohol, tobacco, etc. The categories to be used might include: anti-psychotics, anti-depressants, stimulants, sedative-hypnotics (soporifics), anxiolytics, anti-manics, analgesics, and perhaps a set of categories for those drugs which might result in symptoms which might also be associated with senility, confusion, concentration problems, memory decrements, hallucinations or delusions, anxiety, depression-lethargy and other possible drug consequences as well.

If the drug use appears to be appropriate in terms of the above-stated criteria, then misuse or abuse should be considered in terms of the consequence and dependence criteria which will be discussed briefly. If the individual is taking a psychoactive drug or a substance or combination of substances which result in some psychoactive effect and if that individual reports being dependent on this substance use and if the individual is not being specifically treated by a physician with these drugs for a condition which is consensually accepted as being properly treated with long-term drug therapy involving this psychoactive effect, then inappropriate use may be said to presumably be taking place. A recent study reported that in a large-scale survey, self-expressed craving and frequency of drug use were fairly reliable estimates of dependence on abused drugs. If an individual is taking a drug or set of substances which might have a given undesirable consequence, and if there is a potentially less harmful alternative, and if the individual reports the experience of the undesirable physical, psychological or social consequence, it may be said that inappropriate use is presumably taking place even if the undesirable consequence is not invariably caused by the substance use and could be caused by other factors, including age or physical deterioration. For example, if an elderly person reports some memory difficulties and if memory problems could possibly result from the drug or drugs which they are taking, and if there is a potentially less harmful drug or nondrug alternative available, then it may be said that inappropriate use is presumably taking place. This criteria would also include consequences such as arrest for driving while intoxicated, deterioration of one's social network, physical inability to handle household responsibilities, etc.

If inappropriate use is identified for a given individual, it must then be determined whether the inappropriate use will be classified as a case of "substance misuse" or a case of "substance abuse." All instances of inappropriate drug use are at least instances of drug misuse. While it will not always be possible to determine whether a given instance of inappropriate use is misuse or abuse, it will be possible in many cases.

In order for an instance of inappropriate use to be reasonably classified as abuse, three conditions must obtain. First, the perpetrator must be aware that improper use is occurring. Second, some degree of intention to inappropriately use the drug(s) must have been present at the time of the improper use. In most cases, any indication of knowledge that improper use is occurring would be sufficient to demonstrate intention. Third, there must be at least a potential undesirable physical, psychological or social consequence of the inappropriate use. This would include a consequence in which an individual did not receive or seek a more desirable treatment or course of action because they used the inappropriate drug(s).

Unlike most of the inappropriate drug use which may occur with younger individuals, elderly inappropriate drug use will often involve a perpetrator who is someone other than the elderly drug user. Typically, although not always, this other person will be the physician or physicians who prescribe medications for the elderly individual. Therefore, the categories of misuse and abuse can be viewed as each having two subcategories defined by whether the elderly user or another individual is the perpetrator of the inappropriate substance use.

The discrimination between misuse and abuse will be made by trying to fit the circumstances of the inappropriate drug use of a given individual to the closest model or hypothesized pattern of misuse or abuse.

Misuse, which is perpetrated by a person other than the actual elderly user of the drug(s), is characterized by inadvertency. The perpetrator believes that they are providing the proper drug-use specifications, directions and/or assistance. If the perpetrator is a physician, then the misuse might occur because of drug or patient misinformation, insufficient information or simple error. The physician might be unaware that the elderly individual is seeing another physician for some other specific problem not related to the one he is treating and may prescribe some medication which duplicates or interacts with a medication prescribed by the other physician. The elderly react to and metabolize many drugs differently than younger patients, and the physician may, out of ignorance, over- or underprescribe a medication or may prescribe a medication which is less safe than an alternative for an elderly person though appropriate for a younger person. The physician may give confusing or incomplete directions for the use of the medication and this may lead to inappropriate use; this is a particular problem with PRN prescriptions. The physician might prescribe a medication when a nondrug therapy is available or may prescribe an unnecessary drug not knowing that a patient's age-related complaint may not be pathological but normative for an elder individual (such as sleeping fewer hours per night than previously).

If the perpetrator is a family member or friend who assists the elderly user with his or her medication, then the misuse might occur because of a misunderstanding about drug use or some lack of knowledge on the part of the perpetrator, or a simple error. They may also initiate some use or change in use of medications under the belief that they are helping the elderly person, being unaware that harm may result.

Misuse may be perpetrated by the elderly themselves and again the misuse is characterized by inadvertence. The misuse may occur because of a misunderstanding, misinformation, error, ignorance, confusion or a memory problem. They may not be aware that they are taking substances which interact or that they are using an inappropriate amount of a drug, etc.

One special subset of misuse is the failure to use or the underuse of appropriate medication. This may be because of financial reasons, concern over dependence or the appearance of weakness, or some other reason. Inappropriate use of this type should be classified separately. Inappropriate underuse may result in undesirable physical, psychological or social consequences and can be a serious problem. If the underuse is perpetrated by a physician or family member etc. and it has an undesirable consequence, then misuse has taken place if there was no awareness that the underuse was inappropriate; if there was knowledge of the inappropriateness, then abuse occurred. If the elderly person is the perpetrator of the underuse and if there is no undesirable consequence to that individual's drug underuse, then the original prescribed drug dosage may have involved drug misuse or abuse on the part of the physician; however, the underuse would not be called misuse. If the elderly person is the perpetrator of the underuse and there is an undesirable consequence, then, regardless of whether the elderly person was aware of the inappropriateness or not, this would be a case of "passive drug misuse." If the elderly person is the perpetrator and if there is a consequent psychoactive effect of the underuse other than the alleviation of an undesirable consequence of the original prescribed drug regimen, then drug abuse has occurred.

Abuse which is perpetrated by a person other than the actual elderly user of the drug(s) is characterized by awareness that the use is inappropriate with some understanding that there may be at least a potential undesirable consequence. In most cases, awareness that the use is inappropriate would be sufficient to indicate awareness of at least a potential harmful consequence. If the perpetrator is a physician, the abuse may involve unnecessary or over prescriptions or any of the misuses that have been described as those that a physician might commit. The difference is that the abusing physician has some knowledge of the inappropriateness. Considering the large-scale efforts that have been made to educate physicians about the special needs and medication problems of the elderly, it seems reasonable to assume that any given physician will have been made aware that special care and information is necessary in order to appropriately and safely prescribe for the elderly. Therefore, unless there is reason to believe otherwise, it should be assumed that an inappropriate prescription or drug use direction is the result either of intention or of negligence, both of which would be considered to be a form of abuse. If the inappropriate drug use is perpetrated by a care provider, family member, or friend of the elderly drug user, then the inappropriate use should be considered to be misuse unless there is some indication that the perpetrator would have had some information that inappropriate use was taking place. If inappropriate use is taking place, even though it was not committed by the physician, caretaker, family member or friend, and if any of these individuals are aware of the inappropriate use but do not attempt to correct it, then it may be said that abuse is taking place.

If the elderly user is the perpetrator of the inappropriate use, then abuse may be identified according to a number of criteria, all of which indicate that the elderly user was aware of the inappropriateness. Abuse may occur because of an inappropriate source of the substance. Any use of an illegal drug is abuse. Any use of an illegally obtained drug (for instance, through a falsified prescription, etc.) would be abuse. Obtaining multiple prescriptions for a drug or for drugs with similar effects would constitute abuse. The use of a drug prescribed for another person is abuse. Hoarding drugs and using them in a manner that was not prescribed is abuse. Using a drug for a purpose for which it was not prescribed is abuse. Inappropriate drug use that may involve a violation of prescription directions, a deviation from the intended quantity and/or frequency of use, or a drug combination or interaction may be misuse or abuse and there will not necessarily be a way to distinguish the two. The elderly person may take more of a drug or may take it more often than was intended; they may take a PRN drug more often than the medical consensus would indicate is appropriate. They may drink too much alcohol (depending on the individual's age and physical condition, more than 2½ or 3 "standard drinks" of alcoholic beverages per day), too many caffeinated beverages (amount to be determined by reference to the scientific literature), smoke more tobacco than is consensually accepted as being safe for an elderly person, or take more of an OTC drug than is recommended by the OTC use directions. They may inappropriately take a drug with another prescribed drug, with an OTC drug, or with alcohol or they may inappropriately take alcohol with an OTC drug. They may take a drug or a combination of drugs which is inappropriate in terms of the physical condition or nutritional situation of that elderly user. If it may be said that the elderly person probably was aware that the drug use was inappropriate, then it may be said that abuse occurred. Unless there is a strong reason to believe that the elderly person's inappropriate substance use was the result of an error of which they were unaware, if the inappropriate drug use could result in a psychoactive effect, or if it appears to have resulted in a consequence which had psychological or social impact on the elderly user, then it may be said that abuse occurred.

Obviously, there will often be a difficult decision to be made in the determination of whether inappropriate use has occurred and whether that use is misuse or abuse. Although it is hardly a traditional scientific guideline, it is recommended that the researcher err on the side of the false positive, as even in an exacting study designed to detect and identify misuse and abuse, many cases will be missed.

Whenever possible, it is desirable to further define the patterns of inappropriate substance abuse; in particular, the cases of abuse, in terms of their onset history, their relation to mental health factors, and their relation to demographic variables.

There are a number of different possible onset histories of abuse involving various combinations of onset of use, onset of abuse, etc. The most likely abuse onset histories are as follows:

Pre-elderly years	*Elderly years*
substance use →	substance abuse
substance abuse →	use (or nonuse) only
substance abuse →	substance abuse

There are other abuse history patterns as well as a variety of use and abstention patterns. As much as possible, each subject should be classified as to their use/abuse history pattern for alcohol and for drugs (including both legal and illegal and the use of alcohol in combination with drugs). Subjects should also be classified according to the traditional demographic and background factors as well as to their mental health status. In those instances where an abuser appears to report life factor difficulties (e.g., social isolation, insufficient income, etc.) or psychological difficulties (e.g., depression, anxiety, etc.), it may be possible to make some inference as to whether the substance abuse is more likely to be related to recreational use or coping difficulties.

The suggested strategy for the coding of the drug usage data involves coding each subject's usage information according to several different classification schemes. With the first scheme, probable cases of inappropriate usage would be identified and, when possible, these cases would be further identified as involving misuse or abuse. Those cases not identified as involving probable inappropriate usage might be designated as to whether they can be identified as cases involving probable appropriate usage as opposed to cases where insufficient information was available to determine the appropriateness of the usage. This scheme is more traditional and more conservative in its estimation of the problematic usage.

As many cases of inappropriate use will be difficult to identify with certainty from the available data, it is suggested that each subject should be rated in terms of the risk of inappropriate substance use which their use of drugs and alcohol entails. With the second coding scheme, subjects' drug usage would be rated in terms of the risk of inappropriate usage in terms of a number of simple indices as well as a single more complex and comprehensive index. This could be done using two types of indices.

With the first type of index, subjects would be classified with a set of simple indices according to the number of prescribed drugs they took, the number of psychoactive drugs, the number of drugs which are in the same drug family, the number of drugs which have a similar effect, the number of drugs with psychoactive side effects, the number of OTC drugs, the amount of alcohol consumed, etc. Some rating could also be done in terms of the amounts of the substances which were used.

With the second type of index, factors such as the ones described for use with the first type of index would be weighted in terms of an estimate of the risk involved and combined to produce a single comprehensive index. This index should also reflect the interaction of the factors; for example, taking both a psychoactive drug and alcohol should increase the risk index by more than just the sum of the risks assigned to the two factors individually. Psychological, social and health ratings might also be included as factors in the index. Similarly, an index which reflects the likelihood that a potential consequence of inappropriate substance use has occurred would be very helpful. A separate index reflecting psychological stress and/or difficulties and an index reflecting life factor and life events stresses would be useful for a general exploration of possible correlates of various types of inappropriate substance use.

SUMMARY

While drug abuse is generally thought of as a problem of young populations, older adults are increasingly becoming involved in inappropriate drug use. This trend, given the current demographics of drug use, is likely to continue over the next several decades.

Methods employed for assessing levels and types of drug abuse among young populations may not be as effective or reliable with elderly populations because of some of the characteristics of older individuals and their patterns of inappropriate drug use. The elderly are less willing to admit to drug abuse than younger groups. Some have cognitive and perceptual difficulties. Health problems may limit participation. A number are difficult to contact by virtue of living in isolated and anonymous residences or being in a variety of institutional settings. Inadvertent inappropriate use (misuse) is more common in the elderly than intended inappropriate use (abuse) and the most prevalent form of misuse is underuse. In addition, inappropriate use by the elderly more often involves licit than illicit drugs and may be perpetrated by the individual or by others.

Different strategies are required for understanding, research, and treatment of elderly populations. Examples, guidelines, and research needs are described in the context of a practical classificatory scheme.

REFERENCES

1. Glantz, M., Petersen, D., and Whittington, F. *Drugs and the Elderly Adult.* Rockville, MD: National Institute on Drug Abuse, 1983 (forthcoming).
2. Glantz, M. Predictions of elderly drug abuse. *Journal of Psychoactive Drugs,* 1981, 13, 117–126.

3. Gomberg, E. *Drinking and Problem Drinking Among the Elderly.* Ann Arbor, Michigan: University of Michigan Institute of Gerontology, 1980.

4. Petersen, D., Whittington, F., and Beer, E. Drug use and misuse among the elderly. *Journal of Drug Issues,* 1979, 9, 5–26.

5. Cisin, I., Miller, J., and Harrell, A. *Highlights from the National Survey on Drug Abuse.* Rockville, MD: National Institute on Drug Abuse, 1978.

6. Winick, C. Maturing out of addiction. *Bulletin on Narcotics,* 1962, 14, 1–7.

7. Maddux, J., and Desmond, D. New light on the maturing out hypothesis in opioid dependence. *Bulletin on Narcotics,* 1980, 32, 15–25.

8. Capel, W., and Peppers, L. The aging addict: A longitudinal study of known abusers. *Addictive Diseases,* 1978, 3, 389–404.

9. Capel, W., Goldsmith, B., Waddell, K., and Stewart, G. The aging narcotic addict: An increasing problem for the next decades. *Journal of Gerontology,* 1972, 27, 102–106.

10. Fracchia, J., Shepard, C., Canale, D., Ruest, E., Cambria, E., and Merlin, S. Combination drug therapy for the psychogeriatric patient: Comparison of dosage levels of the same psychotropic drugs, used singly and in combination. *Journal of the American Geriatrics Society,* 1975, 23, 508–511.

11. Castleden, C., Houseton, A., and George, C. Are hypnotics helpful or harmful to elderly patients? *Journal of Drug Issues,* 1979, 9, 55–61.

12. Covert, A., Rodrigues, T., and Solomon, K. The use of mechanical and chemical constraints in nursing homes. *Journal of the American Geriatrics Society,* 1977, 25, 85–89.

13. Ingman, S., Lawson, I., Pierpaoli, P., and Blake, P. A survey of the prescribing and administration of drugs in a long-term care institution for the elderly. *Journal of the American Geriatrics Society,* 1975, 23, 309–316.

14. Raffoul, P., Cooper, J., and Love D. Drug misuse in older people. *The Gerontologist,* 1981, 21, 146–150.

15. Prentice, R. Patterns of psychoactive drug use among the elderly. In *National Institute on Drug Abuse, the Aging Process and Psychoactive Drug Use.* Washington, DC: U.S. Government Printing Office, 1979.

16. Guttmann, D. *A Survey of Drug-Taking Behavior of the Elderly.* Rockville, MD: National Institute on Drug Abuse, 1977.

17. Petersen, D., and Thomas, C. Acute drug reactions among the elderly. *Journal of Gerontology,* 1975, 30, 552–556.

18. Zimberg, S. Alcohol and the elderly. In D. Petersen, F. Whittington, and B. Payne (Eds.), *Drugs and the Elderly: Social and Pharmacological Issues.* Springfield, Illinois: Charles C. Thomas, Publisher, 1979.

19. Harford, T., and Mills, G. Age-related trends in alcohol consumption. *Journal of Studies on Alcohol,* 1978, 39, 207–210.

Chapter 9

THE AGING: DRUG USE AND MISUSE

Peter P. Lamy

GERIATRIC DRUG THERAPY

The major goal of geriatric drug therapy should be to delay, to the extent possible, a patient's dependency (institutionalization). Chronic disease management, pervasive for older adults, should aim at health maintenance/recovery. Drugs can be used effectively and economically in chronic disease management. Yet, drugs and their effects can be hazardous to the elderly, and a secondary goal of geriatric drug therapy must be to minimize that hazard. Drugs can, and often do, impact adversely on an elder's mental, functional, nutritional, and psychosocial status.

Thus, while drugs have the ability to soften the ravages of multiple diseases and disabilities (1), they also have the ability to decrease a patient's quality of life.

Geriatric drug therapy remains complicated, potentially dangerous, and inadequately understood (2). There is a "medicalization" of longer-term care (3), and care given to older patients is often deficient, superficial, and indifferent (4). Many older patients apparently receive drug treatment unnecessarily (5) for which a lack of coordination of responsibility in the management of chronic drug use is likely responsible (6). The increasing prescribing and consumption of drugs has caused widespread anxiety regarding possible inappropriateness of prescribing and adverse drug reactions (7). The question of drug misuse and possible abuse in the care of the elderly has been raised with increasing frequency. Misuse, more so than abuse, probably occurs, involving both prescription and non-prescription drugs, as well as many other

9-I, 9-II, & 9-III). An understanding of the factors leading to possible misuse and its elimination awaits a deeper understanding of the remarkable demographic changes that have taken place and continue to take place (See Tables 9-IV & 9-V), the contribution by the patient (See Table 9-VI), the provider (See Table 9-VII), the system, and the drugs and their dosage forms themselves. Finally, the emerging chronic care system may well play a contributary role in drug misuse.

TABLE 9-I
DRUG MISUSE AND THE ELDERLY

1. Misuse/abuse of legal drugs

   a. Active (overprescribing: unjustified, inappropriate).

   b. Passive (No re-evaluation, of need).

   c. Incorrect chronic use of drugs.

2. Non-use of alternate treatment methodologies (heat, fluids, etc.).

THE DEMOGRAPHICS

The World Health Organization has defined health as a "state of complete physical, mental, and social well-being, and not merely the absence of disease" and has subsequently been criticized for an unnecessarily broad definition. Yet, it seems that this definition is particularly apt for the elderly (8), who are often afflicted with a disease (congestive heart failure, for example) but should be more rationally approached in terms of their "illness." This approach would include a consideration not only of the specific disease but the patient's illness and health behavior and the impact of the

TABLE 9-II
UNJUSTIFIED OR INAPPROPRIATE DRUG USE (OVERMEDICATION) IN THE ELDERLY

Unjustified drug use	a.	There is no proper indication.
	b.	Drug is ineffective for condition being treated.
Inappropriate drug use	a.	A more effective or less hazardous drug is available.
	b.	Drug is used in excessive amount or for excessive duration.
	c.	A less costly drug is available.

TABLE 9-III
THE CHRONIC USE OF DRUGS

The chronic use of a drug is justified only if:

1. Overall morbidity/mortality of disease process is decreased by the drug.

2. There is no substantial toxicity.

3. The beneficial effects of drug therapy are not outweighed by toxic effects.

TABLE 9-IV
THE CHANGING DEMOGRAPHICS

1. Nearly three of every four persons who reach 65 can also expect to turn 75. In 1940, that ratio was only three of five.

2. Life expectancy of the newborn has reached 73.6 years, three years higher than in 1970 and 19.5 years higher than in 1920.

3. The infant mortality rate has fallen to barely 12 deaths per 1,000 births, compared with 20 per 1,000 in 1970.

4. The death rate from heart disease, the leading cause of death, dropped 18 percent in the 1970s. The toll from cancer, the second leading cause of death, has been rising slowly for people over 50, but has been decreasing for those under 50. The death rate from stroke, the third leading cause of death, declined 32 percent in the last decade (it is likely to decrease further wtih the introduction of the beta-blockers).

disease on the patient and, presumably, on the patient's family.

It is generally younger people who assess the health status of the elderly and measure it against their perception. Consequently, the elderly are often looked upon as sick, sickly, and poor. Yet, most older persons living in the community are quite healthy (3), even though more than 80 percent may suffer from one or more diseases. It is the very old who are most at risk to multiple pathology. A brief look at recently published population statistics

TABLE 9-V
THREE STAGES OF LIFE AFTER 65

Stage	Age Range (years)	Characteristics/ Needs
I	65 - 74	Little age change. Normal activities continue, unless there is specific and debilitating illness or disability.
II	75 - 84	Most persons continue with normal activities but many begin to show effects of primary, secondary, and sociogenic aging even without overt disease.
III	85+	Few can maintain full and normal activities of daily living without assistance.

shows that while there is an increase in the elderly population and greater increases are projected, that segment of our population which is 85 years and older has grown, since 1970, by a spectacular 40 percent and is projected to grow even faster, perhaps by 85 or 100 percent over the next 20 years (9–12). In short, the population most at risk to multiple pathology is increasing most rapidly and is, therefore, also most at risk to polymedicine and its possible adverse effects.

DRUG USE AND THE ELDERLY: POLYMEDICINE

In 1967, the average number of prescriptions filled for aged recipients of supplementary medical insurance (SMI) was 13.4. By 1977, that number had increased to 17.9, an increase of almost 34 percent. Not only did the number of prescriptions per SMI recipient increase but so did the size of each prescription. The use of maintenance drugs for the management of chronic diseases such

TABLE 9-VI
POSSIBLE CAUSES OF MISUSE OF DRUGS BY PATIENT

1. Patient takes too much: Overuse.

2. Patient does not take enough: Underuse or omission.

3. Incorrect self-medication.

4. Use of duplicate drugs, possibly because of multiple physician use.

5. Patient does not (cannot) give good history, gives only chief complaint.

TABLE 9-VII
POSSIBLE CAUSES OF MISUSE OF DRUGS ATTRIBUTABLE TO PROVIDER

1. Inaccuracies in diagnosis.

2. Inaccuracies in drug treatment.

3. Failure to consider drug interactions

   a. drug-drug

   b. drug-disease

   c. drug-laboratory test value

   d. drug-nutrition

4. Failure to consider alternate patient management procedures.

5. Failure to provide clear instructions, and to assure that patient understands them and intends to cooperate.

as arthritis and cardiovascular conditions was an important determinator of that increase (13).

Many surveys have been published addressing the use of drugs, both prescription and nonprescription, by the elderly (14–20). In general, all surveys agree that the elderly are prescribed more drugs than are younger people, considerably more. Nonprescription drug use also increases with age, and women receive more drugs than do men (21–23), a particularly disturbing note, since it is the white women over 50 years of age who is most susceptible to adverse drug reactions (24). When one considers that among the very old, women outnumber men by a ratio of 2:1 in the community and 3:1 in skilled nursing facilities, it is easy to see that this particular aged population is doubly jeopardized by polymedicine. To compound this problem, it should be noted that elderly women are far more likely than elderly males to live alone, and those living alone are likely to make more medication errors than those living with others. Some surveys report that females reported drug use 2½ times more frequently than males. The antihypertensives, vitamins, analgesics, cardiac drugs, cardiovascular dilators, diuretics, laxatives and tranquilizers, in that order, were found to be used most frequently in one survey. Another study found that the analgesics, cardiovascular medications, laxatives, vitamins, antacids, antianxiety agents and diuretics were most often used. In one study, 14 percent of those surveyed reported use of between seven and 15 different drugs (25, 26). Apparently, polymedicine, while traditionally roundly condemned, appears to be widely practiced including the widespread use of nonprescription drugs which, too often still, are viewed as innocuous by both prescriber and user. Polymedicine may well often be necessary, but it also may well be hazardous to the patient. One of the most pervasive problems in geriatric medicine, in fact, is the difficulty in separating disease effects, age-related effects and drug effects, which often present in the same or similar manner. It is also noted that elderly, much more often than younger people, receive drugs for somatic conditions but do not receive prescriptions for sedatives, stimulants and antianxiety agents as often as do younger people. On the other hand, many of the drugs the elderly receive have a very narrow therapeutic indices (See Table 9-VIII) which makes avoidance of drug misuse very important.

TABLE 9-VIII
DRUGS WITH A NARROW THERAPEUTIC INDEX

Anticoagulants

Anticonvulsants

Antidepressants

Antihypertensives

Digitalis glycosides

Hypoglycemic agents (oral)

ADVERSE DRUG REACTIONS

It is feasible to eliminate polymedicine by applying rational pharmacotherapy, as recently demonstrated with anticonvulsants, where a reduction in dose and number of anticonvulsants actually increased the well-being of patients (27), while, in other patients, use of multiple anticonvulsants exacerbated seizures. No doubt, similar considerations would apply to the use of psychotherapeutic drugs, particularly the use of more than one antipsychotic drug simultaneously. Phenothiazines cause extrapyramidal side effects relatively often in elderly patients—effects which can be particularly severe with thiothixene and haloperidol (28); yet, use of these drugs is frequent. It is the unexpected and sometimes bizarre effect of drugs which cause the greatest concern, since they will often be overlooked. Among them should be counted the atypical presentation of digoxin toxicity in the elderly and the taste impairment reported by 30 percent of elderly, particularly women, who take drugs. (Incidentally, hypogeusia may also be caused by diabetes mellitus, infections, zinc deficiency, and chronic renal failure.) The antibiotics and their possible adverse effects may also serve as an example. Severe adverse reactions to antibiotics may include anaphylaxism, aplastic anemia and potential nephrotoxicity (high peak concentration with gentamicin), ototoxicity (high trough concentrations with gentamicin), hepato-toxicity, and psychotoxocity. Psychotoxic reactions in the elderly have been reported with penicillin and chloramphenicol, and hepatotoxicity with many, including carbenicillin, isoniazid and rifampin, among others. Of deep concern should be the fact that many drugs can cause confusion and depression in the elderly. A whole host of drugs, ranging from amantadine to trihexyphenidyl, can be responsible for an altered mental status in the elderly, including visual hallucinations, delusions, aggressive behavior, excitement, suicidal thoughts and others. Drug-induced depression can and is easily confused with "senility." Often, it is the cumulation of common side effects that is responsible for adverse reactions. Among those might be mentioned the possible atropine-like psychosis which can occur when several drugs with anticholinergic action or side effects are given simultaneously. The clinician caring for elderly must always exhibit a high Index of Suspicion. For example, it was just recently reported that elderly persons on cimetidine who consume a diet too high in cellulose (fiber is very popular among the elderly) may form phytobezoars (29). Most often, adverse drug reactions in the elderly, though, are due entirely to factors that could be eliminated: excessive dose and excessive duration of treatment. Therefore, the dictum long ago advanced still holds: "Whenever a sick person is seen, irrespective of the nature of the illness, the doctor should ask himself, 'Could this be drug related?' " (30). To eliminate the "illness of medical progress," i.e., the disease that would not have occurred had sound therapeutic measures been employed, it is necessary for the prescriber to be familiar with the therapeutic and toxic effects of any therapeutic agent to be prescribed for the elderly, a process which involves knowledge of a multiplicity of objective and subjective variables. This, it is suggested, is still a very formidable task, particularly in view of the fact that at present only 50 of the 126 medical schools in the U.S. offer geriatric courses, including geriatric pharmacology, and only 2 percent of those require that students enroll in some geriatric studies.

DRUG FACTORS

The elderly differ from younger adults in the quantity of drug delivered to the target organ and, possible, in the sensitivity of that organ to the drug (31). Yet, despite the knowledge that the pharmacology and pharmacokinetics of drugs in the elderly are often altered and the drug-handling capability of the elderly is altered (32–34), many drugs are still being prescribed for the elderly in doses similar to those utilized for younger people, which often results in overdosages and toxic effects in the elderly. It has been estimated that about 20 percent of older patients being hospitalized display symptoms attributable to the effects of pre-scription drugs (35, 36). In addition, the incidence of drug inter-actions, and thus adverse effects, increase with the number of drugs taken (37). The most important physiological changes with age which may be responsible for altered drug action are probably a change in the ratio between lean body weight and fatty tissue, with fatty tissue increasing, more so in females than in males. This would change the volume of distribution of drugs. More importantly, even in apparently healthy older adults, functional kidney changes are the rule rather than the exception. The cumu-lative and additive effects of primary aging (physiological changes with age) and secondary aging (pathophysiological changes with age) often create an impaired kidney function. Impaired renal function then can lead to impaired drug clearance (See Table 9-IX) and increased prevalence and severity of drug toxicities. It is not at all clear that impairment of renal function and the conse-quent slowing of that elimination of many drugs is generally appreciated. Apparently, though, it is even less appreciated that there may be large interpatient and intrapatient variations in drug clearing capacity as a result of equally large variations in the severity of renal disease (38). Suggestions on how to use drugs in renally impaired patients have been published (39, 41).

Quite often overlooked is the fact that it is not only the drug entity that can be the cause of problems in the elderly but also, importantly, the dosage form. Capsules, more so than tablets, can be delayed in the esophagus for up to five minutes and more (42), possibly causing irritation, ulceration, stricture, or even more

TABLE 9-IX
DRUGS WITH DECREASED CLEARANCE IN THE ELDERLY

Acetaminophen	Levopromazine
Amobarbital	Lithium
Ampicillin	Lorazepam
Aspirin	Methotrexate
Carbenoxolone	Netilmicin
Cefazoline	Nortriptyline
Cefradin	Phenylbutazone
Chlordiazepoxide	Propranolol
Chlormethiazole	Protriptyline
Chlorthalidone	Quinidine
Cimetidine	Sulfamethizole
Desmethyldiazepam	Sulfisomidine
Diazepam	Theophylline
Digoxin	Tobramycin
Doxycycline	Tolbutamide
Gentamicin	Warfarin

Adapted from: Ritschel, W.A.: Disposition of Drugs in geriatric patients. Pharmacy International 1: 226-229, 1980.

serious consequences. Patients at risk are those with hiatus hernia, stricture, and enlarged left atrium from mitral valve disease, even though quite often the delay occurs with no abnormal esophageal characteristics. Ophthalmic preparations may cause problems, simply because an elderly with arthritis, tremor and/or reduced visual acuity may not be able to administer them correctly. Fluids often cause problems, particularly if not taken in sufficient quantity. Aspirin may then cause more and more severe gastritis, and bulk laxatives, instead of swelling and producing bulk, may form hard masses which, on occasion, have to be removed surgically in older adults. Lack of sufficient fluid intake with dosage forms, particularly capsules, may cause erratic dissolution and, therefore, drug disposition. Chewable tablets may be swallowed without being chewed, and their formulation will not permit them to be dissolved in the stomach. They have been surgically removed from older patients. The incorrect choice of dosage form may also be responsible for misuse of drugs. Some antibiotics will deliver the necessary blood levels only when given in parenteral dosage form but may be given instead in the oral dosage form, which would be entirely insufficient. Many antibiotics also contain relatively high amounts of sodium, which at times may be sufficient to destabilize elderly CHF patients. Misuse may also occur when vague instructions such as "take on an empty stomach" are given, which many elderly interpret as the time when they sit down to eat.

One more factor, related to drugs and dosage forms, needs to be stressed. Particularly in geriatric medicine, one must be concerned not only with the effectiveness but also with the safety of drugs. The therapeutic ratio based on the differences between therapeutic and toxic levels is, clinically, very critical. While it is often economically advantageous to use generic drugs for the elderly, at other times it is not. Many drugs are simply not bioequivalent. Bioequivalence simply means that, on drug interchange, there will be a predictable and precise therapeutic outcome. When drugs are bio*in*equivalent, this may not be true, and bioinequivalence can possibly lead to overdoses and underdoses. It may then not be surprising that aberrations in clinical symptoms may be ascribed to the widely scattered response to drugs often seen in geriatric patients and not to differences in drug products (43). Among drugs for which bioinequivalence has been demonstrated are digoxin, tolbutamide, phenytoin, griseofulvin, chloramphenicol, prednisone, furosemide, chlorpromazine and thioridazine.

Diagnostic Difficulties

The elderly patient is often a "hoarder of illness," being unwilling to give information and incorrectly ascribing problems to old age. Older adults may also present in the oft-described but still not well-recognized atypical fashion. Many laboratory test values change with age, such as the tests for antinuclear antibodies, cholesterol, erythrocyte sedimentation rate, glucose tolerance, pernicious anemia, rheumatoid factor, and serum globulin.

Fever, which may be absent in the elderly in certain infectious diseases, pain, which with increasing age presents increasingly as referred pain and may be absent when it is expected, and thirst are no longer good indicators of disease in older age. Yet, such apparently age-related complaints as confusion, falls and fatigue could well be important indicators of disease. Fatigue, "expected" in old age, may be due to anxiety or depression, anemia, thyroid disease, infections or heart disease. Many beta blockers cause fatigue in the elderly. Even constipation, a frequent complaint among the elderly, may have several origins and they should be treated, rather than the resulting constipation. Among causative problems may be cancer, diverticulosis, fissures, hemorrhoids, hypokalemia, hypothyroidism, inadequate bulk or fluid intake, depression, diminished physical activity and emotional stress. Additionally, such drugs as the anticholinergics, iron salts and others may cause constipation. Most often missed in the elderly are urinary incontinence and depression, which can also be caused by drugs such as the barbiturates, some beta-adrenergic blockers, clonidine, digitalis, guanethidine, indomethacin, methyldopa, phenothiazines, procainamide and reserpine.

PATIENT FACTORS

As previously mentioned, the effects of primary, secondary and sociogenic aging combine to reduce the elderly's capability to handle drugs as efficiently and effectively as can younger adults. There will be a wider scatter in response to drugs and an increased divergence from the norm.

The reduced immunological function of elderly persons may

illustrate this. The elderly's response to infections may be compromised due to pre-existing immunosuppressive diseases or therapy. Furthermore, older adults may not respond as quickly as younger persons to antimicrobial therapy due to their reduced immunoglobulin levels. Even if an organism is reactive to the selected antibiotic, the response may not be as anticipated if the patient's normal defenses do not function well. It is important to remember that the elderly patient may not manifest the typical signs of an infectious process (i.e., fever and leucocytosis). On the other hand, changing mental status without signs or symptoms may reflect an acute infection such as bacterial endocarditis.

Many of the commonly used antibiotics are bacteriostatic rather than bactericidal. The use of bacteriostatic antimicrobial agents requires the host defenses to eliminate the infectious organism and, since the normal immunological functions decline with age, such therapy may not be adequate. Therefore, in evaluating appropriateness of therapy, it is important to remember that the aminoglycosides, cephalosporins, penicillins, and polymyxins are bactericidal agents. The tetracyclines, chloramphenicol, and low concentrations of clindamycin and erythromycin are bacteriostatic.

The fact that drug sensitivity and patient variability increases with age can also be illustrated using the gastrointestinal system as another example. Overlooking the possible consequences in the decline of effective functioning of that system also may lead to drug misuse. With aging, the esophageal sphincter will function less effectively and administration of xanthines, such as theophylline, can then be the cause of esophagitis. In the presence of hypochlorhydria or anacidity, not uncommon among the elderly, administration of antibiotics may cause candidiasis. Gastritis is more common among elderly than young persons, and anticoagulants can cause a greater incidence of gastric bleeding in the elderly, therefore. In the small intestine, there will be decreased fat absorption and prolonged administration of isoniazid may induce osteomalacia. IgA deficiency in the duodenum, which can occur with increasing age, could induce giardiasis when phenytoin is administered (44). Thus, it is clear that aging itself and the higher incidence of disease processes in aging patients tends to change the function of many organs and, thus, the action of many

drugs (45). This can be exacerbated by the widely occurring protein-
calorie malnutrition among elderly, even those who can feed
themselves (46–48), which not only exposes the elderly to greater
risk to infection but also to still further changed drug action.
More problems are being recognized. Dietary disaccharides have
to be hydrolyzed into their component monosaccharides before
absorption, a task accomplished with the help of specific enzymes,
the disaccharidases, such as lactase. In the presence of lactase
deficiency, alactasia (very rare) or hypolactasia (common among
elderly and seemingly on the increase) occur. Protein-calorie malnutrition may be responsible for hypolactasia, as may giardiasis
and other diseases not uncommon among elderly.

Symptoms of hypolactasia include cramp-like abdominal pains,
flatulence, abdominal distension and diarrhea. Stools are generally watery. A new strip test, developed in Finland, utilizes urine
samples and a specially prepared test paper to detect hypolactasia.

THE HEALTH CARE SYSTEM

The health care system is not responsive to the elderly. It is an
acute care system, dedicated to "success" in terms of patient recovery,
most often not concerned with such facts as the impact of a person's
disease on that person's family, but is dedicated to the use of
high-cost, high technology. These factors are not applicable to
chronic disease management where success should be viewed as
successful care, in terms of delaying dependency and avoiding a
diminishing of a patient's quality of life.

Elderly patients present with more problems and take longer to
give and receive information, yet the length of encounters between
physicians and patients declines with age. Preventable infectious
disease is common in skilled nursing facilities, leading to unnecessary use of antibiotics (49). Those trained in acute care often do
not recognize that chronic care is constantly changing care. For
example, it is relatively easy to forget that in patients with sub-
clinical malnutrition, chronic drug use can cause a depletion of
vitamins. This can lead to symptomatology often ascribed to "old
age" rather than the vitamin deficiency that could and should be
treated. Symptoms such as weakness, breathlessness, difficulty in

walking, bone pain, auditory dysfunction, confusion, muscular weakness and others can result from chronic administration of drugs such as the antituberculars, phenytoin, some cardiovascular drugs and others.

Those trained in acute care also are likely to pursue therapeutic goals not consistent with the overriding goal in geriatric medicine. Perhaps it would be better, in some circumstances, not to raise the dose of an antihypertensive to achieve the desired blood pressure goal, particularly when this might cause increased drug toxicities, as might happen with increased doses of diuretics, or when it may induce other problems.

Elderly residents of skilled nursing facilities often suffer from infections, yet laboratory facilities are often not available. The laboratory is needed both to identify the pathogens responsible for an infectious disease and for selecting an appropriate antibiotic for treatment and monitor its use.

Identification of a disease state or infecting organism is often more difficult in the elderly. For example, skin tests in the elderly are often falsely negative. In general, laboratory reports correlate with but cannot predict clinical outcome. In short, serological test results must be interpreted discriminatingly, in full knowledge of the clinical circumstance, if false conclusions are not to be drawn. For example, even if all steps are pursued correctly, the sensitive organism may not be eradicated because:

1. The antibiotic is not absorbed properly and adequate blood levels are not achieved (tetracyclines and milk).
2. The antibiotic may not diffuse sufficiently into the site of infection (in osteomyelitis or lung abscess).
3. The original organism may be eradicated but may have been replaced by a new one, without a change in clinical signs (urinary tract infections).

It is important to re-emphasize two of these points. Often, it is not enough to identify the antibiotic to which a particular pathogen is sensitive. It may be necessary (in prostatitis, for example) to consider the penetrability of the antibiotic. It is also necessary to consider whether an antibiotic can be carried to the site of infection. Poor circulation in and to infected sites may necessitate a longer than usual duration of treatment, and any patient-care technique aimed at improving perfusion should be used. In other instances (pressure sores, for example), diffusion may be so impaired that systemic administration of an antibiotic could be of no value.

It is also most important to realize that proper selection of the antibiotic entity, itself, will not necessarily lead to the desired clinical outcome. Selection of an oral carbencillin, for example, to treat a surgical wound infection would be useless and even dangerous to the patient, even though the infecting organism may be sensitive to carbenicillin. What would be needed is the selection of the parenteral, and not the oral dosage form, to achieve the necessary blood levels.

Many primary providers do not inquire about the many substances with therapeutic, pharmacological or even toxic activity that an elderly person is likely to purchase in outlets such as health food stores. Vitamins A and E rank high on the list, and their toxic effects, if taken in large doses, have been well documented. Particularly worrisome is the fact that some surveys have indicated that as many as 25 percent of the elderly may purchase potassium supplements, which could lead to serious consequences when a physician then prescribes a potassium supplement or when a patient is given a potassium-sparing diuretic like spironolactone.

There is frequent non-communication between specialist and primary provider, leading to such problems as encountered with timolol. Providers, in general, are little concerned about the cost of drugs, yet some of the newer dosage forms can cost as much as $1 per tablet, and older patients, particularly those living in cities in socioeconomically disadvantaged areas, may well not be able to purchase these drugs, being forced to choose among energy, food, and drugs. Patients tend to use multiple pharmacies and different physicians, which would, if not established, promote drug misuse and abuse.

SUMMARY

Chronic diseases require disease management rather than cure, with an understanding of the appropriate balance between acute and long-term care, particularly long-term care of older adults living in the community. Drugs, although cost-efficient in the management of chronic diseases, must be used appropriately if they are not to be hazardous to the elderly patient. Yet, geriatric drug therapy remains complicated, potentially dangerous and inadequately understood. There is a "medicalization" of long-term care, and care given to older patients is often deficient, superficial and indifferent. Polymedicine, while roundly condemned, is widely practiced and the increasing prescribing of drugs for older adults causes widespread anxiety. To eliminate the hazard of drugs to the elderly, one must understand the system, various patient and health-care-provider characteristics, and the characteristics of drugs and dosage forms used for the elderly.

REFERENCES

1. Lamy, P. P. Drugs and the elderly: a new look. *Family & Community Health,* 1982, 5(2), 34–44.
2. Lamy, P. P. *Prescribing for the Elderly.* Littleton, MA: PSG Pub Co, 1980.
3. Eisdorfer, C. Care of the aged: the barrier of tradition. *Ann Intern Med,* 1981, 95, 256–260.
4. Rabin, D. L. Physician care in nursing homes. *Ann Intern Med,* 1981, 94, 126–128.
5. Kane, R., Solomon, D., and Beck, J. et al. The future need for geriatric manpower in the United States. *N Engl J Med,* 1980, 302, 1327–1332.
6. Kiernan, P. J., and Isaacs, J. B. Use of drugs by the elderly. *J Roy Soc Med,* 1981, 74, 196–198.
7. Williamson, J., and Chopin, J. M. Adverse reactions to prescribed drugs in the elderly: A multicentre investigation. *Age Ageing,* 1980, 9, 73–80.
8. Ouslander, J. G., and Beck, J. C. Defining the health problems of the elderly. *Ann Rev Public Health,* 1982, 2, 55–83.
9. Rosenwaike, I., Yaffe, N., and Sagi, P. C. The recent decline in mortality of the extreme aged: An analysis of statistical data. *Am. J. Public Health,* 1980, 70, 1074–1080.
10. Brotman, H. B. The aging society: A demographic view. *Aging,* 1981, 315–316.
11. Soldo, B. J. America's elderly in the 1980s. *Population Bulletin,* 1980, 35(4), 3–47.
12. Reidenberg, M. M. Drugs in the elderly. *Bull NY Acad Med,* 1980, 56, 703–714.
13. Medicare: Use of Prescription Drugs by Aged Persons Enrolled for Supplementary Medical Insurance 1967–77. HCFA Pub No 03080, Baltimore, MD, Health Care Financing Administration, 1981.
14. Vener, A. M., Krupka, L. R., and Climo, J. J. Drug usage and health characteristics in noninstitutionalized retired persons. *J Am Geriatr Soc,* 1979, 27, 83–90.

15. Chambers, C. D. *An assessment of drug use in the general population.* New York: NY State Narcotic Addiction Control Commission, 1971.

16. Mellinger, G. D., Balter, M. B., and Manheimer, K. I. Patterns of psychotherapeutic drug use among adults in San Francisco. *Arch Gen Psychiatry,* 1971, 25, 385–394.

17. Parry, H. J., Balter, M. B., and Mellinger, G. D. et al. National patterns of psychotherapeutic drug use. *Arch Gen Psychiatry,* 1973, 28, 769–783.

18. U.S. Public Health Service: Working with Older People: A Guide to Practice. Vol. II: Biological, Psychological, and Sociological Aspects of Aging. Washington, D.C.: US Government Printing Office, 1970.

19. Warheit, G. J., Arey, S. A., and Swanson, E. Patterns of drug use: An epidemiologic overview. *J Drug Issues,* 1976, 6, 223–237.

20. Zawadski, R. T., Glazer, G. B., and Lauerie, E. Psychotropic drug use among institutionalized and non-institutionalized Medicaid aged in California. *J Gerontol,* 1978, 33, 835–844.

21. May, F. E., Stewart, R. B., and Hale, W. E., et al. Prescribed and nonprescribed drug use in an ambulatory elderly population. *So Med J,* 1982, 75, 522–528.

22. Smith, C. R. Use of drugs in the aged. *Johns Hopkins Med J,* 1979, 14, 61–64.

23. Guttman, D. Patterns of legal drug use by older Americans. *Addictive Diseases,* 1978, 3, 337–356.

24. Lamy, P. P. Drug prescribing for the elderly. *Bull NY Acad Med,* 1981, 57, 718–730.

25. Hale, W. E., Marks, R. G., and Stewart, R. B. Drug use in a geriatric population. *J Am Geriatr Soc,* 1979, 27, 374–377.

26. Chien, C., and Townsend, E. J. Substance use and abuse among the community elderly: the medical aspect. *Additive Diseases,* 1978, 3, 357–372.

27. Fischbacher, E. Effects of reduction of anticonvulsants on wellbeing. *Br Med J,* 1982, 285, 423–424.

28. Caranasos, G. J. Drugs in the elderly. *Hospital Formulary,* 1982, 17(1), 123–130.

29. Nichols, T. W., Jr. Phytobezoar formation: a new complication of cimetidine therapy. *Ann Intern Med,* 1981, 94, 70.

30. Cluff, L. Diagnosing adverse drug reactions in outpatients. *Hospital Physician,* 1971, 5, 56.

31. World Health Organization: Health care in the elderly: Report of the technical group on use of medicaments by the elderly. *Drugs,* 1981, 22, 279–294.

32. Lamy, P. P. Comparative pharmacokinetic changes and drug therapy in an older population. *J Am Geriatr Soc,* 1982, 30, SH–S19.

33. Vestal, R. F. Pharmacology and aging. *J Am Geriatr Soc,* 1982, 30, 191–200.

34. Greenblatt, D. J., Sellers, E. M., and Shader, R. I. Drug disposition in old age. *N Engl J Med,* 1982, 306, 1081–1088.

35. Wynne, R. D., and Heller, F. Drug overuse among the elderly. *Perspectives on Aging,* 1973, 2, 15–18.

36. Pascarelli, E. F. Drug dependence: An age-old problem compounded by old age. *Geriatrics,* 1974, 29, 109–115.

37. Adverse interactions of drugs. *Med Letter,* 1981, 23, 17–28.
38. Vesell, E. S. The influence of host factors on drug response: VII. renal diseases. *Rational Drug Therapy,* 1981, 15(11), 1–9.
39. Bennett, W. M., Muther, R. S., and Parker, R. A. et al. Drug therapy in renal failure: Dosing guidelines for adults. Part I. *Ann Intern Med,* 1980, 93, 62–71.
40. Bennett, W. M., Muther, R. S., and Parker, R. A. et al. Drug therapy in renal failure: Dosing guidelines for adults. Part II. *Ann Intern Med,* 1980, 93, 286–293.
41. Rowe, J. W., Andres, R., and Tobin, J. D. et al. The effect of age on creatinine clearance in man: A cross-sectional and longitudinal study. *J Gerontol,* 1976, 31, 155–159.
42. Herxheimer, A. (ed.). Tablets and capsules that stick in the oesophagus. *Drug and Therapeutic Bulletin,* 1981, 19(9), 33.
43. Cabana, B. E. The need for establishment of bioavailability and bioequivalency of psychotropic drugs. Paper presented to the Am Coll Neuropsychopharmacology, San Juan, Puerto Rico, Dec. 16, 1980.
44. Johnson, P. C. Gastrointestinal consequences of treatment with drugs in elderly patients. *J Am Geriatr Soc,* 1982, 30, S52–S57.
45. Vesell, E. S. Why are toxic reactions to drugs undetected initially? *N Engl J Med,* 1980, 18, 1027–1029.
46. Bistrian, B. R., Blackburn, G. L., and Hollowell, E. et al. Protein status of general surgical patients. *J Am Med Assoc,* 1974, 230, 858–860.
47. Bistrian, B. R., Blackburn, G. L., and Vitale, J. J. et al. Prevalence of malnutrition in general medical patients. *J Am Med Assoc,* 1976, 235, 1567–1570.
48. Tomaiolo, P., Enman, S., and Kraus, V. Preventing and treating malnutrition in the elderly. *Journal Parenteral Enteral Nutrition,* 1981, 5(1), 46–49.
49. Garibaldi, R. A., Brodine, S., and Matsyumiya, S. Infections among patients in nursing homes: Policies, prevalence and problems. *N Engl J Med,* 1981, 305, 731–735.

Chapter 10

PSYCHOPHARMACOLOGY OF AGING: USE, MISUSE, AND ABUSE OF PSYCHOTROPIC DRUGS

Walter W. Baker

Drug Usage by Elderly

By 1980, aged Americans over 65 years of age (elderly) comprised about 11 percent of the population, some 23 million Americans. This number is expected to exceed 31 million by the turn of the century, representing 13–15 percent of the population. It has been estimated that approximately one-fourth of all drugs prescribed in this country are consumed by the elderly, with a disproportionately large expenditure for psychotropic drugs (1–3). Clearly, there is an impression that older people use drug resources to a greater extent than do other adults. Furthermore, it has been estimated that half of the costs of medications went for the treatment of chronic illnesses. Yet, there was a large amount of medication used for acutely ill elderly patients, who occupied almost one-third of the hospital beds.

However, despite these statistics on the wide use of medications in the aged, the premise is generally agreed upon that aging per se is not a disease and therefore should not be treated arbitrarily with drugs (4). Equally significant is the considerations that the incidence of drug-related side effects and adverse reactions increase proportionately with age and thus supports the proposition that the elderly are prone to have more frequent and more serious drug mishaps (5).

In one study, almost one-third of the elderly patients hospitalized for medical or surgical illnesses in a general hospital received at least one psychotropic drug (6). It may be relevant that since elderly patients are reported to have a higher incidence of psychiatric disorders (7), an inordinately large percentage of psychotropic drugs are prescribed for the elderly (8). It is interesting to note that many older people have come to believe that their daily performance depends on the use of psychotropic agents (9). Over-the-counter preparations may account for as much as 40 percent of all drugs used by the elderly; more than half of these over-the-counter drugs are analgesics (8, 10).

Altered Physiology/Pharmacology

Some of the physiological changes associated with aging and their related effects on the various aspects of the pharmacokinetics of psychotropic drugs are summarized in Table 10-I (11, 12). Although the changes in GI physiology are significant in the aged, their effects on absorption of psychotropic drugs still remain unsettled and require additional study. Also, it has been argued that the variations in absorptions are negligible, especially since most of the psychotropic drugs are passively absorbed (13, 14).

The distribution of psychotropic drugs frequently is altered with aging since lean body mass and total body water both decrease; whereas, the relative amount of total body fat increases (13). This phase disparity results in a higher serum concentration of water-soluble drugs and a lower one for lipid-soluble drugs. Moreover, serum albumin tends to be generally reduced in the aged. For drugs with a high degree of protein binding, one might anticipate a proportionately higher percentage of the drug in the circulation to be in the unbound form which pharmacologically represents the active component (14).

During aging, hepatic blood flow is reduced and liver mass is decreased. These changes are also accompanied by an age-related impairment of enzyme-induced hepatic microsomes (15). The duration of action of most psychotropic drugs, with the exception of lithium, is dependent primarily on the rate at which they are metabolized by liver microsomal enzymes. Reduced hepatic metabolism, thus, may not only significantly increase drug plasma blood levels but also contribute to cumulative toxicity, especially when the drugs are taken over an extended period of time.

TABLE 10-I

RELATIONSHIP OF ALTERED PHYSIOLOGY TO DRUG PHARMACOKINETICS IN ELDERLY

Pharmaco-kinetic Effects	Altered Physiology	Clinical Significance
Absorption	Elevated gastric pH Reduced GI blood flow Reduced number of absorbing cells Reduced GI motility	Not sufficiently documented; incon- clusive

Distri-bution	Body composition
	Reduced total body water
	Reduced lean body mass/
	kg body weight
	Increased body fat
		Higher concentration of
		unbound drugs distri-
		buted in body fluids
		  Longer duration of action
		  of fat soluble drugs

	Protein binding Reduced serum albumin	Higher free fraction of highly protein-bound drugs
Elimin-ation	Hepatic metabolism Reduced enzyme activity Reduced hepatic mass Reduced hepatic blood flow	Slower biotransformation of some drugs
	Renal excretion Reduced glomerular filtration rate Reduced renal plasma flow Altered tubular function (40-50% "Normal)	Slower excretion of some drugs

Perhaps, the best documented change in the elderly is the diminution of kidney functions with reduced renal blood flow, glomerular filtration (40%–50% in the aged), and tubular excretory capacity. If renal excretion is delayed and/or liver metabolism is impaired, the elimination half-life will be markedly prolonged. Examples of psychotropic drugs with more prolonged half-lives in the elderly include tricyclic antidepressants, lithium and the long-acting benzodiazepines, e.g., diazepam (16).

Apart from altered pharmacokinetics, other significant changes are apparent in the aged. For example, cardiac output declines in a linear manner with age to about one-half at 80 years of age (17). Paralleling this, peripheral resistance and circulation time are increased with notable diminished cardiac reserve along with critical shifts in regional blood flow which can alter the distribution of the psychotropic drugs to target sites in the brain (18). Also with advancing age, homeostatic and compensatory mechanisms are less effective (19). As a result, overall responses to psychotropic drugs become more exaggerated (sedation) and side effects uncompensated (orthostatic hypotension). Changes in the end organs and target receptors develop so as to alter their responsiveness to psychotropic drugs, e.g., increased hypersensitivity of dopamine receptors during treatment with neuroleptics, resulting in tardive dyskinesias (20).

Adverse Drug Effects

Prescribing for the elderly is complex and, more often than not, poses a number of problems. For example, the combination of old age, one or more chronic illnesses, along with the consumption of several medications, predispose the aged to a high potential for adverse side effects and drug toxicity (21). Thus, it would appear that the incidence of drug-induced side effects and adverse reactions would rise steadily and proportionately with advancing age and with the number of drugs prescribed.

It has been shown by and large that the elderly are more likely to react adversely to medications, even when administered at average adult doses (22, 23), and they experience substantially more side effects than do younger populations (24). According to the survey conducted at Johns Hopkins, patients over 70 years of age developed twice as many adverse reactions as did patients under 50 years of age (25).

Older patients were particularly vulnerable to cardiovascular and psychoneurological side effects; e.g., orthostatic hypotension, cardiac arrhythmias, extrapyramidal reactions (parkinsonian-like), confusion, disorientation (pseudo-dementia), etc.

Furthermore, when these side effects develop they tend to be more severe than in younger patients (26). Some of these common and severe reactions to psychotropic drugs are listed in Tables 10-II and 10-III.

Guidelines for Prescribing Psychotropic Drugs in Aged

As a rule of thumb, psychotropic drugs should be prescribed at doses 30–50 percent as large as those for younger adults (11, 27, 28). The drug dosage should be titrated on an individual basis, based on the individual's pharmacokinetics and physiological state. Partial improvement often may be the only realistic therapeutic objective in the elderly. Most frequently, the development of adverse side effects become the limiting factor and thus set the upper limit to which the drug dosage can be increased. Also, when feasible, restrict the number of psychoactive drugs, including over-the-counter preparations, that the patient is taking so as to reduce the incidence of adverse drug interactions (29).

Antianxiety Agents/Sedative-Hypnotic Agents

By and large, the benzodiazepines are the most widely prescribed anxiolytic drugs for the elderly. These agents are also frequently the most overprescribed and misprescribed of the psychotropic drugs, producing the common central nervous system side effects listed in Tables 10-II and 10-III. Prolonged and excessive use of the benzodiazepines and other sedative medications may cause delirium, aggravate dementia or even worsen a depression.

Some of these have been used where a sleep medication is indicated (flurazepam-Dalmane®, temazepam-Restoril). Barbiturates should be avoided in geriatric patients, because they frequently produce paradoxical excitatory reactions. In addition, the barbiturates suppress rapid eye movement (REM), which may result in rebound excitation (nightmares) if the drug is withdrawn. Chloral hydrate represents a better alternative to the barbiturates as a hypnotic in the elderly, lacking the undesirable side effects associated with the latter (11, 27).

Antidepressants

Tricyclics: It has been estimated that at any given time, at least 10 percent of the elderly are depressed (27, 28). This figure may be

TABLE 10-II

PSYCHOTROPIC DRUG SIDE EFFECTS THAT MAY BE MORE COMMON
AND MORE SEVERE AMONG ELDERLY PATIENTS

Effect	Class of Drugs	Clinical examples
Sedation	Most psychotropic drugs either produce sedation or enhance sedation of other medications	Increased daytime sedation and napping, increased confusion and irratability at night
Confusion	Anticholinergic properties of tricyclic antidepressants and neuroleptics; lithium; secondary to increased sedation	Disorientation, visual hallucinations, agitation, assaultiveness, loss of memory (pseudodementia)
Orthostatic hypotension	Tricyclic antidepressants and neuroleptics	Falling when getting out of bed or chair suddenly
Cardiac toxicity	Primarily tricyclic antidepressants	Increase in heart rate and in frequency of irregular heart beat rhythms, altered EKG patterns
Extrapyramidal symptoms	Neuroleptics (phenothiazines, haloperidol)	Akathisia, (restlessness) parkinsonian-like reactions, tardive dyskinesias with chronic use

as high 50 percent in the presence of physical illness (29). Depression secondary to some other psychiatric or medical disorder or to multiple medications are not usual in the elderly (30). Depression can be misdiagnosed as "dementia" (pseudodementia) or it can be dismissed as a "normal" aspect of aging which does not require therapeutic intervention. Adverse anticholinergic (atropine-like) side effects are likely to be produced by tricyclic antidepressants, especially if the patient is also receiving other drugs possessing atropine-like activity, e.g., neuroleptics, antiparkinsonian compounds. Centrally, this anticholinergic toxic reaction manifests itself as loss of memory, disorientation, confusion, agitation and often has been erroneously designated as "dementia." The anticholinesterase physostigmine is effective in reversing these effects. Peripherally, the aged are more prone to develop constipation (fecal impaction) and urinary retention, often compounded by hypertrophy of the prostate. Orthostatic hypotension and tachycar-

TABLE 10-III

SIDE EFFECTS COMMONLY ASSOCIATED WITH VARIOUS CLASSES
OF PSYCHOTROPIC MEDICATIONS IN THE ELDERLY

Class of drug	Side effects
Antianxiety agents:	
Usually benzodiazepines	Sedation (especially due to those with longer half-lives) (diazepam) Depression Dementia; delirium; confusion
Barbiturates-seldom indicated	Induction of hepatic micro-somal enzymes Habituation Rebound delirium
Sedative hypnotics:	
Usually benzodiazepines	Same as listed above-shorter half-life compounds have fewer of these side-effects (Lorazepam)
Occasionally chloral hydrate	Induction of hepatic microsomal enzymes, which may increase metabolism of other drugs
Barbiturates-seldom indicated	Same as listed above under Antianxiety agents
Antihistamines	May induce delirium
Antidepressant agents:	
Usually tricyclic antidepressants	Sedation; anticholinergic, including cardiovascular toxicity and induction of delirium pseudo-dementia
Monoamine oxidase inhibitors	Hypertensive crises in combination with tyramine or other sympatho-mimetic compounds
Antipsychotic agents:	
Usually phenothiazines or haloperidol	Sedation, extrapyramidal movement disorders, central and peripheral anticholinergic effects, alpha-adrenergic blockade (ortho-static hypotension)
Lithium carbonate	Gastrointestinal, tremors, delirium, coma, thyroid dysfunction, ECG changes, renal dysfunction

*Adapted after Moran and Thompson, 1982

dia may present serious problems in the aged and may remain unrecognized until the elderly patient falls, develops a myocardial infarction or has a cerebrovascular accident. The dealkylated metabolites of amitriptyline and imipramine (nortriptyline and desipramine) have less anticholinergic properties, are less sedating than the parent compounds, and may be preferable in some of the elderly (24).

Monoamine Oxidase Inhibitors

These antidepressants are used sparingly in this country because of the associated dietary restrictions (avoid foods containing tyramine) and adverse interactions with sympathomimetics (hypertensive crisis) and with several other classes of drugs. As a second option in patients who fail to respond to tricyclic antidepressants, the monoamine oxidase inhibitors are proving to be valuable, especially in patients with "atypical" depression who do not present the vegetative symptoms classically associated with a major depression (27).

Antipsychotic Agents

In addition to their primary indication for chronic schizophrenia in the elderly, antipsychotic drugs (neuroleptics) also are frequently helpful in managing symptoms of delirium, dementia, manic-depression and in the treatment of agitated depression. The relatively more potent neuroleptics (haloperidol and fluphenazine) cause the highest incidence of extrapyramidal side effects, particularly parkinson-like symptoms. Of more concern is the progressively increased risk for the more serious, late development of tardive dyskinesias with the aged (31). To minimize the incidence of tardive dyskinesia, antipsychotic drugs should be prescribed most judiciously in the elderly at the lowest effective doses, frequently re-evaluated, and the practice, when feasible, of "drug holidays" introduced. In general, the less potent antipsychotics (chlorpromazine and thioridazine) produce more sedation and greater anticholinergic actions, both centrally and peripherally. Also, the hypotensive episodes they frequently cause often predisposes to falls, myocardial infarction or cerebrovascular accidents.

Lithium carbonate

Prophylactically, lithium carbonate may be taken for years by the elderly to prevent manic episodes. Levels of renal functioning should be monitored closely in the elderly because of suspected progressive renal damage during chronic use of lithium (24). It is well established that lithium clearance decreases with aging and along with comparable changes in creatine clearance (32). For example, the serum half-life of lithium may be doubled in the elderly with corresponding elevation of blood levels if doses are not adjusted. Side effects in elderly include tremors and GI dysfunctions. At higher toxic serum levels of lithium, the neurological susceptibilities of the elderly are evident in the development of confusion, delirium and coma (33).

Polypharmacy and Drug Interactions

The incidence of polypharmacy increases with age (28). Frequently, the elderly have to take psychotropic drugs in combination with other medical (nonpsychotropic) drugs (10), as well as often with other psychotropic drugs (34, 35). Furthermore, it has been recognized that geriatric patients as a group have an increased propensity for drug interactions simply because they often suffer from a combination of chronic medical problems, each of which may require its own regimen of medications, thus presenting the potential for interactions (36, 37). To further compound this situation, many elderly rely on their own self-medications with over-the-counter (OTC) drugs to treat such problems common to the aged, such as sleep disorders, chronic pain, gastrointestinal complaints, anxiety, depression, fatigue, etc. (38).

In Table 10-IV, the illustrated drug interactions may be viewed as extensions of the common side effects of the psychotropic drugs. For example, the combination of sedative/hypnotics with neuroleptics results in a potentiation of the CNS depressant actions of the latter. On the other hand, acute ingestion of ethanol inhibits oxidative but not conjugative metabolism of other drugs probably, only acutely potentiating the depressant actions of the psychotropic drugs. By contrast, chronic consumption of large amounts of ethanol increases the clearance of the psychotropic drugs, probably by the induction of microsomal drug-metabolizing enzymes (39).

TABLE 10-IV
POTENTIAL INTERACTIONS BETWEEN COMMON PSYCHOTROPIC DRUG
AND MEDICAL DRUG COMBINATIONS IN THE ELDERLY

Drug combinations	Possible clinical outcome
Narcotics or barbiturates and neuroleptics, tricyclic antidepressants, or benzodiazepines	Enhanced sedation, depressed mood, confusion, and disorientation
Atropine-containing medications (antihistamines, antiparkinsonian drugs) and tricyclic antidepressants or neuroleptics	Severe anticholinergic toxicity, confusion, agitation, hallucinations, irritability, sh˕rt-term memory loss
Antihypertensive medication and tricyclic antidepressants	Decreased effectiveness of guanethidine leading to elevated blood pressure
Thiazide diuretics and tricyclic antidepressants	Exacerbated orthostatic hypotension leading to an increase in falling
Thiazide diuretics and lithium; low sodium diet and lithium	Reduced lithium clearance leading to lithium toxicity
Neuroleptics and ethanol, se'ative/hypnotics; neuroleptics and antihypertension, neuroleptics and narcotic analgesics	CNS depression Hypotension Analgesic potentions Respiratory depression

"Displacer" drugs have a high affinity for serum albumin drug-binding sites and thereby reduce the binding of other drugs. Non-narcotic analgesic (e.g., salicylates, indomethacin), commonly taken by the elderly for pain and arthritic conditions, are potent displacers of psychotropic drugs, increasing the ratio of the unbound active drug. Drugs such as phenylhydantoin and disulfiram, as well as acute ethanol intake, may inhibit the metabolism of psychotropic drugs. It is interesting to note that the barbiturates may facilitate their own metabolism by induction of hepatic microsomal enzymes (40).

Often, the tricyclic antidepressants and the neuroleptics block some of the hypotensive effects of guanethidine, probably by competing for presynaptic neurotransmitter reuptake mechanisms utilized by the latter (41).

Guttman (10) found that about 69 percent of 447 elderly patients used over-the-counter medications, compared with 10 percent of the general adult population (42). Interestingly enough, less than 20 percent of elderly patients consulted their physicians concerning the use of these agents. About 55 percent of these over-the-counter preparations were analgesics. It has been estimated that unprescribed drugs probably account for as much as 90 percent of all drugs used by the elderly (8). The complexities of drug interactions are thus further enhanced by these unprescribed drugs, many of which are not called to the attention of the physician. Perhaps, this may be attributed to the fact that the elderly may not necessarily view over-the-counter preparations as drugs. Thus, the onus is on the physician when taking a history of the patient to inquire specifically as to the patients' self-medications practices.

SUMMARY

The elderly not only receive more psychotropic drugs than other adult patients but are also more susceptible to their adverse side effects, both in frequency and intensity. Appropriate prescribing of psychotropic drugs in this population must take into account: physiological status of the elderly pharmacokinetics of the drugs in this age group, interactions of these drugs with other agents prescribed for other medical illness, and interaction with over-the-counter preparations taken for self-medication. In the final analyses, because the elderly present a heterogenous group, drugs must be prescribed cautiously, monitored frequently and on an individual basis (43).

REFERENCES

1. Crook, T., and Cohen, G. (Eds.). *Physicians handbook on Psychotherapeutic Drug Use in the Aged.* New Canaan, Conn.: Mark Pawley Assoc., 1981.

2. Zawadski, R. T., Glazer, G. B., and Lurie, E. Psychotropic drug use among institutionalized and non-institutionalized medicaid aged in California. *J. Gerontology,* 1978, 33, 825–834.

3. Schuckit, M. A., and Moore, M. A. Drug problems in the elderly. In O. J. Kaplan (Ed.), *Psychopathology of Aging.* New York: Academic Press, 1979.

4. Fries, J. F. Aging, natural death and the compression of morbidity. *N. England J. Med,* 1980, 303, 130.

5. Freeman, J. T. Some principles of medication in geriatrics. *J. Am. Geriatrics Soc.,* 1974, 22, 289–295.

6. Salzman, C., and van der Kolk, B. A. Psychotropic drug prescriptions to elderly patients in a general hospital. *J. Am. Geriatr. Soc.,* 1980, 28, 18–22.

7. Kovar, R. E. Health of the elderly and use of health services. *Public Health Rep.,* 1977, 92, 9–19.

8. Chien, C. P., Townsend, E. J., and Ross-Townsend, A. Substance use and abuse among the community elderly: The Medical aspects. *Addict. Dis.,* 1978, 3, 357–372.

9. Kalchthaler, T., Coccaro, E., and Lichtiger, S. Incidence of polypharmacy in a long term care facility. *J. Am. Geriatric Soc.,* 1977, 25, 308–313.

10. Guttman, D. Patterns of legal drug use by older Americans. *Addict. Dis.,* 1977, 3, 337–355.

11. Thompson II, T. L., Moran, M. G., and Nies, A. S. Psychotropic drug use in the elderly. Part 1. *New Engl. J. Med,* 1983, 308, 134–138.

12. Vestal, R. F. Pharmacology and Aging. *J. Amer. Geriatrics Soc.,* 1982, 30, 191–200.

13. Crooks, J., O'Malley, K., and Stevenson, I. H. Pharmacokinetics in the elderly. *Clin. Pharmacokinet.,* 1976, 1, 280–296.

14. Greenblatt, D. J., Sellers, E. M., and Shader, R. I. Drug Therapy: Drug disposition in old age. *New England J. Med,* 1982, 306, 1081–1088.

15. Kato, R., and Tanaka, A. Metabolism of drugs in old rats: Metabolism in vivo and effects of drugs in old rats. *Jap. J. Pharmacol,* 1968, 18, 389–396.

16. Salzman, C. Key concepts in geriatric psychopharmacology. *Psychiatric Clinics of North America,* 1982, 5, 181–190.

17. Brandfonbrener, M., Landowne, M., and Shock, N. W. Changes in cardiac output with age. *Circulation,* 1955, 12, 557–566.

18. Goldman, R. Speculations on vascular changes with age. *J. Am. Geriatrics Soc.,* 1970, 18, 765–779.

19. Finch, C. E. Neuroendocrine and automoic aspects of aging. In C. E. Finch and L. Mayflick (Eds.), *The Handbook of the Biology of Aging,* 262–275. New York: Van Nostrand-Reinhold, 1977.

20. Klawans, H., Goetz, C. G., and Perlik, S. Tardive dyskinesia: Review and update. *Am. J. Psychiat.,* 1980, 137, 900–908.

21. Avorn, J. L., Lamy, P., and Vestal, R. E. Prescribing for the elderly—safely. *Patient Care,* 1982, June 30, 14–53.

22. Jarvik, L. F., Greenblatt, D., and Harmon, D. (Eds.). *Clinical Pharmacology and the Aged Patient.* New York: Raven Press, 1981.

23. Raskind, M., and Eisdorfer, C. The use of psychotherapeutic drugs on geriatrics. In L. L. Simpson (Eds.), *The Use of Psychotherapeutic Drugs in Treatment of Mental Illness.* New York: Raven Press, 1978.

24. Moran, M. G., and Thompson II, T. L. Increased psychotropic side effects in geriatric patients. *Hospital Formulary,* 1982, 17, 1513–1521.

25. Seidl, L. G., Thornton, G. F., and Smith, J. N. et al. Studies on the epidemiology of adverse drug reactions. Reactions in patients on a general medical service. *Bull. Johns Hopkins Hosp.,* 1966, 119, 299–303.

26. Prien, R. F. Problems and practices in geriatric psychopharmacology. *Psychosomatics,* 1980, 21, 213–223.

27. Thompson II, T. L., Moran, M. G., and Nies, A. S. Psychotropic drug use in the elderly. Part 2. *New Engl. J. Med,* 1983, 308, 194–199.

28. Salzman, C. L. Basic principles of psychotropic drug prescriptions for the elderly. *Hospital and Community Psychiatry,* 1982, 33, 133–136.

29. Hollister, L. E. General principles of psychotherapeutic drug use in the aged. In T. Crook and G. Cohen (Eds.), *Physicians' Handbook on Psychotherapeutic Use in the Aged,* 1–10. New Canaan, Conn.: Mark Pawley Assoc., 1981.

30. Butler, R. N. *Why Survive? Being Old in America,* 198–200. New York: Harper & Row, 1975.

31. Task Force on Late Neurological Effects of Antipsychotic Drugs. Tardive dyskinesia: Summary of task force report of the American Psychiatric Assoc. *Am. J. Psychiat.,* 1980, 137, 1163–1172.

32. Prien, R. F., and Gershon, S. Lithium therapy for the elderly. In T. Crook and G. Cohen (Eds.), *Physicians' Handbook on Psychotherapeutic Drug Use in the Aged,* 39–47. New Canaan, Conn.: Mark Pawley Assoc., 1981.

33. Davis, J. M., Fann, W. E., El-Yousef, M. D., and Janowsky, D. S. Clinical problems in treating the aged with psychotropic drugs. In C. Eisdorfer and W. E. Fann (Eds.), *Psychopharmacology and Aging,* 111–125. New York: Plenum Press, 1973.

34. Fracchia, J., Sheppard, C., and Canale, D. et al. Combination drug therapy for the psychogeriatric: Comparison of dosage, levels of some psychotropic used singly and in combination. *J. Am. Geriatr. Soc.,* 1975, 23, 508–511.

35. Salzman, C. Polypharmacy and drug-drug interactions in the elderly. In L. L. Simpson (Eds.), *Geriatric Psychopharmacology,* 117–125. New York: Raven Press, 1979.

36. Kenny, A. D. Designing therapy for the elderly. *Drug Ther.,* 1979, 9, 49–59.

37. Salzman, C. A primer on geriatric psychopharmacology. *Am. J. Psychiatry,* 1982, 39, 67–74.

38. Schuckit, M. A., and Moore, M. A. Drug problems in the elderly. In *Psychopathology of Aging,* 229–241. New York: Academic Press, 1979.

39. Sellers, E. M., and Holloway, M. R. Drug kinetics and alcohol ingestion. *Clin. Pharmacokinetics,* 1978, 3, 440–452.

40. Burrows, G. O., and Davies, B. Antidepressants and barbiturates. *Brit. Med. J.,* 1971, 4, 113.

41. Woosley, R. L., and.Nies, A. S. Guanethidine. *N. Engl. J. Med,* 1976, 295, 1053–1057.
42. Parry, H. J., Butler, M. B., and Mellinger, G. D. et al. National patterns of psychotherapeutic drug use. *Arch. Gen. Psyciatry,* 1973, 28, 769–783.
43. Lamy, P. P. *Prescribing for the Elderly.* Littleton: PSG Publishing Co., 180.

Chapter 11

USE, MISUSE, AND ABUSE
OF PSYCHOACTIVE DRUGS

Robert H. Fortier

INFLUENCE OF SOCIAL NETWORKS,
HEALTH, AND PERSONALITY ON PATTERNS OF
LEGAL DRUG USE BY THE ELDERLY

E lderly persons (60 years and older) are about 15 percent of America's population. Yet, they obtain 25 percent of the prescription drugs (PDRG) and an equal percentage of the over-the-counter drugs (OTCD) distributed in this country (1). This increase in the use of medication by the elderly has been justified by the thesis that, after all, the incidence of treatable disease rises with age. If this thesis is correct, a logical hypothesis is that the use of medication by the elderly should be relatively homogeneous throughout the aged population, responsive only to age. This chapter explores that hypothesis.

STUDY POPULATION

The authors report here on a small portion of the data collected through the implementation of a grant obtained in 1978 by Maxie C. Maultsby, Jr., M.D.[1] The title of the grant is OLDER (Older

[1]Robert H. Fortier is Associate Professor of Psychology, Purdue School of Science, Indianapolis, IN. Maxie C. Maultsby, Jr., is Director of the Rational Behavior Therapy Center, University of Kentucky Medical Center, Lexington, KY. Maxie C. Maultsby, Jr., was awarded Grant # 1-H81 DA 01884-01 by the National Institute of Drug Abuse. Robert H. Fortier began collaborating in the research in 1980 during sabbatical leave at the Rational Behavior Therapy Center. He has primary responsibility for the preparation of this chapter. Maxie C. Maultsby, Jr. and Robert H. Fortier plan a series of papers based upon this research.

Life Drug Experience Research.) The Secretary of the State of Kentucky provided the voter registration list of all men and women 60 years and older living in Fayette County (Lexington and suburbs), nearly 1,500 names. Additional names were obtained through mass media appeals and as referrals from physicians, clergy, and other professionals. Some 800 of these individuals indicated their willingness to serve as research subjects. Transportation was at no cost to participants, and minimum wage for time spent in the research was paid.

After screening for both physiological and psychological characteristics, a relatively psychologically and physically normal, non-disabled population having adequate competencies for coping with life's daily events was obtained. No individual is included in this study who was institutionalized or hospitalized or had untreated medical problems. There is nevertheless sufficient heterogeneity in the population with respect to physical, psychological, and social functioning, as well as in age, to allow the testing of the influence of these variables upon patterns of drug use. In this chapter, we are concerned with only the Caucasian component (slightly more than 90%) of those subjects indicating interest in participating in the study. There are 126 males and 161 females. Age ranged from 60 to above 90. Although the research population included the extremes of educational levels and income, our population is above the national average in both. The vast majority of both males and females were or had been married. As is typical of an aged population, a larger percentage of females were widowed.

ESTABLISHMENT OF PERTINENT DRUG USE PATTERNS

A fairly wide range of recently published research studies were reviewed. These included papers by Petersen, Whittington, and Beer (2), Petersen and Thomas (3), Petersen, Dale, and Dressel (4), Petersen and Whittington (5), Petersen (6), Guttman (7), Whittington, Stephens, Haney and Underwood (8), Temin (9), Beck and Sullivan (10), Glantz (11), and Knapp and Capel (12). Careful analysis of these studies yielded four patterns of drug use which appeared relatively stable and of major interest to a number of investigators. These patterns are described briefly:

    a. Frequencies of over-the-counter (OTCD) and prescription (PDRG) drugs purchased and then actually used, and the combined total of drugs purchased (TDRG) and used.

    b. Use of CNS drugs, including alcohol. Of primary interest here was the possession of both OTCD and PDRG affecting the central nervous system. Alcohol was also included in this pattern. Utilizing NIMH guidelines, we divided our population into four groups: abstainers, light, moderate, and heavy drinkers.

    c. Misuse of Drugs: Under- or overuse of OTCD and PDRG, or not using at all one or the other category of purchased drugs (referred to as "wasted" drugs).

    d. Massive Non-Compliance: A "non-compliance" was scored whenever an individual departed from instructions, whether this be using a drug at more or less than recommended, prescribed usage, or not using it at all.

Specially trained social workers visited all subjects in their homes, inventoried all drugs (including alcoholic beverages), and determined both recommended or prescribed usage and actually practiced usage.

ESTABLISHMENT OF PSYCHO-SOCIAL NETWORKS

In addition to collecting the usual demographic data, numerous questions were asked regarding many aspects of the subjects' present or past lives. Questions regarding physician and hospital use and a scale reflecting overall physical and psychological disability were administered. Subjects were also given several measures of personality functioning: (a) POMS (13); (b) SCL-90-R (14); (c) Quality of Life Scale (15); and (d) YIPTIS (16).

Factor analyses were executed within each sex and then of the combined male and female group. The first set of factor analyses involved demographic data and those questions and scales pertaining to life-style and health. The second was based upon the battery of personality tests. The first set of factor analyses yielded essentially the same cluster of factors within each sex and for the total group, although individual items varied within each factor. These socio-psychological factors are: (a) marital status and/or residence; (b) sociability; (c) work or prior work; (d) present economic status; and (e) health.

The factor analyses of personality data yielded three factors for males and four for females. The three male factors are: (a) STRAIN (composed of CON from the POMS and eight of the scales from the SCL-90-R; (b) FATIGUE (composed of -VIG and FAT from the POMS, SOM from the SCL-90-R, and the Life Satisfaction Scale); and (c) AGITATED–DEPRESSION. The four female factors are: (a) STURM (composed of six scales from the SCL-90-R, and the YIPTIS); (b) AGITATED–FATIGUE (composed of five of the POMS scales); (c) SOMATIC (composed of three of the SCL-90-R scales and the Life Satisfaction Scale); and (d) VIGOR (VIG from the POMS).

STATISTICAL STRATEGIES

The analyses performed were essentially the result of a 4×6 matrix, where each of the four patterns of drug use were analyzed in turn by the five socio-psychological factors, plus personality. The number of analyses is considerably greater than that which is suggested by the above matrix, since each of the socio-psychological factors was defined by several items. Personality, as has been indicated, is represented by three male factors, four female, and four for the total group. Three sets of analyses were performed, one for each sex, and then for the total group.

RESULTS

Space limitations prohibit full tabular presentation of results. A good schematic overview is nevertheless available from Tables 11-I, 11-II and 11-III, where the number of significant comparisons obtained within each cluster for males, females, and the total group are indicated. While the effects of many of the individual networks within the factor clusters will be discussed in the narrative later, the schematic overviews merit attention in themselves.

TABLE 11-I
SUMMARY OF SOCIO-PSYCHOLOGICAL NETWORKS FOR MALES

SOCIO-PSYCHOLOGICAL NETWORKS	NUMBER OF SIGNIFICANT ITEMS			
	DRUG PATTERNS/ FREQUENCIES	CNS	MISUSE	NON-COMPL
MARITAL STATUS	NONE	3x.15	1x.05 3x.10	1x.08 2x.10
SOCIABILITY	3x.04 1x.11	NONE	1x.08 2x.10	1x.15
WORK	1x.01 2x.09	1x.02 1x.09	NONE	NONE
ECONOMICS	1x.03 1x.11	NONE	NONE	NONE
HEALTH	2x.03 1x.13	1x.07	1x.01	1x.10
PERSONALITY	3x.001 1x.06	2x.01 1x.06 1x.13	1x.008	1x.10

*These tables show the relative degree of influence the socio-psychological networks exert upon the different drug patterns.

Although not indicated in the tables, it should be noted that Massive Non-Compliance was a general rule with both males and females. Those individuals following directions in the use of all their drugs are in a distinct minority. There is a high correlation between the number of drugs possessed and massive non-compliance $(r > 0.84)$

TABLE 11-II

SUMMARY OF SOCIO-PSYCHOLOGICAL NETWORKS FOR FEMALES

NUMBER OF SIGNIFICANT ITEMS

SOCIO-PSYCHOLOGICAL NETWORKS	DRUG PATTERNS/ FREQUENCIES	CNS	MISUSE	NON-COMPL
MRITAL STATUS	3x.03	1x.08	1x.01	2x.02
	1x.12	2x.12	1x.05	2x.10
SOCIABILITY	1x.07	NONE	1x.07	NONE
WORK	1x.05	1x.02	1x.12	1x.11
	1x.07	1x.04		
	1x.10			
ECONOMICS	NONE	2x.11	1x.13	1x.08
				1x.10
HEALTH	2x.0001	1x.02	2x.02	1x.002
	1x.055	1x.06	1x.07	1x.04
	1x.10		1x.08	1x.065
				1x.08
PERSONALITY	1x.002	NONE	1x.10	NONE
	1x.07			

*These tables show the relative degree of influence the socio-psychological networks exert upon the different drug patterns.

Male Overview

ECONOMICS is the least influential of the clusters. PERSON-ALITY and HEALTH are clearly the more powerful clusters, exerting an influence on all drug patterns. The drug pattern most susceptible to influence is FREQUENCIES. The least susceptible is NON-COMPLIANCE. There are seven empty cells in the Male analyses, i.e., the networks exerted no influence on those drug patterns.

TABLE 11-III
SUMMARY OF SOCIO-PSYCHOLOGICAL NETWORKS
FOR MALES AND FEMALES—A COMPARISON

NUMBER OF SIGNIFICANT ITEMS

SOCIO-PSYCHOLOGICAL NETWORKS	DRUG PATTERNS/ FREQUENCIES	CNS	MISUSE	NON-COMPL
MARITAL STATUS	1x.001	NONE	1x.06	1x.10
	2x.05			
	2x.09			
SOCIABILITY	NONE	1x.11	1x.10	NONE
WORK	1x.03	1x.008	2x.04	1x.03
	1x.05	1x.01		
		1x.06		
ECONOMICS	2x.11	1x.09	1x.03	1x.03
			2.x.07	
HEALTH	2x.02	2x.07	NONE	NONE
	1x.07			
	1x.10			
PERSONALITY	1x.04	1x.04	NONE	NONE
	1x.056			

*These tables show the relative degree of influence the socio-psychological networks exert upon the different drug patterns.

Female Overview

Although three of the network clusters—MARITAL STATUS AND/OR RESIDENCE, WORK OR PRIOR WORK, and HEALTH—exerted influence over all four drug patterns, HEALTH is by far the most powerful. SOCIABILITY and PERSONALITY are the lesser influential clusters but affect the same two drug patterns, FREQUENCIES and MISUSE. Although FREQUEN-CIES has one empty cell and MISUSE none, both those drug patterns seem rather susceptible to influence by the network clusters. The Female Overview has only five empty cells, as contrasted to seven for Males.

Total Group Overview

It must be remembered that this is a direct male-female comparison, since the two sexes were here compared on precisely the same *individual* cluster items. This was not the case in the within-sex analyses. Thus, where there are empty cells, this indicates that males and females defined in exactly the same way were functioning in exactly the same fashion. Where significant P-values are shown, males and females defined in the same way behaved differently. Many individual cluster items yielded no differences between the sexes on any of the drug patterns. Some of these have special significance and will be discussed later.

WORK OR PRIOR WORK is the most powerful differentiating network cluster, with ECONOMICS being the next more influential. The drug pattern most differentiating between the sexes is FREQUENCIES. NON–COMPLIANCE is the least differentiating, with MISUSE next.

In the next sections, results for the most significant individual network items will be reported, within clusters and across drug patterns.

Individual Network Items, Males

MARITAL STATUS AND/OR RESIDENCE × MISUSE and NON–COMPLIANCE: Males 70 years and over who do not own their homes waste (i.e., not use purchased drugs) more PDRG than those owning their homes. These same men also tend to deviate more from prescribed usage of their PDRG than those owning homes.

SOCIABILITY × FREQUENCIES and MISUSE: More social males, defined both by number of visits and number of people contacted, use more OTCD and TDRG than less social people. These more social individuals also tend to waste more PDRG than less social ones and tend to use more OTCD at *less* than the recommended rate.

WORK OR PRIOR WORK × FREQUENCIES, CNS, and MISUSE: Retired males who had worked as administrators or higher were compared to retired males who had worked in positions no higher than laborers. The first group tended to use *fewer* PDRG and fewer CNS drugs but drank more alcoholic beverages. Retired persons compared to those still working full time tended to use more PDRG (ascending age is *not* related to PDRG) while still wasting more of these drugs. Men under 70 working part time used far more OTCD than similar retired men.

ECONOMICS × FREQUENCIES: Males in the two highest income groups, incomes covering needs and allowing purchases of extras, were compared to those in the two lowest income groups claiming neither ability to purchase necessities nor extras. The latter group used far more OTCD than the former. There was *absolutely no difference* in PDRG used.

HEALTH × FREQUENCIES, CNS, MISUSE, and NON–COMPLIANCE: Those males believing they needed more medical care, in comparison to those that didn't, used far more PDRG, although at *less* than the prescribed rate, but tended toward more non-compliance in the use of those drugs. Males having two or fewer visits to physicians and no hospital days in the last six months were compared to those having three or more physician visits and two or more hospital days. The latter group used far more PDRG and tended to use more CNS drugs.

PERSONALITY × FREQUENCIES, CNS, MISUSE, AND NON–COMPLIANCE: Males falling in the lower two quartiles on all three of the personality factors (least troubled) were compared to those falling in the top two quartiles (most troubled). The latter group (most troubled) used far more PDRG and TDRG, more CNS drugs, wasted fewer of their PDRG, and tended to be more careful in taking their drugs. When the comparisons were made more stringent (lowest quartile on all three personality factors vs. top quartile), the differences were even more extreme. The least troubled group used no PDRG, fewer TDRG, and no CNS drugs.

Individual Network Items, Females

MARITAL STATUS AND/OR RESIDENCE × FREQUEN-CIES, CNS, MISUSE, and NON–COMPLIANCE: Women 65 and over, widowed, retired, living with children, and almost never lonely were compared to those living with grandchildren and frequently being lonely. The latter group used far more PDRG and TDRG, tended to use more CNS drugs, used OTCD at less than the recommended rate, and were more careful in using their PDRG but less careful in using OTCD. That same group used more OTCD, wasted more OTCD, and were less careful in following directions in using their drugs than similar women living alone.

SOCIABILITY × FREQUENCIES and MISUSE: Women having more contact with others through visits and by telephone tended to use more OTCD, while wasting more, than more isolated women.

WORK × FREQUENCIES: Women, 70 and under, married and living with their spouses, having worked longest as technicians or higher, were compared to similar women having worked longest as skilled laborers or lower positions. The higher employed group used fewer OTCD but tended to use more PDRG. Women still working part time used fewer CNS drugs.

ECONOMICS × NON–COMPLIANCE: Women, 70 and under, married and living with their spouse, owning a home and in the two lowest income quartiles were compared to similar women in the top two income quartiles. The wealthier women tended to be less careful in their PDRG use. There was *no* difference between these two groups in any measure of frequency of drug use.

HEALTH × FREQUENCIES, CNS, MISUSE, AND NON–COMPLIANCE: Women believing they needed more medical care were compared with those that didn't. The former group tended to use more PDRG and used more TDRG. They used more CNS drugs, were less careful in the use of their OTCD, but more careful in using PDRG. Women with no more than one physician visit in the last six months and no hospital days were compared to those with four or more physician visits and at least one hospital day. The latter group used far more PDRG and TDRG, wasted fewer PDRG, and were more careful in their use of those drugs.

PERSONALITY × FREQUENCIES: Women falling in the lower two quartiles on all four personality factors (least troubled) were compared to those in the higher two quartiles (most troubled). The most troubled women used far more PDRG and tended to use more TDRG.

Individual Network Items, Male and Female Comparisons

MARITAL STATUS AND/OR RESIDENCE × FREQUEN-CIES and MISUSE: Married and living with spouse: Women tended to use more TDRG but did not differ on any other measure of drug use frequency. Living with grandchildren: Women used more OTCD, PDRG, and TDRG but wasted more of their PDRG.

WORK × FREQUENCIES, CNS, MISUSE, and NON–COM-PLIANCE: Men and women working part time differed only in the extent to which they underused PDRG, with men using PDRG at less than the prescribed rate. Retired men and women differed in their use of PDRG and TDRG, with women being the higher users. Males drank more than women (a rather typical finding). It should be noted that a group of 34 men and 15 women (all now retired), in or above the third income quartile, with some college education, having worked longest as administrator or higher, did *not* differ on a *single* drug use pattern. A small group of men and women who were still working full time differed only in the care with which they were using their OTCD (men were more careful).

ECONOMICS × CNS, MISUSE, AND NON–COMPLIANCE: Men and women, 70 and over, who owned their own home, did not differ in frequency of drug use. Such women underused their PDRG and were generally less careful in their use of such drugs. Men and women, 70 and under, owning their own homes only differed in their underuse of OTCD (women more).

HEALTH × FREQUENCIES and CNS: Men and women having no physician contact nor hospital days differed in the use of PDRG (women more) and use of CNS drugs (women more). Men and women with four or more physician contacts and at least one hospital day differed only in their use of TDRG (women more).

PERSONALITY × FREQUENCIES and CNS: Men and women, claiming good or excellent mental health, never feeling lonely, and placing in the first two quartiles on all four group personality factors, differed in use of PDRG and TDRG and in the use of CNS drugs (women more).

DISCUSSION

The broad hypothesis stated at the beginning of this chapter — that the use of medication by the elderly should be relatively homogeneous throughout the aged population, responsive only to age — is categorically rejected. Numerous socio-psychological networks and personality factors critically influence all four of the major drug patterns studied. Beyond this, the relatively healthy aged in our study do *not* require an increasing number of either OTCD or PDRG in order to remain well.

There are two messages to those who prescribe or supervise the aged who take legal drugs: (1) The physician who practices polypharmacy is inviting massive non-compliance with his or her directions (correlation between total number of drugs taken and massive non-compliance is 0.88 for males and 0.84 for females). (2) There are numerous factors which affect what kinds of drugs are being consumed and their pattern of use. Although the influence upon patterns of drug use by the kind of networks utilized in this study must be confirmed in other studies, it is highly likely that this influence will be intricate and pervasive. Very careful monitoring of outpatient drug use seems essential. Little can be taken for granted.

In more specific terms, the state of health, and even the *belief* in the state of health, is highly related to the use of drugs by both males and females. Those males who differed only in their belief that they needed more medical care did not differ in their actual contact with the health care system. Nevertheless, they differed in their pattern of drug use.

Personality functioning is more likely to affect patterns of drug use among men than among women. The question can legitimately be asked: Does the difference in personality functioning determine the differential use of drugs among males or does the use of drugs contribute to the poor personality functioning of some males? When the consumption of CNS drugs was carefully analyzed, it was noted that several of the males in the poor functioning personality quartiles had obtained CNS drugs from several different physicians (in some cases, the same drug) and were taking them at more than the prescribed rate. These findings suggest two things: (1) personality deviancy may lead to excessive procurement and consumption of CNS drugs; and (2) the consumption of CNS drugs does not appear to alleviate personality deviancy.

Most researchers appear to believe that all older women consume more drugs than older males, including CNS drugs. Petersen, Whittington and Beer (2) caution against that conclusion, suggesting that appropriate demographic controls may not yet have been used. When several relatively large groups of men and women were carefully defined in our study, it was indeed found that no or virtually no differences in any pattern of drug use existed. We suggest that rather than assuming such sex differences, there be continued careful searches for those circumstances which yield sex differences and for those that do not.

A number of investigators have claimed that poorer individuals use a larger number of OTCD because they cannot afford PDRG. Our investigation show that it is true poorer males buy more OTCD than wealthier males, but there is *no* difference in the amount of PDRG purchased. Neither does ECONOMICS affect PDRG used by females. We suspect that far more is involved in this matter than economics. That this may be so is seen in the high use of OTCD by more social men and women. The purchase and use of OTCD drugs may be an act of assertion and independence.

CONCLUSIONS

Psycho-social networks, health, and personality clearly influence broad patterns of legal drug use. Practitioners ignore this finding at their (and their patients') peril. Those practitioners who accept what may appear to be greater use of drugs by women as simply being a "women's way" are ignoring those factors which may be contributing to those particular women's possibly excessive use of medication.

Knapp and Capel (12) call into question "the practice of prescribing and/or using drugs to relieve symptoms when what is required is understanding, counseling, and/or insight to get at the causes" (12). "Thus the symptoms of aging continue to be treated with drugs which provide unwanted effects, which in turn, lead to more serious complications" (12). We suggest that one way to reduce the number of drugs in working with the elderly is through use of the approach developed by Maxie C. Maultsby, Jr.: Rational Behavior Therapy (17).

SUMMARY

Socio-psychological data collected from a relatively physiologically and psychologically normal group of elderly men and women were factored, yielding four clusters: (1) marital status and/or residence; (2) sociability; (3) work or prior work; and (4) economic status. An additional two clusters were generated based on state of health and on personality functioning. We then determined the degree of influence of each cluster upon four patterns of drug use developed from the literature. These patterns are: (1) frequency of use of over-the-counter drugs, prescription drugs, and total drug use; (2) possession of CNS drugs; (3) misuse; (4) non-compliance. The analyses were performed separately on each sex; the sexes were then compared. All clusters were found to influence some of the patterns. Although some clusters differentiated the two sexes, several relatively large groups of men and women were indistinguishable in their pattern of drug use—a finding contrary to that predicted by the literature.

REFERENCES

1. Wynne, R. D., and Heller, F. Drug overuse among the elderly: a growing problem. *Perspective on Aging,* 1973, 11, 15–18.
2. Petersen, D., Whittington, F. J., and Beer, E. T. Drug use and misuse among the elderly. *Journal of Drug Issues,* 1979, 9, 5–26.
3. Petersen, D., and Thomas, C. W. Acute drug reactions among the elderly. *Journal of Gerontology,* 1975, 30, 552–556.
4. Whittington, F., Petersen, D., Dale, B., and Dressel, P. Sex differences in prescriptive drug use of older adults. *Journal of Psychoactive Drugs,* 1981, 13, 175–181.
5. Petersen, D., and Whittington, F. J. Drug use among the elderly: A review.

Journal of Psychedelic Drugs, 1977, 9, 25–37.

6. Petersen, D. Editor's introduction. *Journal of Psychoactive Drugs*, 1981, 13, 111–116.

7. Guttman, D. Patterns of legal drug use by older Americans, *Addictive Diseases: An International Journal*, 1978, 3, 337–356.

8. Stephens, R., Haney, A., and Underwood, S. Psychoactive drug use and potential misuse among persons aged 55 years and older. *Journal of Psychoactive Drugs*, 1981, 13, 185–193.

9. Temin, P. *Taking your medicine: Drug regulation in the United States.* Cambridge, MA: Harvard University Press, 1980.

10. Beck, K., and Sullivan, D. Self-image, medicine and drug use. *Addictive Diseases: An International Journal*, 1978, 3, 373–382.

11. Glantz, M. Predictions of elderly drug use. *Journal of Psychoactive Drugs*, 1981, 13, 117–126.

12. Knapp, R., and Capel, W. Drug use among the elderly. *Journal of Drug Issues*, 1979, 9, 1–3.

13. McNair, D., Lorr, M., and Droppleman, L. *Profile of Mood States.* Educational and Industrial Testing Service, CA 92107, 1971.

14. Derogatis, L. R. SCL-90-R, *Administration, Scoring and Procedures Manual-Revised Version.* Baltimore, MD: Johns-Hopkins University, 1977.

15. Maultsby, M. Procedures for "OLDER" Research. Unpublished Manuscript, 1978.

16. Maultsby, M. C. *Handbook of Rational Self Counseling.* Association for Rational Living, 1971.

17. Maultsby, M. C. *Rational Behavior Therapy.* Englewood Cliffs, NJ: Prentice-Hall, 1984.

Chapter 12

INSTITUTIONAL DRUG ABUSE: THE OVERPRESCRIBING OF PSYCHOACTIVE MEDICATIONS IN NURSING HOMES

Howard M. Waxman
Melissa Klein
Robert Kennedy
Patricia Randels
Erwin A. Carner

A discussion of the over-prescribing of medications for nursing home patients might at first appear inappropriate in a volume primarily devoted to drug and alcohol abuse and addiction. The potential misuse of prescription drugs by nursing homes seems less notorious and less pernicious than the comparable misuse of drugs and alcohol by individuals. We believe, however, that a strong analogy can be made between drug addiction by an individual, and medication misuse by an institution. Furthermore, since medication misuse in the elderly is such a serious and as yet unanswered problem, a fresh perspective on this issue is required. We will argue that the very need for these medications claimed by many long-term care facilities makes it clear that institutions themselves become and can remain addicted to prescribing drugs, in much the same way, and for some of the same reasons, that individuals become addicted to consuming them. The maladaptive use of medications by an organization, like the maladaptive use of drugs by an individual, can stem from overwhelming preoccupaton with using a substance to the detriment of other concerns. Instead of being an individual addiction to consuming drugs, medication overuse in nursing homes can be thought of as an institutional addiction to prescribing them.

It is our thesis that much of the medication administered in nursing homes, especially the psychotropic medications, are used less for the treatment of an ailing patient than for the treatment of an ailing institution—the long-term care industry. This chapter will initially review what is known about psychotropic drug use in nursing homes, and then argue that this high level of use is the result of complex social and organizational forces that operate in long-term care facilities.

While only five to six percent of those over 65 years of age are in long-term care facilities, this represents approximately 1,000,000 people nationwide. Moreover, these numbers will grow steadily as more and more of our population lives to an older age. Today's nursing home population is composed of ailing elderly who are unable to care for themselves, and who lack the necessary social support system to care for them. The majority of patients in nursing homes are frail, elderly, tired in mind as well as body. Most of these patients are women and have been diagnosed as having some form of mental incapacity. Many current nursing home patients were formerly institutionalized with psychiatric disorders. Most have been classified as being "senile." Severe physical impairment is also prevalent, especially in association with poor mental functioning. Approximately one-third of these patients are either bed-fast or chair-fast and one-third are incontinent. Their requirements for care are great, and include toileting, grooming and dressing. In skilled nursing facilities especially there is little likelihood that such patients will "get well" and return home. They are a difficult population to work with, and the demands on the nursing home staff and system can be great.

In an authoritative review of the nursing home industry, Rango recently wrote that the overuse of medications is probably the most common "error of commission" in nursing homes today (1). Survey after survey consistently reveals a very high level of medication use (2, 3). Some nursing home patients take as many as 8 to 12 different medications per day (2). A common practice in nursing homes is pro-re-nata or PRN prescription. This form of medication is, of course, discretionary, with the nurse being instructed to administer the drugs on an "as needed" basis. Approximately one-half of all the drugs administered to nursing home patients are prescribed PRN (3). One study reviewed the records of several nursing homes and found as many as 14 PRN drugs administered to a single patient (3). The most commonly prescribed PRN drugs were found to be cathartics, analgesics, psychotropics, and hypnotics, in that order (3).

Psychotropic drugs are used extensively in nursing homes, with as many as 43 to 55 percent of nursing home patients having a prescription for one of them (4). The antipsychotics (major tranquilizers) and antianxiety drugs (minor tranquilizers) are used with some regularity, and are often prescribed on a PRN basis. One study reported that 74 percent of patients in skilled nursing facilities had a prescription for at least one of these drugs (5).

Naturally, there are some legitimate arguments for the use of psychotropic drugs in nursing homes. Elderly nursing home patients are usually older and more frail than elderly who live independently. Also, a large proportion of nursing home residents have a diagnosable psychiatric condition. Many were formerly cared for in large state mental institutions and have been on antipsychotic medications for many years. In addition, antipsychotic medications remain the most effective means of treating acute or active psychoses (6).

The concern, then, is whether this high level of psychotropic drug use is proper and beneficial to nursing home patients or whether it constitutes overuse or serious misuse. To begin to address this question, we need to examine some of the consequences of using these drugs in elderly patients.

CONSEQUENCES OF DRUG MISUSE

As recently as ten years ago, Peter Lamy wrote that very little was known about drug therapy and the geriatric patient's response to drug treatment (7). While some progress has occurred since then, most authorities agree that we still fail to properly medicate the elderly person in a variety of medical settings.

One of the more common problems with medication delivery to the elderly in all settings is polypharmacy. It is well recognized that the non-institutionalized elderly may receive multiple prescriptions from different physicians, each ignorant of the others' actions. It is less well known, however, that the elderly in long-term care institutions may also receive multiple medications prescribed by several physicians treating different problems. While polypharmacy can cause ill effects in persons of all ages, the elderly are most sensitive to such overmedication, primarily because they are not able to digest and absorb the drugs as readily as younger individuals.

Drug-drug interactions are particularly important in this population, since these patients are apt to receive several drugs at once as a consequence of multiple problems. The process of biological aging causes a decrease in the level of physiological functioning, which in turn can cause unanticipated adverse effects when elderly people are taking medications. Some drugs may interfere with the desired effects of other drugs, or the effects may be addictive or potentiated, leading to the loss of drug benefit or to excessive effect. Since many of these drugs have sedative properties that reduce mental function, it is not unusual to find elderly patients who are overmedicated (8). One study that reviewed the records of 188 nursing home patients found 100 causes at risk for drug-drug interactions (9).

Psychotropic drugs, including antipsychotic drugs and tricylic antidepressants, as well as antiparkinsonian drugs, possess anticholinergic properties and combinations of these drugs can lead to a central anticholinergic syndrome, an acute confusional state. Severe adverse reactions can occur at night time. Drugs that increase confusion or decrease cognition may increase symptoms such as hallucination or delusional behavior. Elderly patients are particularly susceptible to developing such a toxic psychosis from anticholinergic drugs, and the symptoms of this syndrome may lead to the addition of yet more drugs. Or conversely, the drugs may be stopped altogether, and the patients are left without the benefits of needed agents (8).

A number of clinical investigations have shown that the use of antipsychotic drugs even for short periods of time can lead to the syndrome of tardive dyskinesia. Obvious symptoms of tardive dyskinesia are rapid but jerky movements that seem to be well coordinated but are involuntary, and slow writhing movements that are also involuntary (10). If the antipsychotic drug is discontinued, the symptoms of tardive dyskinesia may or may not subside. Irreversible tardive dyskinesia, however, most often occurs in elderly individuals (10).

Antipsychotic drugs can produce similar but reversible extrapyramidal side effects in the early weeks of treatment. In fact, recognition of such symptoms at the earliest possible stage is extremely important, in order to differentiate them from the symptoms of tardive dyskinesia (which occurs much later in the course of treatment and is irreversible). Reversible extrapyramidal symptoms, for the most part, tend to disappear during sleep and are exacerbated by strong emotional feelings. EPS symptoms which may be caused by antipsychotic drugs include pseudoparkinsonism, akinesia, rigidity, tremor, drooling, and heart intolerance. Akathisia, or symptoms of not being able to sit still, insomnia, or feelings of restlessness are additional symptoms that may be caused by antipsychotic drugs. Acute dystonic reactions can also occur, and include uncoordinated spastic movements and involuntary muscle spasm (8).

While it is recommended that the elderly be given 1/4–1/3 of the usual adult does, inadequate dosages of psychopharmacologic medications may lead to confusion. On the other hand, toxic side effects, especially neurologic and cardiovascular ones, can occur even at very low dosages with these drugs in elderly patients.

While antipsychotics, properly used, can improve the quality of life in patients with dementia, they cannot restore their cognitive faculties. Furthermore, improper use of antipsychotics can worsen the confusion and disorientation in dementia. In general, patients with dementia or a physical illness require less drugs. In some cases, apparent psychotic symptoms can result from illness or other medications, making the use of antipsychotics inappropriate and potentially harmful. The utility of continuation of antipsychotic therapy is also now being questioned, with evidence that relapse after withdrawal can be rapidly handled in most cases with continuation of the antipsychotic medication (11).

WHY ARE SO MANY DRUGS PRESCRIBED?

Several major factors have previously been identified as permitting the overuse of medications among nursing home residents. One factor is the use of discretionary PRN drugs. With such a high level of PRN medications, the primary care of the patient is left with the nurse, not the physician. In some cases where responsibility of medication supervision is abdicated by the physician, inappropriate medications, no longer appropriate medications, or inappropriate amounts of medications may be delivered to the patients. One study found higher levels of PRN drug use in nursing homes without a full time physician, than in homes with one (12).

The high use of PRN medications is also related to a lack of physician visits to nursing homes. Most physicians pay less attention to patients in a skilled nursing facility compared to other patients who make office visits or who are hospitalized. As a result, there exists considerable doubt as to whether these physicians are able to keep accurate and current medical charts on their nursing home patients (13). This is reflected in the quality of medical records maintained for nursing home patients. A review of patient records in one study revealed over one-third to be poor or very poor with regard to their adequacy and correctness (13). In the same study, more than 50 percent of the psychiatric records were rated as poorly.

There is also a correlation between the number of nursing home patients physicians have, and their drug prescribing patterns. Physicians with larger nursing home practices (ten or more patients) prescribe many more antipsychotic medications and more medications per patient than physicians with smaller nursing home practices (14). These practices may reflect physicians' attitudes toward nursing home patients in general. In one survey, only 21 percent of the physicians interviewed believed that they should continue to be in charge of their patient when that patient has been placed in a nursing home (2).

Another possible factor leading to drug misuse is the misuse of renewal of order forms. In many cases, the consulting physician does not take the time to carefully review a patient's renew order before placing his signature on the form. It is not uncommon for such forms to accumulate in a patient's medical record. As a result, prescription drugs are often administered when in fact they were prescribed months before, for a specific problem. A patient could thus be taking a medication that was prescribed for a health problem that no longer existed. Also, with this practice, a patient could be taking several unneeded drugs, depending on the number of renew orders that had accumulated and had been administered instead of terminated.

Many nursing home personnel are quite uncomfortable with patients who have mental disorders (13). Many nurses and nurses' aides do not have experience in geropsychiatry and therefore do not know how to meet the emotional needs of their residents. Moreover, psychiatrists are generally not available to patients in the nursing home. This may lead to an overuse of psychotropics as the only known response to symptoms of mental disorder in nursing home patients.

By comparison, one study found that those nursing home patients who were displaying the greatest degree of mental impairment were not those who were receiving the most drugs. In fact, the more active and least impaired nursing home residents were those who were receiving the most medication (15). Furthermore, the administration of drugs for behavioral problems may actually be based more on the interactions of the elderly resident, nurse's aide, nurse, physician and relatives than on the patient's exact symptoms (15). Other studies have found similar results and in addition, have found that while female patients are more likely to receive tranquilizers than male patients in long-term care facilities, men who have impaired mental status, who exhibit unfriendly behavior and who are perceived as a threat to the staff, are given the most tranquilizers of all (16).

NURSING HOME POLITICS

While many factors may permit the misuse of psychotropics in nursing homes, we believe that the real causes of the problem and of its maintenance are to be found in the dynamics of long-term care institutions. The environment of nursing homes is the result of a complex set of social and economic forces. These forces interact to set the stage for a home to be at high risk for what we are calling institutional addiction to prescribing drugs. This is not to suggest that the owners and administrators at such homes are *ipso facto* uncaring or unfeeling. For a variety of reasons, it has been difficult to attract staff to work in nursing homes where the pay is low, the physical conditions are often less than desirable, and there is less glamor than at a center city hospital. The work is demanding, dirty, and often degrading. For these reasons, nursing home staff often lack the qualifications and training one would find among their counterparts in other health care settings.

Perhaps the most important trait of a nursing home, and one that has often been ignored, is the fact that over 90 percent of the actual patient care is delivered by nurses' aides. Physicians are usually not present at these facilities and confine their visits to emergencies or routine monthly or weekly checks and chart maintenance. Registered nurses are difficult to attract, are consequently in short supply, and often provide more administrative than health care functions. Also, many nursing homes are forced to make extensive use of agency nurses to meet their nursing requirements. Temporary agency nurses, no matter how skilled, are simply not familiar enough with the patients to provide the proper guidance. These factors leave the medical and psychological care of the patients to the nurses' aides, the unsung and much maligned heroes and heroines of long-term care.

Nurses' aides typically have at most a high school education, often have no pre-employment professional training for their careers, receive very low wages, work very hard and typically fall at the bottom of the nursing home hierarchy. In many nursing homes, and especially those in urban areas, almost all the aides are Blacks or other minorities and are often from impoverished economic backgrounds. Recently, Asian immigrants have been added to the aide staffs. With a predominantly white ownership and administration, there are often racial overtones to relations between the administration and the staff. Stereotypical assumptions abound, as when an administration perceives the aides as being lazy, irresponsible, and dishonest. Aides, on the other hand, perceive the administration and charge nurses as being cheap, demanding, unreasonable, and uncaring. Conflicts often arise, unions enter the picture, relationships are often strained, formal, and "to the letter." Otherwise caring people are often forced into situations where they are not necessarily proud of their behavior.

Against this background, we also must consider the special characteristics of the nursing home patients, the nature and quality of their interactions with the aide level staff, and the obligations and pressures facing nursing home owners and administrators. It is well known that many former mental institution patients have been absorbed by nursing homes and boarding homes following the de-institutionalization movement. Many of these patients are chronic schizophrenics, who for many years have been on neuroleptic medications. Other patients suffering from organic brain syndrome or affective disorders may pose behavior problems that the aides do not understand and are not trained to deal with. Racial issues are present in patient-aide interactions as well. Many Black aides commonly report being referred to as "boy" and treated as servants by the nursing home patients. This can be especially frequent in settings with more affluent patients who formerly had domestic help working in their private homes. Patients and their families can often be quite demanding and strain the patience of even the most dedicated aide. "Working with difficult patients" we found was identified as the single biggest on the job problem by over 80 percent of a sample of 150 nurses' aides (17).

One serious consequence of these conditions in nursing homes is an astronomically high turnover rate of aide level staff. This averages near 40 percent annually nationwide, and can be as high as 70 percent in some homes. Turnover rates this high create problems with economic, medical and social consequences. For each aide who quits, it costs a year's salary equivalent to replace, orient and train another. The experience of being short staffed so often makes it even more difficult to deliver proper care. The attachments that form between patient and aide also suffer when the aide leaves. A related consequence is extremely high absenteeism which is rated by supervisors as the largest administrative problem they have with their aides. The high turnover and absenteeism rates make running a nursing home an administrative nightmare.

Maintaining staff morale and employee-employer relations is perhaps the most difficult task facing the nursing home industry. With conditions favoring disharmony and high turnover and the serious consequences of these conditions, there is tremendous pressure to keep aides content and to try to maintain stable employment. In such adversarial conditions, there is often very little "give" on either side. Nursing home administrators are answerable to owners and governing boards on the one hand and are faced with the day-to-day pressures from their staffs on the other. The aides, frequently unionized, have their own voice and are becoming more aware of their position and of the power they possess.

In a system with these pressures and conditions, it would not be surprising to find some give in another part of the system where there is less strength. We believe that the overuse of psychotropic medications for the elderly in nursing homes is a symptom reflecting these other pressures. It is not difficult to understand how psychotropic medications, particularly the major tranquilizers, are quite effective in reducing a patient's activity, and thus reducing their burden on the staff. The ease of administering medication to constrain a patient's behavior makes this form of abuse highly prevalent. Patients who are drowsy, asleep or slowed down are quite simply less of a management problem. There exists therefore the temptation to misuse drugs that have legitimate, beneficial utility for some of the patients. In a very real sense, the overmedication of nursing home patients with psychotropic drugs helps to keep the whole system in operation. This stress-reducing function of psychoactive drug prescribing at the institutional level defines our analogy to substance addiction at the individual level.

Some important questions need to be addressed if institutional addiction is to be controlled. First, we must frankly decide whether this overuse of medications might not be justified. Arguing against this use are the deleterious effects of these drugs on patient well-being. On the other hand, we must ask ourselves if patients might actually be better off overmedicated, given the staff turmoil that might result if the use of these medications for behavior control were restricted. Could a case be made that it is in the patients' best interest to be overmedicated, rather than risk the possible abuse of an overworked, discontented aide in an understaffed institution?

It seems that we need to know the short-term and long-term consequences of "institutional withdrawal" from current prescribing practices. For the short term, how would the patients react to the reduction of their neuroleptic medications? How would the nurses and the aides react? How much of the staffs' reaction would be due to actual changes in patient behavior, as a result of medication reduction, as opposed to perceived changes stemming from the staff's own attitudes and expectations? Would the staffs' reaction to reduction in drug prescribing actually influence patient behavior itself? Long-term effects have to be assessed and planned for by developing a better understanding of the dynamics that foster medication misuse. For it is only with an understanding of these forces and their resolution that institutions will be able to permanently free themselves of their patterns of addictive behavior, that have such destructive influences on the lives of everyone involved.

SUMMARY

A thesis is presented that equates medication misuse by a long-term facility to substance abuse by an individual. Both can serve a stress relieving function but are potentially destructive. There is abundant evidence that psychotropic medication use in nursing homes is less for the relief of a patient's symptoms than for behavior control and thus staff utility. There is also growing evidence that overuse or misuse of such medications can result in a variety of medical and psychological complications for the nursing home resident. Socioeconomic factors in nursing homes are cited as a strong influence in the development and maintenance of a nursing home's addiction to prescribing drugs.

REFERENCES

1. Rango, N. Nursing-home care in the United States. *The New England Journal of Medicine*, 1982, 307, 883–890.
2. Lamy, P. Misuse and abuse of drugs by the elderly, *American Pharmacy*, 1980, 20, 14–17.

3. Howard, J. et al. "Medication procedures in a nursing home: Abuse of PRN orders, *Journal of the American Geriatric Society*, 1977, 25(2), 83–84.
4. Ray, A. Study of antipsychotic drug use in nursing homes: Epidemiologic evidence suggesting misuse, *American Journal of Public Health.* 70.
5. U.S. Department of Health, Education and Welfare Office of Long Term Care. Physicians drug prescribing patterns in skilled nursing facilities, LTCF Improvement Campaign, Monograph #2, June, 1976.
6. Baldessarini, R. J., and Lipinski, J. F. Risks versus benefits of antipsychotic drugs, *New England Journal of Medicine*, 1973, 289, 427.
7. Lamy, P., and Kitler, M. Drugs and the geriatric patient, *Journal of the American Geriatric Society*, 1971, 19(1).
8. Lamy, P. *Prescribing for the Elderly.* Mass: PSG Publishing Co., Inc., 1980.
9. Brown, M. M., Brosinger, J. K., Henderson, M., Rife, S. S., Rustia, J. K., Taylor, O., and Young, W. W. Drug-drug interactions among residents in homes for the elderly. *Nursing Research*, 1977, 26, 47–52.
10. Portnoi, V. A., and Johnson, E. Tardive dyskinesia. *Geriatric Nursing*, 1982, Jan/Feb, 39.
11. Gardos, G., and Cole, J. O. Maintenance antipsychotic therapy: Is the cure worse than the disease? *American Journal of Psychiatry*, 1976, 133, 32.
12. Aycock, E. K. PRN drug use in nursing homes. *American Journal of Hospital Pharmacy*, 1981, 38, 105.
13. Teeter, B., Garets, F. K., Miller, W. R., and Heiland, W. F. Psychiatric disturbances of aged patients in skilled nursing homes. *American Journal of Psychiatry*, 1976, 133, 12.
14. Ray, W. A., Federspiel, C. F., and Schaffner, N. A study of antipsychotic drug use in nursing homes: Epidemiologic evidence suggesting misuse. *American Journal of Public Health*, 1980, 70, 485–491.
15. Ingman, S. R., Lawson, I. R., Pierpaoli, P. G., and Blake, P. A survey of the prescribing and administration of drugs in a long term care institution for the elderly. *Journal of the American Geriatrics Society*, 1975, 23, 309–316.
16. Millieien, J. W. Some contingencies effecting the utilization of tranquilizers in long term care of the elderly. *Journal of Health and Social Behavior*, 1977, 18, 206–211.
17. Marter, L., Waxman, H. M., and Carner, E. A. The initial needs assessment, foundation of a training model. In E. A. Carner and H. M. Waxman A Training Program for Nursing Home Aides. A symposium presented at the 35th Annual Scientific Meeting of the Gerontological Society of American, Boston, Mass., November 19, 1982.

SECTION IV
COPING TACTICS OF
ELDERLY SUBSTANCE ABUSERS

Chapter 13

WHAT HAPPENS AS THE ALCOHOLIC AND THE DRUG ADDICT GET OLDER?

Harriet L. Barr

This report differs from most others in the conference in that it does not deal with the epidemiology, special manifestations or particular treatment issues of substance abuse in older people. Rather, it is about individuals identified as drug and alcohol abusers who received residential treatment at Eagleville Hospital, and what happens as they get older. Using a therapeutic community model, Eagleville takes a generic approach as it treats drug addicts and alcoholics together. I am reporting here findings taken from two of the treatment outcome studies that we have conducted of former inpatients (ex-residents). One is a study of mortality among our ex-residents and the other is a long term followup study in which we interviewed a sample of ex-residents seven years after their first treatment episode at Eagleville. From the latter study, we will consider individual cases of people who, by the end of the followup period, were in their fifties and sixties.

The general conclusions to be drawn from these studies, insofar as there are any, can be stated simply in advance. As they get older, they either recover or they don't. If they don't stop being substance abusers, they are very likely to die prematurely so that they do not get to be much older.

The mortality study was conducted in collaboration with Donald

The work reported here was supported by NIMH Staffing Grant 1 H19 MH 17831 and NIDA Demonstration Grant 1 H81 DA 01864.

193

J. Ottenberg, Derry Antes and Alvin Rosen.[1] The study cohort
was all first admissions to Eagleville's inpatient program in 1970,
724 subjects in all, 503 with a primary presenting problem of
alcoholism and 221 with a primary presenting problem of drug
abuse.[2] Their past histories and level of functioning on admission were generally poor; 9 percent were women and 24 percent
were Black. At the time they entered treatment, the average
alcoholic was 42 years old while the average drug addict was 23
years old (This is no longer true; in recent years the age dis-
tributions of drug and alcohol abusers overlap much more than
formerly.). A two-year treatment outcome study was conducted,
and mortality data were obtained for a period of eight years after
treatment.

Substance use or abuse was ascertained for each subject at the
time of his or her two-year follow-up or, in the case of those who
died within the first two years, up to the time of death. This
information was obtained for 92 percent of the study cohort. Each
subject was then classified as either "sober" or "abusing" alcohol,
drugs or both. Those classified as sober were, in practically all
cases, abstinent from both alcohol and drugs. They did include,
however, a few recovered drug addicts who were drinking in a
controlled manner, and even fewer alcoholics who reported that
they smoked a joint or drank occasionally; none of these individuals reported any problems related to their limited use. Those
classified as persistent substance abusers were either consuming
excessive quantities of substance(s) of abuse or experiencing significant life problems as a result of their use; for most, both were
true. In practice, classifying a person as either sober or abusing
was hardly ever a problem.

During the eight years of observation of the mortality experience of this cohort, 108 persons died. Among the alcoholics, 0.182
percent had died, amounting to a death rate of 25.9 per 1,000 years
at risk. Of the drug addicts, 7 percent had died, representing a

---

[1] A comprehensive report of this study will appear in a forthcoming issue of the *Journal
of Studies on Alcohol.*

[2] Fewer than 2 percent were actively abusing both alcohol and other drugs on admission, a
marked contrast to recent years when the rate has varied between 35 percent and 40 percent.

death rate of 8.8 per 1,000 years at risk. The difference in mortality between the two groups is attributable, for the most part, to the age difference between them. When these rates are compared with those found in the general population, controlling for age, race and sex, the ratio of observed to expected deaths is 2:5 for alcoholics and 3:1 for drug addicts, with the excess mortality significantly above expectancy ($p < 0.001$) for both groups.

The most important finding of this study is the difference in the mortality rates of those who had achieved sobriety by the two year followup and those who had not. Excess mortality was found only among the persistent substance abusers; deaths among those who were sober at two years did not exceed the expected number. Among the unrecovered alcoholics, deaths from both disease and violence were well in excess of general population rates. Among the unrecovered drug addicts, however, it was only violent deaths (including drug "overdose" deaths) that exceeded population expectancy. Comparisons between the alcoholics and the drug addicts must necessarily be very tentative, particularly in view of the small number of drug addicts in this study and the fact that they were young and thus not followed into the stage of life when diseases become the major cause of death. Nevertheless, in this study, violent deaths, i.e., deaths due to accidents, suicide and homicide, were excessive in both groups, with excessive disease deaths being found only among the alcoholics. Both alcoholism and drug abuse are clearly associated with the impaired judgment, loss of control, deviant life-style and risk-taking behavior that predispose to accidental death, suicide and homicide. While our data confirm the results of many other studies in showing that alcohol damages the body, contributing to degenerative disease processes, it provides no support for the conclusion that drug abuse does. Considerably longer periods of observation of much larger samples are needed to address this issue.[3]

The average alcoholic in this study had been a daily drinker for 16 years, while the average addict had been a daily drug user for 4

[3]Eagleville is currently conducting a study of the mortality of identified drug abusers in which 6,000 drug abusers will be followed for from 7–13 years (average time = 8.4 years after intake). This study is funded by NIDA, under Research Grant #1-R01-DA03254.

years. It is thus striking that the impact of such long-standing substance abuse on mortality can be halted by achieving sobriety, including the effect of years of excessive drinking on disease processes. Of the 108 deaths, 66 may be considered "excess deaths," attributable to substance abuse and the associated way of life. On the other hand, among the 254 people who were sober on follow-up, there were 19 deaths, rather than the 51 that would have been expected from our data if they had continued their substance abuse. Thus, an estimated 32 individuals were alive eight years after treatment who would have died if they had not achieved sobriety.

In the seven year follow-up study, my collaborator was Derry Antes. We drew a stratified sample of first admissions to Eagleville's inpatient program in 1971, comprised of 158 alcoholics and 133 drug addicts. Of the 291 subjects sought, 43 were confirmed as deceased, 15 were located but refused to be interviewed, and 42 could not be located. The interviews took place, on the average, $7\frac{1}{2}$ years after discharge from the inpatient program. The interviews were very comprehensive, and examined a number of aspects of functioning on a month-by-month basis over the entire post-treatment period, including employment, subsequent treatment, schooling, medical history, illegal activities, involvement with the law, personal relationships, and a very detailed substance abuse history which included both the use of all types of substances of abuse and problems related to that use. In addition to looking at these components separately, we summarized the data into an overall rating of each person's status for each period of time. This made it possible to derive a time curve for each subject over the seven years of followup, as well as average time curves for groups of subjects.

It was noteworthy that the time curves of older subjects were, typically, different from those of the younger subjects. Although the older clients were more likely to be alcoholics and the younger clients drug addicts, we believe that the differences are attributable more to the age at which the person entered treatment than to the particular substance of abuse. For those under 30 years on entering treatment, very few (15%) did well at first, but there was consistent improvement, in many cases associated with further treatment, and by about the fourth year after treatment over 50 percent were doing well, a level that was maintained to the end of the seven year period of observation.

With those coming into treatment after the age of 30, the curve was typically rather flat, a trend even more apparent in those over 40 years of age. Almost half had good outcomes from the beginning and by the end of the seven years somewhat over half were doing well. Whatever the level of functioning right after treatment, it was much more likely to continue over the entire seven years than was the case with the younger group.

When treatment is effective with younger substance abusers, what it does, we may conjecture, is to enable them to resume a process of growth and development that had been arrested when they began to abuse drugs or alcohol. Often, this takes several years in which various ways of living may be tried, some of them misguided. Among those coming into treatment at an older age, we more often find those who have once achieved a certain level of functioning, particularly as regards employment and personal relations. It may be that when treatment is effective with them, its effect is to stop or reverse a downward slide from previous levels. Whatever the explanation, the older patient, in our experience, is more likely to either make it soon after treatment or not at all, although there are many exceptions. Specific examples of ex-residents followed past the age of 50 may clarify the picture.

Consistently Poor Outcomes.

Those whose status throughout the followup period was consistently poor were usually long-term chronic alcoholics. In many of these cases they had become totally dependent by the end of the seven years because of the deterioration of the physical condition. Some wound up in the care of the Veterans Administration, in many cases because they had long since lost family ties, while others were dependent on relatives. A man who was 53 when he entered Eagleville and 61 when he was interviewed right here in the Coatesville V.A. Hospital drank alcoholically throughout the entire period. He gave various reasons: "Bored, nothing else to do; my wife left me, I might as well drink, there's no reason not to." When interviewed he was poorly groomed, emaciated, with a variety of medical problems and some mental confusion. He had been in and out of the V.A. Hospital and drank whenever he was out on pass. But when the interviewer asked whether he was happy or unhappy, he said, "I'm perfectly happy. I have the V.A. to look after me now and I have no more problems."

Another man with a similar condition and history, 62 years old when interviewed, had lived off and on with his mother and in hotels, doing odd jobs. He described his most serious problem as not having friends. A year before the interview his mother died, at which time he entered the V.A. Hospital. Another man was house bound and totally dependent on his wife because of epileptic seizures. Another man was almost blind and partially paralyzed, totally dependent on an aunt and uncle with whom he lived. The interviewer thought that his helplessness could be alleviated by therapy, but he appeared unable to mobilize himself to partake of such help.

Poor Initial Outcome, Later Improvement.

Improvement following initially poor status was sometimes motivated by actual or threatened physical breakdown, or other life cycle changes. A man who was 62 years old on admission and 69 when interviewed appears to have always been a loner, leading a rather empty life, but he appeared intact and abstinent when interviewed. During the first three years following treatment, he had several very bad episodes, and was in and out of state hospitals and halfway houses. With the help of Alcoholics Anonymous he stopped drinking for a year, but then drank alcoholically for a year after that. He reported that he had set himself a goal of one year of abstinence to prove to himself that after that he could drink safely. When his experiment failed and his drinking went out of control, he decided that this was his last chance and that he would not be able to make another recovery if it should fail. With the help of A.A., he then stopped drinking and had been abstinent for four years when interviewed.

Another man, 49 years old on admission and 56 when interviewed, also continued problem drinking for three years after treatment, a period during which his mother was dying of cancer and a brother died. He then became active in A.A. and his church and had been abstinent for four years except for one binge ("boss was giving me a hard time"). Although single and living alone since his mother died, his family is supportive and he is close to his siblings.

Consistently Good Outcome.

A number of people did change following treatment. In many cases the support of spouse, family and church appear to be important, but we cannot rule out the possibility that the maintenance of such ties may in itself be a manifestation of the better status of these individuals. Whatever the cause and effect relationship, they exhibit generally more positive relationships to life. A woman, 53 years old on admission and 60 when interviewed, was abstinent the entire time. She worked first as a housekeeper, then as a nurse's aid. While working she took a training course for private duty nursing and for a year and a half before being interviewed was employed in that capacity. She is very active in her church, and describes her hobbies as baseball and crochet. She was described by the interviewer as well-groomed and energetic; when interviewed she was papering her apartment and laying new carpet.

Others in this group describe improvement in their life situations stemming from their sobriety, such as enjoying renewed family relationships and enjoying retirement.

The examples cited have been of alcoholics because they constitute the majority of our cases in the older age bracket. Two brief comments may be made about the aging drug addict. First, the mortality data suggest that if drug addicts survive the risk of violent death, their medical complications may not be as severe as those of older alcoholics. The data reported here, however, refer primarily to narcotic addicts; data is needed on those who have abused non-narcotic drugs.

The second comment is about a particular subgroup of drug addicts, most of them Black, who decide to quit around age 40 to 45. They tend to be rather bright, street-wise people, who have finally decided that it's time to give up the hassle. They include some of our outstanding treatment successes. Some of them become drug counselors or therapists, and their personal backgrounds contribute to their effectiveness. They are a special group, and worthy of deeper study to determine what underlies the genuinely positive outcomes we have seen.

In conclusion, the generalizations that can be drawn from our experience with the older substance abuser are rather few. Some recover with treatment and others do not. They do not, however, have the luxury of being able to make as many mistakes as the young can make and get away with. Their long-term treatment outcome is more likely to become evident shortly after they leave treatment. If they achieve sobriety, their lives can be enhanced, but if they do not, the probable outcome is either progressive deterioration or premature death.

SUMMARY

Alcoholics and drug addicts treated at Eagleville Hospital were followed up at two and eight years. Alcoholics were found to have significantly higher mortality rates from disease and violence than the general population, whereas drug addicts had increased rates only from violence. The excess mortality occurred only among those who persisted in their substance abuse following treatment.

For those older substance abusers who recover, improvement is often evident shortly after they leave treatment, and despite long histories of abuse they do not evidence increased mortality rates. For those who do not recover, the probable outcome appears to be progressive deterioration or premature death.

Chapter 14

OLD AGE AND ADDICTION:
A STUDY OF ELDERLY PATIENTS IN
METHADONE MAINTENANCE TREATMENT

Don C. Des Jarlais
Herman Joseph
David T. Courtwright

Old age and opiate addiction are generally believed to be mutually exlusive choices. Only very rarely does a person who has reached "old age" begin using illicit opiates (1). If a person has reached the age of 25, he or she is very unlikely to begin using heroin (2). Persons who do become addicted to heroin are not expected to live to an old age. Estimates of death rates for untreated heroin addicts generally range from 35 deaths per thousand addicts per year to 80 deaths per thousand addicts per year (3).

Those heroin addicts who do not die are often believed to discontinue their use of heroin as they become older. Winick (4) noted that relatively few addicts past 40 appeared in official records of treatment agencies and the police. He hypothesized that these "maturing" addicts had resolved the developmental problems that led them to become addicts and thus no longer needed to use heroin.

The conventional wisdom that an addict either dies from addiction related causes or discontinues use of heroin is perhaps best seen in a death study of Musto and Ramos (5). They followed up persons who were enrolled in the New Haven morphine maintenance clinic from 1918 to 1920. They noted that these addicts typically did not die from addiction related causes and lived to an average age similar to other persons from the same social class backgrounds. From this they concluded that the addicts must have discontinued their use of narcotics.

There have been a few studies that reported the existence of elderly heroin addicts (e.g., 6–9), but the tactics that heroin addicts might use to achieve old age are largely unknown. In this chapter we will present self-report data on such tactics and a brief pheno-monological description of what it means to be both elderly and addicted to narcotics.

METHODS

The study originated when we first noticed significant numbers of elderly patients enrolled in New York City methadone mainte-nance programs. In 1979 there were 286 patients between the ages of 55 and 59, 282 patients between 60 and 69, 53 patients between the ages of 70 and 79 and five patients between 80 and 86. An oral history project was implemented to obtain the life histories of these elderly patients. The primary purposes of the project were to determine the needs for special services of elderly methadone patients and to complement the history of addiction in America with data from the addicts' own experiences. (See 10 for a more detailed description of the oral history project.)

The sampling strategy was to obtain life history interviews of all patients with 20 or more years of illicit addiction over age 55 who were willing to be interviewed. The subjects were offered $15 for the initial two hour interview session, and an additional $10 for any additional sessions that were needed. We have received excellent cooperation from the subjects, with only five refusals out of 78 non-Chinese who were approached. Because of language and cultural barriars, only three of the twenty Chinese subjects who were asked to participate agreed. To date we have obtained 81 interviews. For convenience reasons, we first went to clinics that had relatively larger numbers of eligible subjects. The only bias that this convenience strategy apprears to have caused is a rela-tively higher percentage of Chinese subjects approached in the early stages of the data collection than would have occurred had subjects been approached in a randomly selected order.

The interviews were semi-structured and wide ranging. They covered such topics as early development, family relationships, drug use history, criminal and work history, the perceived effects of various historical events on their addiction careers. Supplementary interviews were also conducted with clinic staff to assess the status of the patients within the clinic and to obtain the staffs' perception of any special problems that these elderly patients may have.

RESULTS

Prior to World War II, most narcotic addicts in New York City were white; after the war, the ethnicity of low income areas where narcotics are available changed, and Black and Hispanic addicts came to outnumber Whites. These trends are reflected in the year of onset of addiction among our subjects. Whites predominate among those who were addicted prior to World War II, and Blacks and Hispanics predominate among those who were first addicted after the war. Eighty-six percent of the Whites we interviewed were addicted prior to 1945, while only 38 percent of the Blacks were addicted by then.

In terms of the longevity of these subjects, seven reasons emerged that appear related to their achieving their present age. First, the parents of these subjects also were long-lived. The subjects typically reported one or both parents living into their seventies, eighties or nineties. We have not yet estimated the expected life span of these subjects from the life spans of their parents, but the subjects do appear to have a strong genetic advantage towards long life.

Second, they reported being able to obtain good supplies of narcotics throughout their life of addiction. We had first hypothesized that long-lived addicts might be those who used narcotics relatively infrequently, with long periods of abstinence between periods of addiction. The opposite was the case. These addicts reported that they were almost always able to obtain supplies of good quality narcotics, even during periods of relative scarcity such as World War II. These subjects did not survive by using narcotics relatively infrequently, they probably used greater quantities of purer narcotics than their peers who did not survive to old age.

A third reason for longevity was the ability of most of the subjects to obtain narcotics while largely avoiding the violence common in the street narcotic subculture. Many were middle-level narcotic dealers, high-class prostitutes, confidence men, or "businessmen" dealing in stolen merchandise. They generally lived by their wits rather than their willingness to use force to obtain money. Consequently, they were more able to avoid associating with persons prone to resolve interpersonal disputes through violent means. This undoubtedly contributed to both physical and mental health.

The fourth apparent reason for longevity among this group was their concern for cleaning the needles used for injecting narcotics. Contaminated needles are often the reason for a wide variety of infections in narcotic addicts. These include hepatitis, tetanus, endocarditis, and numerous other infections that lead to skin abscesses. The majority of the subjects we interviewed in this study showed a concern for clean needles that verges on fanaticism compared to typical addicts. Most of our subjects would refuse to share needles with other addicts and used alcohol and/or boiling water to disinfect the needles. They were well aware of the health risks associated with frequent injections and took all reasonable measures to reduce those risks while continuing the injections.

The fifth apparent reason for the longevity of this group of narcotic addicts was their moderate use of non-opiate drugs, particularly alcohol. Many addicts today are addicted to alcohol as well as heroin. Most subjects in this study who were 60 and older reported very moderate use of alcohol. Patients between the ages of 55 and 60 often had life-threatening alcohol-related health problems. We honestly do not expect many of these patients in the 55 to 60 age group to reach age 65. The alcohol problems were particularly severe among Black males.

The sixth apparent reason for longevity among these subjects was the manner in which they moderated their use of heroin. It was noted above that these subjects used consistently without great periods of abstinence. When they were using, however, they "were not greedy" in their use. Most used enough to avoid withdrawal and to obtain some degree of a high, but did not go on binges where they would quickly use all of the heroin available to them at a given time. They did not try to get the biggest high possible by injecting very large amounts of heroin, and they were capable of saving heroin for use during the latter part of a day or the next morning. This manner of using heroin would greatly reduce the chances of overdosing. Since they were using short acting opiates, the subjects had to develop a strict daily routine for injections or else tolerate mild early withdrawal symptoms if taking a shot at a particular time became inconvenient. To have a reliable supply and reserve of narcotics that could be used at their discretion was an important factor in their day to day functioning. This style of using illicit narcotics implies that the person had a reasonable degree of control over his or her use, despite physical dependence upon the drug.

The final reason for longevity in this group of addicts is the availability of methadone treatment within the last fifteen years. Many of these subjects were among the patients who entered methadone treatment during the late 1960s and early 1970s. They were becoming too old to hustle drugs in the illicit market. Many of them had developed networks of physicians who would supply them with narcotics. These physicians, however, also tended to be older and were either retiring or dying. Thus the patients were rapidly losing their ability to obtain a supply of high purity narcotics. What they would have done if they had not been able to enter methadone maintenance treatment is not clear, but after a long life of using narcotics (including many short periods of abstinence), it is unlikely that they would have been able to function well without a supply of high quality narcotics.

The patients' participation in methadone maintenance not only is a major factor in their current physical health, but also in their current social lives. Most of these patients have outlived their peers. For many of them, the methadone maintenance clinic is their major place of social interaction. They live alone and tend not to participate in organized activities for senior citizens because of fears of social discrimination if their status as methadone patients were to become known. Even those patients who have living relatives will often hide their status as patients from relatives because of the fear of disapproval. An interesting example of this is a 65 year old woman who has not told her mother, who is over 90, that she is on methadone. The clinic is thus the one place where they may be open about their addiction history and their current status as methadone patients without fear of social disapproval.

One program, the Lower Eastside Service Center, has established a lounge for its elderly Chinese methadone patients. These patients were generally isolated within the Chinese community, and the lounge provides the patients primary opportunity for social interaction. The men meet daily at the lounge and prepare meals together.

Most patients interviewed were in good physical health. Some did have serious health problems. The medical problems among these patients are those often found among the aging, and include cardiac diseases, arthritis, cancer and diabetes. The clinic physicians' opinions were that the prevalence of these conditions among these patients occurred at approximately the expected rates for their age group. As noted earlier, alcohol related health problems were rare among the patients over 65. Over 90 percent of the patients had been heavy smokers during their lives and smoking-related health problems (cardiac illness and cancer) were relatively frequent among those who were disabled. It is ironic that after using illicit narcotics for most of their adult lives, it is the use of tobacco that will be a major cause of death for many of these patients.

The economic situations of these patients are generally marginal. Most depend upon public assistance payments. Some are able to supplement public assistance with part-time employment. Only four were economically comfortable, a retired businessman, a patient who is currently employed and earning $20,000 per year, and two writers. Again, there is some similarity among these patients and the elderly in the nation as a whole, who are often living at a mere subsistence level. The frequency of economic deprivation among these patients does, however, appear to be higher than the general population.

Within the clinics, the elderly are usually considered to be "model" patients. They do not abuse non-opiate drugs, they do not commit crimes, and they do not cause difficulties for the staff. The only administrative problem associated with these patients comes from trying to obtain proper medical and nursing home care for them when this is needed. Medical personnel outside of the clinics often share the same prejudices against methadone patients that are found in society in general. They also often do not have any specialized knowledge in how medical treatment for a patient on methadone should differ, or *not* differ, from medical treatment for a patient not receiving methadone.

The bias against methadone patients is most clearly seen in the former nursing home regulations in New York. Under these regulations, any person receiving medical treatment for narcotic addiction may be arbitrarily barred from a nursing home. Trying to get nursing homes to accept methadone patients and to provide a means of supplying their needed medication was a difficult task. The State Division of Substance Abuse Services has worked to change the nursing home regulations and new regulations were to be adopted in 1983.

DISCUSSION

A life history research design does not permit a rigorous determination of the relative importance of the various reasons that appear related to longevity among these subjects. Nevertheless, the attitudes towards narcotics and their methods of use deserve special comment. The standard image of narcotic addiction is a combination of seeking intense euphoria and of avoiding the discomforts of withdrawal. All other aspects of life are to be subordinated to these two motivations. These long-lived narcotic users seem to have had a very different style of using narcotics. It might best be described as a "self-maintenance" program. As noted previously, they "were not greedy" in their use of narcotics. They were capable of spacing their available narcotics over time, rather than having a binge use pattern aimed at staying as high as possible until the supply was exhausted. Also as noted above, since they were using short acting narcotics they had to have a reliable supply, develop a strict daily regimen for use or tolerate mild symptoms of withdrawal if they veered from their schedule. These subjects did not merely alternate between being stoned and being in withdrawal. Their use of opiates was "controlled" to the extent that they were capable of effective functioning in a wide variety of life areas.

Creating a self-maintenance program with an illicit, short acting narcotic such as heroin, morphine or dilaudid is not an insignificant accomplishment. Many who tried became binge users; many did not not survive to the ages of our subjects. It is not a task that is socially valued in our society, however, and even though they no longer use illicit drugs, they still face severe social discrimination and limitations in their access to needed health care.

SUMMARY

Although old age and opiate addiction are often considered to be mutually exclusive, there are considerable numbers of elderly addicts attending methadone maintenance clinics. In order to study the tactics involved in their ability to reach old age, patients from 55 to 86 years of age, with a history of 20 or more years of addiction, were interviewed. Seven major factors emerged. These were: genetic advantage, living by wits rather than by force, ability to obtain good supplies of narcotics, concern for cleanliness of needles, moderate use of non-opiate drugs and alcohol in particular, ability to hold drugs in reserve and not binge, availability of methadone maintenance treatment.

REFERENCES

1. Stephens, R. C., Haney, C. A., and Underwood, S. *Drug taking among the elderly.* P. Washington, D.C.: U.S. Dept. of Health and Human Services, 1982.
2. Kandel, D. B. Convergences in prospective longitudinal surveys of normal populations. In D. B. Kandel (Ed.), *Longitudinal Research on Drug Use.* New York: Hemisphere Publishing Corp., John Wiley, 1978.
3. Des Jarlais, D. C. Research design, drug use and death: Cross study comparisons, (in press).
4. Winick, C. Maturing out of narcotic addiction. *Bulletin on Narcotics,* 1962, 14(1), 1–7.
5. Musto, D., and Ramos, M. Notes on American History: A follow-up study of the New Haven Morphine Maintenance Clinic of 1920. *NE J of Medicine,* 1982, 304(118), 1071–1077.
6. Capel, W. C., and Peppers, L. G. The aging addict: A longitudinal study of known abusers. *Addictive Diseases,* 1987, 3, 389–403.
7. Capel, W. C., Goldsmith, B. M., and Waddell, K. J. et al. The aging narcotic addict, an increasing problem for the next decades. *J. Gerontology,* 1972, 27, 102–106.

8. Pascarelli, E. F. Drug abuse and the elderly. In J. H. Lowinson and P. P. Ruiz (Eds.), *Substance Abuse: Clinical Problems and Perspectives.* Baltimore: William and Wilkins, 1981.
9. Pottieger, A. E., and Inciardi, J. A. Aging on the street: Drug use and crime among older men. *Psychoactive Drugs,* 1981, 13, 199–210.
10. Courtwright, D. T., Joseph H., and Des Jarlais, D. C. Memories from the street: Oral histories of elderly methadone patients. *Oral History Review,* 1981, 9, 47–64.

Chapter 15

THE ELDERLY IN METHADONE MAINTENANCE

Emil F. Pascarelli

Ten years ago, few of us involved in the treatment of addictive disorders would have imagined a meeting such as this taking place. Furthermore, we did not comtemplate having to deal with a population of elderly people on methadone maintenance therapy now facing the progressive losses associated with growing older. One of the early papers to recognize this problem appeared in the Journal of Gerontology in 1972. In it Capel and Goldsmith (1) interviewed a group of elderly methadone patients in New Orleans, recognizing that very little was known about this group. They discerned that a substantial number of elderly opioid addicts remain hidden in the community continuing either to use heroin or legally manufactured substances such as Dilaudid, usually obtained through street sources. At that time a number of them began to trickle in to the methadone programs, in a sense happy to find a more economically feasible haven. In 1974 we began to recognize the problem and its potential for growth when we looked at the New York City statistics. At that time 0.005 percent of 34,000 persons on methadone were over 60 years of age (171 people). By 1976, 0.007 percent of 35,000 persons were over 60 years of age (245 people). By 1979 1.1 percent of 30,000 people on methadone were over 60 (340 people). Today that figure has gone up to around 2 percent. With substantial numbers of people in methadone treatment between the ages of 50 and 60, it is easy to see that the number of elderly opioid users will continue to increase substantially.

In the early sixties, when methadone was becoming an acceptable tool in the treatment of opioid addiction we still held to the maturing hypothesis, which espoused the idea that opioid addicts burn out or die before they get old. While to a certain extent this may be true, we are now aware that there is a significant elderly opioid addicted population as well as those abusing other drugs and alcohol. Obviously, if the maturing out process were entirely true, there would be no need for me to be speaking today.

Let us examine some interesting new data to come out of the New York State Division of Substance Abuse Services (DSAS) conducted by Herman Joseph and Don DesJarlais of that organization in conjunction with David Courtwright, Chairman of the History Department of the University of Hartford (2). Their direct tape interviews with over 80 Methadone clients aged 58 to 81 and the establishment of a tape archive represent an important contribution to this field. And while they confirm many of our own observations they have brought many new and fascinating facts to light. From a historical standpoint they note from these interviews that cheap and pure drugs were available in port cities like New York during the 1920's and 1930's. This allowed many addicts to support their habits without resorting to crime. This ties in with our earlier observations at Roosevelt Hospital regarding the requests by elderly addicts for high doses of methadone, even up to 180 mg daily—this, of course, until federal regulations lowered the maximum dose. During the 1910s and 1920s in New York City, narcotic traffic was dominated by Jewish and Chinese entrepreneurs who operated in a non-violent and businesslike fashion. During the 1930s the Italian Mafia took over the drug traffic in a violent manner. The result was an increase in price and a decrease in drug purity. Another interesting fact was the existence until 1940 of a wealthy elite subculture of white opium smokers which included successful gangsters, businessmen, politicians, union leaders, chorus girls and prostitutes. Of course, among the Chinese, both opium and heroin smoking took place, the latter being called "chasing the dragon." Indeed it is this preference for non-invasive routes of drug administration that may account for the large number of elderly Chinese addicts. Courtwright, Joseph and DesJarlais' interviews (2) also yielded the interesting fact that the widely held concept of a panic during World War II relating to a lack of available drug supply was not entirely true. Many had sufficient connections to obtain adequate supplies during that period and not just by boiling down paragoric or by stealing medical supplies. It should be noted that during this period all countries suffered from a shortage of naturally grown supplies. Indeed, this led the Germans to the synthesis of methadone in 1946.

After WWII, the price of drugs continued to climb. Groups like the Chinese continued in their old patterns in a socially condoned environment. Others were forced into the streets to become petty criminals and commit crimes against property to pay for their drugs.

The next question we must ask ourselves is what are the characteristics of these surviving older addicts that allowed them to reach old age? While virtually all in this population are cigarette smokers and many actually died of that addiction, the indiscriminate use of other drugs by older opioid addicts, alcohol included, has not been a severe problem. We have noted that a few of the elderly continue to use marijuana and have even described two cases of antidepressant abuse. (3) Certain characteristics emerge in this group. These include:

1. A history of scrupulousness in the use of needles and syringes, thereby avoiding the dangers of abscesses, endocarditis and hepatitis. Again, the Chinese group tends to use the non-invasive routes.
2. A history of purchase of supplies from reliable contacts or physicians. Furthermore, they indicated that they were not greedy about their drugs. Alcoholism was not a severe problem, although some had a history of periods of drinking. This undoubtedly contributed to survival since alcoholism far eclipses opioid abuse as a devastating problem even among the elderly.

Finally, we must attempt to describe the present day characteristics and problems of the elderly now in methadone treatment:

1. Our observations and the interview studies suggest that elderly patients in methadone treatment are poor and socially isolated. They tend to be secretive about their past history and their present status in methadone maintenance. In other words, they don't tell friends or relatives about their drug involvement.

2. Patients, especially those in their 60's or 70's, have difficulty coping with progressive physical and social losses.
3. The home and family and friends have always been secondary in these people's lives; consequently, the aging addict relies on public assistance and often lives alone in substandard housing. This magnifies the importance of the methadone clinic as a place where these people don't have to cover up and can let down their hair and socialize among peers.
4. The day comes for many when a nursing home placement must be addressed. The New York State Hospital Code (Chapter V, Subchapter A, Article 4) allows nursing home operators to restrict "a patient suffering from narcotic or alcohol addiction or habituation to depressants or stimulant drugs." While a substantial number of old or disabled methadone patients find their way into nursing homes, their placement has not always been easy. Finally, experience at the Roosevelt Hospital program has shown us that prior to placement, many formerly pleasant and cooperative patients become uneasy, belligerent, hostile and manipulative, reflecting the stress they were undergoing as a result of relocation. This stress is compounded by a tendency on the part of the hospital or nursing home staff to want to detoxify the patient. It is important that these patients be allowed to remain on the maintenance program.

All the answers are not yet in on the elderly opioid addict and clearly, new problems will emerge as new groups of methadone patients mature; however, a profile is emerging and a way to proceed has been defined. This can lead to better care for the increasing numbers of elderly in methadone treatment.

SUMMARY

By the mid-seventies, it became clear that the "burn out" hypothesis for old opioid users could not be supported. All drug addicts did not just mature out or die, they indeed grew older and are now a part of our aging population. This paper explores the adaptive life styles of these addicts and the support systems which allow them to survive. In addition, the characteristics of this special population which demand the attention of health care planners are outlined.

REFERENCES

1. Capel, W. C., Goldsmith, B. M., and Waddell, K. J. et al. The aging narcotic addict, an increasing problem for the next decades. *J. Gerontology*, 1972, 27:102–106.
2. Courtwright, D. T., Joseph, H., and DesJarlais, D. C. Memories from the street: oral histories of elderly methadone patients. *Oral History Review*, 1981, 9, 47–64.
3. Pascarelli, E. F. In Substance Abuse, Clinical Problems & Perspectives Ed. Lowinson, J. H. and Ruiz, P. The Elderly, Chapter 60. Williams and Wilkins, Baltimore, 1981.

Chapter 16

AGING AND ALCOHOLISM:
A 15-YEAR FOLLOW-UP STUDY

Merton M. Hyman

INTRODUCTION[1]

A number of issues regarding the course of alcoholism have elicited wide differences of opinion among those involved in the treatment and study of alcoholism. These include: (1) Is the typical course of alcoholism one of progressive deterioration, "maturation" in middle age, or a leveling off of problems until death? (2) Do some alcoholics become moderate non-problem drinkers in later years? (3) What are the relative contributions of patient characteristics and of treatments (or other interventions) to various outcomes? (4) How valid are the results of short-term follow-up studies?

Because my study entailed a 15-year follow-up of a cohort of alcoholics, all of those who were aged 60+ at follow-up had already had serious alcohol-related problems, before middle age. In addition, for purposes of analysis, the "older" alcoholic group included those who would have been aged 60+ at follow-up if they had lived, as well as those aged 60+ who were still alive.

I am indebted to Mr. Frank Durkin M.S.W., Director of Social Services of Roosevelt Hospital, who gave me permission to examine clinic files, and the official backing of the Social Service Center for the study; and to his Assistant, Ms. Mary Lawrence, who interviewed wives and sisters of former clients

[1]Space restrictions will only allow for presentation of selected data from some of the analyses that were done; complete information and data tables may be obtained by writing the author.

INTAKE

Characteristics of Clients at or Before Intake

The study group consisted of all the white male residents of Middlesex County, NJ, aged 30–54, who had made one or more visits to the Alcoholism Treatment Center (a County-run outpatient clinic of Roosevelt Hospital, Metuchen, NJ) and whose cases were closed for the first time in 1958. The number of cases in this cohort was 54.

Characteristics of the cohort included: Education—26 percent had completed, and 22 percent had some high school; Occupational level—19 percent had white-collar and 33 percent had skilled manual occupations; Work status—33 percent had no regular work and 30 percent experienced poverty during most of the two years before intake; Living arrangements—63 percent were living with wives and 19 percent with kin during most of the two years before intake; Medical condition—56 percent had had recorded respiratory, 56 percent digestive, 62 percent neurological (including past detoxications) impairments or symptoms, and 25 percent had had adult civilian injuries (including healed fractures); Antisocial behavior—37 percent had reportedly been physically belligerent and 46 percent reportedly had serious or repeated (3+ arrests) trouble with the law; Previous treatment involvement—48 percent alcoholism rehabilitation (REHAB) hospitals, 26 percent psychiatric hospitals, 9 percent pastoral counseling, 43 percent Alcoholics Anonymous (AA), and 15 percent ambulatory professional psychological help.

For the analysis I wished to do, such public REHAB samples or cohorts, especially outpatient, are much superior to samples or cohorts defined by a particular problem (e.g. arrests, detoxications) or confined to particular characteristics such as being employed, married or well-to-do or living on skid row. I wished to analyze these variables in relation to outcome as well as to each other. It is also less hazardous to generalize about treated alcoholics with such varied samples or cohorts.

A cluster analysis (based on third order correlation matrices) of social and medical characteristics and experiences at or before intake (but not including early life-cycle achievement characteristics such as education and occupational type before downward mobility) yielded three clusters: 1. overall social-economic-health deterioration, 2. aggression-conflict, and 3. hospitalization.

Acute crises such as loss of regular work, debts, and marital separation during the year before intake did not cluster with general deterioration. Furthermore, these acute crises were not associated with unfavorable outcomes as were long-term lack of regular work, poverty, and separation from spouses.

Clinic-Client Interaction

The sources of referral were medical in 52 percent, external authority (employers, welfare or correctional agencies) in 26 percent, and informal in 22 percent. Direct medical outpatient help (e.g., vitamins, tranquilizers, physical examinations) were given to 54 percent, referrals to medical facilities (usually in-patient REHAB) to 59 percent, and social intervention with other parties (e.g. employers, welfare and correctional agencies) were provided for 28 percent. One visit to the clinic was made by 22 percent; 2–4 by 32 percent; 5–10 by 22 percent; and 11+ by 24 percent. The duration of contact was one day in 22 percent from two days to 3.9 months in 31 percent; from 4 months to 2.9 years in 26 percent; and 3+ years in 29 percent. Relatives or friends of 63 percent of the clients visited the clinic at least once.

A cluster analysis of clinic-client interaction variables yielded two clusters: (1) *pressures* (to visit the clinic) including external authority referrals to the clinic, visits by relatives or friends to the clinic, and medical referrals by the clinic, and (2) *services* (rendered by the clinic) including direct outpatient medical help and social intervention by the clinic, numbers of visits to the clinic, and durations of contacts between clients and the clinic.

It appears that pressures by others to visit the clinic may induce a few visits, but clients will only visit frequently if they make use of tangible benefits available.

My impression, in examining clinic files, is that clinic personnel view psychological help (chiefly counseling and group therapy) as the primary function of the clinic. Direct medical help, medical referrals, and social intervention services are viewed as decidedly auxilliary functions. This was quite contrary to the motives of clients: they visit the clinic because of pressure by others or because of desire for direct medical help, medical referrals, or social intervention by the clinic. Desire for "psychological" help (or even for rehabilitation in general) appears to be a very secondary motive (for about 1/3 of the clients).

Age in Relation to Other Antecedent Variables

At intake there were 21, 17, and 16 men aged 30–39, 40–44, and 45–54, respectively. As compared to the younger groups, the older men were less educated (p = 0.003) possibly reflecting historic trends in education, similar in the highest occupational level ever achieved, more often without regular work during most of the two years before intake (p = 0.019), living in poverty (p = 0.088), not living with wife or relatives (p = 0.092), and more frequently had respiratory (p = 0.007) and neurological (p = 0.143) impairments or symptoms. Thus, there was a clear pattern of age being associated with fewer social and economic resources and more health impairments or symptoms, albeit some of the correlations (phis) were only of borderline or marginal significance.

In addition, the older group was more frequently referred to the clinic by medical sources (p = 0.190) or by external authorities such as employees, welfare and correctional agencies (p = 0.044), and made greater use of social intervention services provided by the clinic (p = 0.065).

Most of the variables not describing resources entail some sort of intervention by agencies and institutions in the lives of clients. I had hypothesized that age would be consistently related to interventions, since age was associated with greater general deterioration. The findings show a general trend in that direction but not nearly as strong as that of diminished social, economic, and health resources among the older men.

FOLLOW-UP

Outcomes

Fourteen to sixteen years after intake I was able to locate or certify as dead 48 (89%) of the 54 former clients. Forty were located through phone books, street address and city directories, New Jersey traffic records (Division of Motor Vehicles) or New Jersey death records (Department of Health). Eight (15%) former clients were located, or questions regarding identify on death records resolved, with the help of relatives and friends of former clients (names, phone numbers and addresses of some of these were available in the files of most clients).

All of the six unlocatables were either unemployed at intake or had lost their jobs within a month after intake, and all were living alone at intake or were so within a few months. These characteristics were associated with unfavorable outcomes and probably most unlocatables had had unfavorable outcomes.

Eighteen of the clients had died prior to follow-up. On the basis of previous research[2] I classified nine of the deaths as being probably alcohol-implicated (e.g., cirrhosis, cancer of the upper digestive tract, exposure).

Thus, there were 30 living locatables at follow-up. Four of the men refused to be interviewed and one had been a patient at a psychiatric hospital for 10 years with severe alcohol-related brain damage and could not be interviewed. Interviews were conducted with both the former clients and their wives or relatives in 14 of the cases, with only the clients in 9 cases, and with only relatives in 2 cases. I interviewed the former clients and a woman social worker from the clinic interviewed wives or sisters.

Topics covered by the interviews were: family relations (extended as well as nuclear); leisure and organizational activities; employment and income; health and hospitalizations; ambulatory contact with formal agencies, AA, and helping persons; trouble with the law; traffic accidents and citations (data for the previous 5 years

---

[2]The main investigators relied upon were Schmidt and Delint (1), Brenner (2), and Goodwin (3).

were also available from the N.J. Div. of Motor Vehicles); and drinking practices and changes in these. Some of the questions were focused on the 3 years before follow-up and some on the 14–16 years since intake.

Four of the clients appeared to me, a sociologist with no psychiatric training, as grossly mentally deteriorated. Interviews with kin confirmed these impressions. One seemed borderine deteriorated and one former client had been a "bedfast" psychiatric patient for ten years. These six were considered to constitute a mentally deteriorated group.

Of the 20 mentally alert locatables at follow-up, on whom adequate information was available (there were 4 "refusers"), 5 had been total abstainers during the previous three years and 2 were abstainers with occasional "slips" with very great improvement in life functioning. Seven were frequent drinkers (at least once a week, usually more often) with no reduction in quantity of alcohol consumed and continuing severe problems (alcohol-implicated hospitalizations, lack of regular work or physical belligerence). Five were frequent, but moderated drinkers with great reductions in alcohol consumption (but usually drinking more than the average adult male in the U.S.) and no apparent alcohol-implicated problems. One frequent drinker had less severe alcohol problems at follow-up than at intake, but could not be confidently classified as a non-problem drinker.

Outcome in Relation to Antecedent Variables

Twelve of the cases (5 total abstainers, 2 near-abstainers, and 5 moderated drinkers) were classified as having favorable outcomes, 15 as having unfavorable outcomes which were irreversible (6 mentally deteriorated, 9 alcohol-implicated deaths), and 8 as having unfavorable but reversible outcomes (mentally alert but with continuing problem drinking).

Preliminary tabulations showed that, in relation to antecedent variables, those with irreversible unfavorable outcomes were quite different from those with reversible unfavorable outcomes. Likewise, among those mentally alert, in relation to antecedent variables, abstainers were very different from moderated drinkers. A series of comparisons are presented to examine these different relationships.

IRREVERSIBLE UNFAVORABLE OUTCOMES: There was no clear pattern of non-alcohol-implicated death in relation to antecedent variables. Alcohol-implicated deaths (9 cases) and mental deterioration (6 cases) in relation to antecedent variables showed clear patterns which were similar to each other. I combined these 15 cases under the concept of irreversible unfavorable outcome.

The "irreversibles" as compared to the rest of the cohort (less the 6 unlocatables and 9 who died form non-alcohol-implicated causes) were older ($p = 0.007$), less educated ($p = 0.014$), and lower in occupational level (P = 0.0057); were more often without regular work (P = 0.040), living in poverty (P = 0.127), and not living with wives (0 = 0.070) or any kind of relative (P = 0.133) during most of the two years before intake; and more frequently had digestive ($p = 0.027$) and neurological ($p = 0.142$) impairments or symptoms. They also received lower scores on composite scales of early achievement ($p = 0.018$) and social resources ($p = 0.017$).

Clearly, those with fewer resources before intake were more likely to have irreversible unfavorable outcomes, even if some relations were only of borderline or marginal significance. The future "irreversibles," on the whole, were much older, had much lower early achievements, and had much lower levels of social, economic, and health resources before intake. These differences would surely have been much smaller if the duration between intake and follow-up had been, say, only five years instead of 14–16 years.

A few "intervention" variables were very marginally associated with irreversible unfavorable outcome. However, this analysis provided little support for a hypothesis that interventions by agencies and institutions in the lives of alcoholics were associated with fewer irreversible unfavorable outcomes. As will be seen further on, interventions are indeed associated with fewer irreversible outcomes, but the relationships are quite complex. By contrast, the relations of high levels of resources—as has been presented above—to fewer irreversible unfavorable outcomes are quite straightforward.

ABSTAINERS VS. FREQUENT DRINKERS: Among the 20 mentally alert men on whom adequate data on drinking were available, 7 were abstainers or near-abstainers during most of the three years before follow-up, and 13 were more frequent drinkers. For this analysis, the frequent drinkers included both the continuing problem drinkers and the moderated, non-problem drinkers since they were similar on most antecedent variables.

As compared to the frequent drinkers, the abstainers were older ($p = 0.094$), were more often less educated ($p = 0.044$), and lower in occupational level ($p = 0.048$); without regular work ($p = 0.007$), living in poverty ($p = 0.007$), and less often living with wives or other relatives ($p = 0.176$), during most the two years before intake and more frequently had respiratory ($p = 0.199$) and neurological ($p = 0.146$) impairments or symptoms.

Clearly, future abstainers were much more likely to have fewer resources before intake than future frequent drinkers (among the mentally alert). The future abstainers were older and had lower levels of early achievement, social, economic, and health resources. Men with low levels of resources before intake who did not become total or near abstainers were dead or mentally deteriorated 14–16 years later. It seems surprising, though, that hardly any clients with high resources before intake were abstainers at follow-up.

On the intervention variables, the abstainers had more frequently had stays in REHAB ($p = 0.146$) and psychiatric ($p = 0.199$) hospitals, been in contact with AA ($p = 0.129$), more often used social intervention services provided by the clinic ($p = 0.029$), made more visits to the clinic ($p = 0.176$), and had been in more trouble with the law ($p = 0.054$).

There seems to be some support for a hypothesis that interventions by agencies and institutions in the lives of alcoholics are related to future abstinence. But this pattern is not nearly as strong or consistent as the pattern observed for low levels of resources at or before intake to be associated with abstinence at follow-up.

ABSTAINERS VS. IRREVERSIBLES: The preceding comparisons reveal that both the abstainers and the irreversible subcohorts displayed markedly similar patterns of diminished antecedent resources. Since there was also an indication that the subcohorts tended to differ with respect to the intervention variables, the abstainers (N = 7) and the irreversibles (N = 15) were compared with each other on each of the intervention variables.

As compared to the irreversibles, a greater proportion of abstainers had had trouble with the law ($p = 0.054$), had been in REHAB ($p = 0.098$) and psychiatric ($p = 0.149$) hospitals, and had used the social intervention services provided by the clinic ($p = 0.149$). When these four items were combined into a simple additive scale of Diversified Institutional Intervention, six of the seven future abstainers had scores above 3, whereas 14 of the 15 future irreversibles had scores below 3. This difference in the extent of institutional involvement was highly significant ($p < 0.001$).

CONTINUING PROBLEM DRINKERS VS. MODERATED DRINKERS: Among the 13 mentally alert frequent drinkers, there were 7 continuing problem drinkers, 5 moderated non-problem drinkers, and one client who had reduced problems at follow-up and did not fit into either of the preceding categories. The continuing problem drinkers did not differ from the moderated drinkers at even marginal significance on age or any of the "resource" antecedent variables. The only really strong predictor was physical belligerence. Five of the seven continuing problem drinkers, but one of the five moderated drinkers, had any past indicators of physical belligerence ($p = 0.053$, two-tailed test). Because of the isolated nature of this finding, my interpretation has to be phrased in a very conservative way:

It is not enough for alcoholics to be at a low level of social-economic-health deterioration to become moderated non-problem drinkers after a period of abstinence. They must *also* have not been physically belligerent, which is an aspect of alcohol problems that is not related to general deterioration.

IMPLICATIONS FOR INTERVENTION AND RESEARCH

As most follow-up studies explicitly or implicitly involve evaluations of treatment, the implications of these findings for intervention and research will be discussed jointly.

First, although neither legal pressures, stays in non-REHAB psychiatric hospitals or units (usually for detoxification), and social intervention services are alone adequate for favorable outcomes, each of these adds to its likelihood, Hence, the concept of "interventions' is more useful than that of "treatment" (vis à vis alcoholism, this usually means inpatient or outpatient REHAB).

I speculate that all of these experiences make it harder to deny one's alcoholism; also, in jails and psychiatric hospitals alcoholics meet others who are more deteriorated than themselves, providing a grim picture of their own possible fates if they continue to drink as they have been doing.

Second, if the impacts of different types of interventions are associated with favorable outcomes in a cumulative fashion, the role that a particular intervention experience plays in relation to outcome may not be adequately delineated. It is not surprising that, in a review of 260 studies published during 1952–1971 on follow-ups of alcoholics treated by psychological means, Emrick (4) found no substantial evidence that some types of treatment have, on the whole, higher success rates.[3] Combining experimental or case/control variables with other pre-intake and post-intake interventions should provide investigators with more accurate assessments of the roles that different types of treatment have in relation to outcome.

Third, though alcoholics with fewer resources before intake are more likely than other alcoholics to have irreversible unfavorable outcomes, interventions (especially different types at different times) are not wasted on them. It is among such former clients that institutional interventions are most strongly associated with favorable outcomes. This is one reason to include social data in evaluation studies even when such information is of only peripheral interest to the investigators.

Fourth, some alcoholics do become moderated, non-problem drinkers (almost as many as become abstainers) but they are a "blue ribbon" subgroup. They are characterized by relatively high

---

[3]Pattison (5) suggests that as different types of patients need different types of treatment, some treatments most effective for some alcoholics will not be for others and vice versa. This, he hypothesized, is the reason for weak results in comparing the overall efficiency of different types of treatment. My finding that diversified institutional intervention is strongly associated with favorable outcome among those of lower economic resources at intake is compatible with this view.

levels of social-economic resources and fewer health impairments or symptoms at or before intake[4] and no indication of extent or past physical belligerence (an aspect of problem drinking quite independent of social-economic-health deterioration).

It is important to note that the ideology of the clinic as well as of the Alcohol Treatment Unit of the N.J. Neuropsychiatric Institute of Skillman, NJ (a State-run inpatient REHAB facility, to which at least 80 percent of the clients had gone either before or after intake), was one of recovery through total abstinence.[5] Since almost as many clients recovered via moderated drinking as via abstinence, it does not appear that in order to recover via moderated drinking alcoholics need to be treated in settings wherein recovery via moderate drinking is an acceptable goal. I see a way out of the acrid controversy regarding moderated drinking by former alcoholics. Gear treatment toward abstinence, but don't be surprised or feel that such outcomes represent failures if as many of those treated recover via moderated drinking as via abstinence.

Fifth, antisocial behavior, especially physical belligerence, is not related to the general dimension of social-economic-health deterioration. Antisocial behavior, especially physical belligerence, may require interventions that are not necessary for other alcoholics at similar levels of general deterioration. Furthermore, legal pressures, of limited use regarding general rehabilitation of alcoholics, might be quite effective in reducing antisocial behavior. No assumption should be made that to reduce antisocial behavior, alcoholics must be rehabilitated.

Sixth, what is the more typical course of alcoholism, progressive deterioration or maturation in middle age? The 15 former clients who had died from alcohol-implicated causes or had become

---

[4]Popham and Schmidt (6) also found that those with higher levels of resources at intake were more likely to improve via moderated drinking than were others. The length of time to follow-up was, however, only one year.

[5]As abstinence is the ideological goal of the great majority of REHAB settings, it is quite likely that most of the subjects investigated in the Rand report (7), who had improved via moderated drinking rather than via abstinence have been treated in abstinent-oriented milieux.

Alcoholism, Drug Addiction and Aging

mentally deteriorated by follow-up fit the scenario of progressive deterioration fairly well. They were characterized by a combination of low levels of resources before intake *and* low levels of institutional intervention. The seven total or near abstainers do not at all fit the model of "maturation" in middle age; all of them had been the recipients of a diversity of institutional interventions in their lives (and they are almost all characterized by low levels of resources at or before intake). The five moderated frequent and one borderline drinker were characterized by little general deterioration and no physical belligerence at or before intake. Though not receiving as much institutional intervention as the abstainers, five had been at REHAB hospitals either before or after intake and four had either had serious or repeated trouble with the law or stays at psychiatric hospitals. "Spontaneous" maturation receives little support from these data. The seven continuing problem drinkers, though not yet irreversibly deteriorated, have certainly not "maturated" out of alcoholism.[6]

SUMMARY

A follow-up was conducted circa 15 years after intake on 54 men who had been clients of a public outpatient alcoholism clinic in New Jersey during the late 1950s. Six were unlocated; 18 had died (9 from alcohol-implicated causes); 6 were mentally deteriorated; 4 refused to be interviewed; 7 were abstainers; 7 were continuing problem drinkers; 5 were moderated drinkers; and 1 had reduced problems. Both alcohol-implicated deaths and mental deterioration and abstinence were associated with age, low early achievement, and social-economic-health deterioration at intake. Abstainers, however, had received a variety of institutional interventions in their lives.

---

[6]The most systematic attempt to support the concept of "maturation" in middle age with empirical data was that of Drew (8). However, Drew takes the position that there is not substantial proof that treatment makes a difference in outcome of alcoholics. Even if this were true for one treatment at a time, it might not be true for cumulations of diversified institutional interventions, as the present data suggests.

REFERENCES

1. Schmidt, W., and Delint, J. Causes of deaths of alcoholics. *Quart. J. Stud. Alc.*, 1972, 33, 171–185.
2. Brenner, B. Alcoholism and fatal accidents. *Quart. J. Stud. Alc.*, 1967, 28, 512–528.
3. Goodwin, D. Alcohol in suicide and homicide. *Quart. J. Stud. Alc.*, 1973, 34, 144–156.
4. Emrick, C. A review of psychologically oriented treatment of alcoholism. II The relative effectiveness of treatment vs. non-treatment. *J. Stud. Alc.*, 1975, 36, 88–108.
5. Pattison, E. (Ed.), *Selection of Treatment for Alcoholics.* New Brunswick: Rutgers Center of Alcohol Studies, 1982.
6. Popham, R., and Schmidt, W. Some factors effecting the likelihood of moderate drinking by treating alcoholics. *J. Stud. Alc.*, 1976, 37, 868–882.
7. Pollich, J., Armor, D., and Braiker, H. *The Course of Alcoholism: Four Years After Treatment.* Santa Monica: Rand Corporation, 1980.
8. Drew, L. Alcoholism as a self-limiting disease. *Quart. J. Stud. Alc.*, 1968, 29, 956–967.

Chapter 17

THE EPIDEMIOLOGY OF LATE-LIFE
PROBLEM DRINKING: WHAT A SURVEY SAYS

Allan R. Meyers

INTRODUCTION

For the past several years, my colleagues and I have studied the relationships among drinking, problem drinking, optimism, locus-of-control, and life satisfaction in a random sample of the adult population of Metropolitan Boston, Massachusetts (U.S.A.) (1–2). More recently, we have turned our attention to the drinking behavior of the sub-set of older adults (60 years and older) (3–5).

This chapter begins with a review of the methods and results of our earlier papers, followed by a more detailed analysis of those older respondents who reported that they had drinking problems at the time of the research (late 1977–early 1978). The analysis addresses four of the main themes of the 1982 Coatesville-Jefferson Conference: (1) the prevalence of problem drinking in the sample and the social demographic and psychological risk factors associated with problem drinking; (2) components of the aging process which engender or exacerbate problem drinking among older people; (3) the age at onset of late-life problem drinking; and (4) the alcohol treatment experiences of a general sample of older adults.

This project was supported by grant number R01-AA21333-03 from the National Institute on Alcoholism and Alcohol Abuse. I have received substantial technical advice and constructive criticism from my colleagues at Boston University, most notably Dr. Ralph Hingson, Marc Mucatel, and Timothy Heeren. Neither the funding agency nor my colleagues bear any responsibility for my analysis nor the conclusions I have drawn from the research.

METHODS

Earlier papers provide more detailed descriptions of sampling, surveys, and the characteristics of both the general study sample (N = 5314 adults, aged 18 or older) and the sub-set of those who were at least 60 years old (N = 928) (1–2, 4–5).

Briefly stated, the data were derived from structured interviews with a random sample of the adult population of the Boston, Massachusetts, SMSA. The interview protocol included extensive data on respondents' demographic characteristics, and their assessments of life satisfaction, optimism, and locus-of-control in seven life areas: work, leisure activities, finances, and relationships with spouses, children, other family members, and close friends. There was also a series of questions about respondents' past and current drinking behaviors, contexts of drinking, reasons for drinking, past and current drinking problems, experiences with alcohol treatment programs, and the effects of alcohol upon respondents' lives in reference to seven life areas: work, income, health, and relationships with spouses, children, other family members, and friends.

REVIEW OF PREVIOUS STUDIES

The earlier studies of the older respondents have shown that they drank significantly less alcohol than younger ones, and report significantly fewer alcohol-related problems, both at the time of our survey and in the past (1–4). The reported prevalences of both alcohol use and alcohol-related problems are significantly correlated with age, gender, and national origin — both are more common among young-old (70 years and younger), native-born males. Moreover, each group of older drinkers — those with and without reported alcohol-related problems — showed characteristic patterns of reasons for drinking and contexts of drinking — in terms of time, place, person — and reasons for alcohol use (6). Predictably, those who report problems are significantly more likely than others to drink to the point of inebriation; they also drank significantly more for reasons of "escape" or "mood elevation," and less for reasons related to "sociability" or because they like the taste of alcohol.

Other relationships between late-life drinking and problem drinking and respondents' demographic and social psychological characteristics defy much of the conventional wisdom of both gerontology and the alcohol treatment field (4–5). For example, prevailing theories suggest that older adults who experience such stressful life events as widowhood or forced retirement are more likely to use alcohol and more likely to have alcohol-related problems, as are those who are dissatisfied, frustrated, or bored (7–9). Our data are limited by the fact that they are cross-sectional rather than longitudinal. However, they indicate that older people who are retired, widowed, relatively poor, and generally dissatisfied and pessimistic are, in fact, significantly more likely to abstain from alcohol than their counterparts (5). There are no significant relationships between retirement, widowhood, employment, and alcohol-related problems among older people and only very specific relationships between respondents' social psychological characteristics and the prevalence of alcohol-related problems in old age: those with alcohol-related problems are significantly more likely to be dissatisfied with their relationships with family members, spouses, and close friends; otherwise, their profiles of satisfaction, optimism, and locus-of-control did not differ significantly from those of their counterparts (4).

The previous study of alcohol-related problems among older people included two kinds of problem drinkers: those who indicated that they had a "drinking problem" at the time of the survey (N = 9) and those who, while denying that they had such a problem, indicated that their drinking had made their lives "worse" in at least one of six life areas: marriage, work, income, health, relationships with children, and relationships with close friends (N = 31). Since there were too few respondents to justify separate statistical analysis of either category, they were combined for purposes of analysis. Moreover, their demographic and social psychological profiles are, in most cases, the same (4). There are, however, clear differences between the two, at least in terms of their own images and conceptions of their drinking problems. There is therefore some value in a detailed analysis of each group.

The present analysis concerns only those nine individuals who reported that they had "drinking problems." The small number precludes statistical analysis and poses serious problems of external validity. At the same time, it allows a more careful review of respondents' answers to the formal interview protocol, and also their spontaneous open-ended comments to the interviewers. The sample has another important advantage: it was identified in a general, rather than a clinical population. Respondents are therefore free of the selection bias that characterizes much of the earlier research in the field (4–5).

RESULTS

Demographic and Social Risk Factors
Associated with Problem Drinking among Older Adults

In terms of demographic characteristics, the older problem drinkers in the sample were highly homogenous; they were significantly more likely to be "young-old" (i.e., 70 years old or younger) than their counterparts, native-born, and male. Only one problem drinker was a woman, and the oldest was 70 years old. They were also significantly more likely to be White, Irish or Irish-American, and Catholic. This is not to say that there were no problem drinkers with other ethnic, religious or racial backgrounds: there was, for example, one person of Eastern European background, one Black person, one Jewish person, and one who identified himself as a member of the Society of Friends. However, none of these appears more than once.

In this respect, it is very important to stress that Older Bostonians are a special population in terms of ethnicity and national origin: there is a very large Irish-American component and a relatively small number of non-Whites (10). It is therefore extremely important to resist any temptation to generalize about ethnic differences in late-life drinking on the basis of these results.

Individual problem drinkers reported that they had had alcohol-related problems with spouses and children (see page following). However, aggregately, there was no significant relationship between problem drinking and such other important demographic variables as marital status, household composition, social interaction, income, occupation, or employment status (i.e., whether a respondent was employed or retired). In fact, older problem drinkers live in a range of family circumstances. Two lived alone and reported that they had little social interaction, but others reported that they lived in conjugal households of two individuals, two-generational households with parents or children, and in one case, a three-generation household with spouse, children and children-in-law, and a grandson. In the same way, some were retired, some disabled, and some gainfully employed. They had, or had had, a range of occupations which included a trucker, a maintenance person, a dietician, a teacher, two attorneys, and an architect. Their incomes reflected a corresponding range, from those who relied upon Social Security payments as their sole sources of income to those who reported annual incomes of $25,000 or more (1977–1978 dollars). However, in no case was there a systematic relationship between any of these factors and problems with alcohol use.

Social Psychological Risk Factors

The only significant differences in life satisfaction between problem drinkers and other older adults in the sample concerned their reported levels of satisfaction with human relationships rather than income or work: those who were problem drinkers were significantly more dissatisfied with their relationships with family members, with spouses, and with close friends. Unfortunately, since these are cross-sectional data, it is not clear whether the deterioration of human relationships was a cause or a consequence of drinking. Moreover, respondents' comments indicate that problem drinking may be either a consequence or a cause of interpersonal stress. In the first case, for example, one person said that, "I married an alcoholic and was a potential alcoholic, so it [the drinking problem] became worse." On the other hand, another said, in reference to his children, that, "They resent it [his drinking]. It can be unpleasant." A third noted that, "My wife doesn't approve. I've already told you [the interviewer] more than she knows about my drinking. Occasionally, when I come home and show signs of having been drinking, she is upset; she doesn't understand why I can't have just one drink. But then, she is a very controlled person in all ways." Finally, one respondent noted, in reference to the effect of drinking upon her friendships, that drinking made her "emotionally unstable—I was quarrelsome and nasty when I drank."

Effects of the Aging Process

Problem drinkers reported reasons for drinking that were significantly different from those of their problem-free counterparts. Though most reported that they drank for "social" reasons, they were much more likely to report that they drank for "hedonistic" reasons or for reasons of escape (e.g., "oblivion," or to "forget about the rest of the world").

In two cases, their reported reasons for drinking pertained directly to elements of the aging process or the consequences of being old. In one case, a respondent indicated that his main reason for drinking was "health reasons." He elaborated upon this comment later in the questionnaire: "I'd say health reasons [were the most important reasons for drinking]. It's a crutch, of course—but it's the only thing that helps my condition . . . I'm in a lot of pain and medication doesn't seem to help and the only thing that helps is having two or three beers and that's not permanent relief." This same respondent also acknowledged that his drinking complicated his health problems: "I got a lot of ailments [sic] associated with alcohol—diabetes, cirrhosis . . . hypertension. The doctor attributes drinking to part of it."

In the second case, a respondent indicated that the prospect of forced retirement exacerbated a previous drinking problem and caused him to drink in greater quantities than he had previously done before. After a long discussion, in which he told the interviewer that he drank mainly for reasons of "conviviality," he added that the prospect of forced retirement was another factor in his tendency to drink: "There's a certain amount of frustration involved in my drinking . . . my job is quite frustrating at times, especially because of this age thing. My drinking does dull my frustrations."

Age at Onset of Problem Drinking

The interview did not ask explicitly about the age at onset of the respondents' drinking problems. It did ask whether they had had drinking problems in the past. All of the respondents who indicated that they had current drinking problems also indicated that they had had such problems in the past. In some cases, their responses showed that they had such problems for many years and probably for all of their adult lives: one, for example, said, "I have always been an alcoholic," and another indicated that he had been an alcoholic at least from the time of his first marriage.

In other cases, their responses indicated that they had drinking problems at least from the time of middle adulthood. One person, for example, who identified himself as a "recovering alcoholic," who had not drunk in at least ten years, indicated that his drinking problems had begun before marriage and continued until the time of his decision not to drink. What is most significant is the fact that no one of the nine individuals indicated that he or she had begun to drink or had begun to drink in a problem pattern in response to the stresses of aging and old age.

One respondent also made an interesting point about the age at which one identifies the fact that he or she has a drinking problem. This individual, who indicated that the stresses of a threat of forced retirement had exacerbated an existing drinking problem (see previous pages), said that his drinking behavior had not changed substantially, but that his evaluation of that behavior had: "I never got to the point where I acknowledged that it [my drinking] was a problem or an addiction, but the fact is that I never have just one drink. I always have two or three."

Treatment Experiences

Three of the nine problem drinkers indicated that they had controlled their problems and that they were currently abstainers, although all three acknowledged the possibility that they could backslide and resume drinking at any time. One said, quite explicitly, that for her, the temptation was very strong. Two of the three and six others who had not controlled their drinking had received treatment for their drinking. Six had received help from Alcoholics Anonymous (AA) only, one from AA and a psychiatrist, and one from a physician only. One of those who had controlled her drinking problem indicated that she had done so without formal treatment.

Those who had sought treatment were asked to explain why the treatment programs had succeeded or failed. The strongest comments, both positive and negative, concerned A.A. On the one hand an advocate stated, "Had I not gone to A.A., I wouldn't have developed an understanding of myself. . . . Nothing resolves anyone's drinking problem, but . . . A.A. laid out a program and [I] used it and [my] life became better." On the other hand, a detractor felt that "they [the members of the A.A. group] just talked; I didn't need that."

Of those who reported that they had drinking problems, only one was in treatment at the time of the survey, from A.A. He was unenthusiastic about the results: "I called up A.A. a few times, but they weren't very helpful. I got a little message on the phone, but that's it." Of the others, three felt that they had control of their drinking problems, in one case with A.A. assistance (this section), and one was uncertain whether he actually had a drinking problem. Four gave no reasons for not seeking treatment, and one, who reported that he had often participated in A.A. groups, said, quite simply, "Nothing could help me now."

Discussion and Conclusions

The survey data provide a limited profile of the older problem drinkers in terms of age, gender, and certain forms of life satisfaction, but otherwise, they suggest no preeminent social or psychological traits. This is not to say that there may not be other common traits which were not measured by our survey: for example, some critics have suggested that we did not measure respondents' personalities (for example, using the MMPI or another similar inventory) or that we did not measure such traits as boredom, frustration, or loss.

The data also suggest that most older problem drinkers have

relatively long-term drinking problems, though the study cannot specify the actual length of time. Although there is some evidence that factors associated with social and biological aging may aggravate or, perhaps, reactivate pre-existing drinking problems, there is no evidence that people develop new problems in response to the stresses of aging and old age.

Finally, the study suggests that most older problem drinkers have had experience with formal treatment programs, but that they have had only mixed success. What is more significant, only one of those with an uncontrolled problem was seeking treatment at the time of the research.

These data must be interpreted with considerable caution. Although the sample was large, the number of problem drinkers was small, so the possibility of sampling error is great. Moreover, there is the problem of reporting bias that is inherent in any survey research. Finally, there is a danger of making longitudinal inferences from cross-sectional data. However, taking into account all of the problems and all of the caveats, the study suggests certain conclusions about the study and treatment of problem drinking in old age.

First, in reference to treatment for older problem drinkers, the data suggest that most such people are not receiving treatment, though they accept that they have problems. It is not clear whether they need special programs or whether they simply need better access to existing ones. Moreover, insofar as they may need special programs, it may not be for reasons of age. In fact, they are distinguished as much by the fact that they are a group with long-term, residual drinking problems, which have defied previous treatment, as they are by their ages. Therefore, the resilience of their problems may have as much to do with their special need as their old age.

Secondly, since older problem drinkers appear to have long-term problems, rather than problems of more recent onset, the data suggest that the etiology of problem drinking may have more to do with early experiences than with the experiences of aging and old age. We have made a similar point about differences in drinking between younger and older people and among older people in the Boston sample; we have suggested that late-life drinking patterns reflect more the effects of personal and social historical factors (for example: Prohibition, the First and Second World Wars, and ethnic, social, and gender differences) than they do the situational factors of late life (3–5). The same may also be true of problem drinking in old age.

Thirdly, our data suggest that there is no simple process which leads to late-life drinking, nor is there any simple way to characterize those who are at risk. Rather, late-life problem drinking appears to be a contingent response, the essential element of which appears to be a previous history of problem drinking or alcohol-related problems earlier in life: i.e., people with specific demographic and psychological characteristics and histories of problem drinking turn to alcohol in response to certain circumstances. Others, with similar patterns of demographic and psychological characteristics, but without histories of problem drinking, respond to the same circumstances in different ways. This is not to say that they experience less dissatisfaction, frustration, or sadness, but only that they manage those phenomena and respond to them in different ways.

Survey research of general populations will probably not reveal the complexity of this kind of multiple contingent process (11–12). As we have suggested in other papers, these will be elucidated only by more intensive studies, mainly longitudinal studies, of both general populations and those who appear to be at particular risk.

The Veterans Administration (VA), the co-sponsors of the Coatesville-Jefferson Conferences, deal extensively with one apparent high-risk population: young-old, native-born males. Therefore, there is a unique opportunity to contribute significantly to our understanding of the etiology and natural history of problem drinking in old age. One very useful outcome of this conference will be the development of collaborative research using the VA populations, which could contribute significantly to our understanding of the relationships among the use and abuse of alcohol, the process of aging, and the experiences of old age.

SUMMARY

Nine (of 928) older respondents (60 years and older) in a probability sample of the population of Metropolitan Boston, Massachusetts, reported that they had drinking problems at the time of the study (1977–1978). A comparison between their responses to a structured interview protocol and those of their counterparts who reported no problems shows that older problem drinkers are more likely to be young-old (70 years and younger) native-born males; they are also more likely to report low levels of satisfaction with their relationships with family and friends. In some cases, they report that they use alcohol for reasons related to old age and aging, though all of them indicated that their drinking problems had begun earlier in life. Eight of the nine had sought treatment for their drinking problems, two of them with some success. One had controlled a drinking problem without formal treatment, and one was in treatment at the time of the survey.

REFERENCES

1. Hingson, R. et al., Life satisfaction and drinking practices in the Boston metropolitan area. *Journal of Studies in Alcohol*, 1981, 42, 24.
2. Hingson, R. et al. Seeking help for drinking problems: A study in the Boston metropolitan area. *Journal of Studies in Alcohol*, 1982, 43, 273–288.
3. Meyers, Allan et al. Evidence for cohort or generalized differences in the drinking behavior of older adults. *International Journal of Aging and Human Development*, 1981–1982, 14(1), 31–44.
4. Meyers, A. R. et al. The social and psychological correlates of problem drinking in old age. *Journal of the American Geriatric Society*, 1982, 30, 452–456.
5. Meyers, A. R. et al. The social epidemiology of alcohol use by urban older adults. *International Journal of Aging and Human Development*, in press.
6. Meyers, A. R. Reasons for drinking contexts of drinking, and alcohol-related problems in old age. Paper presented at the Annual Meeting of the Northeastern Gerontologic Association, Albany, NY, April 30, 1982.
7. Gomberg, E. L. Drinking and problem drinking among the elderly. In *Alcohol, Drugs, and Aging: Usage and Problems*, No. 1, Institute of Gerontology, University of Michigan, 1980.
8. Brody, J. Epidemiological characteristics of alcoholism in the elderly. *Advances in Alcoholism*, 1981, 2, 7.

9. Schuckit, M. Alcohol and the elderly. *Advances in Alcoholism*, 1980, 1(16), 1–3.
10. Branch, L. *Boston Elders: A Survey of Needs, 1978.* Boston, Mass: Commission on Affairs of the Elderly, 1978.
11. Finney, J., and Moos, R. Life stressors and problem drinking among older adults. In M. Galanter (Ed.), *Recent Developments in Alcoholism* (Vol. II). New York: Plenum, forthcoming.
12. Mishara, Brian.

SECTION V
TREATMENT STRATEGIES

Chapter 18

WHAT WE KNOW, DON'T KNOW AND NEED TO KNOW ABOUT OLDER ALCOHOLICS AND HOW TO HELP THEM: MODELS OF PREVENTION AND TREATMENT

Brian L. Mishara

What is so unique or atypical about older alcoholics? Is it justifiable to create special programs for older persons with alcohol problems, or would it be better to ignore the widespread prejudice that older persons are different and have to be treated specially? Perhaps, older persons are not as unusual as common beliefs suggest, and perhaps the nature of alcohol problems in old age is such that age-related differences are of minimal importance. If this is true, then we are wasting our time seeking specialized books on the topic and had better stop proliferating the false belief that older means different. But, before you return this book to the publisher to demand your money back, perhaps we can spend a few minutes considering what we know and don't know about the effect of adding the adjective "older" to "alcoholic."

Rather than just listing a series of findings and hypotheses without a frame of reference, this chapter presents several models of the development of alcoholism in later life. It is hoped that these models will serve as an interesting basis for discussion. However, it should be noted that they are derived from a highly individualized and prejudiced view of alcoholism and the aging process. While the author must admit that he thinks his point of view is the only logical and sensible approach one could take,

Special thanks are expressed to Francois Labelle for drawing the tables and figures in this chapter.

243

various and sundry skeptics exist who fail to grasp the logic and beauty of the author's conceptualization.

The model starts (see Fig. 18-1) with the development of individual characteristics or traits which may predispose some persons toward abstention and others toward occasional drinking and potential alcoholism. This list is by no means all inclusive, and a debate on the relative influence of these various factors is far beyond the scope of this brief presentation. Of particular note for gerontological issues is the factor, "cohort/generational." This refers to the unique characteristics of people born the same year—hence members of the same cohort group. People born and raised at the turn of the century, because of differences in culture, history, nutrition, education, etc., are different from people born at other historical times. For example, as the generation of persons born during the depression years becomes old, the entire picture of the nature of the elderly population and their behaviors could change. Thus, when we refer to "*the* older alcoholic," we are speaking of a population of persons from a limited number of cohort groups who will be replaced by members of completely different generations.

Thus, according to Figure 18-1, we have early life identifications as abstainers, occasional drinkers, and potential alcoholics. The abstainers start their adult life as non-drinkers, the occasional drinkers consume alcoholic beverages without obvious problems, and the potential alcoholics may either develop alcohol problems or avoid alcoholism because of the nature of their psycho-social environment and the type of experiences they encounter. A potential alcoholic whose business allows for frequent cocktail parties and stints away from home at conferences in places like Coatesville may find it easy to slip into a pattern of alcoholism, especially if things are not going well at home. On the other hand, his life experiences may be such that the opportunity and the extra motivation to turn to a pattern of alcoholism are not present. The question of whether occasional drinkers in early life can slip into the category of "potential alcoholic" is debatable and not of particular gerontological concern at the moment. What interests us here is what happens in later life.

According to several community surveys, most abstainers tend to continue to avoid alcohol, except when a physician suggests that medicinal use to help with sleep or other health problems is indicated. Whereas, it is theoretically possible that abstainers could develop into potential or actual alcoholics, there are no reports indicating a sizable incidence of this developmental change (thus the dotted line in Figure 18-1).

Many people continue occasional drinking patterns throughout their lives. In fact, research suggests that people who drink occasionally have average life expectancies which are *longer* than the life expectancies of abstainers. Still, many older persons who no longer drink report that they stopped drinking as they grew older either because of concern for their health or because they experienced displeasure at the loss of control or diminished cognitive capacities while under the influence. If one conceives of all drinkers as potential alcoholics, this group of occasional drinkers may still benefit from primary prevention efforts (to be described later).

A potential alcoholic who does not develop an alcohol problem in later life is a prime candidate for primary prevention efforts before a pattern of problem drinking occurs. Differentiating between potential alcoholics and occasional drinkers is a very tricky diagnostic question, which will be discussed in a little more depth later on.

The major causal factor related to the development of alcoholism in the later years is the experience of a loss. This loss can be the death of a spouse, loss of a job through retirement, loss of health or physical capacities, or loss of a home due to relocation. Persons who develop alcohol problems in later life enter into the secondary prevention system.

It should be noted that the possibility exists for potential alcoholics to lose their potential or even give up drinking entirely as they experience negative effects of aging or develop health concerns.

People who have long-standing chronic alcoholism problems often do not survive into old age. The high mortality rate among chronic alcoholics is one explanation for the low rates of alcoholism in old age. A second explanation suggests that a number of chronic alcoholics stop drinking because of health concerns, changes in their social situation, or institutionalization (where they simply

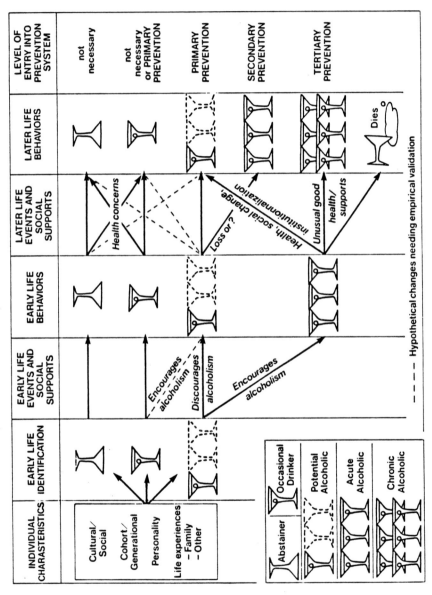

Figure 18-1. Models of the development of alcoholism in later life is portrayed in this illustration.

no longer have access to alcohol). Some find substitutes in psychotropic medications.

Nevertheless, a certain number of chronic alcoholics survive into old age. To do so requires almost superhuman physical stamina coupled with some form of social or institutional support. A good Veterans Administration health-care program with periodic short-lived "cures" would be an example of such a support system for older chronic alcoholics.

Treatment of alcoholism in old age may be divided into the classic typology of primary, secondary and tertiary prevention (see Table 18-I). Primary prevention is aimed at inhibiting the development of alcohol problems before they begin. Primary prevention programs may be focused on the entire population or certain target groups of persons identified as having a high risk. A crucial task for future research is the development of criteria for determining who is at risk and when it is best to intervene. One primary prevention strategy would involve preparation for aging or interventions focused upon nipping alcoholism in the bud before old age. Other primary prevention activities may focus upon certain "alcoholgenic" life events, such as bereavement. Since members of the target population in primary prevention have not yet developed drinking problems, these efforts may be cost effective since one does not have to deal with the presence of addiction to alcohol.

Secondary prevention efforts focus upon new problem drinkers. Unfortunately, candidates for secondary prevention programs are often seen well after the problem has started. People usually seek help when they have a medical crisis (which may or may not be alcohol related) or when they are somehow convinced that they need help. There is the potential for organic impairment, either in the form of a concurrent difficulty or a problem exacerbated by drinking or nutritional deficiencies resulting from the substitution of alcoholic beverages for adequate nutrition. Denial is a common defense, and alcoholics, their families, and various professionals who have contact with them need to be educated to recognize when an alcohol problem is present.

"Tardive referral syndrome" is a term coined by the author to describe the pattern of family protection and denial which leads to late detection and treatment of alcohol problems. For a variety of

TABLE 18-I

MODELS OF PREVENTION AND TREATMENT OF ALCOHOLISM IN OLD AGE

	CLIENT CHARACTERISTICS				
	FOR WHOM?	WHEN?	CLIENT'S COGNITIVE CAPACITIES	CLIENT'S IDENTIFICATION AS HAVING AN ALCOHOL PROBLEM	SPECIAL CLIENT RESOURCES
PRIMARY PREVENTION	- Entire population - High risk groups	- Before old age - Early old age - Specific life events (eg. retirement, bereavement)	Usually not a factor	None	- Cultural and cohort group characteristics - Lack of alcohol dependance
SECONDARY PREVENTION	New problem drinkers	- Medical crisis - Person/family identifies problem as needing help	Possible organic impairment	- Education necessary for identification - Frequent denial - Tardive referral syndrome	- Family/social supports - Willingness
TERTIARY PREVENTION	Chronic problem drinkers: - Life long alcoholics - "Chronicized" in later years	- Social supports fail - Medical crisis - Police/agency insists (- Winter approaching)	- Usually organic impairment - Possible "psychopathic" manipulative behaviors	Identification already present (with or without denial)	Experience at survival

reasons, families and clients often seem to conspire to avoid seeking help until the problem is so severe that there is little choice — something must be done. The frequent existence of family support and the client's possible willingness to seek help are special resources which increase the potential for success.

Tertiary prevention efforts do not attempt to cure alcoholics — the goal is simply to reduce the impact of alcoholism on the life of the alcoholic and society. Chronic alcoholics may enter the tertiary prevention system when social supports fail, they are picked up by the police, or they enter a hospital in a medical crisis.

In tertiary prevention, organic impairment is almost always present. Only the most skilled neuropsychologists can differentiate between organic impairment due to alcoholism, concurrent organic impairment unrelated to alcoholism, and reversible brain syndromes which are readily treatable. Older chronic alcoholics have tremendous survival skills, which allow them to successfully manipulate many an unsuspecting professional.

Primary prevention programs consist of efforts to reduce the incidence of alcoholism. As shown in Table 18-II, programs can involve society at large or specific target populations defined as "at risk." The definition of what constitutes a high-risk group remains an important task to accomplish before efficient primary prevention programs can be undertaken. Do certain types of people have a predisposition toward alcoholism in old age? On the other hand, should high-risk groups be defined on the basis of critical life events or social-environmental circumstances? Primary prevention of alcoholism need not be conducted by people in the alcoholism treatment business. Perhaps interventions such as improving housing quality, pre-retirement planning, outreach to the isolated elderly, new career programs in later life, and aid to families with dependent older persons could all reduce the incidence of alcoholism in old age. Other more radical and controversial prevention efforts might include making psychotropic medications which are less harmful than alcohol readily available. For example, marijuana might offer a viable alternative for older persons who wish to seek a chemical solution to their miseries with fewer negative health implications.

Secondary prevention efforts are aimed at reducing the prevalence of alcoholism. The focus is upon acute alcoholics and the goal is a lasting cure. Clients need to be convinced to seek help. When a family is involved, it is often a family member rather than the potential client who makes the initial contact. If family and social supports are limited, the client is typically pressured into

TABLE 18-II

MODELS OF PREVENTION AND TREATMENT OF ALCOHOLISM IN OLD AGE

	PROGRAM CHARACTERISTICS			
	FOCUS	ACTIVITIES	PROGRAM IDENTIFICATION WITH ALCOHOL ABUSE	CASE FINDING
PRIMARY PREVENTION	- Society - High risk groups	- Education - Consultation - Advocacy - Social change	Not necessary	- Society wide programs - Identify high risk groups - Identify critical life events (crises?) or developmental stages
SECONDARY PREVENTION	- Families - Clients	- Outreach - Family support - Crisis intervention - Direct treatment - Follow-up and follow-through - Medical care	Debatable	If has family/support system: - family initiates contact - client is convinced or pressured to obtain help If limited social supports: - client is convinced to seek help (e.g. by physician) - crisis event leads to treatment (e.g. accident/hospitalisation)
TERTIARY PREVENTION	Clients	- Sheltered environment - Direct treatment - Medical care - Creating non-institutional alternatives	Necessary	Habitual referral methods: - self - police - interested parties - social service agencies - hospital/medical

getting help by some other interested party, such as a physician or case worker. Often, a medical crisis leads to the realization that alcoholism is a problem.

In the secondary prevention model it is subject to controversy whether an intervention effort should or must be labeled as a special "alcoholism" program. For many families and clients, the idea of going into a general hospital for some "physical care" seems more socially acceptable than telling friends that you are going to the "addiction treatment program." Others feel that unless the problem is openly identified as "alcoholism," avoidance or denial of the nature of the problem inhibits treatment. Alcoholics Anonymous, which can be considered as providing both secondary and tertiary prevention services, strictly adheres to this point of view.

Tertiary prevention is aimed at the chronic alcoholic. Often, the client is coerced into accepting treatment. The activities in tertiary prevention constitute the majority of available services for older alcoholics.

Now, let us turn to a comparison of the three models of prevention (see Table 18-III). Each level of prevention suffers from inherent difficulties. In primary prevention, cultural and cohort group characteristics are often so strong that efforts to change cultural patterns are futile. People who are used to drinking regularly may resist suggestions that it would be best to cut back for health reasons as they age. On the other hand, cultural differences may also inhibit certain populations from developing alcohol problems in the later years.

Similarly, the alcohol industry is so solidly entrenched in our society that it may be difficult to avoid the tendency to overindulge in such a widely available and inexpensive a means of self-destruction. So far, there have been few major efforts to alleviate the social differences between older and younger persons. Is it possible to prevent alcoholism without attacking the major causes of discontent for the elderly in our society?

Despite these difficulties, primary prevention efforts seem the most promising of the three levels of intervention. If alcoholism can be prevented *before* it begins, the costs of alcoholism in resources and social ramifications would be greatly reduced. Although primary prevention seems like the most fruitful route to follow, very little is being done due to a general lack of resources provided for primary prevention activities. We live in a society where we are more willing to spend thousands of dollars to try to cure or support a chronic alcoholic but are unwilling to spend hundreds

TABLE 18-III

MODELS OF PREVENTION AND TREATMENT OF ALCOHOLISM IN OLD AGE

	PROGRAM CHARACTERISTICS		
	INHERENT DIFFICULTIES	RESULTS ANTICIPATED	OUTCOMES IF UNSUCCESSFUL
PRIMARY PREVENTION	- Cultural and cohort group characteristics - Societal resistance to social change - Lack of resources	- Reduced incidence - Continued controlled drinking - Abstinence - Enhanced quality of life	- No reduced incidence - Increase in alternative problems (e.g. dependence on psychotropic medication)
SECONDARY PREVENTION	- Tardive referral syndrome - greater physical danger - well established behavior patterns – resistance to change - Return to same psycho-social environment	- Reduced prevalence - Abstinence (controlled drinking ?) - Improved quality of life	- Premature institutionalization - Chronicization - Treatment drop-out - Return to problem drinking after interventions
TERTIARY PREVENTION	Conflict between institutional goal of cure vs client goal of survival	More extended time before next institutional involvement	- Premature death - Immediate re-entry into treatment system following discharge - Permanent institutionalization

to prevent the incidence of alcoholism in the future.

A major difficulty for successful secondary prevention efforts is the "tardive referral syndrome." Families and individuals tend to avoid seeking help until it is almost too late. This tendency results in a higher proportion of physical illness related to alcohol abuse and increased difficulties in providing successful treatment. A second major problem is the common practice of returning clients to the same psycho-social environments which brought about their problems in the first place.

In tertiary prevention the major inherent difficulty is the basic conflict between the institutional goal of curing the alcoholic of his illness and the client's goal of surviving to drink again. Clients learn quickly that they must pretend to go along with the institutional goal in order to get out, and institutional staff are usually unable to accept the fact that a success involves simply a more extended time before the client's next institutional involvement.

The results if successful or unsuccessful listed in Table 18-III should be self-evident. It is important to note that both the positive results anticipated and the nature of possible unsuccessful outcomes are different for each of the three levels of prevention.

Now, let us turn to some basic issues. First, who are the potential clients for efforts at prevention and intervention? With regard to primary prevention, we know very little of who becomes an alcoholic in later life. We do know, on the basis of retrospective case reports, that a loss of some type is frequently associated with the onset of drinking problems in old age. Thus, one promising approach to primary prevention would be to focus upon individuals who have experienced a recent loss.

Although we do not have much hard data concerning who becomes an alcoholic, we are beginning to learn about several factors which are related to the amount of alcohol consumption reported by people who are not alcoholics.

For example, in a recent unpublished study that the author completed (with the urban planner, Martin Wexler) of the housing adjustments of a random sample of heads of households over age 65 in the Montreal area, we found that the volume of weekly alcohol consumption was significantly related to housing satisfaction. People less generally satisfied with their housing and people with fewer confidants tended to consume more. Also, among the people who moved recently, those who tended to drink more were those who were less satisfied with their family relations. Among people who had not moved for at least ten years, people who drank more tended to have a greater number of members of their support network living at a distance of over 10-minute's drive away from them. This suggests that the absence of immediate family supports may influence drinking patterns.

For secondary prevention, diagnostic criteria need to be developed to identify older alcoholics. Defining an alcohol problem in old age is not an easy task. Usual criteria for evaluating problem drinking are often not applicable to older persons. For example, consider the constellations of symptoms suggested by Carruth (1973) and their criticisms by Mishara and Kastenbaum (1980):

1. Symptoms developed as a result of drinking, such as debilitating hangovers, blackouts, memory loss and "shakes." When older persons have these symptoms, they may simply be attributed to "growing old" rather than suggestive of an alcohol problem.
2. Psychological dependence on alcohol, defined as the inability to conduct normal everyday tasks without drinking or planning one's life around drink. Persons who are retired are less likely to have much in the way of everyday tasks they need to do. Since older persons tend to drink alone, the psychological dependence may go unnoticed.
3. Health problems related to alcohol use. Older persons tend to have more chronic health problems anyway.
4. Financial problems related to alcohol use. The majority of older persons already have financial problems.
5. Problems with spouse or relatives as a result of alcohol use. Widowhood is common in old age and the solitude resulting from a loss of spouse or relatives may initiate a drinking problem.
6. Problems with friends and neighbors as a result of alcohol use. This is limited by patterns of drinking alone.
7. Problems on the job as a result of drinking. What about people who are retired?
8. Belligerence and problems with police or the law as a result of drinking. A tendency to drink at home and protection from families may limit these problems.

More adequate means of identifying older problem drinkers need to be developed. Williams (1973) found that many older problem drinkers are not recognized as alcoholics by treatment agencies even through they receive help for medical or social problems stemming from their drinking.

Although it is clear that losses have been endured by a large proportion of older persons who develop alcohol problems, there are no hard data which allow us to determine why some older persons turn to the bottle while others are able to endure and flourish despite the losses sustained. In the process of bereavement following loss, it is normal to go through an extended period of time when one's emotional life is disrupted (Mishara & Riedel, 1984). Perhaps, the nature of the social support system available to the individual is an important variable. When people are bereaved, they often experience the loss of a part of themselves (this is literally the case when the loss is of a bodily function or capacity). The extent to which personal self-esteem is linked to the lost person or functions and the availability of alternative sources of self-esteem may be crucial variables in determining the adequacy of adaptation to the loss. The choice of alcohol as a negative adaptive means may also be related to cultural beliefs about drinking as well as practical considerations, such as the easy availability of reasonably priced beverages or the opportunity for social contact which is offered at the local pub.

Identifying the clients for tertiary prevention (i.e., chronic problem drinkers) involves identifying the personality characteristics which allowed them to survive so long despite their drinking problem. Such individuals must possess a practical wisdom which allows them to establish a life as an alcoholic within a society which marginalizes this sub-population. They must also be capable of resisting any attempts by society and/or their families to reform them and eliminate their "difficulty." Or, they may use society's interventions to help them survive and continue to drink later. For example, passing the cold Montreal winter in a veterans' hospital might be an effective survival strategy; or having a "cure" might temporarily avert a physical problem and mean that it will be a while before the volume of alcohol one needs to drink to get "high" is so great that it poses a financial problem.

To date, there is little indication that there is a high incidence of acute or chronic alcoholism in old age. Perhaps this is related to research results which clearly prove that to become an alcoholic is one of the most effective means of foreshortening one's life expectancy (Metropolitan Life Insurance, 1977). Alcoholism is associated with a wide range of medical problems ranging from malnutrition and vitamin deficiencies to liver disease and chronic heart disease (Mezey, 1974). This proven relationship leads to the hypothesis by Drew (1968) that there are relatively few older alcoholics because a person with an alcohol problem has a poor chance of surviving into old age. For Drew, alcoholism is a "self-limiting" problem; after age 50 the proportion of alcoholics by age group decreases continually.

While it is accurate to link chronic alcohol abuse with increased mortality, Drew's hypothesis can be challenged from several perspectives: First, although frequent heavy drinkers are more likely to suffer a premature death, moderate alcohol consumption has been consistently related to *greater* average life spans, when compared to groups who abstain from alcohol consumption.

For example, studies by Shurtleff (1970) and Belloc (1973) found a tendancy for light drinkers to show the *lowest* mortality rates of all the drinking and non-drinking groups. However, before running off to the liquor store to buy some "eau de vie," you might wish to consider that a correlation between moderate drinking and longevity does not prove that alcohol is the cause of the greater life expectancies. People who abstain from drinking in our society are unusual. Perhaps, non-drinkers engage in other unusual health-related behaviors which result in a foreshortened life span.

A second criticism of Drew's hypothesis is based on Amark's (1951) research and review of several other Scandinavian authors. He found that many alcoholics, at around age 50, improve spontaneously. Studies in Japan (Moore, 1964) and North America (Wallgren & Barry, 1970) confirm the observation that at least some alcoholics either give up drinking or reduce their consumption to a moderate level some time after age 40. Perhaps, for those who do not succumb early to an alcohol-related disease, as people age they develop a wisdom which leads to reduced consumption.

A third problem with the hypothesis that there are few older alcoholics (regardless of the reason) stems from criticisms of current data on alcohol use and abuse. Most data derive from survey studies where someone knocks on the door and asks, as part of an interview, how much the person drinks. Do subjects in these studies tell the truth; or, without bad intent, do people tend to minimize or forget the extent of their excesses when talking to the interviewers? If the tendencies to hide or forget alcohol abuse are stronger among older persons, this would account, in part, for the reduced proportion of alcoholics reported among the elderly.

Another major source of data are records concerning those who receive treatment for alcohol problems. Clearly, older persons are rarely seen in alcohol rehabilitation programs. But, does this mean that there is not a need for such interventions? Perhaps, older persons avoid treatment programs because of lack of knowledge, prejudices against professional help, fear of institutionalization, rejection by treatment staff who do not feel that it is worthwhile to help them, or lack of adequate programs to meet their needs. Or, maybe its just more difficult to recognize older problem drinkers.

It would be nice to be able to say that treatment programs for alcoholics have great success, but it would also be dishonest. Long-term follow-up studies of alcohol treatment programs are rare, and follow-up a year later invariably shows high recidivism rates. With regard to older clients, there are so few research reports that any conclusions must be considered speculative. Many studies do not report on age differences in results involving older and younger clients. Other studies on older clients often involve such highly specialized samples that their generalizability for other groups may be questionable. Furthermore, since relatively few older persons receive treatment, there may be an inherent sampling bias. Perhaps, since only the most motivated persons end up in treatment programs, there is a tendency to have more successful outcomes. Still, the unfounded prejudice that older persons respond less well to therapeutic interventions argues in favor of limited success rates. Also, the tardive referral syndrome mentioned earlier would tend to make treatment more difficult, since the problems would be quite severe before treatment is started.

To date, there is no evidence that older clients respond less well to interventions. In fact, results from the available studies often report *better* improvement rates when compared to younger clients. For example, Blaney, Bradford and MacKenzie (1975) found that in one hospital over a six-month follow-up, persons over 60 had the same success rates as adults 30–39 and rates somewhat better than younger clients. In a second hospital, the elderly group had a 77 percent improvement rate, compared to only 36 percent for the youngest clients, aged 20–29.

Of course, treatment results depend upon what is considered to be "improvement." Total abstinence has been criticized as a necessary outcome (Davis, 1962; Kendall, 1965), and there is a trend toward seeking criteria for success which look at success in family relationships, job performance, and control of drinking. But, where does the happiness of the client fit in? Can a person stop drinking and be more miserable?

One of the major problems with secondary and tertiary prevention programs is the fact that help stops after the "cure." Even in programs where follow-up is available, the amount of time devoted to after-treatment contact is usually quite limited, and the environment which supported, enhanced or caused the drinking problem is generally left untouched. For this reason, Alcoholics Anonymous offers a viable alternative to professional interventions. Alcoholics Anonymous provides the type of extensive and continued support needed to develop an alternative life-style.

Also, there is an important point regarding treatment of alcoholism in the elderly which is often ignored. To date, we have no hard data which suggests that older alcoholics need special types of treatment programs or respond better to certain approaches than younger clients. Until such data are available, there is no justification to support the segregation of older alcoholics into specialized programs "for their benefit."

Alcoholism among older persons is rarely an entirely individual problem. Alcohol abuse may be a response to societal pressures or may be supported by the nature of the society in which one lives. In our society, excessive drinking is one of the few simple and inexpensive means of emotional escape available to older people. A major step toward the primary prevention of alcohol abuse would be the development of a wide range of alternatives for persons who feel isolated, are grieving, suffer from incapacities, or experience a loss of social roles.

Any talk on alcohol and old age would not be complete without some mention of the use of alcohol in moderation. Alcohol use does not imply abuse. A distinction must be made between the massive negative effects of excess drinking and the consistent research findings on the positive effects of moderate intake of alcoholic beverages. Experiments in institutions and with independent older persons living at home show a general lack of negative effects and often suggest a wide range of positive effects of wine and beer taken in moderation. For example, a glass or two of wine a day may enhance sleep, general feelings of well-being, and possibly cognitive functions. (For a full review of this research, see Mishara, Kastenbaum, Baker & Patterson, 1974 and Mishara & Kastenbaum, 1980.)

Epilogue: Future Prospects

Compared to other areas of research, there are relatively few studies on alcohol and the elderly. Furthermore, research results available today may be less relevant for older persons in future generations. The values in society are constantly changing, and there may be a general trend toward increased consumption and availability of mind-altering chemicals (alcoholic beverages included). The tendency to drink less as one ages may diminish as time goes on. On the other hand, drinking problems may be replaced by the use of other "recreational" drugs such as marijuana, which does not have the disastrous ramifications on health as excess alcohol intake does.

Today, there is a tendency for practitioners to fail to diagnose and treat alcohol problems in old age and a reluctance on the part of older problem drinkers and their families to seek help. This mutual avoidance leads to a dearth of therapeutic contact, often explained away by the notion that the effort to help an older person or the effort to seek help is not justified "at that stage in life." This explanation ignores the major findings in gerontology research in recent years. Older persons respond positively to a variety of interventions, often better than younger clients. Regardless of the losses endured, it is possible to continue to develop and have a meaningful and joyous life in the later years.

It is important to have a balanced view about alcohol and old age. There are no indications that alcoholic beverages taken in moderation have negative effects, and there is research suggesting that restrained alcohol use should be encouraged. However, when faced with an older alcoholic, interventions may be warranted and appropriate. It is easy to brush aside problem drinking in old age by observing that alcohol offers the only solace for an individual. It is harder to help create social alternatives which would improve the quality of that person's life. Yet, if we seek the easy way out and brush aside the difficulty, we miss an opportunity not only to help someone with great potential but also avoid a chance to help assure ourselves of a better life when we grow old.

SUMMARY

A model is presented tracing development of abstainers, occasional drinkers, potential alcoholics, and chronic alcoholics. The prevalence of alcoholism in old age is not high. Some individuals with long-standing alcoholism problems may give up their drinking for a variety of reasons; many do not survive. Survival requires great physical stamina plus some form of social or institutional support (e.g., financial, health care). For those that develop alcoholism in the later years, the major causal factor is considered to be the experience of a loss. Primary, secondary, and tertiary treatment techniques and difficulties are discussed in some detail.

REFERENCES

Amark, C. A study in alcoholism. *Acta Psychiatrica Scandinavia,* 1951, Suppl. 70, 273–279.

Belloc, N. Relationship of health practices and mortality. *Preventive Medicine,* 1973, 2, 67–81.

Blaney, R., Radford, I. S., and MacKenzie, G. A Belfast study of the prediction of outcome of alcoholism. *British Journal of Addiction,* 1975, 70, 41–50.

Carruth, B. Toward a definition of problem drinking among older persons: Conceptual and methodological considerations. In E. P. Williams et al. (Eds.), *Alcohol and Problem Drinking Among Older Persons.* Springfield, Va: National Technical Information Service, 1973.

Davis, D. L. Normal drinking in recovered alcohol addicts. *Quarterly Journal of Studies on Alcoholism,* 1962, 23, 94–104.

Drew, L. R. H. Alcohol as a self-limiting disease. *Quarterly Journal of Studies on Alcoholism,* 1968, 29, 956–967.

Kendall, R. E. Normal drinking by former alcohol addicts. *Quarterly Journal of Studies on Alcoholism,* 1965, 26, 247–257.

Metropolitan Life Insurance. Mortality from alcoholism. *Statistical Bulletin,* 1977, 58, 2–5.

Mezey, E. Medical problems associated with alcoholism. *Primary Care,* 1974, 1, 293–316.

Mishara, B. L., and Kastenbaum, R. *Alcohol and Old Age.* New York: Grune and Stratton, 1980.

Mishara, B. L., Kastenbaum, R., Patterson, R., and Baker, F. Alcohol effects in old age: an experimental investigation. *Social Science & Medicine,* 1975, 9, 535–547.

Mishara, B. L., and Riedel, R. *Le Vieillissement.* Paris: Presses Universitaires de France, 1984.

Moore, R. A. Alcoholism in Japan. *Quarterly Journal of Studies on Alcoholism,* 1964, 25, 142–150.

Shurtleff, D. Some characteristics related to the incidence of cardiovascular disease and death: Framingham study, a 16 year follow-up. In W. B. Kannel and T. Gordon (Eds.), *The Framingham Study,* Section 26. Washington, D.C.: U.S. Government Printing Office, 1970.

Wallgren, H., and Barry, H. III. *Actions of Alcohol.* New York: Elsevier, 1970.

Williams, E. P. Alcoholism and problem drinking among older persons: Community Agency study. In E. P. Williams et al. (Eds.), *Alcohol and Problem Drinking Among Older Persons.* Springfield, Va.: National Technical Information Service, 1973.

Chapter 19

SHORT-TERM FAMILY ORIENTED MODELS
OF TREATMENT FOR THE ELDERLY

Fredrica Mann Friedman
C. Jack Friedman
Thomas E. Skoloda

B eing elderly in America today can mean forced isolation and
restriction—not only in terms of retirement from jobs but
disassociation from the social community and family as well.
"Breakfast, lunch, the TV room, dinner and back to bed again.
What a way to live!" is the expression of a resident in a modern
nursing home with a relatively busy schedule of activities. This
sixty-four-year-old woman had been seen by two psychiatrists and
two psychologists, each of whom concluded that her mental and
emotional functioning were within the normal range, yet the
diagnoses on her medical chart was psychosis and Alzheimer's
disease. Contrary to the recommendations of these four consultants over a one-year period, this elderly woman is still being
administered antipsychotic drugs on a regular basis. This case
illustrates the plight of thousands of elderly citizens who have
been seen by our consultants (Creative Human Services) over the
past two years. This chapter describes an approach which incorpo-
rates psychological evaluation and short-term family therapy. This
combination has been found to be a useful adjunctive treatment
for elderly residents of nursing homes. At the present, the use of
psychotropic medication is often the major treatment available to
physicians for nursing home residents perceived as having emotional and/or adjustment problems. The type of treatment described
in this chapter may help physicians decrease the often heavy use

of psychotropic drugs to manage patients' problems in nursing homes.

Before describing the Creative Human Services (CHS) family therapy approach, it will be helpful to point out several of the factors which have served as barriers to effective treatment for the elderly. The barriers fall into three general categories. The first is lack of information about aging itself. There is a great deal of misinformation about the phenomenon of old age as a stage of life, about the term senility, about the problems caused by loss or deprivation of sensory information as we age, about the effects of common food and medication, and about the new needs of increasingly larger numbers of elderly Americans. In addition to these, there are many other areas which reflect our society's misperception of aging and our lack of knowledge related to aging.

The second major barrier to effective treatment of the elderly is a lack of understanding of the psychology of the elderly. What are the exact effects of physiological deterioration on the emotions and mental functioning? What are the avoidance techniques, compensatory mechanisms, and other adaptive behaviors used by older people to make up for the loss of function? How does the psychology of the elderly differ from the psychology of other age groups? What type of treatment is effective with the elderly? These are just a few of the questions to which we do not have complete and satisfactory answers.

The third major barrier is a lack of appreciation for the significance of family relationships in the treatment of elderly patients. A thorough understanding of family dynamics, family patterns, such as family myths and repetition phenomenon and "futuristic time bombs," are all prerequisites to effective diagnosis and treatment of the elderly, whether at home or in institutions (1). A host of unresolved continuing family conflicts, role changes and financial interdependence issues also complicate the treatment of the elderly. Emphasis on the complexities of understanding and correctly diagnosing problems of the elderly is needed because the simplistic view of "poor memory, poor balance, she keeps repeating herself, I guess mom's senile" is an all too common approach to dealing with the problems of the elderly. When Lowell Thomas rambled on about his memoires, with obvious lapses in memory, he was characterized as charming and witty.[1] When grandma does the same, a family upheaval ensues and we take her to the doctor.

The Short-Term Family Oriented Model of treatment stresses the significance of a thorough evaluation of the medical-psychological-social problems of the patient. It would indeed seem difficult, at best, to try to do therapy when having little, if any, idea as to a correct diagnosis (i.e., what specifically is the problem to be solved or resolved). Because there is still such limited real understanding of the phenomenology of aging, or of the conditions described as Alzheimer's disease, organic brain syndrome, brain damage, or the ever-popular "senility," the process of therapeutic intervention or patient management presents a considerable challenge.

The first logical place to begin a treatment process is with the determination of a correct and meaningful diagnosis of medical, psychological and social problems. The medical problem is addressed by a review of the present diagnosis, a review of the medical history including past problems and treatment, consultation with the physician and nursing staff, and interviews with the patient and family members. It is often found that the patient and/or family have a poor understanding of the medical situation and may not have attempted to clarify these issues. In fact, in some cases, this lack of information may be the major problem, resulting in the patient experiencing symptoms which are unexpected and frightening. Both patients and their family members can have unrealistic expectations of treatment. For example, let's say that in a particular case, the most likely result of treatment is to arrest or slow down deterioration; but the patient and family expect total and complete rehabilitation. In this case, unrealistic expectations can result in frustration, anger, or depression in response to the perceived lack of progress. The patient may, in fact, hide or deny important symptoms in order to appear to be making progress. The physician then is unaware of the symptoms and considers progress to be adequate. This situation can often result in family

---

[1]Acceptance speech at annual dinner of the Chapel of the Four Chaplains, honoring Lowell Thomas and General Alexander Haig, 1981.

complaints about the physician, the medication, the nursing staff or the environment of the nursing home itself. The example given is only one of many instances where appreciation and review of the medical history is required in order to determine the basis for patient problems.

Medical problems can also interact with or result in psychological difficulties, such as depression, guilt, and anger, and in order to understand and treat these psychological symptoms, it is necessary to understand the physical problems confronting the patient. The psychological evaluation is the next step in this procedure. With the elderly, this first step is not easily achieved by observations of behaviors or symptoms. Current psychological and psychiatric tests of mental and emotional functioning are, for the most part, not appropriate for administration to the elderly, who often have problems in hearing, vision, and motor skills due to arthritis and other strictly physiological-medical problems. Many recognized psychological tests that we call standardized are based upon a sample size of less than 250, spanning a 15-year age range. One has only to look at the test stimuli to appreciate the predicament for the psychological examiner when testing the elderly. By way of example, the Wechsler Adult Intelligence Scale (WAIS), which was standardized using only a sample of 35 people over 65 years of age, has visual stimuli which are so small that people with cataracts, regardless of superior brain functioning, might perform as though they had brain damage.

However, professionals who have had respect for the dignity of elderly patients and have taken the time to work around their sensory deficits have often discovered a wealth of overlooked intellectual and cognitive strengths in these patients. Many new tests and modifications of already established tests and questionnaires have been recently developed by Friedman and Friedman (2) for use in the evaluation, diagnosis and treatment of the elderly. If decrements in brain function and structure are viewed as part of a continuum that starts at birth and continues to death, the more incapacitating manifestations of brain damage that appear with increasing age are not seen as being so frightening nor so unreasonable. From this viewpoint, memory loss and mental confusion assume a different significance. Our stereotypes of the absent-minded, yet brilliant professor, the scatter-brained young housewife who is always forgetting where she put her keys, or the empty-headed gossip who never has anything new to say, are indications of contradictions, inconsistency, and irrational thinking in our society. These same people, at age 60, who cannot remember where they put something, or who repeat themselves in conversation, will be described as "senile." "Senility" must change in definition from being an age dependent entity to a concept representing a more noticeable and handicapping form of a condition present and continually increasing in all of us. Otherwise, we must bury the word itself and not use it as a label with which to indict the elderly.

As the clinician becomes more comfortable with the concept of a continuum of brain damage as applying in varying degrees to all human beings in different stages, he/she can look past the overtly disconcerting behaviors of many elderly persons. Underneath the confusion, memory deficits, loss of balance, incontinence, verbal repetition and hearing and visual deficits is a human being who may be as horrified, frightened, and disgusted by any of these symptoms as we may be. Consequently, we see a complete range of avoidant, denying, and compensatory behaviors which manifest themselves in as broad a spectrum of abnormal-seeming symptoms as one would expect to find in a mental institution. For example, an elderly person trying to mask his hearing loss may answer your questions with apparently incomprehensible and confused responses, since he is only guessing at what we heard. One of the more frequently perplexing symptoms is the on-again, off-again confusion. "Sometimes, she seems perfectly lucid and answers competently and other times, she seems confused and doesn't make any sense" is a familiar statement characterizing the elderly. Simply calling such a condition "brain damage" does not take into account that anxiety, fear, maladaptive adjustment reactions, medication, metabolic imbalances at different hours of the day, and deafness are all possible contributors to apparent "senility," OBS, or organic psychosis.

The second step in our model involves clarification of presenting symptoms. Obvious deterioration of functioning, increasing dependence on others for basic life-support services, and removal to a nursing home facility are emotionally laden processes which have the ability to evoke behavioral reactions mimicking psychosis or OBS, as traditionally defined. The symptoms which warrant professional intervention are so diverse that we are including here a reproduction of the Creative Human Services Presenting Symptoms Checklist (see Table 19-I).

More often than not, acting-out behavior, violence, aggression, yelling, paranoia, hallucinations, delusions, and wandering are the most disturbing and predominant reasons for referral for evaluation and treatment. Secondly are the depressive-type reactions, such as sadness, lack of participation in activities, or withdrawal. Thirdly are behaviors, such as refusing to eat or take medication, which cause the physician, nurse, or family member to worry about the survival of the patient. And then there are a range of disruptive-behavioral, affective-emotional and cognitive-confusion memory problems, all of which frighten and worry the caretakers and present reality management problems as regards the elderly member at home or in an institution.

Although in the interest of clarification, we have divided the Creative Human Services Presenting Symptoms Checklist into ten discrete categories, any single symptom or combination of symptoms might be idiosyncratic reactions to one or more personal family themes relative to that person's life. For example, mental confusion, a term subject to much bias, may be due to a lesion in a specific part of the brain although other areas are functioning well; or it may be the result of poor circulation with sudden changes in movement; or it may be a reaction to a particular medicine, such as digitalis or inderol; or it may be a misconception due to value differences, language difficulties, intelligence, or type of memory deficit; or it may be due to a lack of hearing which one is trying to mask; or it may be a way of getting attention when one is feeling lonely and abandoned; or it may be a manipulative characteristic to stir up trouble and get visits from family; or it may be the result of a characteristic way of treating people one does not like, by ignoring them, and on it goes.

There are three major steps in our Short-Term Family Oriented Model of treatment: (1) determination of a correct and meaningful diagnosis of medical, psychological and social problems; (2) delinea-

TABLE 19-I
CHS Presenting Symptoms Checklist

BEHAVIORAL REACTIONS
___aggressiveness, violence
___self mutilation
___disruptiveness
___belligerance
___extreme negativism
___ritualistic behavior
___screaming
___threatening
___withdrawal
___hyperexcitability
___temper outbursts
___destructiveness
___impulsivity
___violation of rules
___nocturnal disruptiveness
___safety violations
___runaway attempts
___sexual acting out
___hoarding
___provocative behavior
___hyperactive behavior
___Other:_____

DISTURBANCES IN FUNCTION
___eating
___digestion
___initial insomnia
___delayed insomnia
___loss of mobility
___problems in self-care
___toilet behavior
___dressing
___grooming (hair, shave)
___ambulation
___regression
___messiness

PSYCHOSOMATIC REACTIONS
___gastrointestinal
___respiratory
___cardiac
___muscular
___sensory
___dermatological
___urologic
___Other:_____

THOUGHT DISTURBANCES
___delusions
___hallucinations
___irrational beliefs
___paranoid thinking
___suspiciousness
___poor reality testing
___ideas of reference
___persecutory ideation
___obsessiveness
___Other:_____

AFFECTIVE DISTURBANCES
___depression
___emotional withdrawal
___despair, hopelessness
___emotional lability
___anxiety, fearfulness
___hostility
___guilt, shame
___boredom
___loneliness, isolation
___loss of libido
___loss of motivation
___loss of spontaneity
___concern over object loss
___jealousy
___feelings of alienation
___bland indifference
___hysteria
___Other:_____

HYPOCHONDRIASIS
___Specify:_____

SPECIAL PROBLEMS
___apandonment
___self isolation
___family crisis
___financial
___no family
___legal problems
___alcoholism
___substance abuse

MEDICAL PROBLEMS
___convalescence
___chronic illness
___terminal illness
___disfigurement
___chronic pain
___acute pain
___fear of death
___fear of treatment
___medicine side effect
___pain medicine addiction
___pain medicine dependence
___dependence on life support
___sensory handicaps

COGNITIVE IMPAIRMENT
___memory failure
___time disorientation
___place disorientation
___recognition problems
___spatial confusion
___disorganization
___miscomprehension
___episodic confusion
___illogic
___dementia
___mental retardation
___perseveration
___pleasant incompetence
___perplexity
___unintelligible speech
___Other:_____

PSYCHOSOCIAL PROBLEMS
___staff relationships
___family relationships
___interests, hobbies
___treatment services
___adaptation to facility
___friendships in facility
___heterosexual relationships
___outside friendships
___Other:_____

The problems of concern for this reason for psychodiagnostic evaluation are checked under their respective categories above.

tion of the complex of symptoms which warrant professional intervention; and (3) interviews and meetings with family and staff.

For patients in a nursing home and for the person facing old age in their own home, the phenomenology is a unique combination of lifelong individual, family and social experiences with all the attendant values, dynamics, perceptions, biases and misconceptions that characterize their unique family, cultural background and their idiosyncratic way of synthesizing all of this. This synthesis is reflected in the way each person manages daily routines, activities and relationships.

Consequently, the family interviews and meetings are the third and, in some ways, most important part of the Short-Term Family Oriented Treatment Model. Family involvement is often crucial to the treatment of the elderly, and we have noted a high degree of family involvement with elderly residents of nursing homes. It is important to interview all significant members of the family, since there are often individual observations and interactions which contribute to the problems being experienced by the patient. Particular attention can be paid to the number of family members involved and their interrelationships, the family's interpretation of the presenting problem, and past attempts to deal with this or similar problems. Of course, this approach does not differ significantly from the use of family therapy in many other situations. One of the major ways that this approach does differ is that the staff of the nursing home can also be considered as part of the extended family. Elderly residents often respond to staff, particularly nursing staff, the same way they respond to family members. For example, nurses can be frustrated by unsuccessful attempts to please the patient, or staff can be put through the paces by the number of requests and demands that the resident makes in order to achieve a greater feeling of control over his/her life. Nursing home staff members who are involved with the patient are interviewed and their perceptions of the resident and the problems are also considered. For some nursing home residents, the staff constitutes the only family remaining for the resident. This can occur when other family members are deceased or too distant to be considered family. In these cases as well as with residents with family contact, the staff of the nursing home often represent family ties and can be considered as supportive, rejecting, concerned, cold, etc. The staff and family are interviewed and the presenting problem is redefined in objective measurable terms. Thus, the complaint "We can't satisfy her!" can be translated into Mrs. M does not accept the disabilities resulting from her illness and needs education and information concerning her disorder, it's disabling characteristics, and realistic expectations of treatment.

Attempting to redefine the presenting problem into objective measurable terms requires knowledge of the medical problem, and the degree of psychological impairment. At this point, short-term goals can be established. An important way of improving chances for success is by limiting goals to short-term measurable outcomes. This stage is often one of the most crucial in the Short-Term Family Oriented Model because of the tendency to set goals too high too quickly. Establish short-term goals, then check progress, assess the progress, and establish new procedures if necessary. The process involves trying different approaches until we see some success, then continuing along those lines. Constant reassessment is required for several weeks until visible quantifiable progress is seen. At this point, the therapist explains to the staff, family members, and patient the process by which success was achieved and indicates how this approach might be used to help solve problems in the future. The therapist then withdraws from active involvement except for periodic follow-up visits which help reinforce the treatment and avert future problems. The clinician must take the time to perceive and treat each patient as a unique individual, part of a unique family system, and must be willing to use trial and error to ferret out the central and peripheral problems and to test and re-test hypotheses to maximize the effectiveness of treatment.

SUMMARY

The CHS Model of family therapy for the elderly starts with a comprehensive evaluation of the presenting problems in such a way that the problems are defined as workable entities. Using checklists such as the Creative Human Services Presenting Symptoms Checklist and psychological tests, clear, workable treatment goals can be established. In addition, family members and nursing home staff are also interviewed, since each can provide valuable material to help clarify the diagnosis and the range of possible treatment options. After this information-gathering stage, meetings are established with the patient and other important family members to communicate the results of the evaluation and to explore treatment alternatives. The family therapist serves as the hub of a wheel of communication to effect the treatment alternatives identified by the evaluation. Finally, the therapist withdraws and demonstrates to the family how it has worked to solve the problems identified and leaves the family with the knowledge that similar problems can be dealt with in the future. The approach may help to broaden the range of treatment available to residents of nursing homes and may provide a more effective treatment than the heavy use of medications and drugs often seen in nursing homes.

REFERENCES

1. Friedman, C. Jack. "Uncovering Spouses' Future Oriented Fantasies." In Alan S. Gurman, Ph.D. (Ed.), *Questions and Answers in the Practice of Family Therapy.* New York: Brunner/Mazel, 1981.
2. Friedman, C. Jack, and Friedman, Fredrica Mann. *Psychological Report Record.* Ardmore, PA: Creative Human Services, 1983.

Chapter 20

SERVICES FOR THE ELDERLY
WITH ALCOHOL-RELATED PROBLEMS:
A SYSTEMS APPROACH

John Bland

This chapter is a brief description of activities in the state of Maryland between 1975–1979 designed to respond to the needs of the elderly. The recognition early on was that there would be no new funds generated to expand services for the elderly alcoholic or problem drinker. Additionally, there was the recognition that ideally some form of evaluation would be important; however, after much consideration it was decided that, although evaluation was desirable and important, it would have to be a later consideration. The focus therefore was to determine if existing services provided by personnel serving the elderly and personnel treating the alcoholic or problem drinker could be employed to treat the individual who was over 55 with a drinking problem.

The effort to develop a coordinated capacity to provide treatment, rehabilitation and prevention services for the older person who is alcoholic or who has alcohol-related problems began in 1975 with a strong push from the Maryland Legislature. The Alcoholism Control Administration (ACA) was admonished through a House Joint Resolution to insure that persons who were elderly must have equal access to available alcoholism services as are enjoyed by all other citizens in the state. Several legislators had received complaints from their constituents that they had experienced difficulties getting older friends and relatives into state-funded alcoholism treatment programs. The resultant investigation served as a springboard for the state of Maryland to begin a process of seriously facing up to the fact that first there was a problem and, second, the fields of alcoholism and aging needed to come together if the needs of this age group were to be met successfully.

The initial investigation revealed that the attitudes of alcoholism treatment personnel toward the elderly were generally negative. Some were concerned about the fact that treatment goals of intermediate-care facilities directed the individual to get his life in order by remaining totally abstinent and this would be the platform to launch one back into gainful employment, resumption of family living, and other activities expected of persons between 25 to 55 years of age. Another concern was related to the decrease in mobility of the elderly person as compared with the younger individual. Additionally, the increase in medical problems, frequently requiring more medical supports than halfway houses for alcoholics had been accustomed to addressing, was problematic. Other program directors or counselors expressed the opinion that the prognosis for "old people" was always poor. Clearly, the attitude of the treatment providers toward the elderly person seeking treatment was negative.

Seeking some positive approaches to address the twofold problems of limited accessibility of alcoholism services and limited knowledge on the part of alcoholism treatment personnel of services to the aged, I called together representatives of both fields serving the Greater Baltimore area. These include the:

1. Baltimore City Department of Social Services, Adult Division
2. Baltimore City Health Department (BCHD), Alcoholism Center
3. BCHD Mobility Transportation
4. BCHD Geriatric Evaluation Services (GES)
5. Baltimore City Housing and Community Development (BCHCD)
6. Maryland Commission on Aging
7. Maryland Department of Health and Mental Hygiene
   • Alcoholism Control Administration (ACA)
   • Aging and Chronically Ill Administration (ACIA)
18. Baltimore City Alcoholism Directorate (Provider Group)
9. Levindale Geriatric Research Center

10. Waxter Senior Center
11. Meals on Wheels

In a series of meetings, representatives of these agencies formulated several goals.

1. To provide consciousness raising and sensitizing experiences for alcoholism personnel working with elderly in a variety of settings, including: senior centers, eating together centers, high-rise apartment living, briefings provided by GES staff and such like. Conversely, affording personnel who worked with the elderly experiences within alcoholism treatment activities, visiting a detox center, touring an intermediate-care facility, a long-term-care facility, open AA meetings, outpatient centers, ride with the Good Samaritan Team as it made rounds to pick up public inebriates and such like.
2. To provide workshops and seminars to enhance the knowledge base of each group, including up-to-date resource lists which had key contact persons pinpointed. At each step an evaluation form was filled out in an effort to assess the effectiveness of the experiences.
3. To train a cadre of trainers within the alcoholism provider network and the geriatric provider network.

The first two goals were given the greatest amount of attention. We conferred with Erma Polly Williams of the Rutgers Center of Alcohol Studies, who participated with Bruce Carruth et al. (1) in a community study and Dr. Sheldon Zimberg, who has also made major contributions in his explorations of alcohol abuse among the elderly (2). A major workshop resulted from their consultation and participation during the spring of 1976. Seven goals in mobilizing the community to act on the problem were considered:

1. Establishing that problem drinking among older people is a problem in and for the community.
2. Developing an interest in the problem and a commitment to action on the part of the community power structure, caretakers, and interested citizens.

3. Coordinating an effective care-providing system for older problem drinkers in the community.
4. Developing special programs to fill the gaps in the current care-providing system.
5. Developing an effective outreach and identification program.
6. Establishing programs for prevention and early detection.
7. Establishing an effective research and evaluation program and mechanisms to disseminate new knowledge about the problem.

After two years or more of training and information exchange, the Steering Committee, or faculty as we called ourselves, developed a consensus around the following factors as being useful in understanding alcoholism among older people.

There is evidence gathered from contacts with the elderly in a variety of situations, in addition to the limited research data available, to suggest several factors which may contribute to alcoholism among older people.

- The elderly appear to be a high-risk group for problem drinking and alcoholism. Changes in metabolism and in central nervous system functioning may increase the intoxicating effect of alcohol, and the presence of chronic illness may tend to exacerbate the body's response to the ingestion of alcohol.
- Social and psychological aspects of aging can become predisposing conditions causing older people to drink with harmful effect. These include the necessity of living on a limited and fixed income, reduced income, reduced mobility, changes in role and social status, and the feelings of loneliness and isolation associated with the death of friends and family members.
- Problems stemming from the combined use of alcohol and other drugs occur more frequently among the elderly than in younger age groups. Prescription and over-the-counter drugs are both heavily used by older Americans, thus increasing the incidence of interactions between alcohol and other drugs that may have toxic or lethal effects.

- People experiencing drinking problems in old age are generally classified as either late-onset or early onset drinkers, with the latter known as "hardy survivors." Late-onset drinking problems usually occur as a result of situational problems, exacerbated by failing physical and mental health, and emotional and environmental stresses. Early onset drinkers are those who began to have drinking problems prior to old age, usually during their thirties and forties.
- Diagnostic problems constitute a substantial barrier to treatment of older alcoholics. Medical personnel often mistake as signs of frailty, senility, or brain disorders conditions which may in fact be signs of alcohol abuse and alcoholism.
- Evidence suggests that older people may be more responsive to treatment and prevention strategies than younger populations.

Our records show that since 1979, there has been an increase in the number of patients age 60 or over who were admitted to treatment. In 1979, there were 601 and in 1980 there were 796, which represented 5.4 percent of the total admissions for that year. Individuals received services in emergency rooms, outpatient services of the local health department alcoholism unit, intermediate residential care as well as long-term care. However, the largest number were seen on an outpatient basis.

Hospital data for the period January 1, 1981 through December 31, 1981 indicated that individuals with a primary diagnosis of alcoholism over age 59 who were admitted numbered 381 with an average length of stay of 10.08 days. Additionally, individuals over age 59 admitted with a diagnosis of liver cirrhosis numbered 342 and had an average length of stay of 9.32 days. Although the data is somewhat sketchy, there is the general belief that caregivers have made more referrals of older alcoholics to acute general hospitals statewide with increasingly more success.

SUMMARY

This chapter is a description of the procedures used by the Maryland State Alcoholism Control Administration (ACA) to implement a 1975 Maryland Legislative resolution issued to insure that the elderly had equal access to available alcoholism services as other citizens in the state. In its initial investigation, the ACA found negative attitudes among alcoholism treatment personnel toward providing treatment for elderly clients. In order to change these attitudes, representatives from the alcoholism field and the agencies dealing with the elderly were brought together in a series of meetings to facilitate information exchange and provide cross training over a period of two years. An analysis of the data on the number of hospital admissions for individuals over 59 with a primary diagnosis of alcoholism showed a definite increase. It appeared that this approach was successful and resulted in increased treatment for elderly alcoholics.

REFERENCES

1. Carruth, B., Williams, E. P., Mysak, P., and Bourdreaux, L. Alcoholism and Problem Drinking Among Older Persons: Community Care Providers and the Older Problem Drinker. Rutgers Center of Alcohol Studies, 1973.
2. Zimberg, S. Diagnosis and Treatment of the Elderly Alcoholic. *Alcoholism: Clinical and Experimental Research*, 1978, 2, 27–29.

Chapter 21

OUTPATIENT TREATMENT
OF OLDER ALCOHOLICS

Henry Pinsker

The existence of alcohol abuse as a significant problem among the elderly has received increasing attention in recent years (1, 2) and there has been increased concern about the elderly alcoholic. Rathbone-McCuan and Bland (3) observed that until recently, studies focused on the youthful or middle-aged drinker and that alcoholism services are generally not geared to aged alcoholics. "At the same time," they continued, "geriatric services have not faced up to the severity and prevalence of alcohol-related problems among their clientele." Meyers et al. (4) concluded that late-life drinking problems appear to be residual ones that have resisted efforts at treatment. Most of the older alcoholics interviewed in their study had not received any formal assistance for alcoholism and most of those who had received treatment said that it had not helped. The authors suggest that there may be need for programs designed especially for older alcoholics. Zimberg (5), on the other hand, reported that older individuals with alcohol problems responded well to treatment aimed at their current social and emotional problems.

SPECIALIZED OPC ACTIVITIES FOR OLDER ALCOHOLICS

The Beth Israel Medical Center Alcoholism Treatment Program's Outpatient Clinic is located on the edge of Manhattan's Bowery. Most of the clinic's patients are on public assistance, with almost half admitting to irregular work to supplement their incomes. Those who cannot attend sober or who cannot keep appointments are eventually referred to more traditional Bowery facilities, so continued enrollment in our clinic reflects some ability to maintain commitment and to maintain some sobriety. On both 1981 and 1982 census, 27 percent of the 400 enrolled patients were age 50 or more, but only 2 percent were over 60. Table 21-I portrays some of the characteristics of the clinic patients by age group. The patient who is over 55 in our clinic is likely to be a white or Hispanic man who did not complete high school and who never used opiates or other substances. He is likely to live alone and to have been attending the OPC for a year. Younger patients were more likely to have had psychiatric admissions in the past, to have abused other drugs, and to have only transient living arrangements.

When we were persuaded by what we read in both the newspa-

TABLE 21-I
SELECTED CHARACTERISTICS BY AGE GROUP

age group	18-49	50-54	55+
Number of individuals	293	53	55
Male	78%	74%	90%
White	39	49	44
Black	34	29	25
Hispanic	27	22	31
Undomiciled or lives in transient hotel	11	9	1
Lives alone	53	69	73
Lives with marital/sexual partner	15	15	20
Completed high school	54	49	32
Former opiate user	40	20	11
Enrolled in OPC 1 year or more	30	49	62
Enrolled in OPC 3 years or more	7	20	11
Active in A.A. outside OPC	47	40	35

pers and the scientific literature that our older patients were an underserved minority, we organized an activity which we called the 55+ Club. The designation "club" was used to emphasize that this was not just another approach to group therapy. The focus was always on activity and socialization, refreshments were served at meetings, and from time to time the club went on trips out of the clinic. It was hoped that issues and difficulties commonly associated with aging would become topics for discussion, but conversation among club members was limited to small talk and problems of coping with "the system." The most frequent topics were the welfare department, housing, and politics. Feelings were never mentioned. Issues often explored in geriatrics groups (i.e. declining health, loss of family, reduced ability to perform) were touched upon only when introduced by the leaders. These older alcoholics had developed an identity as alcoholics and were responsive to alcoholism-related issues. They did not, apparently, identify themselves as senior citizens.

Membership in the club was always small. Patients who spoke only Spanish were for the most part in the appropriate age group but could not be included. Many counselors seemed reluctant to refer their patients, and even though the meetings and trips of the 55+ Club were openly scheduled, patients did not ask to be referred.

As time went on, the group's membership dwindled. Two died, but the magnitude of denial was so great that the significance of these deaths was never explored. The healthier members gradually stopped attending, leaving only the most passive and impaired. Excursions away from the clinic were popular, yet there were always empty places as there were always men who had promised to participate but still stayed away on trip days. While reluctance to accept commitments is not unusual in this population, it was disheartening to the leaders. Some members also went on trips with various senior centers that were able to provide more elaborate services. With declining membership and no indication of interest from other patients or staff, the 55+ Club was dissolved. The individuals involved continued to participate in their usual groups and individual sessions.

Although not classified as a senior activity, the groups conducted in Spanish were composed primarily of patients who were over 50.

In these groups, as in the 55+ Club, involutional problems were never aired. Denial may have been more vigorously practiced by the older Hispanic men. Group therapy sessions conducted in Spanish invariably included a certain amount of mirthful, boasting talk about women and sex, with emphasis on current prowess. Most of the older Hispanic men began treatment as a condition for continued eligibility for welfare. Once engaged, they were consistent in attendance but not likely to take part in any clinic activity other than their weekly group. Although scheduled as therapy, the Spanish-only groups seem to have had a useful, club-like social function.

DISCUSSION

The patients who were invited to participate in the specially organized activity for those over 55 were people who had been unemployed for at least several years and who were recipients of public assistance. By the time the public assistance alcoholic reaches 55 (the age at which one becomes a senior citizen), he has already experienced many of the losses ordinarily associated with aging. He has become accustomed to having no regular work, so he doesn't have the fear of losing his work. For some, reaching the age at which getting a job is unlikely is a positive event, for it legitimizes inactivity. A variety of physical problems have already been experienced. Since clinic attendance is associated with sobriety, health is usually improving. If not involved with family members, the contacts, including contact with children, had been disrupted for years. The future may be ominous, but it is dealt with by denial. He will not talk about the possibility that he might become ill or disabled and have no support from family, friends, savings, or insurance.

The term "senior citizen" is sometimes used as a euphemism for the aged, sometimes as a marketing strategy. An important concern of those who talk to and about senior citizens is that they should not feel depreciated or useless in our youth-oriented society. *Modern Maturity*, the publication of the American Association of Retired Persons (eligibility begins at 55), "focuses on the joys, problems and opportunities that interest mature people; hobbies, travel, health care. . . . " Mailings from this organization include information about bargain travel (for which the senior is seen as a prime market) and insurance to protect against the ill health that lurks ahead. None of these issues has much pertinence for the resourceless alcoholic who has recently become sober.

The fact that older patients in our clinic were not willing to face the problems of age does not minimize the usefulness of group discussion as a technique for helping older people to deal with fears and problems associated with becoming old. It may be that an alcoholism clinic is not the place to carry out this discussion. The reiterated emphasis on alcohol as the cause of life's troubles and the emphasis on the individual's own day-by-day sobriety as the foundation of coping is one of the strengths of an alcoholism facility. When the alcoholic has achieved enough improvement to be ready to deal with all the problems that are not specifically related to sobriety, it may be best that he be encouraged to obtain services from other specialists. Once recovery is well under way, the individual can see himself as more than an alcoholic. As such, it is appropriate that he learn to use all the community's resources, not expecting all to be provided in the context of alcoholism treatment. In fact, this is what our patients elected to do.

CONCLUSION

The 55+ Club in our clinic was never successful. It appealed to neither staff nor to the patients who participated. Problems of aging, often discussed in geriatric therapeutic groups, were not discussed, either because they had occurred earlier, in the context of alcoholism, or because the need to deny precluded worrisome talk about possible future troubles. The individuals in this group were over 55, but few were over 62. In the working world, they would not be candidates for retirement or special privilege. In sum, these men had not assumed a senior identity and saw no need to do so. We cannot say whether some form of special program might have made it possible for us to engage a larger number of alcoholics who were over 60 or whether some special program might be useful for older alcoholics who were still drinking.

SUMMARY

A socialization and activity, "club" was established for patients of ages 55 and older who were enrolled in an alcoholism outpatient clinic. The participants avoided discussion of problems of aging, never spoke of feelings, and did not see their status as "senior citizens" as reason for a group experience apart from other alcoholics attending the clinic. Physical and social problems that many people face, or begin to worry about, when they approach the sixties had been experienced earlier as consequences of alcoholism. Some participated in senior activities in other facilities, not because such activities met a need, but because they were recognized as additional resources.

REFERENCES

1. National Institute on Alcoholism and Alcohol Abuse. Third Special Report to Congress on Alcohol and Health. Washington, D.C.: U.S. Department of Health, Education, and Welfare, 1978.
2. Mishara, B. L. *Alcoholism and Old Age.* NY: Grune & Stratton, 1980.
3. Rathbone-McCuan, E., and Bland, J. A treatment typology for the elderly alcohol abuser. *J Am Geriatrics Soc.,* 1975, 23, 553–557.
4. Meyers, A. R., Hingson, R., Mucatel, M., and Goldman, E. Social and psychological correlates of problem drinking in old age. *J Am Geriatrics Soc.,* 1982, 30, 452–456.
5. Zimberg, S. Two types of problems drinkers: Both can be managed. *Geriatrics,* 1974, 29(8), 135–138.

Chapter 22

TREATMENT OF THE ELDERLY ALCOHOLIC

Sheldon Zimberg

Introduction

In recent years there has been an increasing awareness that alcohol abuse and alcoholism are significant problems among the aged. This awareness has been supported by studies that looked at this problem from a variety of viewpoints, including community-based prevalence studies, hospital admissions, arrests for public intoxication, outpatient treatment programs, and interviews with the staff of health, social service, and information and referral agencies.

In the Washington Heights area of Manhattan, a household-prevalence survey was conducted which involved questions related to alcoholism (1). This study noted that for individuals aged 20 years and over, a peak prevalence of 23 per 1,000 population occurred in the 45–54 age group. The prevalence decreased to 17 per 1,000 for the age group 55–65 and then increased to a prevalence of 22 per 1,000 at the 65–74 year age group. This study noted that elderly widowers had a rate of 105 per 1,000 in contrast to the overall rate of 19 per 1,000. In addition to this study, a sample of United Automobile Workers Union members 21 years of age and over was conducted in the Baltimore Metropolitan area (2). This study found that 10 percent of the men and 20 percent of the women age 60 and over were heavy escape drinkers and considered to be alcoholics.

A study conducted on 534 patients over age 60 admitted to a psychiatric observation ward in San Francisco General Hospital noted that 23 percent were alcoholic (3). Another study conducted at a county psychiatric screening ward in Houston, Texas noted that 44 percent of 100 consecutive admissions age 60 and over were alcoholic (4). A prevalence study on alcoholism conducted at Harlem Hospital Center in New York City noted that 60 percent of the male admissions to the medical service and 43 percent of the female admissions were alcoholic; 5 of the male patients (56%) in age group 70 and over were alcoholic, but none of the women were (5). A survey of patients 65 years of age and over admitted to the acute medical ward of a California Veterans Administration Hospital noted that 18 percent of these patients were alcoholic (6).

In San Francisco it was noted in a study of 722 individuals age 60 and over arrested for minor crimes, that 82.3 percent were charged with drunkenness (7). This proportion of drunkenness arrests was much higher than in any other age group.

In an outpatient geriatric psychiatry program conducted at Harlem Hospital, 12 percent of the elderly patients were noted to have a drinking problem (8). In a medical home-care program, 13 percent of the elderly patients requiring psychiatric consultation were diagnosed as alcoholic (9). The author noted that 17 percent of patients age 65 and over admitted to a suburban New York community mental health center had alcohol abuse as a problem on admission.

Interviews of the staff of health, social-service, and criminal justice agencies were conducted in three communities representing urban, rural, and mixed urban-rural populations regarding the extent of problem drinking among their elderly clients (10). The authors found that 45 percent of those interviewed had had contact with an elderly problem drinker in the previous year. They also noted that the alcoholism information and referral services surveyed reported that 30 percent of all calls were for persons over age 55.

Mishara and Kastenbaum (11) presented an excellent review of literature on alcohol use and problem drinking in the elderly. They concluded that elderly people tend to drink less than young people, but there are some elderly who have significant problems with alcohol.

It can be seen that a great deal of data has been accumulated from a variety of sources indicating that a significant problem among the elderly has been ignored. It is not possible to determine an actual prevalence of alcoholism among elderly people.

However, a reasonable estimate would seem to be 10–15 percent, with a higher proportion occurring among the institutionalized elderly.

With this recognition of the problem, we must develop a useful classification of problem drinkers among the elderly, questions regarding possible causal factors, and effective treatment approaches. It is clear that elderly alcoholics carry the double stigma in our society of being old as well as alcoholic. This chapter will discuss these questions and describe effective treatment methods with this population of alcoholics in order to dispel stereotyped conceptions that have resulted in the rejection by health-care professionals of alcoholics in general and the elderly alcoholic in particular.

CLASSIFICATION OF ELDERLY ALCOHOLICS

A number of authors have noted that elderly alcoholics can be differentiated into several diagnostic groupings. Simon et al. (3) and Gaitz and Baer (4) made distinctions between elderly alcoholics with and without an organic mental syndrome. Such a distinction would imply differing prognoses and treatment approaches. Simon (3) indicated that alcoholics with an organic mental syndrome had a poor prognosis with respect to dying at an earlier age than elderly alcoholics without an organic mental syndrome. Simon (3) also noted that of the 23 percent of elderly alcoholic admissions, 7 percent became alcoholic after age 60 and 16 percent became alcoholic before age 60 and had long histories of alcohol abuse, thus indicating that about one-third of these patients developed a drinking problem in later life and two-thirds were long-standing alcoholics.

In developing a classification of elderly alcoholics, it would appear that a distinction between late-onset problem drinking and early onset problem drinking would be a more useful approach than one based on a distinction of psychiatric diagnosis, particularly the presence or absence of an organic mental syndrome. The late- and early onset problem-drinking classification can permit observations regarding the effects of the stresses of aging that contribute to the onset of other mental health problems in the aged in contrast to factors that existed in alcoholics long before they became elderly and may be unrelated to the developmental problems associated with aging.

Rosin and Glatt (12) reviewed 103 cases of patients age 65 and over who were seen in psychiatric home consultations or admitted to a regional alcoholism unit or to a hospital's geriatric unit. They also found two distinct groups of alcoholics and noted, as did Simon et al. (3), that two-thirds of the patients were long-standing alcoholics, with their alcoholism persisting as they grew older, the other one-third representing patients who developed their alcoholism in later life. The long-standing alcoholics had personality characteristics similar to those found among younger alcoholics, but the late-onset alcoholics seemed to have developed their drinking problems associated with depression, bereavement, retirement, loneliness, marital stress, and physical illness. Alcoholism in the late-onset alcoholics seemed related to the stresses of aging.

Based on their data, Carruth et al. (10) reported three distinct types of alcoholics. One type consisted of individuals who had no history of a drinking problem prior to old age and who developed the problem during old age (late onset); a second group consisted of individuals who intermittently experienced problems with alcohol but in old age developed a more severe and persistent problem of alcohol abuse (late-onset exacerbation); the third group consisted of individuals who had a long history of alcoholism and continued their problem drinking into old age (early onset). The authors did not indicate the relative percentages in the three groups described. It seems possible to conclude, however, that the two latter groups could be considered alcoholics of long standing with different drinking patterns in their younger years. The terms late onset, late-onset exacerbation, and early onset are this author's designations.

The concept of early onset alcoholism (two-thirds) and late-onset alcoholism (one-third) among the elderly appears to be a more useful classification. First, it is possible to determine, through the history of the use of alcohol in relation to problems, in which group an elderly alcoholic might be classified. Second, the long-standing alcoholics are more likely to be experiencing medical complications of alcoholism and therefore require medical care. Third, recognizing factors contributing to the development of the problem may make interventions more effective.

Important questions arise, however, if we accept this classification of early and late onset of alcoholism among the elderly. These questions deal with different treatment approaches for these two groups based on differing psychological and social characteristics that may be found among these patients.

DIAGNOSIS OF ALCOHOLISM IN THE ELDERLY

The author has developed an alcohol-abuse scale (see Table 22-I) that has proved clinically useful in establishing the diagnosis of alcoholism based on level of severity and can measure changes in severity over time due to spontaneous remission or as a result of the effects of treatment.

TABLE 22-I
SCALE OF ALCOHOL ABUSE

Severity Level	Characteristics
1. None	Drinks only on occasion if at all.
2. Minimal	Drinking is not conspicuous; occasional intoxications (up to 4/yr). No social, family, occupational, health, or legal problems related to drinking.
3. Mild	Intoxications occurring up to once a month, although generally limited to evening or weekends and/or some impairment in social, family relations, or occupational functioning related to drinking. No physical or legal problems to drinking.
4. Moderate	Frequent intoxications, up to one or two times per week and/or significant impairment in social, family, or occupational functioning. Some suggestive evidence of physical impairment related to drinking, such as tremors, frequent accidents, epigastric distress, loss of appetite at times. No history of DTs, cirrhosis, nutritional deficiency, hospitalization related to drinking, or arrests related to drinking.
5. Severe	Almost constant drinking (practically every day). History of DTs, cirrhosis, chronic brain syndrome, neuritis, or nutritional deficiency. Severe disruption in social or family relations. Unable to hold a steady job but able to maintain himself on public assistance. One or more arrests related to drinking (drunk or disorderly). One or more hospitalizations related to drinking.
6. Extreme	All of the characteristics of severe impairment plus homelessness and/or inability to maintain himself on public assistance.

There are generally less physical sequelae and less evidence of signs and symptoms of alcohol addiction in the elderly. Therefore, level 3 of the scale is the most likely point of severity among elderly alcoholics in contrast to levels of 4–6 in younger alcoholics. This observation is based on the fact that elderly people tend to consume smaller quantities of alcohol, possibly because they cannot metabolize it as readily as younger people (13).

The problems elderly alcoholics encounter are primarily social rather than those medical problems that would require detoxification and extensive medical care. Although some elderly alcoholics have medical problems associated with their drinking, in most the manifestations of alcoholism are more subtle than in younger people and greater efforts are required to elicit social problems associated with the consumption of alcohol. Organic brain syndromes can be exacerbated by smaller quantities of alcohol consumed by the elderly, and alcohol consumed with the other medications often utilized by the elderly can produce states of confusion out of proportion to the amount of alcohol consumed. These various factors, therefore, make the diagnosis of alcoholism much more difficult in the elderly.

PSYCHOSOCIAL FACTORS IN GERIATRIC ALCOHOLISM

Cahalan, Cisin, and Crossley (14), in their monograph based on a national survey of drinking behavior and attitudes in the United States, discussed some interesting observations concerning the natural history of drinking behavior and problem drinking. They noted that about one-third more individuals had problem drinking in a period before the three-year study period than during the study period itself, suggesting a tendency toward spontaneous remission.

Malzberg (15), Locke and Duvall (16) and Gorwitz, Bahn, Warthen and Cooper (17) presented data that showed a decline in admissions of elderly alcoholics to psychiatric hospitals and psychiatric clinics. These data, based on admissions to treatment, seem to confirm the epidemiological data developed by Cahalan et al. (14) and in fact have been the major basis for assuming that alcoholism is not a significant problem among the elderly.

Drew (18) observed that data concerning mortality related to alcoholism and alcoholism treatment outcome could not account for the observed decreased in alcoholics among the older age groups. He suggested that alcoholism is a self-limiting disease with a significant spontaneous remission with advancing age. Imber, Schultz, Funderburk, Allen, and Flamer (19) described a follow-up of 58 alcoholics who received no treatment for alcoholism. It was noted that the rate of abstinence was 15 percent at one year and 11 percent after 3 years. Therefore, spontaneous remission does seem to occur in alcoholism.

The question arises as to what factors might contribute to a spontaneous remission in elderly alcoholics. It has been established that drugs, including alcohol, tend to stay in the body longer and to have more prolonged and more powerful clinical and toxic effect in the body of an aged person (13). In addition, there is a functional loss of neuronal tissue in the aged which may account for the observed increased sensitivity to drugs of the sedative-hypnotic class (which includes alcohol). Therefore, it is quite possible that the effects of alcohol on mood and behavior become less pleasant and produce more unpleasant side effects in elderly people. Even long-standing alcoholics are likely to give up alcohol if it has become a noxious substance to them because of their diminished tolerance and its increased toxic effects.

If this explanation is correct, then what are the factors that contribute to the continued problem drinking among some alcoholics into old age and the development of late-onset alcoholism among a significant number of elderly people? The author has noted in his experience with both late-onset and early onset alcoholics a significant number of social and psychological factors associated with aging that have affected these patients. Rosin and Glatt (12) and Droller (20) noted in their treatment of elderly alcoholics that depression, bereavement, retirement, loneliness, marital stress, and physical illness were major contributing factors to the drinking problem. Treatment efforts directed at these factors in the elderly, in contrast to treatment efforts directed at the use of alcohol among younger alcoholics, were found to be most beneficial.

Based on these observations it is possible to construct a hypothesis that could account for the spontaneous tendency of alcoholism to remit with advancing age, as well as for the fact that some long-standing alcoholics continue to have problem drinking and that some elderly individuals develop alcohol problems in later life. Both groups of elderly alcoholics are reacting to the stresses of aging, which, in producing a great deal of anxiety and depression, lead to the use of alcohol in the form of self-medication. Apparently, the adverse effects of alcohol use in these aged are less disturbing than facing overwhelming problems, particularly object loss. Therefore, the socio-psychological stresses of aging can prolong problem drinking in long-standing alcoholics into old age and can contribute to the development of problem drinking in later life for some elderly individuals. If this hypothesis is correct, treatment approaches will have to consider primarily the socio-psychological stresses of aging as the focus for intervention.

PSYCHO-SOCIAL TREATMENT TECHNIQUES

Although awareness of alcoholism among the elderly has developed only recently, there have been reports of successful interventions in relation to elderly alcoholics. Droller (20) reported on seven cases of elderly alcoholics he visited at home. He found that in addition to medical and supportive treatment, therapy that was primarily social was the most beneficial to these patients. Rosin and Glatt (12), in their treatment of 103 elderly alcoholics, noted that environmental manipulation and medical services, along with day hospital, and home visiting by staff or good neighbors were the services that were most beneficial.

The author, in his experience in an outpatient geriatric psychiatric program (8), as a psychiatric consultant to a medical home care program (9), and as a psychiatric consultant to a nursing home, noted similar responses to social interventions. The use of group socialization and at times antidepressant medication was effective in eliminating alcohol abuse as a problem among the patients in these programs. The use of disulfiram, AA, or referral to alcoholism treatment programs required by younger alcoholics was not necessary for these patients. It is of even further interest to note that both early onset and late-onset alcoholics responded equally well to these psycho-social interventions, suggesting common etiological factors for these two groups of elderly alcoholics.

The hypothesis that psycho-social factors are the major contributors to alcoholism among the aged has been supported by the successful use of treatment interventions based on a psycho-social model. In young adult and middle-aged alcoholics, the first approaches to treatment are directed at the drinking behavior itself. Only with such directive intervention can the elimination of the use of alcohol be accomplished and an opportunity for learning other coping mechanisms to replace the alcohol be achieved. This direct-intervention approach is designed for the primary alcoholic, that is, in alcoholism that develops as the major behavioral disorder that is influenced by social-cultural, psychological, and physiological factors, but remains the main and overwhelming severe disorder of addiction.

In contrast, the elderly alcoholic is responding to severe social and psychological stresses associated with aging and is drinking in response to these stresses. If these stresses can be eliminated or attenuated, the secondary use of alcohol is diminished, thus leading to sobriety.

Techniques of Therapy

The treatment techniques utilized with such patients are based on the author's experience in a geriatric psychiatry outpatient program and involve the use of group therapy. Prior to admission to the group, every patient should have a complete physical and psychiatric evaluation so that physical or psychiatric disorders can be diagnosed and appropriate treatments instituted.

The group therapy can involve up to 15 to 20 patients and should not be insight oriented or directive as far as alcoholism is concerned. The patients should be elderly persons with a variety of social, psychological, organic mental, and physical disorders, not just alcoholism. The patients with alcoholism should be told that they have a drinking problem and that it is probably related to the difficulties they are having in adjusting to their current life situation.

The group should meet at least once a week and last for one-and-one-half to two hours. Cookies, coffee, and tea should be made available. If meals can be provided, eating together as a group would be helpful. The approach utilized by the group leaders should be supportive and oriented toward problem solving. Drinking problems should be one of the problem areas discussed but not the only one. Members of the group should be encouraged to discuss other members' problems as well as their own and to give advice and suggestions.

The group sessions could be divided into an informal social and/or eating period during the beginning of sessions, then a discussion and problem-solving period, followed by a socializing period at the end. The socializing period could be expanded through the use of activities therapy involving occupational therapy and/or planning for trips and outings, development of a patient government, and establishment of a patient kitty or dues. Patients requiring the institution of medication or medication follow-up can be seen by the physician individually after the group activities are completed.

The staffing of group programs should ideally consist of a psychiatrist who is knowledgeable about the problems of aging and alcoholism, a nurse, and one or two paraprofessional workers. These paraprofessional workers can provide a great many services for the patients, who will have many areas of difficulty. Such services should include visiting the homes of patients who miss clinic appointments; accompanying patient to other clinics and community agencies to act as liaison and patient advocates; observing and reporting patient behavior to the professional staff; contacting department of social services to help with patients' economic and housing needs; interviewing patients' friends, relatives, and neighbors to help support the patients living at home; and participating in the group sessions.

Many of the patients treated in such groups will be noted to be clinically depressed. The judicious use of antidepressant medication can be helpful for such patients.

LOCATION OF TREATMENT PROGRAMS

The question arises as to where these treatments should be provided in order to reach the greatest number of elderly alcoholics. In addition, there is the common question of how one deals with the significant number of elderly unwilling or unable to leave their homes. It has been found that elderly alcoholics perceive their alcoholism in ways different from younger alcoholics. First, older alcoholics generally consume smaller quantities of alcohol because of a lower tolerance and, therefore, have fewer acute medical problems associated with their alcohol consumption. For most elderly alcoholics, the alcohol that is consumed produces social problems but less often acute physical problems. Chronic medical problems such as cirrhosis of the liver or peptic ulcer may be present, but the need to detoxify from alcohol and treat alcohol withdrawal manifestations is quite rare. Therefore, the physical distress associated with alcoholism is seen less in elderly alcoholics, leading to a greater reluctance of the elderly to utilize specialized alcoholism treatment programs.

Denial exists in elderly alcoholics as it does with younger alcoholics, but the confrontation required to reach younger alcoholics to get them to recognize that they are alcoholic has not been found to be necessary. In view of these clinical observations, as well as the responses of elderly alcoholics to socio-psychological approaches related to the stresses of aging and their multiplicity of complex problems, only one of which is problem drinking, it would seem inappropriate to refer such patients to alcoholism treatment programs. Treatment interventions will be much more effective when delivered through facilities serving the aged, such as senior citizen programs, outpatient geriatric medical or psychiatric programs, nursing homes, or home-care programs. It is unlikely that significant numbers of elderly will be willing to go to an alcoholism program to deal with their problem drinking.

The development of specialized AA programs for elderly alcoholics might be an exception to this suggestion. Such AA programs should utilize elderly alcoholics as speakers to help the participants identify with similar problems. In addition, the group nature of an AA meeting could be enhanced by providing socialization and recreational activities after the formal AA meeting. Conducting such meetings in a senior citizen center would be ideal in regard to location and in regard to the availability of recreational activities.

The problems associated with delivering services to the elderly in general will also apply to elderly alcoholics. Many people will be unwilling or unable to leave their homes to go to outpatient programs or to participate in groups once they get there. Therefore, the delivery of comprehensive services to the elderly must include outreach and case-finding services, as well as an effective home-care program. Elderly individuals unwilling to participate in group activities as part of their lifelong life-style and personality have to be dealt with individually in an effort to learn what particular interests and competence the elderly person has that might be utilized to catalyze involvement in some aspect of a program. These considerations apply to the elderly alcoholic, as well.

APPLYING THE CONCEPTS OF THE
THERAPEUTIC COMMUNITY TO THE ELDERLY

Gruenberg (21) developed the concept of the social breakdown syndrome to describe and measure the amount of chronic mental disorder existing in a community and in psychiatric institutional settings. The syndrome consists of social and psychological behavioral deterioration resulting from the loss of social supports in the community or the authoritarian and rigid conditions in an institutional setting.

It is possible through the use of the concepts of the therapeutic community (22, 23) to treat effectively manifestations of behavioral disturbances that result from severe social and psychological deprivation and even improve functional capacities in elderly individuals suffering from organic mental impairment. The concepts of a therapeutic community can be applied in ambulatory settings (clinics and day care) as well as institutional settings (psychiatric hospitals and nursing homes).

The principles and practices embodied in the concept of the therapeutic community involve the recognition that an individual patient is part of a social system in which the individual's efforts toward involvement result in positive feedback from the social system as a necessary condition for maintaining feelings of self-worth and the ability to maintain continued cognitive and emotional involvement with the social system. The organization of an institution can either maximize the individual's involvement and provide positive feedback or strip the individual of all responsibilities and self-worth, resulting in a variety of behavioral disturbances. The isolated individual in the community can also be subjected to a state of isolation and helplessness in relation to the community at large.

The practices of the therapeutic community involve the opportunity for patients to have open and direct communication with the staff. Patients are encouraged to participate actively in their own treatment and to make decisions regarding administrative and therapeutic aspects of the treatment program. Patients are encouraged to participate in the decision-making process through patient-staff meetings and the establishment of a system of participatory patient government. Contacts with the community at large are encouraged and built into activities and recreational programs. The relationship between staff and patient is one of mutual respect and cooperation, with the staff providing guidance and direction rather than authoritarian orders and regulations.

The author provided psychiatric consultations to a county nursing home in Rockland County, New York over a period of two years. Prior to this consultation patients in the nursing home had no say in the various activities that were provided, were often put to bed at 6:30 P.M., and had limited outside activities. All sexual behavior was suppressed. There were several patients with drinking problems, and six to seven patients a year were sent to a nearby state psychiatric hospital because of serious management problems.

The focus of the psychiatric consultation was to establish a therapeutic community at the nursing home, with discussions of various patient problems and the staff rules and attitudes as they related to these problems. The results produced a nursing home where patients made the decisions about the movies they would see and the activities they wanted. Frequent group discussions between staff and patients eliminated some of the areas of patient complaints. Patients' intellectual interests increased so that they asked the local community college to provide courses for them in the nursing home. Behavioral problems including alcohol abuse were eliminated, no longer requiring any patient to be transferred to the state hospital. Married couples who had been placed in separate rooms were permitted to sleep in the same room, and a room was set aside for privacy for patients who had established close relationships. It was apparent that sexual interests in elderly patients were not really absent, only suppressed. The nursing home became in many respects more like a home for the patients, since they had a considerable voice in what went on in the facility. The staff benefited by having many fewer management problems to contend with and no longer had to put patients to bed at 6:30 P.M. in order to have a quiet night. All this was accomplished by changing the social system of the nursing home, opening channels of communication between staff and patients, and permitting patients to exercise much greater responsibility for their own care and the care of the other patients.

SUMMARY

Evidence is presented of the existence of a significant problem of alcohol abuse among the elderly from a variety of sources. The recognition of this problem requires the development of effective treatment interventions for this population of alcoholics.

Elderly alcoholics can be classified into early onset alcoholics with long histories of alcoholism and later-onset alcoholics who develop drinking problems in late life. Among elderly alcoholics, about two-thirds are early onset alcoholics and one-third late-onset alcoholics.

The psycho-social stresses of aging, including depression, bereavement, retirement, loneliness, marital stress, economic hardships, and physical illness, are thought to be the major causal factors of alcoholism among the elderly. There is a tendency for alcohol to be consumed less as one ages; however, the alcoholism in early onset alcoholics and development of alcoholism in late-onset alcoholics can be related to the reaction to the stresses of aging.

The diagnosis of alcoholism in the elderly is more difficult because there are less acute medical problems. Alcoholism is manifested by social, behavioral and organic mental impairments.

The psycho-social treatment techniques of alcoholism among the elderly are described. They include the use of supportive and problem-solving-oriented group therapy, antidepressant medication, group socialization, and recreational activities. Elderly alcoholics are best treated with elderly people who have other problems in programs established for the elderly rather than in separate alcoholism programs. The use of professional and paraprofessional staff in treatment teams can be the most effective approach to treatment.

Establishing therapeutic communities in nursing homes can improve patient behavior and reduce behavioral and management problems, including alcoholism.

REFERENCES

1. Bailey, M. B., Habermen, P. W., and Alksne, H. The epidemiology of alcoholism in an urban residential area. *Quart. J. Stud. Alc.*, 1965, 26, 19–40.
2. Siassi, I., Crocetti, G., and Spiro, H. R. Drinking patterns and alcoholism in a blue collar population. *Quart. J. Stud. Alc.*, 1973, 34, 917–926.
3. Simon, A., Epstein, L. J., and Reynolds, L. Alcoholism in the geriatric mentally ill. *Geriatrics*, 1968, 23, 125–131.
4. Gaitz, C. M., and Baer, P. E. Characteristics of elderly patients with alcoholism. *Arch. Gen. Psychiatry*, 1971, 24, 327–378.
5. McCusker, J., Cherubin, C. F., and Zimberg, S. Prevalence of alcoholism in general municipal hospital population. *N.Y.S.J. Med*, 1971, 71, 751–754.
6. Schuckit, M. A., and Miller, P. L. Alcoholism in elderly men: a survey of a general medical ward. *Ann. Ny.Y. Acad. Sci.*, 1976, 273, 558–571.
7. Epstein, L. J., Mills, C., and Simon, A. Antisocial behavior of the elderly. *Comp. Psychiatry*, 1970, 11, 36–42.
8. Zimberg, S. Outpatient geriatric psychiatry in an urban ghetto with nonprofessional workers. *Amer. J. Psychiatry*, 1969, 125, 1697–1702.
9. Zimberg, S. The psychiatrist and medical home care: geriatric psychiatry in the Harlem community. *Amer. J. Psychiatry,* 1971, 127, 1062–1066.
10. Carruth, B., Williams, E. P., Mysak, P., and Boudreaux, L. Community care providers and the older problem drinker. *Grassroots*, 1975, July Supplement, 1–5.
11. Mishara, B. L., and Kastenbaum, R. *Alcohol and Old Age.* New York: Grune and Stratton, 1980.

12. Rosin, A. J., and Glatt, M. M. Alcohol excess in the elderly. *Quart. J. Stud. Alc.,* 1971, 32, 53–59.
13. Salzman, C., Vanderkolk, B., and Shader, R. Psychopharmacology and the geriatric patient. In R. I. Shader (Ed.), *Manual of Psychiatric Therapeutics.* Boston: Little, Brown, 1975.
14. Cahalan, D., Cisin, I. H., and Crossley, H. M. *American Drinking Practices: A National Survey of Drinking Behavior and Attitudes.* New Brunswick: Rutgers Center of Alcohol Studies, 1974.
15. Malzberg, B. A study of first admissions with alcoholic psychoses in New York State. *Quart. J. Stud. Alc.,* 1947, 8, 276–295.
16. Locke, B. Z., and Duvall, H. J. Alcoholism among first admissions to Ohio public mental hospitals. *Quart. J. Stud. Alc.,* 1960, 21, 457–474.
17. Gorwitz, K., Bahn, A., Warther, F. J., and Cooper, M. Some epidemiological data on alcoholism in Maryland based on admissions to psychiatric facilities. *Quart. J. Stud. Alc.,* 1970, 31, 423–443.
18. Drew, L. R. H. Alcohol as a self-limiting disease. *Quart. J. Stud. Alc.,* 1968, 29, 956–967.
19. Imber, S., Schultz, E., Funderburk, F., Allen, R., and Flamer, R. The fate of the untreated alcoholic. *J. Neru & Ment. Dis.,* 1976, 162, 238–247.
20. Droller, H. Some aspects of alcoholism in the elderly. *Lancet,* 1964, 2, 137–139.
21. Gruenberg, G. M. The social breakdown syndrome and Its prevention. In S. Arieti and G. Caplan (Eds.), *American Handbook of Psychiatry.* New York: Basic Books, 1974.
22. Jones, M. *The Therapeutic Community.* New York: Basic Books, 1953.
23. Stanton, A. H., and Schwartz, M. S. *The Mental Hospital.* New York: Basic Books, 1954.

SECTION VI
ISSUES IN DEALING WITH
SUBSTANCE ABUSERS
AMONG OLDER VETERANS

Chapter 23

SUBSTANCE ABUSE DISORDERS
IN AGING VETERANS

Stewart L. Baker

The general population has increased two-and-one-half times
since the beginning of this century, at the same time the
number of people age 65 and over has increased seven times, with
the result that these elderly now represent 10 percent of Americans.
Due to failing health with advancing age, older individuals represent an even higher proportion of the population seeking medical
care.

Alcoholism is a health problem that affects a significant number of aging individuals. It is important that efforts be made
to examine this problem, with respect to the current level of
knowledge, and to identify issues that have not been addressed
previously. It's my hope and expectation for this conference, with
such well-informed, distinguished figures from the related research,
treatment, and academic communities, that we may experience a
renaissance, a sense of renewed and fresh dedication to the usefulness of early incorporation and implementation of the most current state of knowledge about this large field of human need.
Recently, in a national survey of 225 agencies involved in the
referral or treatment of individuals with drinking problems, 18
percent of the persons being treated were found to be 55 years or
older. Other assays collected from general medical and from psychiatric hospitals indicate that the prevalence of alcoholism among
these older individuals ranges from 18 percent to as high as 55
percent in such treatment centers. General population studies
report the occurrence of alcoholism in elderly persons ranges
from 2 percent to 10 percent. The conclusion reached from such
studies is that alcohol abuse and alcoholism constitute a signifi-

cant psychiatric and medical health problem for the aging population, regardless of whether the sample is drawn from the general
population, the outpatient clinics, medical or psychiatric wards,
or domiciliary centers. Veterans Administration (VA) annual census studies have repeatedly revealed that over 30 percent of all VA
domiciliary residents suffer from alcoholism. As Zimberg has
stressed in several of his published papers, it is a problem that
often goes unrecognized and untreated (1, 2).

To identify the VA's stake in geriatric medicine, I will cite some
demographic data. Nearly 39 million Americans have served in
the uniformed services. Nearly 1.1 million of these died in service
during wartime. Some 87 percent of all veterans served during
wartime: only 13 percent served during peacetime only. Approximately 75 percent of all American veterans are still living – about
30 million. Approximately a half million persons are discharged
yearly from the military services and become new veterans. About
75 percent of this number is offset by deaths of other veterans in
the group of 30 million from five wars, with the growth in total
veterans being about 100,000 annually. However, the reduced size
of military forces during recent years has generated progressively
lower numbers of new veterans, so that last year, for the first time,
the total number of living veterans fell by about 25,000. There are
about a half million World War I veterans, twelve and one-half
million World War II veterans (the largest cohort of veterans),
almost six million Korean War veterans, and nine million Vietnam-
era veterans (the second largest cohort, coming from this nation's
longest war). There are almost 700,000 female veterans.

As veterans age, reach retirement status at age 65, and attempt
to live on fixed-income pensions, social security benefits, or reduced
income from part-time employment, many experience a major
decrease in discretionary income. Given this reduction in discretionary income, an unknown number of such veterans, who did
not utilize VA facilities prior to age 65, will be required to do so
when they are in need of medical, surgical or psychiatric services
after reaching age 65.

Under current law (PL 96-330), essentially all veterans over age
65 who were discharged under honorable conditions are eligible
for inpatient care at VA medical centers. Recently, there has been

indication that Medicare beneficiaries, who are also eligible for VA care, could soon be required to utilize Veterans Administration rather than Medicare resources in obtaining necessary health-care services.

A substantial, almost explosive increase is projected in the number and proportion of veterans 65 years of age and above during the next 10 years. The World War II veteran population is now approaching the geriatric-age group, to be followed in relatively rapid succession by the Korean-era veterans. Presently, there are approximately three million veterans age 65 and older. By 1985, hardly more than two years hence, their numbers will almost double to approximately five million and will continue to increase until 1995 to peak in excess of eight million at that time. One can sense the multiple impacts of such a large population shift on current configurations of VA health service facilities. Currently available data demonstrate that a higher proportion of the veterans over 65 utilize VA health-care services than any other age group. Further, as a group they experience higher rates of hospitalization, longer lengths of stay, have fewer social and community supports, and require a wide range of acute- and long-term-care services. One measure of the projected impact of such a logarithmic rate of growth in this cohort of veterans can be provided by the following: currently 18 percent of all VA outpatient treatment visits are made by veterans over age 65; in the year 2000, approximately 50 percent of all visits will be made by veterans 65 or older. This scale of change in the volume of treatment services for older veterans has urgent implications for changes in the VA health-care-delivery system.

Today, public policy about alcohol and other drug use is in heated debate. Earlier-held assumptions about the social and biological determinants of dysfunctional drug and alcohol use are being reassessed. Research which should ideally precede and help shape public policy in this problem area is finally being accomplished. Up to the present time, public policy in this parameter has been reactive and reflexive, responding to a sense of crisis with actions based on traditional assumptions about alcohol and drug use which are at odds with contemporary social values and practices. We must still make the point that alcohol is a drug.

American drug policy will never be coherent until it is founded on uniform principles, recognizing that all drugs, including alcohol, act according to the same general principles, with little regard to their legitimacy or prescriptive source. Their effects vary with dose. At high dose levels, and for some individuals at much lower dose levels, all drugs may be dangerous.

This brings me to another problem often identified in the aging population: the very real hazard of drug interactions. The elderly consume a disproportionately large amount of prescription and over-the-counter drugs, frequently self-administered in excessive quantities. Our VA outpatient and pharmacy services provide a broad range of medications, often for the same veteran, to speed up bowel action, for sleep, for cardiac arrhythmias, for depression, for appetite, and on and on. These multiple prescriptions, often derived from a number of different clinics, provide a repertoire of fine tunings for more integrated biomedical function and often for support of vital functions. However, there is a need for monitoring the patient's drug use profile. Drug interactions are preventable. Alcohol-drug interaction is a serious potential problem; some combinations can cause death. Of special importance in this regard is the research finding that in elderly patients the action of stimulants is lessened whereas the action of depressants, including alcohol, is enhanced. Problems with antihistamines, with barbiturates, and hypnotics such as Doriden® and Noludar® are often encountered when they are prescribed for aged patients.

Schuckit (3) has cautioned that the elderly are at heightened risk for experiencing adverse reactions to alcohol. The aging process results in a decreased resilience in all body systems with the lessening of physical reserves, accompanied by a decrease in emotional and psychological flexibility, as well. For the older drinker, these changes are aggravated by difficulties in metabolism of all substances, including alcohol. At the same time, the central nervous system in elderly persons is particularly vulnerable to the effects of CNS-depressing medications. Schuckit has shown that as little as one cocktail can decrease the cardiac efficiency in individuals with heart disease and that moderate doses can directly raise the blood pressure.

Higher rates of alcoholism are seen in elderly patients presenting with medical or emotional problems, probably related to the well-documented consequences of persistent alcohol intake. It is estimated that 20 percent of older general medical and surgical patients fulfill the criteria for alcoholism, with similar rates for geriatric populations presenting with emotional problems. And, as I've noted earlier, the prevalence in VA domiciliaries exceeds 30 percent.

Atkinson (4) reports on two frequently identified subtypes of elderly alcoholics: the early onset alcoholics who have their first alcoholic problems before age 40 and who survive, usually by becoming abstinent during late middle age; and the late-onset alcoholics whose drinking problems begin after age 40 and whose drinking continues past age 65. The later-onset alcoholic has relatively fewer interpersonal and social problems. The clinical course is one of remission and return to drinking in an alternating pattern. In comparison with age-matched nonalcoholics, the older alcoholics have higher rates of suicide attempts and more often show signs of mental deterioration. They are also more likely than the age-matched nonalcoholics to live alone, to be unmarried, and they tend to change their residence more often. These facets of the disease tend to worsen the prognosis and create special problems and risks against the completion of a course of treatment. In another study, over 90 percent of the older, actively drinking alcoholics presented with a major health problem, often the consequence of chronic drinking. Chronic obstructive pulmonary disease and confusional states rank high in frequency of occurrence in this group.

The frequency of associated medical problems calls for a comprehensive biomedical assessment of each patient. Reintegration with family is often a highly fruitful treatment goal. Remotivating such isolated persons requires a broad spectrum of treatment activities, ranging from the development of an organizing approach to leisure time, to include the recognition and development of long-unexpressed talents and hobbies, and other skills. The impacts of retirement, and of aging, and the decrease in discretionary funds should be regularly assessed for consideration in the treatment plan.

The medical risks of Antabuse®, the need for an age-appropriate AA group, and a facilitated (on-line) access to medical consultation are common concerns of those who treat elderly alcoholics. But, above all these concerns, the maturation of a warm trust relationship with another person (sometimes staff but perchance another patient) can provide the needed spark, the motivation to readdress a larger community of activities and values, with a more coherent and supportive meaning for life.

Physicians frequently miss the diagnosis of alcoholism in the aging patient and often it is because the possibility is ignored. Zimberg has suggested that alcoholism is one of the five biggest health problems among the aged. The VA's Audio-Visual Center at St. Louis is currently developing a five-part multimedia training tape packet for specialized medical education of physicians for improved recognition and clinical management of alcoholism and the alcohol-related secondary diseases and other complications of alcoholism. We expect that these will be distributed to the VA medical centers for use next spring. A number of reports have observed that physicians have trouble working effectively with older people because of limitations in their own knowledge, experience or skills, and attitudes related to aging. Most physicians in practice today have received little or no instruction about the nature of aging and the special constellation of disabilities that commonly affect the elderly. The average physician has the same misconceptions about aging as the general public. These are some common misconceptions: that there is inevitable physical failing, inevitable mental failing, inevitable sexual failing, that most elderly are in institutions, most are separated from families, most want to live with families, and most want to withdraw from society. All of these myths have been dispelled by studies. We hope to contribute to healthier physician attitudes by the multimedia training packets mentioned earlier.

Another major challenge to treatment and rehabilitation programs for the elderly is the tendency of elderly patients to attribute most health problems and symptoms simply to old age and to think that little or nothing can be done to help. A related problem is the tendency of older patients to have a hopeless view about their problem, such that they "give up" on continuing recommended therapeutic programs, particularly when they relate to changes in diet and physical therapy programs.

· In a foreword to a recently published book, entitled *Elderly Patients and Their Doctors*, and edited by Marie Haug (5), Dr. Robert Butler, who was until recently, the director of the National Institute on Aging, proposes:

> There is an increasing awareness of a compelling need to foster the discovery and application of new knowledge concerning: (1) health promotion and disease prevention in older persons, (2) diagnostic evaluation of older persons, and (3) care and treatment of older persons. Considering the large growth of the population involved, strikingly little is known about age-related illnesses — their causes, physical and psychosocial consequences, and effective therapies. Considering the fact that health costs are escalating at a staggering rate, we must promote the growth of the important field of geriatrics in schools of medicine, nursing, social work and allied disciplines. The complexities of disease and old age have not been appreciated yet in full enough measure by medical and other health schools. Indeed, this failure reflects a devalued view of older persons, one that is often held in the health professions. Ageism is a part of our culture. Despite its humanitarian and scientific roots, medicine has not shaken itself loose from widespread cultural negativism.

In 1975, in part responsive to these critical deficits in information and clinical practices, the VA activated five Geriatric Research, Education and Clinical Centers, called "GRECCS," within the physical boundaries of selected VA medical centers. These centers, now totaling eight, have provided considerable needed focus on aging veterans across the VA's national health service delivery system. A report on the progress of these specialized centers was published in the March 1982 *Journal of the American Geriatrics Society*. In addition to considerable basic or molecular research on the aging process, with over 500 papers published thus far, there are many indications that the centers have been integrated into the VA hospitals' clinical operations and associated activities. Each GRECC operates a demonstration unit of about 20 beds; to date, they have provided geriatric training experience for over 600 health-care professionals, with 24 physicians completing the 2-year fellowship each year. The newly initiated Nurse Scholarship Program, designed to assist in providing an adequate supply of professional nurses for the VA and the nation, has established gerontologic nursing as one of its priority areas and is supporting master's level training in that category of professional skills.

Shortly, a joint research and development/professional services team from central office will site visit three VA medical centers to collect data for use in advertising a proposal for a VA alcoholism research program, which will emphasize the clinical research interface, with special regard for psycho-social parameters of the disease. The mandate for these new alcoholism research centers will include special concerns for the aging veteran. It is scheduled to be competed by VA medical centers this fiscal year and to become operational at the winning sites in FY 1984.

SUMMARY

Substance misuse including alcoholism is a critical problem which must be aggressively addressed by all agencies providing health-care services to the elderly. Issues of special import are professional attitudes towards both the elderly and towards older folks who abuse substances and our lack of knowledge as to interaction of drugs, alcohol and aging as it affects medical/social problems of the elderly. In addition, large medical systems, like the Veterans Administration, with many clinics prescribing to the same patient must coordinate treatment efforts, especially as related to polypharmacy, and must at the same time keep in mind that the elderly are heavy users of over-the-counter medications. In this, health-care professionals must strive to assure that they are part of the solution and not contributors to the problem. The VA has been grappling with the issue of drugs, alcohol and aging for some years. The following chapters briefly describe one of our treatment/rehabilitation efforts. In addition to local efforts, the VA has established five special centers to study aging and is currently developing three centers to research alcoholism with special regard for the psychosocial parameters of the disease. Finally, we are designing a multimedia training packet directed towards improving physician recognition and clinical management of alcoholism and the alcohol-related secondary disease and other complications of alcoholism.

REFERENCES

1. Zimberg, S. The elderly alcoholic. *Gerontologist*, 1974, 14, 221–224.
2. Zimberg, S. Diagnosis and treatment of the elderly alcoholic. *Alcoholism: Clinical and Experimental Research*, 1978, 2(1), 27–29.
3. Shuckit, M. A., and Pastor, P. A. The elderly as a unique population. *Blue Journal Alcoholism: Clinical and Experimental Research*, 1978, 2(1), 31–38.
4. Atkinson, J. H. Alcoholism and geriatric problems (part II) *Advances in Alcoholism*, Raleigh Hills Foundation, 1981, 2(9), 1–3.
5. Butler, R. M., Foreword in M. R. Haug (Ed.), *Elderly Patients and Their Doctors*, VII–IX. New York: Springer Publishing Co., 1981.

Chapter 24

MEDICAL AND PSYCHIATRIC MANAGEMENT OF THE OLDER ALCOHOLIC VETERAN

Luis A. Marco
Patricia M. Randels

.

Introduction

A lcohol is a source of fuel that provides calories for the body. It
is also a drug with distinct pharmacologic properties. Alcoholic beverages are readily available at social gatherings, and
drinking is legally and socially sanctioned. Despite alcohol's strong
addicting properties and its association with adverse biological
and psychosocial effects, it continues to represent an entrenched
indulgence in most advanced societies. Only continual drunkenness and chronic alcoholism are usually cause for disparagement.
Abuse of alcohol is a large and pervasive problem. The number of
alcoholics in the United States is perhaps over 14 million people
(1); alcoholism is listed as the third most serious national health
problem; it is the fourth most common cause of death within the
35–55 age range (2). Of the approximately 100 million people who
use beverage alcohol, 5–10 percent do so irresponsibly and with
negative consequences for themselves and others. Some 20–30
percent of medical-surgical admissions have been attributed to
complications of excessive alcohol use and 50 percent of violent
crimes (e.g., murder, rape) and highway fatalities are thought to
be provoked by alcohol intoxication. These must have been the
figures and kinds of outcomes that prompted Chafetz (3) to assert
that today alcoholism is one of America's major public health

The authors thank Mrs. E. Theresa Snyder and Elsie M. Tripken for typing various drafts
of the manuscript and Mr. Paul Grauer for completing the references.

problems and the largest untreated treatable disease. The pattern of admissions for alcoholism at the Coatesville VA Medical Center, as monitored during the last 10 months, yields the following figures: 20 out of 362 admissions (5.5%) were alcoholics 50 years of age or older and 70/362 (19.3%) were less than 50 years old. For all ages, 90/362 (24.8%) of all admissions were due to alcoholism. This is higher than the estimated 20 percent of the patients in acute-care hospital beds who appear to have an alcohol-related problem. Alcoholics utilize various medical services more frequently than non-alcoholics, but since alcoholism is often denied by the afflicted individual as well as by their relatives, the true cost of these services is often hidden. Nevertheless, alcohol-related illnesses cost society about $77 billion annually (4); $79.5 billion estimated in 1982 (5). Yet, in 1980 only approximately $940.5 million was spent on the treatment of alcoholism (6), which represents only 0.004 percent of the total health dollars.

Alcohol passes from the stomach into the small intestine where it is readily absorbed into the bloodstream and freely distributed in body water. Since alcohol is a simple nonpolar compound, it readily enters all body tissues and diffuses throughout the body in proportion to the water content of the tissues. Most organs contain 70–80 percent of the alcohol plasma concentration at equilibrium. Adipose tissue contains only 10–20 percent of the plasma concentrations of alcohol because of its low water content and poor blood supply. Food and sugar in the stomach delay absorption. Carbon dioxide and bicarbonate (characteristic of sparkling wines) accelerate the process. The duration of effect from alcohol depends upon its elimination from the body. The rate of elimination, in turn, depends upon individual variability, and there are no easy ways to expedite either metabolism or elimination. Age per se appears to have no effect on the rate of alcohol elimination but peak blood alcohol concentration (BAC) at the end of an intravenous infusion of 15 percent (v/v) alcohol, at a rate of 375 mg/m^2/min to healthy male volunteers ranging in age from 21 to 81 years, has been found to correlate with age and to increase 33 percent over the adult age span (7). This correlation seems to be related to age differences in body composition, particularly the increased adiposity with age.

Thus, the same alcohol dose in terms of surface area becomes a higher dose per lean body mass in the elderly than in younger individuals.

The nutritional value of alcohol is negligible. However, when 1 gm of ethanol is metabolized in the body, 7.1 calories are released, and a significant portion of this energy can be utilized to maintain cellular metabolism. Unfortunately, even though ethanol can be considered to be a nutrient, the intake of ethanol interferes with the normal metabolism and absorption of other nutrients by inhibiting gastric emptying, increasing gastric acid secretion, and producing changes in the motility of the intestine. In addition, ethanol directly inhibits the energy-coupled processes involved in the transport of amino acids, vitamins, and minerals across the intestinal mucosa.

The major catabolic pathway of ethanol is via the zinc-containing liver enzyme alcohol dehydrogenase, which, in the presence of nicotinamide-adenine dinucleotide (NAD^+), dehydrogenates ethanol to acetaldehyde. This degradation reduces the blood alcohol concentration at a uniform rate of approximately 100–200 mg/kg per hour, irrespective of plasma concentrations, and gives rise to the common estimate that humans can metabolize about 1 oz whisky/hr (8). The acetaldehyde is converted to acetate by mitochondrial acetaldehyde dehydrogenase and to acetyl coenzyme A which enters the citric acid cycle. There are two other liver enzyme systems, the microsomal ethanol oxidizing system and catalase, whose role in alcohol degradation is less clear (9).

Attitudes toward treatment have varied widely with time. Not too long ago, alcoholics were denied treatment or were rejected as patients, often because they may appear dirty and smell foul in the emergency room. The rationale for treatment approaches has varied less whimsically with time and has usually been based on experimentation or experience. From these scientific insights, there has emerged an increased interest in, and understanding of, the medical and psychological devastation caused by alcohol abuse. Care-related and support systems of the alcoholic and other family members have spread throughout the nation. There are now more than 4,000 alcohol-treatment facilities in this country (2).

The management of the alcoholic patient must be individualized and specialized to be appropriate. The needs of the sporadic acutely intoxicated are found to differ from those of the acutely intoxicated with a background of steady and heavy chronic alcoholism and both from the goals of long-term treatment. It is impossible to outline a single management protocol for alcoholism, whether drug therapy, psychotherapy, or behavioral approaches are primarily entertained. Furthermore, the objectives of drug therapy are as different as the various pathogenetic mechanisms often involved in alcoholism and no single drug can address them all.

The first step in the management of the alcoholic, old or young, is, as elsewhere in medicine, an accurate diagnosis. Although the focus of this chapter is not the diagnosis of alcoholism, we must emphasize that the longer the diagnosis is delayed, the longer needed management will be postponed. Extensive inquiry about the patient's use of alcohol was thought by (Harry S.) Sullivan as being extremely revealing of the patient's personality and possible psychopathology.

Alcoholism and drug dependence are the two disorders most difficult to distinguish from antisocial personality. This is because they are often intertwined: substance abuse leads to antisocial behavior and antisocial personalities often indulge in alcohol and other substances. If these can be disentangled, the determination of a historical, chronological sequence of behaviors is the best lead as to which was present first and which is secondary.

Once the history suggests primarily alcoholism, major criteria for its diagnosis are available and should be evaluated. These include: the National Council on Alcoholism (10), the Michigan Alcoholism Screening Test or MAST (11, 12) and the Diagnostic and Statistical Manual or DSM–III (13).

Alcohol abuse and dependence are hidden disorders; denial is the rule and only about 5 percent of alcoholics fit the striking stereotype of the street bum or "revolving door alcoholic." For the remaining alcoholics, casefinding is made difficult by their own denial and by family cover-up motivated by embarrassment, shame and disgust. Thus, the physician must clear his suspicion to prevent the problem from remaining undetected. The physician must be sensitive to early or frank signs of medical sequelae of heavy alcohol use, including moderate nontender hepatomegaly; frequent bruising in the nonelderly; ulcer disease apparently refractory to usual treatment; elevation in serum uric acid and triglycerides; persistent unexplained elevations in liver function tests; and weight loss. Such problems may provide important cues for the diagnosis of alcoholism and for an integrated treatment. Social or personal complications, such as arrests while driving under the influence of alcohol, work absenteeism, or garrulousness, may suggest need for concern and carefully planned interviewing.

Knowledge of possible predisposing factors to alcohol abuse or unusual reactions to alcohol add to the casefinding armamentarium. For example, alcoholism is more common among Scandinavian, Irish, American Indians, and Eskimos than among Italians, Jews, Greeks, or Orientals. Biologic, rather than cultural, factors may predominate in the latter groups. Last-borns are over-represented among alcoholics, as are children of total abstainers or alcoholics. Certain occupations and social settings such as bartending, the armed services, other mobile work situations, and college seem to be associated with heavy drinking. The rate of alcohol-associated problems among physicians (15%–18%) is somewhat higher than that for the general population (10%).

Although it is difficult to tease apart the contributions of genetics or biology, learning and environment, and the combined effects of these factors in influencing the development of alcoholism, heritability appears to be an important factor in determining drinking behavior, innate tolerance or sensitivity, ethanol metabolic rate, acquired tolerance (metabolic and/or CNS), physical dependence, and susceptibility to medical complications (14). In a series of studies of Danish adoption and intemperance registers, Goodwin and colleagues (15) have found that adopted-away sons of alcoholics, separated from their parents early in life, are four times more likely to become alcoholic than adoptees whose biologic parents were not alcoholic, but a similar effect for the daughters of alcoholics could not be demonstrated (16).

Factors which might alert the clinician to problems with alcohol use include problems associated with developmental landmarks and life changes, e.g., adolescence, menopause, retirement, etc. The elderly constitute an explosively growing proportion of the population and have shown increased alcohol and drug consumption.

There are no major differences between the alcoholism of elderly individuals and that of more youthful persons. But there are important interactions between aging and alcohol abuse. These interactions make the elderly alcoholic unique in terms of medical and psychiatric management. The effects of aging are, in many important ways, similar to those of alcohol. We can only mention them cursorily (see Table 24-I).

Aging brings about neurological compromise which manifests itself in psychomotor slowing and diminished cognitive capacity. Alcohol adds direct CNS damage and diffuse functional loss. Sleep is disrupted by aging and alcohol in similar ways. Both cause frequent awakenings and decrease in REM and deep sleep. It has been said that the sleep pattern of middle-aged alcoholics resembles that of elderly non-alcoholics.

The heart decreases its output by 40–50 percent through the life span, and circulation time increases correspondingly, while alcohol adds to the aging of the heart by decreasing cardiac output and coronary circulation, with high output heart failure or beri-beri heart in advanced cases of alcoholism. Blood flow further slows down with alcohol due to the "sludging" of RBC's.

With aging, the liver undergoes weight reduction, the hepatocytes become larger and less numerous, and protein synthesis, RNA, metabolism of drugs, and albumin levels all decrease with age. Similar effects are observed in the alcoholic liver, with a final outcome of cirrhosis and hepatic failure.

In the gastrointestinal system, aging correlates with hypochlorhydria while hyperchlorhydria is more typical in the drinker. In both, however, the evolution is toward slowed absorption and digestion.

Kidney function in the elderly undergoes a decline in blood flow of about 55 percent and in glomerular tubular function of 46 percent with a resultant decrease in drug clearance. In the alcoholic, there is first diuresis with loss of K, Mg, Ca, P, and Zn and impairment of nerve-muscle function, but later, and particularly during withdrawal, fluid retention and heart overload are the rule.

Nutrition is impaired in both with further depletion of Ca, Fe, and vitamins (A, B, C). Indeed, alcohol has been considered to be a nutrition antagonist or a nutrient with empty calories, since no vitamins and minerals are ingested with it as they would with foodstuffs.

Stress responses become constricted in the elderly in adaptive and homeostatic capacity with greater variations and reduced speed of recovery. Alcohol is a stressor, further adding to this imbalance.

The immune system of the elderly or the alcoholic becomes limited in its capacity with infection.

Even the skin and mucosae of the middle-aged alcoholic resemble remarkably those of the elderly: dry, scaly, reddened, bruised, keratotic, reddened sore mouth and tongue, and the healing of wounds is dampened and prone to infections.

Thus, drinking in many ways is like speaking the aging process. This interplay is what is most unique about the elderly alcoholic. Table 24-I lists these major interactions. Otherwise, as stated above, age per se appears to have no effect on the rate of alcohol elimination.

TABLE 24-I
AGING-ALCOHOL INTERACTION

NEUROLOGICAL

HEART - CIRCULATION

LIVER

GASTRO-INTESTINAL

KIDNEY

NUTRITION

STRESS

IMMUNE

SKIN - MUCOSAE

DSM–III makes no categorical provisions for the diagnosis of alcoholism in the elderly. It divides alcoholic conditions into two major groups, non-organic and organic, with two and seven diagnostic categories respectively as shown in Table 24-II.

TABLE 24-II
DSM–III Alcohol-Induced Diagnostic Categories

NON-ORGANIC	OMD
ALCOHOL ABUSE	INTOXICATION
ALCOHOL DEPENDENCE	IDIOSYNCRATIC INTOXICATION
	WITHDRAWAL
	WITHDRAWAL DELIRIUM
	HALLUCINOSIS
	AMNESTIC
	DEMENTIA

The diagnostic criteria for Alcohol Abuse (305.0%) according to DSM–III are:

A. Pattern of pathological alcohol use: need for daily use of alcohol for adequate functioning; inability to cut down or stop drinking; repeated efforts to control or reduce excess drinking by "going on the wagon" (periods of temporary abstinence) or restricting drinking to certain times of the day; binges (remaining intoxicated throughout the day for at least two days); occasional consumption of a fifth of spirits (or its equivalent in wine or beer); amnesic periods for events occurring while intoxicated (blackouts); continuation of drinking despite a serious physical disorder that the individual knows is exacerbated by alcohol use; drinking of non-beverage alcohol.

B. Impairment in social or occupational functioning due to alcohol use: e.g., violence while intoxicated, absence from work, loss of job, legal difficulties (e.g., arrest for intoxicated behavior, traffic accidents while intoxicated), argu-

ments or difficulties with family or friends because of
excessive alcohol use.

C. Duration of disturbance of at least one month.

Diagnostic criteria for Alcohol Dependence (DSM–III 303.9x):

A. Either a pattern of pathological use (as A above) or
    impairment in social or occupational functioning due to
    alcohol use (as B above).

B. Either tolerance or withdrawal:
    (1) Tolerance: need for markedly increased amounts of
        alcohol to achieve the desired effect, or markedly
        diminished effect with regular use of the same amount.
    (2) Withdrawal: development of Alcohol Withdrawal (e.g.,
        morning "shakes" and malaise relieved by drinking)
        after cessation of or reduction in drinking.

The management of the non-organic alcoholic is usually protracted but promising if intensive and tailored to the individual
needs of the patient. The sections that follow discuss the main
treatment modalities.

A determination of the stage of alcoholism can be made on the
basis of Table 24-III which is based, in a simplified form, on the
work of Jellinek (17) and Pokorny et al. (18). It provides a guideline about level of functioning, complications, and prognosis.
This table is instructive on several counts: It marks the point in
the time sequence of events from initial involvement with alcohol,
through onset of physical damage, seeking medical help, diminished sexual potency, to seeking psychiatric advice. Note that
sexual impotence is the 32nd item in the complete natural history
of 39 developments in alcoholism. This is far down in the list but
even further in the authors' original sequence. Impaired potency
comes just before the stage of giving up (stage 37), the last in a
continuum of dwindling self-esteem. It finally portrays a gloomy
picture for outcome and prognosis following the request for professional help.

The first order of business after deciding upon a diagnosis of
alcoholism is to share the diagnosis with the patient in a non-
judgmental fashion. To judge may serve to alienate the individual.
Attempting to engender fear by describing all the terrible sequelae

TABLE 24-III
STAGING IN ALCOHOLISM

	STAGES
ALCOHOL APPROACH	(1-6)
ALCOHOL DEPENDENCE	
SOCIO-ECONOMIC DETERIORATION	(7-18)
SURRENDER TO ALCOHOL INVOLVEMENT	(19-28)
ONSET OF PHYSICAL DAMAGE	(29-30)
SEEKING MEDICAL HELP	(31)
DIMINISHED SEXUAL POTENCY	(32)
"WHAT'S THE USE?"	(37)
FAMILY URGES PSYCHIATRIC ADVICE	(38)
SEEKS PSYCHIATRIC ADVICE	(39)

may backfire. Scaring the patient too much may generate unmanageable anxiety levels and contribute to further drinking "to calm down." Outpatient detoxification at this point would most likely be fruitless and potentially dangerous. The patient may be tempted to combine a benzodiazepine with drinking, a potentially lethal combination. Outpatient detoxification should only be attempted when the patient has a strong supportive family system that can supervise the schedule of medications. The physician's role is to attend to the medical needs of the patient in a therapeutic alliance that will allow a broad-based treatment plan, including referral to specialized treatment modalities.

Treatment approaches for alcohol dependence cover a broad spectrum of modalities, including self-help groups, residential treatment such as therapeutic communities, psychotherapy (including individual, group, and family approaches), behavioral therapies, and combined approaches. Any of these may be supplemented by pharmacologic ancillary approaches using disulfiram, cross-tolerant sedatives, minor or major tranquilizers, or antidepressant medications depending upon medical and psychiatric indications. But not every approach is appropriate for every patient.

Some other considerations are helpful in the management of the elderly alcoholic: (1) Tremors and shakiness are usually more conspicuous and exaggerated in the old than in younger patients. They can be important indicators of impending withdrawal. (2) Successful disulfiram patients tend to be older, although not necessarily elderly, more socially stable, more highly motivated, better able to form dependable relationships, less depressed, and less likely to have blackouts or sociopathic traits. Perhaps these very traits are associated with better prognosis in chronic alcoholism in the absence of disulfiram, as has been suggested (19). (3) Use of antihistamine and anticholinergic agents should be avoided in the treatment of alcohol withdrawal, particularly in the older patient. Neither hydroxyzine, diphenhydramine, or highly sedating neuroleptics offer any advantages over other agents and they have the disadvantage of readily causing severe side effects and toxicity to which elderly persons are particularly prone. Central anticholinergic toxicity can be indistinguishable from the confusion of severe alcohol withdrawal reactions.

Although heavy drinking appears to decline with age in both women and men (20), the older problem drinker has recently come to the attention of people in the alcohol field. The older problem drinker usually is a person who has been abusing alcohol for 20 to 50 years or has started using alcohol following the typical heavy losses of senescence. The younger members of the family are particularly prone to strong and protracted denial of the alcohol problem in their elders, particularly when the abuse is of relatively recent development. To make management more difficult, the existing supportive services are not tailored to serve the older person. Most older veterans with an alcohol problem have had it for a long time. Some demographic figures from Coatesville VAMC illustrate this contention.

Twenty-three percent of the inpatient population of the combined geriatric and extended-care services at Coatesville VAMC are hospitalized because of alcohol-related problems, mostly chronic organic mental disorders (OMD). This population consists of about 52 patients ranging in age from 50 to 79 (av. 64 years). They have been hospitalized during their current admission for 1 to 21 years (av. 6 years). Some 6/52 (12%) had been discharged from a previous admission here due to alcohol or were transferred to another VAMC or to a nursing home. The period out of our VAMC for this group was usually relatively brief (up to 2 years) before they returned to CVAMC with the same or an exacerbated problem or irreversible condition related to alcohol. Ten out of the total 52 patients (19%) have a diagnosis of alcohol amnestic syndrome (Korsakoff's). The remainder covers the entire spectrum of chronic alcohol deteriorations or complications, including alcoholic dementia, liver cirrhosis, encephalopathy, or conditions frequently seen among alcohol-tobacco abusers (i.e., chronic obstructive pulmonary disease). For this type of patient, often only palliative and symptomatic measures are available.

Treatment modalities for the alcoholic organic mental disorders (OMD, Table 24-II) are most rewarding for the first three categories, less promising for the next two (withdrawal delirium, hallucinosis), and almost non-existing or palliative at best for the last two (amnestic and dementia).

SUMMARY

The alcohol-induced organic mental disorders, as described in the recently published DSM–III of the American Psychiatric Association, can be grouped into four acute disorders (intoxication, withdrawal, delirium, Wernicke's) with immediate risks of complications and relatively concrete pharmacotherapeutic indications and three subacute or chronic disorders (alcohol hallucinosis, alcohol amnestic syndrome, and alcoholic dementia) for which management is more symptomatic and palliative. While drugs may play a primary role in the recovery from acute alcohol-induced disorders, with minor exceptions, they are unlikely to bring about the rehabilitation of the chronic alcoholic. The therapeutic management of the sober chronic alcoholic without any organic mental disorder is kaleidoscopic and complex. Main treatment modalities for this very difficult problem have been outlined. Treatment for major complications requires specialized approaches.

REFERENCES

1. Fourth Special Report to the U.S. Congress on Alcohol and Health, National Institute on Alcohol Abuse and Alcoholism, January, 1981.
2. Carels, E. J., and Kite, W. R. A management approach to alcoholism treatment services. *Psychiatric Annals,* 1982, 12(7), 715–724.
3. Chafetz, M. E. Alcoholism and alcoholic psychoses. In A. M. Freedman, H. I. Kaplan, and B. J. Sadock (Eds.), *Comprehensive Textbook of Psychiatry-II* (Vol. 2, 2nd Edition, 1331–1348). Baltimore: Williams and Wilkins Co., 1975.
4. Berry, R. E. Estimating the economic costs of alcohol abuse. *N Engl J Med,* 1976, 295, 620–621.
5. Cruze, A. M., Harwood, H. J., and Kristiansen, P. L. et al., Economic Costs to Society of Alcohol, Drug Abuse and Mental Illness—1977. Alcohol, Drug Abuse and Mental Health Administration, October, 1981.
6. National Drug and Alcoholism Treatment Utilization Survey. Alcohol, Drug Abuse and Mental Health Administration, June, 1981, p. 24.
7. Vestal, R. E. Aging and pharmacokinetics: Impact of altered physiology in the elderly. In A. Cherkin, C. E. Finch, and N. Karash et al. (Eds.), *Physiology and Cell Biology of Aging (Aging, Vol. 8)*, 185–201. New York: Raven Press, 1979.
8. Westerfield, W. W., and Shulman, M. P. Metabolism and calorie value of alcohol. *JAMA,* 1959, 170, 197–203.
9. Isselbacker, K. J. Metabolic and hepatic effects of alcohol. *N Engl J Med,* 1977, 296, 612–616.
10. National Council on Alcoholism. Criteria for the diagnosis of alcoholism. *Am J. Psychiatry,* 1972, 129, 127.
11. Selzer, M. L. The Michigan Alcohol Screening Test: The quest for a new diagnostic instrument. *Am J Psychiatry,* 1971, 127, 1653–1658.
12. Selzer, M. L. Alcoholics and social drinkers: Characteristics and differentiation, in Alcohol, Drugs and Traffic Safety. Toronto, Addiction Research Foundation, 1975.
13. Diagnostic and Statistical Manual of Mental Disorders, 3rd Edition. The American Psychiatric Association, 1980.
14. Li T-K Enzymology of human alcohol metabolism. In A. Meister (Ed.), *Advances in Enzymology and Related Areas of Molecular Biology.* New York: John Wiley and Sons, 1977.
15. Goodwin, D. W., Schulsinger, F., and Hermansen, I. et al. Alcohol problems in adoptees raised apart from alcoholic biologic parents. *Arch Gen Psychiatry,* 1973, 28, 238–243.
16. Goodwin, D. W., Schulsinger, F., and Knop, J. et al. Alcoholism and depression in adopted-out daughters of alcoholics. *Arch Gen Psychiatry,* 1977, 34(7), 751–755.
17. Jellinek, E. M. Phases of alcohol addiction. *Quart J Stud Alc.,* 1952, 13, 673.

18. Pokorny, A. D., Kanas, T., and Overall, J. E. Order of appearance of alcoholic symptoms. *Alcoholism: Clinical and Experimental Research,* 1981, 5(2), 216–220.
19. Lundwall, L., and Baekeland, F. Disulfiram treatment of alcoholism: a review. *J Nerv Ment Dis,* 1971, 153, 381–394.
20. Cahalna, D., Cisin, I. H., and Crosley, H. M. *American Drinking Practices: A National Survey of Drinking Behavior and Attitudes.* New Brunswick, NJ: Rutgers Center of Alcoholic Studies, 1969.

Chapter 25

THE ELDERLY ALCOHOLIC: NURSING CONSIDERATIONS

Nancy Elliott
Donna G. Smith

U sually, the first thing that new nurses observe in the Alcohol Rehabilitation Program for older alcoholics at this center is the elderly appearance of middle-aged men. Most of our residents tend to appear to be 10 to 20 years older than their chronological age. Neuropsychologic tests have demonstrated significant parallels between alcoholism and aging, suggesting the possibility of "premature aging" as a result of alcoholism. The older alcoholics that we see at this medical center are often weakened and vulnerable, both physically and mentally. Their medical problems are usually of a chronic nature, having been caused or exacerbated by their drinking. Most have suffered a number of losses—home, family, friends, employment—leaving them lonely, depressed and often angry. The nurse caring for the elderly alcoholic must let the patient know that it's "OK" to grieve over his losses without fostering self-pity and help him recognize the strengths he must have in order to have survived living as he has.

Patient education is an important aspect in treating the elderly alcoholic. They are often taking a variety of prescription and non-prescription drugs and are often unaware of the adverse and sometimes fatal outcome of combining these drugs with alcohol. They often deny that their diminishing physical health is related to their alcoholism. The older alcoholic has a great need for socialization. This is a major part of the treatment program. He needs to learn to socialize without the presence of alcohol and to feel that he is a person worthy of friendship.

Placement of the elderly alcoholic following rehabilitation is

326

often hard work. Families are often non-existent or unwilling to cope with this family member who may have caused much of the discord in the family over the years. Halfway houses are usually geared for younger men, and nursing home personnel are often not trained to advance the alcoholic's recovery. This makes place-ment difficult.

While recognizing the special problems of the older alcoholic, the nurse must also be aware that many aspects of alcohol treat-ment are the same, regardless of age. This includes a supportive detoxification process, with rest, nutrition and palliative medi-cation to ease the withdrawal symptoms. Rehabilitation, too, should proceed along the same lines as for the younger alcoholic, utilizing individual and group therapy, behavior modification, pharmacotherapy and Alcoholics Anonymous. A therapeutic com-munity milieu is used here as the center of the treatment program. We feel that it aids the patient in reconstructing family-like affilia-tions while offering an opportunity to enhance socialization skill deficits.

Through our experience with elderly alcoholics, we feel that there are a number of key points that can be addressed by nursing staff such that patient care in this population may be improved.

ATTITUDE. The attitudes you have about alcoholism and aging will greatly influence one's ability to treat elderly alcoholics. In order to improve their health and quality of life, they must be seen as treatable. An attitude of mutual respect and cooperation must be established. This will lead to a more available and approach-able client. By acknowledging the wisdom and strength that have gotten the elderly through the years, you can draw upon their resources. Care plans must be designed in cooperation with the patient to utilize individual strengths.

DIAGNOSIS. Establishing the diagnosis of alcoholism proves to be one of the greatest difficulties in treating them. Careful history-taking from both client and family with attention to alcohol-related details is essential, since normal signs of aging may also be signs of alcoholism. Because of the typical elderly life-style, the usual routes of alcoholic identification such as social isolation, poor work habits and legal problems are often ineffective.

ASSESSMENT. It is particularly challenging for the clinician to differentiate the physiologic effects of aging from those of alcohol ingestion as a cause of sleep impairment or memory problems and to separate alcoholism from depression or dementia. Careful nursing assessment, evaluating the patient holistically and objectively, is essential to determining appropriate treatment. Special attention to onset of disease and surrounding stressors helps the elderly identify specific problem areas. Documentation of specific patterns of memory loss, skill deficits and sleeping and eating habits assist in establishing both differential diagnosis and treatment needs.

DETOXIFICATION. With the decreased metabolism of aging, blood alcohol levels remain higher for longer periods of time. Intoxicated behavior will persist longer and detoxification time will be longer. Sleep impairment may be present, as the elderly patient is often more sensitive to normal doses of sleeping medications. Sedative effects may last longer. Gait disturbances due to acute intoxication and alcoholic neuropathy are common. For these reasons, great care must be taken to avoid physical injury. Memory loss and disorientation present several management problems. Instructions may need to be repeated frequently. Precautions must be taken to prevent wandering off as well as the disturbances of other patients, who frequently find the elderly alcoholic's meddlesome behavior irritating. Enlisting the understanding and assistance of other patients in orienting and protecting the elderly proves mutually beneficial. Reducing environmental changes minimizes memory loss and disorientation.

REHABILITATION. Conventional therapeutic communities work well, as they allow the patient some control over his environment and encourage social interaction. Special emphasis on the specific goals of individual patients invites them to not only be involved in treatment but to assume responsibility for their own health. When memory loss persists, the "buddy" system can be utilized to offer support and frequent reality orientation.

FAMILY. Family contact is essential from day one. Especially when memory gaps and denial are present, the family can facilitate an accurate history. Intervention with the family is necessary to develop a therapeutic support system for when the patient returns home. Issues of enablement and denial can be addressed directly, and referral should be made to AA groups.

FOLLOW-UP. Evaluation of the support system is critical to recovery. If family cannot be used, other community or friendship structures must be suggested. Involvement in the church, community and world promotes feelings of usefulness and self-fulfillment.

EDUCATION. An ongoing process of education geared to the individual begins upon admission. Specific issues geared to the elderly such as medication interactions, time structures, death and loss are addressed in group sessions.

When these points have been applied to the treatment of the elderly alcoholic, our experience has shown that the therapeutic process has benefited in terms of increased efficacy, quality of care and completeness.

SUMMARY

The older veteran alcoholic presents nursing staff with a complex of medical, psychological and social problems. Each must be addressed with special care, as they tend to interact and cause the chronic patient to feel overwhelmed and helpless. The complexity of problems presented by these patients demand special treatment, rehabilitation and aftercare planning. When provided skilled nursing care reinforced by a sense of hope, older alcoholics are responding well and can be very rewarding patients.

Chapter 26

RE-ENTRY HOUSE AND
OTHER DISPOSITIONAL ALTERNATIVES
FOR THE AGING ALCOHOLIC

Alan P. Mittelman

The author has had the opportunity to participate in the care and planning for many aging alcoholics via Re-Entry House. Re-Entry House is a 64-bed unit, staffed by two social workers, a psychologist, nurses, and is augmented by personnel from various departments and services. Re-Entry House serves about 300 veterans per year. Approximately 70 percent to 80 percent of these people are substance abusers. Of these, a substantial but not clearly determined percentage are elderly (chronologically over 55) and unsure as to where they will go when they are discharged from the medical center. The Re-Entry House Program is designed to provide support and counseling appropriate to a client's identified goals.

The Re-Entry House Program is a 90-day program that places high expectations on the client in the effort to fulfill the mission of structured treatment and planning for discharge. These "aging alcoholics" are characterized by limited or lacking financial resources, little family support, an inability to secure or retain employment, poor health, and, frequently, little motivation to live. For many of the veterans who participate in the program, their social skills have deteriorated substantially and their sense of self-pride has been all but extinguished. These are people who are alone and lonely and who see little in their future and frequently live in the past. Their lives generally run from minute to minute and day to day, with little ability or desire to look forward to the future or to plan ahead. Before the veterans are referred to the Re-Entry House Program, they have already begun a course of rehabilitation involving their problems of substance abuse, along with the problems of living and aging. Frequently, these problems are closely intertwined.

Participation in the various therapies, as well as the veterans adjustment to the program, enables the staff to evaluate the dispositional plan which seems most realistic and beneficial. These options are then discussed with the veteran. The client is then expected to arrive at a decision as to what dispositional plan is to be pursued. The therapist is expected to help the client throughout this entire process and provide whatever guidance is needed. The process of discharge planning also tries to consider the veteran's medical and emotional condition. Many of the clients come to our unit expressing the desire to re-enter the community and secure employment and independent housing. For a substantial number of them, this is not realistic. These veterans have not been able to handle the ADL (activities of daily living) of independent living, nor have they been able to establish a durable, productive sobriety. Much of the Re-Entry House treatment process focuses on helping the veteran to assess his/her strengths, as well as limitations. Therefore, much effort is focused toward helping the veteran to identify and expand in ways that will strengthen his/her sense of worthiness. This is accomplished by utilizing the resources of rehabilitative medicine services, vocational counseling services, social work services and nursing services, as well as the dynamics of group and individual therapies. The veteran is encouraged to engage in productive activities that will reinforce a sense of achievement and self-worth. The program is structured so that a maximum level of responsibility is placed on the client. The resident is expected to attend his therapies as scheduled and to utilize the support and counseling of his therapist and other staff members It is expected that the resident will attend to the details of arranging leaves of absence, as well as notifying a therapist that he will be absent. She/he is responsible for the maintenance of his/her personal and environmental hygiene. The thrust of the program is to appeal to a client's health, not illness, and to expect adult, responsible behavior. Residents are encouraged to be assertive about communicating their needs but not to be demanding. Yet, they are also taught to address their rights. In a culture that has been giving lip service to the aged, but not always real service, it is appropriate that these folks be urged to speak up for themselves and not depend on others to speak for them. As mentioned earlier, many clients wish to attempt a life of independence and employment. The job market is not very accessible to an elderly alcoholic who may have a number of medical problems, as well as a poor work history. Thus, it becomes the function of the treatment team to help these people review the options open to them, collect the necessary and appropriate data, and then make a decision about productivity and independence.

The options for dispositional planning for the aging alcoholic include residential care homes, nursing homes, halfway houses, and VA and state domiciliaries. The process of helping these veterans to formulate a dispositional plan involves many factors. A primary limiting factor is financial status. Almost all community facilities are interested in having the potential client in their programs pay a share of the cost of his/her participation. The client may have too little or too much money to utilize available resources. With an income of $450, one may be ineligible for domiciliary placement because of excessive income ($145 is the upper income limit). That same $450, however, may be inadequate for placement in a residential care home. Thus, a good rapport with the patient, a careful assessment of his treatment needs and a thorough knowledge of his/her available financial resources is needed to facilitate long-term care.

Of the available short-term dispositional alternatives, the Residential Care Home (RCH) Program is widely used in the VA system. Essentially, this is a private residence that complies with local, state and VA standards of health safety through repeated inspections. It provides room and board, some genuine caring and the opportunity to reside in a home in the community. All of the homes are different. The physical qualities of the home, the environment and the personality of the owner allow and require the social worker to match the home environment and the personality with patients who have been accepted for placement. Generally, the RCH acts as a short-term residence for helping patients to select longer-term options. While in the RCH, the veteran usually attends the Day Treatment Program. Day treatment strives to provide a base for mental and physical stimulation geared toward improving the clients quality of life. For the aging alcoholic, this program may be financially unattainable. Elderly, chronically unemployed alcoholics may not have the $400–$500 required for these services. Further, their benefits (SSI, DPA) or pensions may not be able to meet these financial demands. If the financial demands cannot be met, the veteran may have to look for other day treatment or residential alternatives as more viable options.

Another referral option is the halfway house. It provides a structured, longer-term supportive environment that encourages (via peer pressure) the alcoholic to stay sober. This facility also focuses on urging (and even requiring) the client to secure employment. Sometimes this is achievable. However, the job market, the client's poor track record, as well as a bias against hiring the elderly, all work toward setting the stage for failure. In addition, halfway house placement is most often complicated by residency requirements and the dynamics of county funding. With only one exception in this geographic area, a client must reside in the county that funds the facility. Consequently, all too frequently, these facilities review the client's application and are not able to offer the aging alcoholic their residential support.

A third option, and our most utilized, is domiciliary placement. There are currently sixteen VA domiciliaries and others that are state operated (sometimes with federal subsidy). Pennsylvania, for example, has two such facilities. The domiciliary concept was an outgrowth of the Civil War. It was then designed to provide room and board to veterans who were not able to adequately care for themselves. Today, the domiciliary is a rehabilitation center that has the goal of helping to restore veterans to production and independence. This has been especially true during the past decade. VA domiciliaries have available, or on site, almost every resource that any medical center could offer. It also has services one would expect to find in a residential placement situation. The domiciliary stresses helping the individual to maximize his strengths and level of independent functioning. The resident is expected to handle his life in a responsible fashion that lends itself not only to the operation of the institution but to the best interest and welfare of the veteran. Ordinarily, the veteran becomes eligible for admission to a "dom" by virtue of medical or psychiatric disabilities. Our experiences have determined that psycho-social deficits will also satisfy that criteria. The domiciliary has proven to be an excellent opportunity for the aging alcoholic to "test his wings." It provides a structure that encourages interaction with the tolerance for others. The veteran can experience acceptance by his peers and then begin to accept others. This is a major step toward a durable sobriety and, perhaps, a return to a more satisfying life. In the "dom" the resident also has available to him the resources of the nearby community. Although many residents remain there for years, many others use it as a means to regroup their internal and external resources before moving on. For some, it becomes an opportunity to develop new social relationships or renew old ones. Others use this facility to refine old skills (social and vocational) to prepare them for community living. The domiciliary is many things to many people. In the final analysis, it provides an opportunity for one to live with dignity and self-respect as one attempts to normalize one's life.

The above options describe those that we have used. They represent sound planning based on finances, psycho-social needs, and the client's will to continue with life. Those people who have opted to return to the streets have not been discussed. When this happens, they usually have decided to quit trying to rebuild their life. These veterans ultimately show up on some future census sheet for admission or are listed on an obituary page. It is unclear to the writer whether it is their aging or their alcoholism that dominates in the decision making.

The literature abounds with studies and statistics that tell us how large the aged segment of our population is and will be. It seems logical to expect that the incidence of alcoholism will continue to be significant for this group. How the needs of the aging will be met in the near and distant future is unclear. We, as social workers, psychologists, physicians, and nurses, must be aware of the problems that face us as treatment people. As "enablers" or "helping people," it is incumbent that we know about available resources. This must also bring to light resource deficits.

SUMMARY

   This chapter outlines the dispositional alternatives for the aging alcoholic at one VA facility. Those options include residential care homes, halfway houses, nursing homes, and domiciliaries. Re-Entry House is a 90-day dispositional planning unit which acts as the vehicle for helping inpatients to select from these options. Financial, medical and health, social and emotional considerations for dispositional planning are reviewed as they relate to the issues of aging and alcoholism.

Chapter 27

DEVELOPMENT AND EVALUATION OF A TREATMENT PROGRAM FOR OLDER VETERAN ALCOHOLICS

Keith A. Druley

Steven Pashko

In 1971, Coatesville VA Medical Center management set out to meet the growing need for substance abuse treatment programs. This resulted in the development of separate units for drug detoxification, drug rehabilitation and alcohol rehabilitation. At that time, the center was a 1,300-bed neuropsychiatric facility. By 1975, these well-established programs had waiting lists and were providing services to young and middle-aged veterans with acute drug and/or alcohol problems. For the most part, these veterans presented few, if any, serious medical problems. They were not psychotic and were typically on their first or second admission to the center. These programs accepted patients directly from outside; almost never from within the center. By 1975, these treatment efforts were well known in the tri-state area, as was attested to by long waiting lists. The medical center management, between 1971 to 1975, had done well in their attempt to meet the needs of younger and middled-aged veterans with drug and alcohol problems. However, we had failed to address the needs of substance-abusing patients within the medical center. Line treatment staff struggled with treatment/management issues as they attempted to provide services to substance-abusing veterans with serious mood and/or thought disorders and to older chronic alcoholics.

The existence of well-respected drug and alcohol treatment programs designed to treat veterans with good prognosis demanded the development of programs for patients who "fell through the cracks" because of mixed diagnosis and/or age. A study completed by McLellan et. al. (1) in 1975 clearly indicated that something needed to be done. They surveyed drug and/or alcohol usage of veterans on psychiatric wards, excluding those on substance abuse treatment programs. Results indicated that 50 percent of the post-Viet Nam veterans reported having a substance abuse problem at some time in their life. Less than half of those having an alcohol problem reported it to staff. Sixty percent reported using alcohol while in treatment and 30 percent reported drinking at least three times a week while on a psychiatric ward.

Top management decided to deal with the problem of the older chronic alcoholic first. Since a program for the treatment of psychiatrically ill substance abusers was to be initiated a year later (2), it was decided that all chronic alcoholics who continued to drink, become intoxicated and cause trouble would be transferred to a locked status and under very close supervision. This plan had its advantages and disadvantages. The main disadvantage was that it collected a group of crafty older alcoholics, who were all "drinking buddies," in one area. This group was quick to demonstrate their ability to procure alcoholic beverages irrespective of the best-laid plans of staff. The advantages were manyfold; three will be highlighted. First, the center clearly communicated to these veterans that they would no longer tolerate their self-destructive behavior and abusive misuse of the system. Second, grouping these men forced staff to take a united front and to develop a cohesive system for dealing with the self-destructive behavior. A study by McLellan et. al. (3) of staff attitudes towards problem drinking patients indicated considerable interdisciplinary conflict as to how drunkenness should be dealt with. For example, physicians, psychologists and social workers tended to take a rather lenient attitude, while nurses reacted in a less lenient and more confrontive manner. These staff conflicts tended to support and at times to even encourage acting out on the part of alcoholic patients. Finally, and most important, this administrative maneuver delivered this particular group of veteran patients almost exclusively into the care of the nursing service. Nursing staff were comfortable with the many medical problems of these patients. Their counseling was reality oriented, and most important nursing staff perceived drunkenness as life-threatening behavior that could not and would not be tolerated either by the patients' physical system or by the staff. In addition, nursing staff were sensitive to their professional limitations and did not hesitate to request psychiatric, social work or psychological consultation when the need arose. From the very beginning, this program was viewed as being run by a head nurse and selected nursing staff. The physician, psychologist and social worker were available as consultants, but the program was clearly the property of the nurse coordinator and her staff.

This Chronic Alcohol Rehabilitation Program was initiated in July of 1975. The ward staff consisted of a head nurse, staff nurses, nursing assistants and a secretary. The staff did not feel "put upon" by having been assigned this group of patients. They willingly changed from a psychiatry ward to become a ward in the Substance Abuse Treatment Unit. The staff were highly skilled professionals with a positive, parental attitude towards their patients. This attitude was often expressed in statements such as: "Oh, they're a good bunch of old boys, all they have to do is learn how to behave" or "they can be gentlemen, if they want to, only nobody expects it of them."

Program staff quickly recognized, however, that they needed special training if they were to meet the demands and needs of chronic alcoholics. In this they were quick to realize that good intentions and top-flight nursing skills were not sufficient in and of themselves. The staff visited the drug and alcohol rehabilitation programs at CVAMC and reviewed the detailed written constitutions of existing two therapeutic communities. As a result of this exposure and a good deal of staff discussion, they came up with three treatment/program options. First, they could remain a locked ward and serve as custodians. The second option was a nursing ward with an emphasis on education, counseling and care for multiple medical problems. Finally, they could develop a therapeutic community, wherein staff and patients would work together to realize program goals. They chose the latter with the goal that their patients had to develop a positive sense of responsibility for their own behavior. As one staff member stated it, "they've got to quit being a slave to demon rum." Subsequently, staff courageously set out to develop a modified therapeutic community for themselves and their patients. A detailed description of the program is presented by Erdlen et al. (4).

What emerged from the dramatic change in therapeutic perspective was a flash herculean struggle. The struggle centered around the issues of self-governance (5) and self-care (6). On the one hand, the patients were wise and crafty in their use of the system to support pathological drinking. Knowing they could come into the medical center when it was too cold or when they were broke and too ill to survive was comforting. All they had to do was come in the medical center, be locked up, behave and be taken care of. Generally, they could lay around the ward, smoke, watch TV, play cards and sleep in the dayroom chairs. The ward was without specific rules and regulations, without a patient-staff organization and without a schedule of activities. Suddenly, these ground rules were changed. In a matter of days the ward became a program with a 60-page constitution and a patient-staff government. Even more remarkable, the doors were unlocked and patients, now known as residents, were allowed at first limited and later total ground privileges by decision of the resident-staff governing body. At first, the patients strongly resisted these changes by refusing to cooperate; many became surly and withdrawn; a few even went out and drank. However, staff held firm to their belief that a therapeutic community could work. Subsequently, after working through this resistance, this group of chronic alcoholics became model residents in a model therapeutic community. Together, staff and residents developed a program comprised mainly of low-key group counseling, community meetings, self-government and the "Bridge Program." The latter allowed them to do piecework for money in a highly supervised work-restoration project. In addition, they became actively involved in an Alcoholics Anonymous program and requested workshops in religion from the chaplain service.

The follow-up studies of this program have been completed. One covered 50 patients discharged between December 1976 through May 1977. Details of this study are available in the 1979 Erdlen et al. article (4). Seventy-six percent of the 50 men who graduated from the program were located. Two subjects were deceased (4%), while five men (10%) refused to be interviewed. Complete interviews were obtained either in person or by telephone for the remaining 31 subjects (62%). Interviews were structured to determine present need for treatment in five problem areas: medical, psychological, social, economic support and alcohol abuse. Seventy-four percent of the follow-up subjects reported no need for further medical or psychological care. Sixty-four percent of the subjects indicated that they were able to "take care of themselves." These men were getting by on pensions. One-half of the subjects were living in domiciliaries, contract nursing homes, or halfway houses. The majority of these former patients indicated that they were satisfied with their living arrangements. Data from this study suggests that improvement in social adjustment was modest. For the most part, these former patients were living a passive existence, within the confines of their living arrangements. Finally, the follow-up data indicated that 64 percent of the men felt no need for further alcoholism treatment. Forty-five percent of the former patients claimed abstinence, while 19 percent indicated reduced drinking behavior. The authors of this study (Erdlen et al., 1979) conclude "generally, the men interviewed seemed to be maintaining themselves well in the areas of health, economic supports and sobriety. Their social situations were the least improved, as they remained relatively passive in forming peer relationships and utilizing their leisure time. It is possible that with their histories of marginal friendships and superficial involvement, a post-discharge placement with a more structured social environment is needed."

A second follow-up study was completed on veterans entering this program during the calendar year 1978. The Addiction Severity Index (ASI) was administered to all patients at the time of admission. Follow-up evaluations were done six months after discharge between an independent research technician and the veteran, either in person or by phone. The ASI is a structured clinical interview developed to assess problem severity in six areas commonly affected by addiction. These areas include medical, legal, substance abuse, employment, family and psychological problems. The instrument and specifics of the follow-up study are discussed in detail by McLellan et al. (7). Table 27-I presents the background characteristics of patients assigned to the Chronic Alcoholism Program (CAP) and for patients on the fast-paced Alcohol Rehabilitation Program (ARP) (for younger, motivated patients). Seventy-two percent of the veterans assigned to CAP were divorced, separated or single. Eighty-five percent had chronic serious medical problems for which 49 percent received medical pensions. Twenty-four percent reported working during the past year and only 29 percent indicated that they were living with someone during this same period. Table 27-II presents follow-up results for veterans in both programs. Of key interest is the reported reduction in days of medical problems, days of psychiatric problems, days drinking and days intoxicated for CAP veterans. Previous to admission, patients assigned to CAP reported drinking 21 out of 30 days (70% of the time) and being intoxicated 16 out of 30 days (over 50% of the time). Post-discharge, they reported drinking 7 out of 30 days and being intoxicated on five.

SUMMARY

A nurse-coordinated program was developed to meet the needs of chronic alcohol patients who were being cared for on psychiatric wards. A therapeutic community which stressed self-care and self-governance greatly reduced the management problems usually created by these patients when they are housed in psychiatric units. These men quit drinking while in the program, stopped going on unauthorized absence, attended assignments and presented fewer discipline problems. Two follow-up studies indicated that program effects carried over after discharge. There was a significant reduction in drinking and days intoxicated. In addition, patients reported reductions in the days they experienced medical symptoms and psychological distress. Significantly, the veterans were feeling better in both mind and body six months after treatment. In concluding, it is also important to note that this program freed up staff-intensive psychiatric beds by developing a cost-efficient/effective nurse-coordinated therapeutic community.

TABLE 27-I
BACKGROUND CHARACTERISTICS

	Alcohol Rehab. Program (ARP) N = 115		Chronic Alcohol Program (CAP) N = 85
DEMOGRAPHICS			
Age	47		54
White (%)	77		75
Black (%)	23		25
Yrs. Education	12	•	10
Yrs. Alc. Prob.	12	•	17
Married (%)	20	•	10
Div. or Sep. (%)	62	••	47
Single (%)	18		25
MEDICAL			
Chronic Med. Prob. (%)	50	••	85
Receive Med. Pens. (%)	30	•	49
EMPLOYMENT			
Have Trade or Skill (%)	54		55
Worked Past Yr. (%)	51	••	24
LEGAL			
On Prob. or Parole (%)	26	•	13
Awaiting Trial/Charges (%)	19	••	0
LIVING SITUATION			
Living w/Parents (%)	11		6
Living w/Spouse (%)	31	•	18
Living w/Friends (%)	6		5
Living Alone	30	•	44
Residence Owned (%)	29		23
PSYCHIATRIC HISTORY			
Prior Treatment (%)	53		44
Serious Depression (%)	54	•	38
Serious Anxiety (%)	59	•	47
Suicide Attempt (%)	14		17
Violent Behavior (%)	28		20

KEY: (• = $p < 0.05$, •• = $p < 0.01$)

TABLE 27-II

ADMISSION TO SIX-MONTH FOLLOW-UP COMPARISON OF MALE VETERANS
TREATED IN TWO ALCOHOLISM REHABILITATION PROGRAMS

	Alcohol Treatment Unit (N = 115)			Chronic Alcohol Unit (N = 85)		
	ADM.		6-MO.	ADM.		6-MO.
MEDICAL FACTOR[1]	343		289	531	••	335
Days of Med. Probs.	9		8	14	•	9
EMPLOYMENT FACTOR	303	•	267	409		391
Days Working	6	••	15	4		4
Money Earned	231		296	148		139
ALCOHOL FACTOR	513	••	196	546	••	154
Days Drinking	19	••	8	21	••	7
Days Intoxicated	10	••	4	16	••	5
DRUG FACTOR	15		19	21		22
FAMILY FACTOR	226		199	213		191
CRIME FACTOR	111	••	46	29		16
Days Crime	4	•	2	1		1
Illegal Income	85	•	23	18		22
PSYCHOLOGICAL FACTOR	210	•	169	188	•	157
Days Psych. Symptoms	12	••	7	10	0.07	7

[1]All criteria were measured during 30 days before admission and before 6-month follow-up. Higher scores equal greater problem severity.

KEY: (• = $p < 0.05$, •• = $p < 0.01$ [by paired t-test])

REFERENCES

1. McLellan, A. T., Druley, K. A., and Carson, J. E. Evaluation of substance abuse problems in a psychiatric hospital. *Journal of Clinical Psychisatry,* 1978, 39(5), 425–430.
2. McLellan, A. T., MacGahan, J., and Druley, K. A. Drug abuse and psychiatric illness. In E. Gottheil et al. (eds.), *Substance Abuse and Psychiatric Illness.* New York: Pergamon Press, 1980a.
3. McLellan, A. T., Hery, D. S., and Druley, K. A. Staff drinking patterns and approach to patient drinking problems within a psychiatric hospital. *American Journal of Drug and Alcohol Abuse,* 1979, 5(4), 271–274.
4. Erdlen, F. R., Sobczynski, E., Broocker, B., and McLellan, A. T. Effective inpatient treatment of older alcoholics. In Gottheil, E., McLellan, A. T., Druley, K. A., and Alterman, A. I. (Eds.), *Addiction Research and Treatment: Converging Trends,* 113–123. New York: Pergamon Press, 1979.

5. Mack, J. E. Alcoholism, A. A., and the governance of the self. In M. H. Bean and N. E. Zinberg (Eds.), *Dynamic Approaches to the Understanding and Treatment of Alcoholism*, 128–162. New York: The Free Press, 1981.
6. Khantzian, E. J. Some treatment implications of the ego and self disturbances in alcoholism. In M. H. Bean and N. E. Zinberg (Eds.), *Dynamic Approaches to the Understanding and Treatment of Alcoholism*, 163–188. New York: The Free Press, 1981.
7. McLellan, A. T., Druley, K. A., O'Brien, C. P., and Kron, R. Matching substance abuse patients to appropriate treatments. A conceptual and methodological approach. *Drug and Alcohol Dependence*, 1980b, 5(3), 189–193.

Chapter 28

FACTORS THAT DIFFERENTIATE TREATMENT PLACEMENT AMONG OLDER CHRONIC ALCOHOLICS

Gary D. Kunz
Thomas W. Stammers
Steven Pashko
Keith A. Druley

The word older, when linked to the term chronic alcoholic, frequently elicits the mental image of a physically debilitated, cognitively impaired, and socially bankrupt individual who owes his critical condition to many long years of excessive drinking. Having suffered innumerable physical, interpersonal and psychological losses related to his addiction, it seems that increasing chronological age serves only to intensify or magnify the clinical problems of the alcoholic, and a significantly lower level of general vitality is expected if not observed.

At this treatment facility, a specialized rehabilitation program exists to serve the needs of the chronic alcoholic, as characterized above. However, it has been observed over a number of years that chronological age, per se, is not a factor for treatment planning when the decision is to be made to assign a particular individual to a slower-paced program for "chronic" alcoholics versus a faster-paced counterpart for less debilitated alcoholics. The question to be addressed by this chapter is: Can historical, psychosocial, or medical markers be identified which differentiate those alcoholic veterans of age 55 or older who are deemed capable of functioning

We thank Ivanell Smith and Nanci Alvarez for their help in developing the attached CLINICAL RECORD SURVEY and for their dilligent effort in tracking down appropriate patients and collecting data.

satisfactorily in a fast-track rehabilitation program from those whom it is felt would be more appropriately placed in a slow-track rehabilitation program?

To some extent the issue of chronicity has been functionally defined by treatment program formats, program pace, and outcome expectations. For the most part, the Coatesville VA Medical Center fast-track program (Alcohol Rehabilitation Program/ARP) and the slow-track program (Chronic Alcohol Rehabilitation Program/CARP) are very similar with regard to basic program structure. Both involve well-organized therapeutic communities based on patient-run governments as well as strong AA components involving step meetings, speaker meetings, and discussion meetings. Thirdly, the primary mode of therapeutic intervention is group therapy which is supported by patient education, therapeutic recreation, and physical activities. Despite the basic similarity in design between these two abstinence-oriented rehabilitation programs, some significant differences in pace and expectations for process and outcome do exist. Whereas the slow-track therapeutic community is very basic in structure and makes somewhat scaled-down demands on it's participants' abilities to organize and manage, the fast-track therapeutic community is highly complex and places significantly higher demands on it's participants. With regard to therapeutic group intervention, the slow-track approach can be characterized as less intensive, reality based, problem-solving-oriented counseling which is supportive in nature, whereas the fast-track approach can be characterized as more intensive and insight oriented, relying upon confrontation and peer pressure to promote self-scrutiny. Finally, different levels of post-treatment outcome are generally expected for participants of the two rehabilitation programs. For graduates of the CARP, a meaningful sobriety with improved quality of life is sought with disposition which may involve domiciliary placement or some other supportive environment, while for graduates of the ARP what might be termed a productive sobriety involving employment and independent living is the goal.

Statistics compiled by McLellan et al. (1) on a total of 200 graduates of the ARP and the CARP are shown in Table 28-I. These comparisons are offered to give the reader a thumbnail sketch of the typical referral to each of the rehabilitation programs in terms of demographic data, psychiatric history, and severity of disturbance on medical, employment, legal, and social factors.

TABLE 28-I
BACKGROUND CHARACTERISTICS

	Alcohol Rehab. Program (ARP) N = 115		Chronic Alcohol Rehab. Program (CARP) N = 85
DEMOGRAPHICS			
Age	47		54
White (%)	77.		75
Black (%)	23		25
Yrs. Education	12	*	10
Yrs. Alc. Prob.	12*		17
Married (%)	20	*	10
Div. or Sep. (%)	62	**	47
Single (%)	18		25
MEDICAL			
Chronic Med. Prob. (%)	50	**	85
Receive Med. Pens. (%)	30	*	49
EMPLOYMENT			
Have Trade or Skill (%)	54		55
Worked Past Yr. (%)	51	**	24
LEGAL			
On Prob. or Parole (%)	26	*	13
Awaiting Trial/Charges (%)	19	**	0
LIVING SITUATION			
Living w/Parents (%)	11		6
Living w/Spouse (%)	31	*	18
Living w/Friends (%)	6		5
Living Alone (%)	30	*	44
Residence Owned (%)	29		23
PSYCHIATRIC HISTORY			
Prior Treatment (%)	53		44
Serious Depression (%)	54	*	38
Serious Anxiety (%)	59	*	47
Suicide Attempt (%)	14		17
Violent Behavior (%)	28		20

KEY: (* = $p < 0.05$, ** = $p < 0.01$)

Table 28-II reflects an admission to six-month follow-up comparison of the same sample of graduates from the two programs rating them for improvement on seven outcome factors. As indicated, graduates of the fast-track ARP showed significant improvement on the factors of employment, alcohol consumption, criminal activity, and psychological functioning, whereas graduates of the slow-track CARP showed significant improvement on the medical factor and psychological functioning, in addition to alcohol consumption. McLellan's findings suggest that each program is relatively successful in accomplishing it's overall treatment objectives, and thus it can be inferred that the clinical judgments which underlie referral of candidates to respective programs are equally sound in maintaining viable therapeutic environments which produce positive results:

Outcome statistics for subsamples of McLellan's subjects aged

TABLE 28-II

ADMISSION TO SIX-MONTH FOLLOW-UP COMPARISON OF MALE VETERANS
TREATED IN TWO ALCOHOLISM REHABILITATION PROGRAMS

	Alcohol Rehab. Program (ARP) (N = 115)		Chronic Alcohol Rehab. Program (CARP) (N = 85)		
	Adm.	6-Mo.	Adm.		6-Mo.
MEDICAL FACTOR[1]	343	289	531	••	355
Days of Med. Probs.	9	8	14	•	9
EMPLOYMENT FACTOR	303 •	267	409		391
Days Working	6 ••	15	4		4
Money Earned	231	296	148		139
ALCOHOL FACTOR	513 ••	196	546	••	154
Days Drinking	19 ••	8	21	••	7
Days Intoxicated	10 ••	4	16	••	5
DRUG FACTOR	15	19	21		22
FAMILY FACTOR	226	199	213		191
CRIME FACTOR	111	46	29		16
Days Crime	4 •	2	1		1
Illegal Income	85 •	23	18		22
PSYCHOLOGICAL FACTOR	210 •	169	188	•	157
Days Psych. Symptoms	12 ••	7	10	0.07	7

[1]All criteria were measured during 30 days before admission and before 6-month follow-up. Higher scores equal greater problem severity.

KEY: (• = $p < 0.05$, •• = $p < 0.01$ [by paired t=test])

55 and older are presented in Table 28-III. These data yield a similar pattern of results for older alcoholic veterans who are referred to the respective treatment programs. These again lend support to the clinical judgments associated with the referral decisions.

TABLE 28-III

ADMISSION TO SIX-MONTH COMPARISON OF MALE ALCOHOLICS
AGED 55 AND OLDER TREATED IN TWO REHABILITATION PROGRAMS

	Alcohol Rehab. Program (ARP) Age ≥ 55			Chronic Alchol Rehab. Program (CARP) Age ≥ 55		
	Adm.	(N = 21)	6-Mo.	Adm.	(N = 51)	6-Mo.
MEDICAL FACTOR[1]	476		409	550	*	392
Days of Med. Probs.	12		10	16	*	10
EMPLOYMENT FACTOR	438	*	385	519		507
Days Worked	5		7	3		3
Money Earned	187	.07	251	109		98
ALCOHOL FACTOR	661	**	220	534	**	144
Days Drinking	24	**	9	20	**	6
Days Intoxicated	14	**	7	12	**	4
DRUG FACTOR	002		005	019		016
FAMILY FACTOR	193		161	205		183
CRIME FACTOR	041		017	031		023
Days of Crime	2		1	1		1
Illegal Income	16		4	10		6
PSYCHOLOGICAL FACTOR	183	**	102	172	.06	141
Days Psych. Symptoms	8	**	4	8		6

[1]All criteria were measured during the 30-day period before admission and before 6-month follow-up. Higher scores equal greater problem severity.

KEY: (* = $p < 0.05$, ** = $p < 0.01$)

To reiterate the research question addressed by this chapter: Can historical, psychosocial, or medical markers be identified which differentiate those alcoholic veterans of age 55 or older who are deemed capable of functioning satisfactorily in a fast-track rehabilitation program from those whom it is felt would be more appropriately placed in a slow-track rehabilitation program? This question required that a retrospective evaluation of demographic, developmental, psychodiagnostic, psychosocial, and medical information on graduates from the two rehabilitation programs be undertaken, in order to detect the presence of some systematic factor(s), which should be linked to the more global clinical judgments discussed above.

In order to accomplish this, a sample of 25 CARP graduates and 21 ARP graduates from the years 1981 and 1982 were selected for whom there were available complete sets of routine admission psychological testing. This admission testing battery consisted of the MMPI, the Shipley Institute of Living Scale, and the Beck Depression Inventory. From these samples it was possible to collect additional demographic, historical, and medical information on subsamples of 11 CARP and 13 ARP graduates from their clinical records. This pool of information provided the basis of comparison for alcoholic veterans aged 55 or older who were referred to either the fast-track ARP or the slow-track CARP.

Results

A comparison of the composite MMPI profiles for the two samples yields remarkably similar clinical configurations. Three points are noteworthy for the purposes of this study. First, all scale scores for the ARP sample are in the direction of greater mental health with respect to the CARP sample. Secondly, the F–Scale is one standard deviation higher on the CARP patients than on the ARP patients. Thirdly, the relative heights of scales 7 and 8 differ for the two groups.

Mean Beck scores for the ARP and CARP samples are 13.24 and 15.76, respectively.

The mean WAIS equivalent IQ as derived from the Shipley Institute of Living Scale was 105.86 for the ARP and 98.12 for the CARP. Verbal to abstract differentials for the two groups yielded cognitive coefficients of 74 and 73, respectively.

A sign test using mean scores of the 13 MMPI scales (K-corrected), the Beck Depression Inventory, and the verbal and abstract differentials from the Shipley was performed. The analysis suggests that fast-track (ARP) patients have significantly better ($p < 0.01$) global psychological health. Of the sixteen variables used to describe the patients functioning, fourteen were in the more healthful direction (see Table 28-IV).

TABLE 28-IV
COMPARISON OF THE TWO REHABILITATION SAMPLES
AND SELECTED PSYCHOLOGICAL VARIABLES

	L	F	K	Hs	D	Hy	Pd	Mf	Pa	Pt	Sc	Ma	Si	
CARP	4[a]	13	11	25	25	25	31	24	13	42	44	24	29	
ARP	4	7	12		22	23	23	29	23	10	40	40	22	24

	MEAN CARP	MEAN ARP
BECK	15.76	13.24*
WAIS EQUIV.	98.12	105.86
SHIPLEY VERBAL	26.08	30.88*
SHIPLEY ABSTRACT	13.84	18.19*
CQ	73	74

[a]MMPl (K-Corrected Scores)

*Sign Test across tests shows a significant difference at the p<0.01 between

CARP AND ARP pateints.

Mean values for medical indices obtained upon admission for the smaller subsamples of the two groups are shown in Table 28-V. The medical markers must be interpreted with caution, as no conclusive pathophysical status could be determined by the medical indicator on admission. The two groups of patients reflect a relatively normal admission pattern to an alcohol treatment unit with no disturbing medical aspects separating each group.

Discussion and Conclusions

While the results of this clinical study must be interpreted with caution and the conclusions derived be limited in scope, some evidence is seen in support of clinical determinations of referral of older alcoholic veterans to either a fast-track or a slow-track

TABLE 28-V
MEDICAL MARKERS

		CARP (N = 11)	ARP (N = 13)
Mean Value			
	Admission B/P	143/90	119/78
	Adm. + 5D. B/P	123/78	121/77
	Glucose	98.09	106.07
	Total Bilirubin	0.72	0.43
	Uric Acid	5.12	4.43
	LDH	128.54	120.76
	SGOT	33.70	27.92
	MCV	93.45	93.69
	MCH	31.27	31.92
	AMYLASE	80.09	69.00

rehabilitation program which are not based solely on age or physical status of the veteran in question. On admission, veterans who are referred to a slow-track program display a significantly higher level of global psychopathology as indicated by the MMPI F-Scale. Their clinical profiles on the MMPI and the results of the Beck Depression Scale and Abstract and Verbal Shipley differentials are consistently in the direction of poorer psychological health in comparison to the clinical profiles of their counterparts who are referred to a fast-track program. In addition, the juxtaposition of relative heights of scales 7 and 8 on the MMPI for these two groups suggests that the psychological problems of the subjects referred to the slow-track program tend to be more refractory in nature and reflect a more severely alienated character disorder, whereas the psychological disturbances of fast-track rehabilitation program candidates tend to be more benign in nature and reflect a higher level of residual effectiveness in defense against the development of more fixed and pathological patterns of disturbance.

Candidates for the fast-track rehabilitation program show a slightly higher level of education and a prior history of vocational status at a higher level than do their slow-track counterparts. Overall, referrals to the fast-track program have demonstrated a positive adaptation to life situations (even during drinking periods) estimated by the ability to maintain longer continuous employment, a more intact interpersonal support system, and a longer period of self-awareness of their problem as indicated by self-ratings.

Clearly, further and more rigorous research is indicated to clarify the issues highlighted here in terms of prevention, diagnosis and treatment of alcohol dependence. Most important perhaps are the implications of this study that apply to matching patients to treatment programs to achieve greatest therapeutic effectiveness based on an evaluation of the candidates ego functioning and a consideration of realistic and appropriate goals for life-style and productivity following treatment. Finally, it is suggested that research efforts be focused on the role that social support networks play both in terms of the development of chronic and debilitating alcohol dependence and the long-term recovery from this disease.

SUMMARY

Previous studies have shown that some alcoholic veterans, who are age 55 or older, perform well in "fast-track" rehabilitation programs. This runs contrary to a belief that older alcoholics are more "chronic" and thus should be placed in "slow-track," longer-care programs.

This preliminary study attempts to identify characteristics in older alcoholics that would yield ways of differentiating program appropriateness. Indications are that medical markers and psycho-social adaptation do not distinguish between veterans who are placed in fast- or slow-track programs. It does suggest that program decisions might be made on the basis of a global trend in psychological health as indicated by MMPI, Beck Depression Scale, and Shipley scores. Although the results are not definitive, we will be gathering more data to confirm our preliminary findings that alcoholic veterans can be placed in fast-track rehabilitation programs on the basis of psychological health and not necessarily on the basis of age.

REFERENCES

1. McLellan, A. T., Luborsky, L., O'Brien, C. P., Woody, G. E., and Druley, K. A. Evaluation of Substance Abuse Treatment. Veterans Administration HRS+D Project #284, 1980, unpublished report.

APPENDIX A

CLINICAL RECORD SURVEY

1. Name
2. Religion
3. Branch of service and rank
4. Age
5. Education
6. Race
7. Trade or skill
8. Employment status
9. Last job title
10. Longest period of employment
11. Date last worked
12. Income:
    a. Current
    b. Pensions or other benefits
    c. Estimated socio-economic class
    d. Higest yearly income (past)
13. Marital status: if
    a. Married: quality of relationship
    b. Divorced: what year?
    c. Widowed: what year?
    d. Separated: what year?
14. Children:
    a. If yes: how many?
    b. If yes: quality of relationship
15. Description of subject's life-style
16. Type of diet
17. Who prepares food?
18. How many hobbies does subject list?

19. Does subject list drinking as a hobby?
20. Year subject began drinking alcohol
21. When did drinking become a problem?
22. Frequency and quantity of drinking
23. Subjects drink of choice
24. a. Date of first blackout
    b. Date of first bout of DT's
    c. Date of first DWI
    d. Date of first alcohol-related arrest (other than DWI)
25. Other addictions
26. Subject's longest period of sobriety
27. Family members with alcohol problems
28. Does subject consider himself a member of AA?
29. Legal problems:
    a. number
    b. type
    c. number of incarcerations
    d. total length of incarcerations
30. Treatment (hospitalization) history
    a. Medical: chief complaint(s)/date(s)
    b. Psychiatric: facility(s)/date(s)
    c. Alcohol treatment: facility(s)/date(s)
31. Previous suicide attempts (number)
    a. Was subject intoxicated at the time?
32. Admission blood pressure
33. Admission + 5 days blood pressure
34. KDA profile
    a. Glucose
    b. Bilirubin—total
    c. Uric acid
    d. LDH
    e. SGOT
    f. SGPT
35. Mean corpuscular volume
36. Mean corpuscular hemoglobin
37. Amylase

INDEX

357